PHILOSOPHY FOR A2: UNIT 3

Philosophy for A2: Unit 3 is the definitive textbook for students of the new AQA Advanced level syllabus introduced in 2008. Structured very closely around the AQA specifications for Unit 3: Key Themes in Philosophy, it is the ideal introduction to each of the core themes:

* Philosophy of mind
* Political philosophy
* Epistemology and metaphysics
* Moral philosophy
* Philosophy of religion.

All chapters are helpfully subdivided into short, digestible passages, and include:

* quiz questions to test core knowledge
* discussion questions to deepen understanding
* 'going further' sections for advanced study
* text boxes highlighting key definitions and arguments
* cross-references to help students make connections.

In addition, a chapter on exam preparation contains a wealth of helpful hints and tips on revision and exam techniques. Written by an experienced philosopher and A level consultant, *Philosophy for A2: Unit 3* is an essential companion for all students of A2 level philosophy.

Michael Lacewing is Director of Research and Senior Lecturer in Philosophy at Heythrop College, University of London. He is founder of the company A Level Philosophy, and a consultant on philosophy at A level for the British Philosophical Association.

PHILOSOPHY FOR A2: UNIT 3

Key Themes in Philosophy

Michael Lacewing

Routledge
Taylor & Francis Group

LONDON AND NEW YORK

First published 2010
by Routledge
2 Park Square, Milton Park, Abingdon, Oxon, OX14 4RN

Simultaneously published in the USA and Canada
by Routledge
270 Madison Ave, New York, NY 10016

Routledge is an imprint of the Taylor & Francis Group, an informa business

© 2010 Michael Lacewing

Reprinted 2010

Typeset in Mixage by
Keystroke, Tettenhall, Wolverhampton
Printed and bound in Great Britain by
the MPG Books Group

British Library Cataloguing in Publication Data
A catalogue record for this book is available from the British Library

ISBN 13: 978–0–415–45822–1

CONTENTS

INTRODUCTION

Deepening philosophical ability

The AQA AS Philosophy syllabus aimed to introduce students to a number of philosophical issues. The aim at A2 is to build upon the knowledge and skills learned at AS, to develop a deeper critical understanding of philosophical theories and an ability to engage in discussions that are conceptually sophisticated.

Philosophical depth does not come easily. *Philosophy needs to be read slowly and, usually, more than once*. Each paragraph is intended to be taken as a thought to be considered, re-read, reflected on. You will probably find, in addition, that you are not able to completely understand a particular theory until you also understand rival theories that oppose it. And so, at the end of each chapter you may feel that you need to return to earlier discussions, to think about them again in the light of what you learned later.

How to use this book

Following the syllabus

Each of the five themes specified in Unit 3 is discussed in a separate chapter. Each chapter opens with a brief synopsis of what the chapter covers and what you should be able to do by the end of it, followed by the AQA syllabus for that issue. The discussion follows the AQA syllabus very closely. Many headings and sub-headings from the syllabus are used to structure the discussion, and each section is further divided by the main ideas, arguments and objections.

Glossary

Philosophical terms are explained when they are first introduced, and there is a glossary providing definitions of the most important ones, so that wherever you start to read from, you can always look up the words you don't understand (words that appear in the glossary are in **bold**).

Features

Alongside the text, there are a number of features in the margin. There are definitions of key terms; further thoughts; references for quotations or to philosophical texts where the argument can be followed up; and questions that test your understanding and your abilities to analyse and evaluate the arguments. To get the most out of the book, stop and answer the questions – in your own words – as you go along.

Understanding is also about being able to make connections. So, there are lots of CROSS-REFERENCES, not only to other discussions in this book but also to topics in AS Units 1 and 2 and A2 Unit 4, so that you can follow up the links and see how arguments and issues connect up. Units 1 and 2 are discussed in the textbook *Philosophy for AS* (indicated by the icon), and Unit 4 is discussed in the textbook *Philosophy for A2: Philosophical Problems* (indicated by the icon).

'Going further' sections provide discussions of more difficult ideas or take the arguments further. So they will broaden your knowledge, and help you 'go further' in your evaluation of the theories and arguments.

At the end of each discussion, there is a list of 'Key points', putting clearly the main issues the section has covered.

The final chapter provides advice on how to revise for the exam, and how to perform well on the day.

Companion website and further resources

You can find further resources, including book lists, helpful weblinks, PowerPoint presentations and material on the philosophical skills you need to argue well, on the companion website http://www.routledge.com/textbooks/philosophy.

The examination

Assessment objectives

The examiners mark your answers according to three principles, known as 'Assessment Objectives' (AOs). They are:

AO1: *Knowledge and understanding*: how well do you know and understand the central debates regarding a particular issue, the positions philosophers have defended and the arguments they use to defend them?

AO2: *Interpretation and analysis*: how well do you interpret and analyse relevant philosophical positions and arguments? Are you able to select and apply relevant ideas, concepts, examples and arguments to support your account of an issue? Do you understand how the argument works and what the implications of a position are?

AO3: *Assessment and evaluation*: how well do you assess and evaluate arguments and counter-arguments? Are you able to construct arguments in support of a particular position, and defend it against objections? Do you understand whether an argument succeeds or fails and why? How well do you compare arguments and counter-arguments to weigh up what the most plausible position is?

In addition, you will be marked on your writing. Do you write clearly and grammatically, so that the examiner can understand what you mean? Does the way you write reflect a proper philosophical engagement with the issue? Are your points made coherently?

Structure of the exam

The exam for Unit 3 is longer than the exams for the other units, lasting two hours. It is divided into five sections, one for each theme. Within each section, there are two questions. You must answer two questions in total, one each from two different sections.

The questions are all essay questions, each worth 50 marks. Here are two examples, from the specimen paper:

Theme: Political Philosophy

To what extent, if at all, could the possession of rights be based on utility?

Theme: Epistemology and Metaphysics

Assess the view that there are such things as universals.

The marks

There are 15 marks each for AO1 (Knowledge and understanding) and AO2 (Interpretation and analysis), and 20 marks for AO3 (Assessment and evaluation).

Acknowledgements

In preparing this book, I have drawn on two excellent reference works: the *Stanford Encyclopedia of Philosophy* (http://plato.stanford.edu/contents.html) and the *Routledge Encyclopedia of Philosophy* (http://www.rep.routledge.com). Thanks to Routledge for providing me with free access during this time.

Thanks also to Katy Hamilton, Gemma Dunn, Priyanka Pathak and Tony Bruce at (or formerly at) Routledge for encouraging this project, and to my colleagues at Heythrop College for supporting my work with A level philosophy. A final and deep thank-you to Lizzy Lewis, without whom A Level Philosophy (the company) would not survive.

PHILOSOPHY OF MIND

In this chapter, we examine three types of answer to the question 'What is the mind?' The first, substance dualism, argues that the mind is a substance that can exist independently of the body. The second approach argues that we can completely analyse and explain 'the mind' – which is not a 'thing' at all – in other terms, such as behaviour, functions or neurophysical processes. The third set of answers holds on to the idea that there is something unique about the mind that cannot be captured in this way. In discussing these theories, we examine a wide variety of topics, such as how we know other people have minds, how the mind can cause physical events (e.g. bodily movements) and the nature of consciousness and thought. Students should be able to argue for and against different positions in these topics and in the three schools of thought.

SYLLABUS CHECKLIST ✔

The AQA A2 syllabus for this chapter is:

Substance dualism

✔ Cartesian, or substance, dualism: the view that mind and body are distinct and separate entities. Reasons for holding this view.

✔ Problems associated with this view of mind, including solipsism; the problem of other minds and the mind-body problem.

✔ Responses to these problems: arguments against the possibility of starting from one's own case, how we learn to self-ascribe and whether there could be a necessarily private language (such as a language describing private mental states); the argument from analogy and inference to the best explanation; accounts of the relationship between mind and body.

Reductive accounts of the mind

✔ Logical behaviourism, the logical analysis of mental concepts in terms of behaviour; identity theories, type and token versions of the ontological reduction of minds and mental processes to brains and brain processes; functionalist theories, machine and teleological versions of the reduction of mental states to a causal role; eliminative materialism, the attempt to rid ourselves of 'folk psychology' completely. Arguments for and against these positions.

✔ The features of consciousness thought to resist reduction: particularly qualia and intentionality.

✔ The hard problem of consciousness: how is it that some physical organisms are subjects of experience, how does the water of the brain give rise to the rich wine of consciousness? Whether zombies are conceivable and possible. Whether artificial intelligence is intelligent.

Non-reductive materialism

✔ The view of consciousness as an emergent or supervenient property of the brain (or other suitably complex physical system). Biological naturalism **or** anomalous monism. Arguments and difficulties for such positions.

✔ Whether such views are materialist or versions of property dualism. Accounts of mental causation: how can we explain, or explain away, the belief that mental states such as reasons, beliefs, sensations and emotions are causes of actions?

I. SUBSTANCE DUALISM

Cartesian, or substance, dualism

A substance is traditionally understood as an entity, a thing, that does not depend on another entity in order to exist. Substance **dualism** holds that there are two fundamentally different types of such entities: material substances, or bodies, and mental substances, or minds. It claims that minds do not depend on bodies in order to exist; for example, that minds can exist separated from any body. People who believe that the mind is the soul, and the soul can continue to exist without a body after death, are substance dualists. If mental substance exists, it will be very unlike matter. For instance, we shall see that Descartes argues that it does not exist in space and does not have any parts.

We can contrast substance dualism with materialism, the view that there is only one sort of substance, matter. According to materialism, everything that exists either is a material thing, or is dependent on some material thing to exist. For example, a materialist might claim that mental properties (including mental states, such as holding beliefs, and mental events, such as having a thought) are properties of a person, and that a person is necessarily a material object (a body). Or again – a more contentious view – they might claim that mental properties are, in fact, properties of the brain.

What is substance dualism?

Key points • • •

- One traditional definition of a substance is something that does not depend on any other thing to exist.
- Substance dualism holds that there are two types of substances, mental substances (minds) and material substances (bodies), each capable of existing without the other.
- Materialism holds that there are only material substances, so that everything that exists either is, or depends on, a material substance to exist.

Reasons for holding this view

Plato's arguments

In the *Phaedo*, Plato argued that death is the separation of the soul from the body. He gave two arguments for thinking that the soul could exist separately from the body.

First, he argued that souls cannot be destroyed. All unseen things are unchanging and 'simple' – that is, they don't have parts. If they don't have parts, they cannot be broken up. To destroy something is to break it into parts. And so something without parts cannot be destroyed. The soul is unchanging and simple. So, it cannot be destroyed.

We can object that perhaps there are other types of destruction than breaking into parts. For example, if souls were created out of nothing, then perhaps they could be destroyed by being annihilated.

Second, Plato argued that everything comes about from its opposite. Whenever you change something, you change it from what it is into what it (currently) is not; for example, if you paint a wall red, you change it from not-red to red. Likewise, life changes into its opposite, not-life, or death, the separation of soul and body. But to become alive is therefore also a change from not being alive. Life must come from 'death' – that is, it must be the *joining* of soul and body. So, our souls must exist in another world first and then are born, or reborn, here.

We can object that there are types of change, such as 'coming into existence', that don't involve change from one opposite to another. If I come into existence, it is wrong to say that I change from not existing to existing. Because if I didn't exist, then I didn't have any properties at all, including that of 'not existing'. If death is the destruction of the soul, rather than the separation of soul from body, birth could be its creation (from nothing) rather than the joining of a soul to a body.

In both these arguments, Plato assumes that souls exist. But this is exactly what we want to prove.

Critically discuss Plato's view that the soul can exist independently of the body.

Descartes' knowledge argument

Plato's views on the soul were very influential, and were combined with Christian doctrine as this emerged two thousand years ago. In the seventeenth century, when Descartes lived, the view that humans are part angel, part beast was almost deemed an orthodoxy. But unlike many of his contemporaries, Descartes defended dualism not (in the first instance) on the basis of theology, but by epistemology.

In his *Meditations*, Descartes raises the question of what kind of thing he is. The question 'what am I?' can be answered by considering the question of what it is for me to exist. Descartes is trying to identify his essence, those properties which, if he lost them, would mean he was no longer what he is. (An island, for instance, must be surrounded by water. If the water dried up, joining it to the mainland, it would cease to be an island.)

Explain and illustrate the difference between properties that are essential and those that are not.

He remarks that he can coherently doubt whether he has a body; after all, he only believes he has a body as a result of his perceptual experiences. However, suppose these experiences were actually hallucinations caused by an evil demon. He could be mistaken, deceived into thinking he has a body. But, he continues, he cannot doubt that he has a mind – that is, that he thinks. He cannot doubt that he thinks, because doubting is a kind of thinking. If the demon were to make him doubt that he is thinking, that would only show that he *is* thinking. Equally, he cannot doubt that he exists: if he were to doubt that he exists, that would prove he does exist – as something that thinks.

So, he knows he exists even though he doesn't know whether or not he has a body. From this, Descartes concludes that it is possible for him to exist without a body. He would not necessarily cease to be himself if he ceased to have a body, but he would necessarily cease to be himself if he didn't have a mind.

This argument doesn't show that substance dualism is true, because it doesn't show that *bodies* exist. But let us assume that they do (Descartes argues for this later in the *Meditations*). In that case, if bodies exist, and minds can exist independently of bodies, then substance dualism is true.

> Outline Descartes' argument that mind and body are different because he knows he has a mind, but does not (yet) know he has a body.

The mind as single substance

Descartes claims that he is a thinking *substance*. Many philosophers have thought he means to show that he is the *same* thing, the same 'I', persisting from one moment in time to the next. But how can Descartes be certain of this? Could it not be that Descartes (or any of us) is *only a succession of thoughts*?

Descartes' response was to say that thoughts logically require a thinker. Properties cannot exist without substances; thoughts are, logically, properties of the mind. But perhaps he is wrong. Perhaps thoughts are substances – things that can exist independently.

> Hume believed that thoughts did not logically need a thinker. See PHYSICAL AND PSYCHOLOGICAL CONTINUITY II, p. 190.

Going further: knowledge and reality

Does Descartes' knowledge argument establish that minds exist independently of the body? We can object that just because Descartes can *think* of his mind existing without his body, this doesn't mean that his mind *really can* exist without his body. Perhaps there is some metaphysical connection between his mind and body that Descartes doesn't know about that would make this impossible.

There are two difficulties facing Descartes' argument. The first relates to claims about whether one thing (e.g. mind) is the same thing as another (e.g. body), or whether they are different. We can illustrate this idea with a different example. Suppose I believe (rightly) that the Masked Man has robbed the bank. I also believe that my father has not robbed the bank. I conclude that my father is not the Masked Man. Is the conclusion justified?

No, and here's why. It is true that if two things (in this case, people) have different properties, then they cannot be identical. If the Masked Man robbed the bank and my father didn't, then my father is not the Masked Man. But it is not true that if I *believe* that two things have different properties, then they cannot be identical. I could be mistaken about the properties things have. Suppose my father is the Masked Man. Then my father did rob the bank, and my belief that he didn't is wrong.

Descartes argues that the mind is independent of the body (and so not the body), because he can conceive of its existing without the body. Now if the mind can exist without the body, then it cannot be the same thing as the body. But from just Descartes' thought, we cannot infer this. If the mind is the body, then obviously it cannot exist independently of the body. In this case, Descartes' conception is wrong.

A second difficulty follows this one. Descartes is using his thought to infer what is possible. If the mind is the body, then it is impossible for the mind to exist without the body. So, to know what is possible here, we first need some independent reason to think that the mind is something distinct from the body, such as the argument from indivisibility (below).

Even then, we need to be very cautious using what we can conceive of as a test of possibility. For example, if my father is the Masked Man, then it is impossible that the Masked Man robbed the bank, but my father didn't. Yet it is easy to imagine precisely this, that the Masked Man robbed the bank, but my father didn't. What I am imagining, though, is that the man who is the Masked Man is not my father; and it is questionable how coherent that is.

Identical things must have exactly the same properties. This is known as Leibniz's Law of the Indiscernibility of Identicals.

? Does Descartes' argument from knowledge support the conclusion that the mind can exist independently of the body?

Indivisibility

Descartes argues, as Plato did, that, unlike the body, the mind does not have any parts and cannot be divided. He argues, 'when I consider my mind, that is to say myself insofar as I am only a thinking thing, I can distinguish no parts'. It is with the *whole* mind that one thinks, wills, doubts and so on. These are just different ways of thinking, not parts of the mind. By contrast, the body does have parts. You can literally lose part of your body, say a hand.

Meditations, 164

Descartes argues that having parts is an *essential* property of bodies. Bodies exist in space, and they can therefore be divided. The essential property of minds, he said in the knowledge argument, is thought. Since minds and bodies have different essential properties, they are entirely distinct types of thing.

Is Descartes' argument sound? It does seem right to say that we will, think, imagine, with the whole of our minds, not a literal part. However, cases of mental illness, such as multiple personality syndrome, might be used to suggest that the mind can be divided. In such cases, it seems that some aspects of the person's mind are unable to communicate with other aspects. Freudian ideas of consciousness and the unconscious suggest something similar: people may desire one thing consciously and the opposite thing unconsciously. While this doesn't make the mind *spatially* divisible, it does make sense of talking about 'parts' of the mind.

Explain Descartes' argument that the body can be divided, but the mind cannot.

However, Descartes could respond that the *way* in which the mind is divisible is entirely different from the way in which the body is. So, his argument that mind and body are different because they have different properties is still valid.

We can respond, though, that the argument assumes that *minds exist*. If minds do not exist as things at all, then we cannot talk about 'their' properties. A materialist will claim that there are no 'minds', only mental properties, which are properties of persons or brains.

Assess Descartes' argument for substance dualism from the indivisibility of the mind.

Key points • • •

- Plato argues that, unlike the body, the soul cannot be destroyed because it does not have parts. We can reply that there can be other kinds of destruction.
- He also argues that all change involves something coming about from its opposite. Becoming alive is a change from not being alive. It is the joining

of the soul to the body; so the soul must exist before life. We can reply that 'coming into existence' doesn't involve one's changing from one thing to another.

- Descartes argues that he can doubt the existence of his body, but not that of his mind, which shows that his mind can exist without his body.
- We can object that he has not shown he/his mind exists as a substance, a unitary thing. He could be no more than a succession of thoughts.
- Another objection is that we cannot legitimately infer from conceiving of the mind existing without the body that it can actually exist without the body. Being able to conceive of two things as different does not guarantee that they are two different things, rather than one thing thought of in different ways.
- Descartes argues that having parts is an essential property of bodies, as things that exist in space. But the essential property of minds is thought; and minds have no parts. Therefore, minds and bodies are distinct.
- We can object that this presupposes that minds exist (so as to have properties).

Problems associated with this view of mind

The mind-body problem

Substance dualism seems to make me, a person with both mind and body, essentially *two* things, connected together. This raises the question of how the two things relate to one another.

We may first object that this idea, that we are two connected things, doesn't do justice to our experience of being just *one* thing, which we might call an 'embodied mind'. It 'splits' our experience, which fundamentally seems unified.

Second, modern work on the brain suggests that the mind is very dependent on the brain to function, and, in the end, to exist at all. Damage to certain parts of the brain can make someone unable to think. So, alterations in the body can affect the essential property of the mind; thus, the mind does not have even its essential property independently of the body. Since this property of thinking defines the mind, we can say that our minds are not independent of our bodies.

Descartes can respond to this that the dependency is merely *causal*, not logical. The mind is still logically independent of the body – that is, it is meta-physically possible for it to exist without the body. Compare: your body needs

See Descartes' response in MIND-BODY INDEPENDENCE AND THE INTERMINGLING THESIS, p. 173.

oxygen to function; without it you die. Yet this does not mean that your body is not a separate substance from oxygen. It is logically distinct, even if there is a causal dependency.

However, third, substance dualism is most often rejected because it cannot give an adequate account of mental causation. Nothing seems more obvious than that the mind and the body interact with each other. I decide to phone a friend and move my body to do so. But how is it that something mental, which is not in space and has no physical force, can affect something physical, which is in space and moved by physical forces?

Solipsism

Descartes argues that he knows 'I think' before he knows anything else. He later remarks that he knows, too, *what* he thinks when he thinks it; for example, he can identify a sensation of cold without mistake. In thinking about and identifying my experiences, I unite them under concepts. If nothing but I and my thoughts exist, then I need to be able to do all this, in language, without depending on anything else. Descartes' knowledge argument supposes that we can make sense of the idea of our minds existing on their own, independently of anything outside. The idea that only my mind exists is solipsism.

From Descartes' starting point emerges a picture of concepts and language that John Locke explicitly endorsed: 'Words in their primary or immediate sig-nification, stand for nothing but the ideas in the mind of him that uses them.' What I mean by 'red', for instance, is not, directly, the colour of the tomato, but the *sensation* I have of the colour of the tomato, or remember or imagine having. How does 'red' get its meaning? It's as though I associate the word with the sensation, saying the word 'red' in my head while keeping the sensation of red in mind as I do so. It is like pointing to a colour chart, but where the chart and the pointing are mental, not physical.

Your sensations, of course, are yours alone; they cannot be experienced by anyone else. This means that what you mean by words is given by something that no one else has access to. Your language is a 'private' language, meaning it is logically impossible for anyone else to get at what you mean by words. Locke accepts this: for communication to occur, we must each mean similar sensations by the same words. Your 'red' must be similar to my 'red'.

Wittgenstein argued that if this understanding of language were right, then solipsism would be *inescapable*. If all words get their meaning by referring to

For further discussion, see ACCOUNTS OF MENTAL CAUSATION, p. 58.

What challenges does the mind-body problem raise for substance dualism?

An Essay Concerning Human Understanding, III.ii.2

my experience, then what I mean by 'experience' is 'my experience'. We have said that it is logically impossible that anyone else could have my experiences. But that means that it makes *no sense* to think of other people having experience – because 'experience' refers to my experience alone. But if no one else has experience, then solipsism is true.

Explain the connection between solipsism and Locke's theory of meaning.

The problem of other minds

There is another reason to think that substance dualism tends towards solipsism. The problem of other minds is the question of how we can know that there are minds other than our own. We each experience our own mind *directly*, from 'within'. I can apprehend my sensations and emotions in a way that is 'felt'. I can know what I want or believe through introspection. But my knowledge of other people's minds, if I have any such knowledge, is very different. I cannot have any phenomenological experience of other people's mental states; nor can I know them through introspection. At first sight, at least, all we have to go on is other people's *behaviour* – what is expressed through their bodies.

This raises an important challenge for substance dualism. If minds and bodies are entirely independent, then how can I infer from seeing a body that there is a mind 'attached'? Other 'people' – other bodies – could all be machines, programmed to behave as they do, but with no minds.

Explain the challenge to substance dualism of demonstrating that other minds exist.

Key points • • •

- Substance dualism entails that we are two things, mind and body, connected together. We can object that our experience is of being just one thing.
- Neuroscience has shown that the mind is very dependent on the brain, which undermines the idea that the mind is a separate substance. Descartes can respond that the dependence is causal, not logical.
- Substance dualism faces the problem of explaining how the mind, given that it is so different from the body, can cause physical events.
- Descartes assumes we can make sense of the idea of our minds existing alone, without any other mind or physical world. This entails that words must get their meaning by referring to our ideas, thoughts and sensations. But if this is true, the word 'experience' means my experience. Since it is logically impossible that anyone else should have my experience,

it is logically impossible that anyone else should have experience. This is solipsism.

- Substance dualism also faces the challenge of showing that we can know other minds exist. If minds are logically independent of bodies, any evidence from someone's bodily behaviour does not prove that they have a mind.

Responses to these problems

There are different answers that philosophers have developed in response to the problem of other minds. We will consider three, and see that the third also forms a response to solipsism.

We will consider another answer when discussing LOGICAL BEHAVIOURISM, p. 20.

The argument from analogy

The argument from analogy runs like this: other people are made of the same stuff as me and behave very much as I do in similar circumstances; I have a mind; by analogy, it's logical to think they do as well. It is perhaps the 'common-sense' position on how to solve the problem of other minds. But we can object to its use of **induction**. The conclusion that other people have minds is based on a single case – mine. This is like saying, 'that dog has three legs; therefore, all dogs have three legs.' You can't generalize from one case, because it could be a special case. Perhaps I am the only person to have a mind (solipsism).

A.J. Ayer reformulated the argument to avoid induction from one case by moving from a single correlation between 'behaviour' and (a single) 'mind' to correlating many behaviours of mine with many mental states of mine. This behaviour is correlated with this mental state; that behaviour with that mental state; and so on. Furthermore, mental states are causes of behaviour; to establish this, we only need our own case. But having established the cause, we may legitimately infer that the behaviour of others is caused by mental states.

But the argument relies on the view that like effects (behaviour) have like causes (mental states), a claim that has been generally rejected. Even if my behaviour is caused by my mental states, that doesn't mean that the behaviour of other people could not be caused by something entirely different (say, brain states without mental states).

Can we solve the problem of other minds using analogy?

Inference to the best explanation

Rather than inferring from one's own case to other minds, we may employ a standard form of theoretical scientific reasoning, *inference to the best explanation*. What hypothesis best explains other people's behaviour? The hypothesis that other people have minds, and that their mental states cause them to behave as they do.

Why believe this? In particular, why think that it is a better hypothesis than the claim that (other) people are machines without minds? One way philosophers have developed the argument is to *define* mental states as the inner states of an organism that respond to the environment and cause behaviour. The theory that there are such 'inner' states that cause behaviour is then said to be the best explanation of behaviour. Pain makes you respond quickly to prevent further damage; desire makes you pursue something you need; belief gives you information you need in order to pursue desires.

This line of argument faces three challenges. First, it depends on functionalism being the right account of what mental states are. But philosophers have argued that functionalism is not the right account either of thought or of consciousness. Second, if we understand the mind in terms of its causal relations to behaviour, then we need to solve the problem of how the mind can cause physical events. As we will see in ACCOUNTS OF MENTAL CAUSATION (p. 58), this is particularly difficult for substance dualism. Third, we can object that the belief that other people have minds is not a *hypothesis*, nor do we *infer*, on the basis of *evidence*, that they have minds. This argument is developed next.

This theory is put forward by FUNCTIONALISM, discussed on p. 16.

See INTENTIONALITY AND ARTIFICIAL INTELLIGENCE, p. 31, and QUALIA AND FUNCTIONALISM, p. 41.

Is the 'theory' that other people have minds the best explanation for the 'evidence' given by their behaviour?

Our experience presupposes other minds: on ascribing mental states

A third solution is to reject the idea that we need to *infer*, in any way, that other people have minds. We can develop this claim in two ways.

First, Wittgenstein argued that we react to people as minded, just as we react to them as alive, and that this reaction is deeper, more fundamental than any beliefs about them. Our 'belief' that other people have minds, then, is not the product of any process of thought (including inference); it is part of human nature, which guides how we think. He also argued that we can have direct awareness of other people's mental states – most particularly, emotions. We can literally *see* anger *in* their facial expression, for example. Again, this is not a process of inference; the 'interpretation' is part of our perception of human faces itself. We experience the mind directly in bodily expressions. This particular response is not easily available to substance dualism, which holds that there is always a logical gap between anything bodily and a mental state.

A different approach argues that to have a mind oneself presupposes inter-action with other minds. Descartes assumes that we can ascribe mental states to ourselves. But what does this ability require? We can argue that, for instance, a child cannot learn that it is angry without also learning what it means to say of someone else that they are angry. The ability to ascribe mental states to oneself is learned, and is interdependent with the ability to ascribe mental states to other people. To learn the meaning of 'anger' is to learn its correct application to both oneself and others, simultaneously. In general, a sense of self (of oneself as a self) develops as part of the same process as the sense of others as selves. If there can be no knowledge of oneself as a mind without presupposing that there are other minds, the problem does not arise.

Do we infer that other people have minds?

A FIRST RESPONSE TO SOLIPSISM

The arguments from analogy and inference to the best explanation assumed that there were other people, or other people's bodies, and we needed to explain their behaviour. Solipsism would reply that there are no other bodies, only my experiences of other bodies. So, those answers to the problem of other minds leave solipsism untouched. This last argument from ascribing mental states, however, provides an answer, as it entails that it is impossible to give an account of the mind, even one's own mind, starting just from one's own case. Solipsism supposes that my thoughts exist independently of anything else. But I could not have these thoughts without other minds existing.

Going further: the private language argument

Wittgenstein famously argued that a 'private' language of the kind described in SOLIPSISM (p. 13) is logically impossible. The words we use to talk about our experiences cannot get their meanings by each of us, individually and privately, referring to a sensation we associate with the word.

First, if it were true, we could not understand each other. Locke says that the sensations to which we privately refer would have to be similar. But this

Philosophical Investigations, §§ 257ff.

comparison is impossible; in fact, it makes no sense. If meanings are given by private sensations, there is no meaning to the phrase 'my sensations are similar to yours'. I cannot meaningfully refer to your sensations or compare them with mine.

Second, words would not have meaning at all. How do I associate a word to a sensation? We suggested it was like mentally pointing at a mental sample. Wittgenstein argues that this is not enough. Meanings are stable, and words can be used correctly or incorrectly. If 'red' means the sensation that comes to mind when I think of the word 'red', how can I check whether the *right* sensation has come to mind?

For instance, can I tell whether it is the same sensation that occurred when I first labelled the sensation 'red'? I try to recall that sensation – but, of course, this is just to think *again* of what I mean by 'red'. I'm not comparing *two* things at all, so I can't check one against the other. Putting the point another way: what is it to remember *correctly* the sensation I originally associated with the word 'red'? It is to remember the same sensation. What do I mean by 'the same sensation'? Well, the sensation of red. But this is a vicious circle. We were trying to fix the meaning of the word 'red' by appealing to a sensation. But now we have to appeal to the meaning of red to identify the correct sensation!

Why does this matter? Because there is no gap between what *seems* right (I think it is the same sensation) and what *is* right (it being the same sensation). This means I can't use the word 'wrongly'; 'red' is whatever occurs to me at the time I'm thinking. But words can be used wrongly – that is, with the wrong meaning. So, this cannot be how words get their meaning.

Wittgenstein concludes that we cannot fix the meaning of words by appealing to private sensations. Instead, we have to use something *public*, available to other people. For example, we might fix the meanings of colour words by using a colour chart. This defeats solipsism, since, as we saw, that presupposes that the meanings of words can be fixed by reference to my experiences alone. If this is logically impossible, solipsism literally makes no sense.

Does Wittgenstein's argument have any implications for substance dualism? Only that Descartes' knowledge argument is unsound, because it presupposes a private language. However, that does not mean that substance dualism is false, only that we cannot use that particular argument in its favour.

Outline and illustrate the private language argument.

Key points • • •

- The argument from analogy claims that I can infer other people have minds because they behave as I do, and I have a mind.
- We can object that we cannot base an inference on one case. I could be a special case.
- The argument from inference to the best explanation claims that the hypothesis that other people have minds is the best explanation for their behaviour. We can develop this by saying that mental states are defined by their causal relations.
- We can object, first, that this account of mental states is false, and second, that it presupposes that we can show that mental states cause behaviour. We can also object that the belief that other people have minds is not a hypothesis at all.
- Wittgenstein argued that we can see mental states expressed in behaviour, for example facial expression, and that this is not an inference.
- We can also argue that the ability to ascribe mental states to oneself presupposes that one can ascribe them to other people. To become a mind presupposes the existence of other minds. This also provides an answer to solipsism.
- The private language argument says that words cannot get their meaning by referring to 'private' sensations or ideas, because this provides no criterion for using the word correctly. That words can be used correctly or incorrectly presupposes a public standard of meaning.

II. REDUCTIVE ACCOUNTS OF THE MIND

The most common alternative to substance dualism is the view that there is only one kind of substance, which is matter. This view is materialism. In recent years, materialism has been supplanted by 'physicalism'. The most important reason for this is that physics has shown that 'matter' is too crude an identification of the most basic substance that exists; for example, matter can be changed into energy. For now, we shall define physicalism as the view that everything that exists is physical, or depends upon something that is physical. 'Physical' means something that comes under the laws and investigations of physics, and whose essential properties are identified and described by physics.

Physicalism is discussed again, and refined on p. 46.

While all physicalist theories of the mind agree that the mind is not a separate *substance*, they can disagree on whether it is right to say that mental events are physical events, or whether mental properties are physical properties. This is the question of 'reduction'. We shall discuss 'reduction' further in IDENTITY THEORIES (p. 23), but the question of whether reductionism in some form is right is the topic of the rest of this chapter. Logical behaviourism reduces mental properties to behaviour, TYPE IDENTITY THEORY (p. 23) reduces them to physical properties, and FUNCTIONALISM (p. 26) reduces them to functions.

Logical behaviourism

Logical behaviourism is a form of physicalism, but it does not attempt to reduce mental states, events and so on to physical ones. Instead, it seeks to reduce them to behaviour.

Behaviourism began as a theory of how psychology should conduct itself to achieve the status of a science. Science can investigate only what is publicly accessible. Hence, psychology can and must aim only at the explanation and prediction of behaviour, as any talk of or appeal to 'inner', and so inaccessible, states cannot be scientific. There is no scientific way to establish their existence or nature. It is no objection to say, 'But we can ask people what they feel/ want/believe.' Behaviourism applies to and includes speech behaviour. What people say does not give us 'direct access' to their inner states; it is just another form of behaviour.

In some ways, this is unexciting. Behaviourism becomes more controversial when it makes either of two further claims:

1. that behaviour can be described and explained *without reference to mental events*; instead, we can explain behaviour in terms of stimuli, learning history and reinforcement (all external and observable); or
2. that talk about the mind and mental states is, or should be, talk about behaviour.

This last claim is the theory of 'logical behaviourism'. It recommends that when we try to describe and explain behaviour, concepts that refer to 'inner' mental states should (and can) either be paraphrased into concepts that refer only to behaviour and external events, or be eliminated.

In its simplest, and very implausible, form, logical behaviourism equates a mental state, such as pain, to actual behaviour: so, to be in pain is to do certain things, such as wince, recoil from the cause of pain, nurse the damaged part of the body, etc. But someone stoical might not show their pain; while an actor might pretend to be in pain. So, this can't be right. The more sophisticated version claims that talk of pain is just talk of the *disposition* to behave in these ways, which the stoic has but the actor does not. When talking of dispositions, we are talking of what the person might do in particular situations.

The appeal of logical behaviourism

Logical behaviourism has a number of advantages. For example, it doesn't face the problem of mental causation. As we discussed in THE MIND–BODY PROBLEM (p. 12), if substance dualism were correct, there is a very perplexing problem about how two things as different as mind and body can causally interact. However, we will see that other ACCOUNTS OF MENTAL CAUSATION (p. 58) also face difficulties. Behaviourism claims that mental states don't cause behaviour, so there is no problem of *how* they cause behaviour. It claims either that behaviour can be explained without reference to mental states or that talk of mental states is just talk of behaviour.

It also avoids THE PROBLEM OF OTHER MINDS (p. 14). Talking about mental states is just talking about dispositions to behave in certain ways. From how someone behaves, we can infer what behavioural dispositions they have. But from this, we don't then infer that they have a mind. The link between behaviour and minds isn't evidential, it is logical. To say they have certain dispositions just is to say they have certain mental states. We can know that other people have minds, because we can know directly that they behave in particular ways.

Objections and replies

Two objections to behaviourism take issue with how it takes into account our experience of our own minds. The first claims that we can tell from *introspection* what mental states – beliefs, desires and so on – we have. This would seem odd if mental states were just dispositions to behaviour. I don't have to infer from how I behave, or how I think I am disposed to behave, what mental states I have. They have some 'inner' aspect as well that reveals their content to us directly.

What is logical behaviourism? How does it differ from the original psychological theory?

How does logical behaviourism solve the problems of mental causation and other minds?

The second objection presses the point: many mental states have an inner aspect that can't be captured by behaviour at all. Pain isn't just a disposition to shout or wince; there is also *how pain feels*, 'what it is like' to experience pain. Or again, couldn't it be that you and I have identical dispositions to behaviour, but 'from the inside' there is something different? Imagine that when I look at grass, I experience the colour that you experience when you look at ripe tomatoes. But we both use the word 'green' for describing grass and 'red' for describing tomatoes.

Behaviourists have countered these objections by again pointing to what our language about the mind means. Take the last example: can we coherently suppose and describe the idea that I see 'red' when looking at something green? I don't have any other way of describing what I see when I see something we call 'green' except 'green'! I can't 'check' whether what occurs in your consciousness is just what occurs in my consciousness when we look at the same colour. But this is because it is *logically* impossible: 'checking your consciousness' here doesn't make sense. So, to try to 'compare' what we see 'in our minds' is literally nonsense.

A similar answer can be given to the first objection. It might be that we can now identify our mental states (= behavioural dispositions) immediately. But how did we *learn* to identify and then describe these states (a desire for chocolate, a belief that dogs have four legs)? As argued in OUR EXPERIENCE PRESUPPOSES OTHER MINDS (p. 16), it must have been from other people, and that means that there must have been a way to correlate something public, available to others – that is, behaviour – with these states in the first place. So, all talk about mental states can be meaningful only if it is tied to behaviour.

A third objection is that we cannot reduce talk of mental states to talk of behaviour. Doing exactly the same thing could, in different instances, be expressions of completely different mental states. I might run towards something because I'm scared of it, and want to surprise it; or I might run towards it because I'm not scared of it. The stoic might be in pain, but not show it – thereby expressing the disposition not to show pain. How can we tell which dispositions someone has and is expressing *without referring to other mental states*? When we try to spell out those states as dispositions to behave, we find the same problem again. But if we always have to refer to other mental states, we haven't reduced mental states to dispositions to behave.

The behaviourist can respond that we are taking 'behaviour' much too narrowly. You can tell – from facial expression, for instance – whether someone is running scared or not scared; or from what happens next; or from just how they go about it. Behaviour is *expressive*, not just 'mere behaviour'.

This qualitative aspect of mental states is discussed further in QUALIA, p. 40.

This is a consequence of Wittgenstein's PRIVATE LANGUAGE ARGUMENT, p. 17.

But this reply is not legitimate: expressive descriptions of behaviour use the very mental terms (angrily, in fear, etc.) that behaviourism says should be replaced. So, we still can't replace talk of mental states by talk of behaviour.

Key points • • •

- Logical behaviourism claims that talk about the mind and mental states can be reduced to talk about behaviour – not actual behaviour, but dispositions to behave.
- Because mental states don't cause behaviour, but are logically analysed in terms of behaviour, the theory solves the problem of mental causation. And because we can witness other people's behaviour directly, it solves the problem of other minds.
- However, we can object that mental states have an 'inner' aspect that is not logically connected to behaviour, such as how they feel.
- Behaviourism responds that these felt aspects of mind must also be linked to behaviour, or we could never have learned to identify and describe them.
- Another objection is that we cannot eliminate references to mental states when trying to analyse what behaviour a mental state is a disposition towards. How someone behaves when they have a particular mental state depends on the other mental states they have.

Identity theories of the mind

Type identity theory

Physicalism claims that everything that exists is dependent on something physical in order to exist. 'The mind' is not a separate substance, a 'thing'. It is more accurate to talk of mental properties, mental events, mental states and processes. We can, then, say that these properties (etc.) are possessed not by a mind, but by a person or a brain, which are physical objects. While they agree on this, physicalists differ on whether mental properties are types of property that are entirely distinct from physical properties.

A swan is a bird and white – but what makes it a bird (a biological property) and what makes it white (a colour property) are different properties, though both are physical properties. Are mental properties a kind of physical property? Can

It is called 'type' identity, because we identify what *type* of thing something is by its essential properties. Mental things turn out to be the same type of thing as physical things – that is, mental properties are actually physical properties.

Ontology is the study (-ology) of what exists, or 'being' (ont-).

Outline and illustrate type identity theory.

We will discuss what 'realised by' means in Functionalism, p. 27.

we analyse, for example, thinking a thought or feeling an itch in terms of neuro-physiological properties?

The view that we can is called 'type identity theory'. It claims that mental properties *just are* physical properties. For example, thinking a thought or feeling an itch is *exactly the same thing* as certain neurones firing. They may not *seem* the same, but that's just because we have different ways of knowing about these properties: through experience and through neuroscience. Many things turn out to be something they don't seem to be. For example, solid objects are mostly empty space, water is just hydrogen and oxygen (who'd have guessed?).

Type identity theory is a form of 'reduction'. An 'ontological reduction' involves the claim that the things in one domain (e.g. mental things) are identical with some of the things in another domain. For example, things that appear non-physical are really physical. Mental properties, it argues, are a subset of physical properties. The identity claim is a reduction because we have 'reduced' mental properties – which we might have thought were a different kind of thing – to physical properties. That is, there is *nothing more* to mental properties than being a certain kind of physical property. The theory doesn't explain what physical properties are; for that, we need some independent explanation, for example from physics.

Type identity theory was developed in the 1960s as neuroscience gathered pace. The evidence is that mental events and states are very closely dependent on the brain, so many people now think that 'the mind' is just 'the brain', and everything mental is actually neurophysiological.

Reductionism and multiple realisability

However, neuroscientific evidence does not establish type identity theory. To see this, we need to think philosophically, not scientifically. The most famous objection to type identity theory says that mental properties cannot be *identical* to physical properties because the *same* mental property can be 'realised by' *different* physical properties. For example, the brain states that relate to pain are different in different species, but pain is the same mental state. Therefore, 'being in pain' cannot be exactly the same thing as being in any *one* of these different physical states. And this is true for all sorts of mental states. Could there be aliens who have thoughts? If having the thought 'snow is white' is identical with having a particular physical property, then it would be *impossible* for an alien to have this thought if it did not have an identical brain to human beings. This is very implausible. This is the argument from 'multiple realisability'.

The identity theorist could argue that we should talk about 'human pain', that this is a different property from 'dog pain'. Or again, if there are intelligent aliens who have thoughts, but different brains, we should talk of 'human thoughts' and 'aliens' thoughts'. But this doesn't seem plausible – pain is pain because of *how it feels*; thought is thought because of *what is thought*. A dog and a human being in pain share something in common, which we identify as the mental property 'being in pain'. If an alien believes that snow is white, and so do I, we have the same type of thought, whatever our physiology. So, mental properties can't *be* physical properties.

This is not to say that there is *no* relation between mental and physical properties. It is just to argue that the relation is not identity.

> The argument was presented in Hilary Putnam's paper 'Psychological Predicates'.

> ? What is the objection from multiple realisability?

Token identity

A different identity theory agrees that mental events are physical events, but rejects the claim that mental properties are identical to physical properties as we have been discussing them; for example, properties investigated by neuroscience or physics. Token identity theory claims that while mental properties are not physical properties, each individual occurrence ('token') of a mental property is identical with the occurrence of a physical property. The occurrence of the mental and physical properties forms one and the same event. An example: the mental property 'being in pain' is not identical with any physical property (the multiple realisability argument). However, each time the mental property 'being in pain' occurs in some creature, it occurs *with and because of* the occurrence of some physical property; for example, in human beings, some part of the brain being activated. In a different species, or on a different occasion, 'being in pain' may occur with and because of the occurrence of a different physical property. However, 'being in pain' always and only ever occurs with and because of the occurrence of *some* physical property of other.

The idea of 'token identity' will become clearer when we look at a specific version of the theory. Functionalism, which we look at next, is usually understood this way.

> Another version, ANOMALOUS MONISM (p. 46), was the first token identity theory.

Key points • • •

- Type identity theory claims that not only is there just one kind of substance, that identified by physics, but mental properties are, in fact, physical properties.
- This claim reduces mental properties to physical ones – that is, what it is to be a particular mental property is to be a particular physical property.
- However, the argument from multiple realisability says that it is possible for two creatures to have the same mental property, for example 'being in pain', but have different physical properties. A mental property that can be multiply realised in this way cannot be identical with any particular physical property.
- Token identity theory claims that mental properties are not identical to physical properties, but the *occurrence* of a mental property on any particular occasion is identical to the occurrence of a particular physical property on that occasion.

Functionalism

Functionalism claims that mental states are logically linked to behaviour, but they are not reducible to it. Mental states are states that exist 'between' input (e.g. stimulus, experience) and output (e.g. behaviour). To characterise a mental state, we need to describe its typical inputs and outputs. For example, what typically causes pain and what pain typically causes are quite different from what typically causes beliefs, and what they cause. In listing these inputs and outputs, we can't refer only to the stimuli and behaviour; mental states have causal relations to *other* mental states. For example, pain normally causes the belief that one is in pain. So, the definitions of mental states will be interdependent. We can't eliminate talk of mental states in favour of talk of behaviour.

On this view, we can say that mental states are *functional* states. Any mental state can be analysed in terms of the links it has with stimuli, behaviour and other mental states. This analysis also rejects type identity theory. That theory claims that mental states and properties just are physical states and properties. This means that a species with a different kind of brain, or no brain at all – that uses something other structure to think, feel, etc. – could not be in the same mental states as us.

This seems just wrong, to the functionalist. The property of 'having the function x' is a property that can occur in many different physical things. For example, 'being a mousetrap' is a functional property. There are lots of different mousetraps, built in different ways, using different methods and materials. 'Being a poison' is a functional property. There are lots of different sorts of poisons, which work in different ways and are made of different chemicals. So, 'being in pain' is also a functional property – lots of different physical ways, different brain states, that could be 'being in pain'. This might not just vary from one species to another; it could vary from one individual to another, or even in one individual, from one time to another.

Causal role (or 'teleological') functionalism

There are different ways in which we can understand the idea of 'function'. In the most popular version of functionalism, 'causal role functionalism', the idea is understood causally. A mental state is a causal disposition to act in certain ways, and to have certain other mental states, given inputs and other mental states. In other words, a mental state has a particular causal role in causing other mental states, and together with other mental states, in causing behaviour. We pick mental states out by their causal role.

This is the idea of function that we find in the examples above. 'Being a mousetrap' involves having certain causal properties, namely trapping a mouse. The idea of 'being a poison' is also a causal idea.

Now, in each of these examples, the functional property depends on a set of physical properties. Some physical state or other (some arrangement of parts) 'realises' – has, on this occasion – the causal role that is 'being a mousetrap'; some chemical state or other, in each case, realises 'being a poison'. Likewise, mental properties such as 'being in pain' are realised by properties playing a causal role. In human beings, perhaps these are brain properties. However, telling us all about what goes on in the brain is not to say anything *essential* about what it is to have a mind (mental properties), for things with very different brains, or with no brains at all, could have mental properties, just as long as they realised the same functional properties – that is, played the same causal role.

How does functionalism differ from behaviourism and from type identity theory?

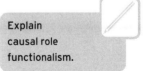

Explain causal role functionalism.

Going further: machine functionalism

As a theory, functionalism began in the 1960s in a slightly different form, with a different meaning of 'function'. It rested on a comparison between the mind and a computer. A computer performs a task by going through a series of states governed by a set of rules or algorithm (a program). It is possible to describe a computer that could perform any task that is computational, meaning that it can be broken down into a series of small steps that can be related by a set of rules. The mathematician and code breaker Alan Turing provided the description, and what he described became known as a Turing machine.

A Turing machine is not a physical object, but a mathematical idea. It is a machine with a finite number of possible 'states' that follows a program that specifies, for any state and event, the next state the machine should go into. Each rule in the program has the form 'if the machine is in State1, and it receives Input1, it should go into State2, and produce Output1'. So, each state is defined functionally.

A drinks machine provides an example of the sorts of rules. Suppose it vends only one drink, at 60p. Its first state (State1) is to display the sign 'Enter 60p'. Some rules it has would be:

1. 'When the machine is in State1, and it receives the input of a 50p piece (Input1), it should go into State2, and display "Enter 10p".'
2. 'When the machine is in State2, and it receives the input of a 10p piece (Input2), it should vend the drink, go into State1, and display "Enter 60p".'
3. 'When the machine is in State1, and it receives the input of a 10p piece (Input3), it should go into State3, and display "Enter 50p".'
4. 'When the machine is in State3, and it receives the input of a 50p piece (Input1), it should vend the drink, go into State1, and display "Enter 60p".'

And so on for all possible combinations of coins adding up to 60p. This set of rules, which specifies every possible state of the machine and every possible transition from that state according to each possible input, is called a 'machine table'.

A drinks machine is very limited in what it can do. A Turing machine can carry out any computation, so its machine table will be huge. But because its number of states, and the number of inputs, is finite, it will be finite.

Machine functionalism is the view that any creature with a mind can be understood as a Turing machine, and mental states can be understood as machine states. These are specified by the machine table – that is, what a state is can be defined in terms of what it does in response to inputs and other states, and what outputs it produces. As functionalism developed, the idea that mental states are machine states of a Turing machine that follow the rules of the machine table was left behind in favour of the less restrictive idea that they are states defined by their causal role.

> What is machine functionalism? How does it differ from causal role functionalism?

Functionalism and reduction

If a mental state is just a state playing a certain kind of function, what is the nature of this state? It could be anything, say functionalists. Functionalism is about what mental states are, not about the nature of the substance that realises those mental states. It is therefore logically compatible with both substance dualism and physicalism.

However, most functionalists are physicalists. If physicalism is true, then mental properties are realised by physical substance and physical properties (e.g. properties of the brain). As we've just seen, perhaps different brain states play the same function in different species. But *on each occasion* the occurrence of the brain state *is* the occurrence of the mental state. This is token identity – each individual instance of a mental state is just a brain state, playing a certain function.

Functionalism reduces mental properties to functional properties; but, even assuming physicalism, it does not reduce them to physical properties. Functional properties occur throughout science; an example is being an eye (there are lots of types of eyes). They are not themselves physical properties – that is, properties identified by physics. However, functional properties are properties that are realised by physical properties operating in causal relationships. They are not, therefore, *radically* different from physical properties. There is nothing unique or strange about them.

Objections to functionalism take the form of arguments that we cannot reduce mental properties to functional properties. The two properties now

> For this reason, most philosophers do not consider functionalism a form of property dualism, on which see THE 'HARD PROBLEM' OF CONSCIOUSNESS, p. 43.

Explain why functionalism embraces token identity theory.

often thought to be the essential mental properties are consciousness and Intentionality. We shall discuss Intentionality in the next section, and return to consciousness starting in CONSCIOUSNESS, FUNCTIONALISM AND QUALIA (p. 39).

Key points • • •

*   Functionalism claims that mental states and properties are functional states and properties. Causal role functionalism interprets 'function' as the role played in a network of causes and effects. Machine functionalism interprets it in terms of the rules governing the machine states.
*   Functionalism avoids the objection to type identity theory from multiple realisability. A functional property (and so mental properties) can be realised by various physical (or even non-physical) properties. Functionalism is compatible with substance dualism, although most functionalists are physicalists.
*   Physicalist functionalism accepts token-identity theory. On each occasion, the occurrence of the functional property is identical with the occurrence of the physical property playing a particular causal role.

Intentionality and artificial intelligence

Intentionality

Many mental states are 'about' something – objects or events in the world. For example, I might have a belief *about Paris*, a desire *for chocolate*, be angry *at the government* or intend *to go to the pub*. In all these cases, my state of mind is 'directed' towards an 'object', the thing I'm thinking about (Paris, chocolate, the government, going to the pub). This idea of 'directedness' is known as 'Intentionality'. Intentionality is not about intentions (to mark the difference, I shall always use a capital 'I' for 'Intentionality'). If I have an intention, I am 'aiming at' *doing* something. With Intentionality, it is the thought or mental state that 'aims at' its object, what it is about, and no 'doing' needs to be involved. Beliefs, desires, emotions all have Intentionality; they are all 'Intentional mental states'.

From the Latin *intendere*, meaning 'to aim at'.

An Intentional mental state is a mental state with Intentional content. So what is this? Whenever we think of, have a belief about or desire something, we always conceive of it in a certain way, under a particular description. For example, in Sophocles' famous play *Oedipus Rex*, Oedipus kills his father and marries his mother. He doesn't want to do this. But it turns out that he doesn't know who his parents are. He doesn't know that the people he thinks are his parents aren't. On his journey, he meets an old man in the road who gets in his way. Oedipus becomes very angry and kills the old man. In fact, the man was his father, Laius. Oedipus was angry at the old man. Was he angry at his father? From his point of view, he wasn't; he didn't think of the old man *as* his father.

So, Intentional states represent the world in particular and partial ways. It's like seeing something from a particular aspect; you can see it, but not all of it. *What* Intentional states represent – Paris, the government, Laius, snow – is called the 'Intentional object'. The *way* they represent that object we can call the 'aspectual shape' of the object. The Intentional object plus the aspectual shape comprise the Intentional content.

We can have different mental states with the same Intentional content if we take different 'attitudes' to that content. For example, I can believe I'm arriving late; I can want to be arriving late; I can fear I'm arriving late; I can be pleased I'm arriving late. An Intentional state, then, comprises a particular 'attitude' or 'mode' towards a particular Intentional content.

> ? What is the structure of an Intentional mental state?

Problems for reduction

Intentionality poses this challenge: how is it possible for anything physical to have the property of Intentionality? Physical things are never 'about' anything. To say what it is for a physical thing or state to be the thing or state that it is doesn't require reference to something else. A particular molecular structure or physical process, described in these terms, is not about anything. But the states and processes of your brain are just chemical states and processes. So how could they ever be about anything? So how could Intentional mental states be states of your brain?

Functionalism claims that Intentionality is a functional property. A physical thing can have the property of Intentionality because of its role in a network of causes and effects. But how do we get from the idea that a belief about dogs, say, is *caused* by certain experiences of dogs and *causes* certain behaviour towards dogs to the idea that beliefs are *about* dogs? Compare: clouds are caused by water evaporating from the sea and they cause rain; but clouds aren't about the sea, and they don't represent rain.

Functionalists maintain that if the causal network is complicated enough, then states within the system are not just causal, but Intentional. The past 35 years have seen large research programmes attempting to develop an account of the necessary causal network.

Going further: reducing Intentionality

Intentional states 'represent' the world. We can understand this in terms of information. So, philosophers have started from thinking how natural things can carry information. For example, smoke carries the 'information' that there is a fire, fingerprints carry 'information' related to the identity of the person and so on. However, notice that it makes no sense to say that smoke is 'mistaken'. By contrast, Intentional states can be mistaken. For example, someone might believe that the capital of Germany is Frankfurt, not Berlin. They would be wrong. Getting this idea of a mistake out of a model of natural 'information' has proven very difficult.

Some philosophers argue the function of beliefs is to represent the world truly. We can get the idea of 'mistaken' (false) beliefs from this; such beliefs are the result of our belief-forming process 'malfunctioning'. We can compare this to biological organs. The function of the eye is to see, yet eyes can malfunction in many ways. We identify the function of something biological in terms of evolution – what was the organ 'selected for'? This gives us a standard by which we can talk about something being (or going) 'wrong'. We can then use this idea of function as a starting point for Intentionality.

However, this is still not enough. For example, the stomach has the function of digestion, and it can fail to perform this function. But states of the stomach are not *about* digestion (or food). They are not Intentional states at all.

Explain and illustrate the difficulty of analysing Intentionality in terms of causal role.

Is artificial intelligence intelligent?

Artificial intelligence is a research project in computer science that aims to create computers that display behaviour that is 'intelligent'. Some philosophers and scientists argue that the test for whether a computer is intelligent is the 'Turing Test'. A person, a computer and another person (the interrogator) are each in a different room. The interrogator puts the same questions, in turn, to the person and the computer, not knowing which is which. If after five minutes the interrogator cannot tell from his or her conversations with the person and the machine which is which, then the machine has passed the Turing Test.

Whether the Turing Test is a good test for intelligence is very controversial. But we shall look just at an objection which claims that, unless we develop computers with consciousness, they cannot be genuinely intelligent.

John Searle argues that Intentionality is not reducible to functions. To illustrate his argument, he describes a room with two holes in the wall; through one, pieces of paper are passed in (inputs), through the other, pieces of paper are passed out (outputs). There is someone in the room, who has to respond to the inputs by sending the outputs. The inputs are questions in Chinese; the person doesn't understand Chinese, but has a huge book that correlates every question with an answer. He finds the output that is that answer, and sends that piece of paper out. The room as a whole – the system – 'behaves' as if it understands Chinese! But it doesn't – the person doesn't, the rulebook doesn't, the room doesn't. Even if the person memorised the rulebook, that person wouldn't understand Chinese; he or she wouldn't know what the questions *meant*. This is what real Intentionality requires. Yet the room performs the same functions as someone who does understand Chinese, answering questions. So, performing functions isn't enough for understanding meaning, for real Intentionality.

Minds, Brains and Programs

Some functionalists have rejected Searle's conclusion; they say that the room (operating as it does, with the person inside) *does* understand Chinese. Consider this development of the thought experiment. Since the person inside the room doesn't understand Chinese, let's just have a computer that does the same thing (it is programmed to follow a rulebook). Suppose we then put the computer inside a robot, which interacts with the world. We add a program for correlating visual input (through cameras in its eyes) to output – so the robot can now 'name' things in Chinese, as well as answer questions in Chinese. Is it now so obvious that the robot doesn't understand Chinese?

Searle would still say that it doesn't. Artificial intelligence isn't intelligence at all; at best, it is a simulation of intelligence. Other functionalists argue that to understand is nothing more than being able to interact with the world (including other people) in the right causal-functional way. Although we haven't been able to give a complete functional analysis of how this is done, this doesn't mean that we will not be able to give one in the future. When we can, we will be able to create genuine robotic intelligence.

Searle replies that the difference between Intentionality and a simulation of Intentionality is consciousness. Without consciousness, a series of functional interactions remains meaningless *to the robot* even when it looks meaningful to us. But Intentional states are meaningful 'from the inside'; they are meaningful to the creature that has them. Without consciousness, meaning is lacking, and therefore so is Intentionality. We will look at the question of whether functionalism can explain consciousness in CONSCIOUSNESS, FUNCTIONALISM AND QUALIA (p. 39).

> Critically discuss whether functionalism can successfully account for Intentionality.

Key points • • •

* Intentionality is the property of a mental state by which it is 'directed' onto some 'object'. An Intentional mental state comprises a particular attitude, e.g. belief, towards a particular Intentional content. Intentional content comprises an Intentional object under a particular aspectual shape.
* Physical states and properties do not seem to have this property of 'directedness'. They are what they are without reference to anything else.
* Functionalism argues that Intentionality is a highly complex causal-functional property. However, deriving Intentionality from causal interactions has proven difficult.
* The Turing Test is a test for artificial intelligence. It tests whether someone can successfully distinguish between a person and a machine after five minutes' conversation.
* Searle argues that Intentionality cannot be reduced to functions, because Intentionality involves understanding meaning, while performing functions does not. What is missing is consciousness. Functionalists respond that complex functions would be enough for understanding.

Eliminative materialism

The views we have discussed so far – substance dualism, behaviourism, type identity theory and functionalism – all assume our usual understanding of mental life, in terms of beliefs, desires, emotions, feelings and so on. Eliminative materialism (aka eliminativism), by contrast, argues that it is not, and that future scientific developments will show that the way we think and talk about the mind is fundamentally flawed. It is so mistaken, in fact, that we should abandon all talk of the mental, and stick to talking about brain processes instead.

This claim is not a form of reductionism; it is a form of *elimination*. Reduction says that there are mental properties, but they are in fact physical, or behavioural, or functional properties. Eliminativism says that there are no mental properties – nothing exists that corresponds to mental terms like 'belief', 'desire' and so on. In fact, nothing corresponds to Intentionality.

'Folk psychology'

The argument for eliminativism goes like this. First, according to eliminativism, our common-sense understanding of mental states and processes – often called 'folk psychology' – is in fact an **empirical** theory about human behaviour. We are using a set of concepts, for example of different types of mental states (belief, desire, emotion, sensation) and processes (thinking, feeling, sensing), and a set of general, very loose laws to describe, explain and predict behaviour. For example, if someone is thirsty, they will – under normal conditions – look for something to drink. If someone believes it is raining outside, and doesn't want to get wet, they will – under normal conditions – pick up an umbrella or other covering to keep them dry. And so on. As functionalism has indicated, the meaning of the concepts is given by the role they play in the network of laws. (Desires motivate behaviour, beliefs represent the world and so on.)

Second, empirical theories can be tested, and if they turn out not to be accurate, then they should be abandoned in favour of a more accurate theory. Because the concepts of folk psychology gain their meaning from the network of laws, if it were shown that our common-sense laws are actually not very good at explaining and predicting people's behaviour, then we should abandon our common-sense concepts as well.

Third, scientific research indicates a strong connection between the mind and brain states and processes, for example that behaviour is caused by events in the brain. Therefore, our common-sense theory of the mind needs to be related to a neuroscientific theory. This is the question of reduction. Will the common-sense ontology of states and processes (beliefs, desires, etc.) reduce to the ontology of neuroscience (brain states and processes)? Eliminativism argues that it will not reduce, because our common-sense theory of the mind is false.

Why believe this?

1. There are many aspects of mental life that folk psychology cannot explain, such as mental illness, the nature of intelligence, sleep, perception and learning.
2. If we look at the history of folk psychology, it reveals no progress since the ancient Greek authors, 2,500 years ago. Meanwhile, neuroscientific explanations are constantly growing in scope and power.
3. We cannot make folk psychology coherent with other scientific theories. In particular, the ideas of Intentionality and consciousness are highly problematic. If it does not fit in with empirically robust theories, such as neuroscience, we have reason to abandon it.

Outline and illustrate the argument for eliminativism.

Objections

We can challenge each of these points, and whether they support eliminativism. To the first point, we can say that folk psychology is not *intended* to be a theory of these aspects of mental life, so it is no criticism that it does not explain them. It is only meant to explain human behaviour or, even more specifically, human action.

To the second, we can say that folk psychology *has* evolved over time. For instance, the Greeks used an idea of fixed and unchanging 'character', whereas now we tend to appeal more to the situation someone finds themselves in. Or again, ideas about unconscious beliefs and desires have become part of folk psychology. And if we look at recent empirical psychology – aside from neuroscience – we find that theories using common-sense concepts and ideas have produced new knowledge. To eliminate the concepts of beliefs, desires and other common-sense mental states from psychology would do away with much scientific psychology as well as folk psychology.

To the third, we can argue – with FUNCTIONALISM (p. 26) and ANOMALOUS MONISM (p. 46) – that folk psychology does not need to be reducible to other scientific theories in order to be compatible with them. Our folk psychological explanations appeal to properties that neuroscientific explanations do not cover; but the two kinds of explanations can be made coherent through token identity theory.

Eliminativism will reply that these points are not very strong. First, we need to know how human action or behaviour relates to the rest of mental life. To have very different *sorts* of theories explaining different aspects of the mind is unsatisfactory. Second, the developments in folk psychology are relatively superficial. Our common-sense explanations of behaviour are still far less powerful than the kinds of explanations we find elsewhere in the sciences. The only way to address this problem is to look to neuroscience. Third, why should we accept an *abstract* functional account of how the mind works based on common sense? Why not start with looking at the *actual workings* of the functional system – that is, the brain – and derive our functional account from it?

How persuasive are eliminativism's three criticisms of folk psychology?

Going further: eliminativism is incoherent

The discussion so far has accepted the suggestion that folk psychology is an empirical theory. But there is good reason to suppose that this is a misunderstanding. We can argue for this indirectly.

Eliminativism, it seems, presents arguments, which are expressions of beliefs and use beliefs about what words mean and how reasoning works, in order to change our beliefs about folk psychology. Yet it claims that *there are no beliefs*. So what does eliminativism express, what is it trying to change? If there are no beliefs, including no beliefs about meaning, no beliefs linked by reasoning, then eliminativism expresses nothing at all; it is meaningless. So if eliminativism is true, it is meaningless. So it can't be true.

Eliminativists say that this begs the question. It presupposes that there are beliefs and meanings in the folk psychological sense. Compare: there was an argument in the nineteenth century between people who thought that to be alive required some special energy, a 'vital force', and those who said there was no such force. The vitalists could argue that if what their opponents said was true, they would all be dead! Yet now we know there is no special 'vital force', that life arises from ordinary chemical reactions.

But we can press the objection. Eliminativism is eliminating Intentionality. The very ideas of meaning, or 'making sense', of 'true' versus 'false' belief, or 'reasoning' itself, are to be rejected, as they all rest on Intentionality. So how we can say that eliminativism is true, or a theory that makes more sense than folk psychology? Just as the opponents of vitalism appealed to chemical reactions, we need some *alternative* to Intentionality according to which it makes sense to say that folk psychology is false. But eliminativism does not give us this. Without it, we *cannot conceive* that folk psychology is false, because that very idea presupposes the folk psychological concept of Intentionality.

The analogy with vitalism fails. The anti-vitalist *agrees* that he must be alive to make his claim (and then gives an account of life). The eliminativist says she does *not* need beliefs in order to make her claim, and gives us no account of how it is possible to make a claim without having beliefs.

Folk psychology turns out not to be an empirical theory (which might be wrong), but a condition of intelligibility, a condition for thinking, reasoning, making claims at all. So, we can't eliminate it. If it can't be reduced – as eliminativism argues – then we must embrace a non-reductive theory of the mind.

Assess eliminativism.

Key points • • •

- Eliminativism argues that 'folk psychology' is an empirical theory of the mind that should be replaced by neuroscience. Folk psychology does not explain many mental phenomena, has not progressed in over 2,500 years, and cannot be made consistent with scientific theories we know to be true.
- We can object that folk psychology does not intend to explain more than people's behaviour, that many developments in psychology use its concepts, and that it does not need to be reducible to other scientific theories to be true.
- A more fundamental objection is that eliminativism cannot be true because it is incoherent. One cannot argue that a theory is false, and so we should not believe it, without presupposing Intentionality. Eliminativism offers us no alternative way of making sense of the idea of meaning. Folk psychology is therefore not an empirical theory, but a condition of saying anything meaningful at all.

Consciousness, functionalism and qualia

A functionalist theory of consciousness

Functionalism claims that mental properties are functional properties. On p. 30, we identified two properties as essentially mental: Intentionality and consciousness. We have seen the difficulties Intentionality presents for functionalism (p. 31). How might a functionalist try to show that consciousness is a functional property?

The first move is to be more precise about what we are explaining. Rather than talking about consciousness, we should try to explain what makes a mental state conscious. Not all mental states are conscious. For example, there are desires and emotions we have that we are not conscious of having; we can discover things about ourselves. What makes the difference between a mental state that is conscious and one that is not? One suggestion is that a mental state is conscious if the person is *conscious of* it. This immediately introduces the idea of a relation, which is what functionalism wants: a mental state is conscious just as a matter of its relations to other mental states and behaviour. For functionalism to succeed, consciousness must be completely reducible to the ways in which mental states interact. So what relations between mental states are involved when a person is conscious of a particular mental state?

David Rosenthal suggests that a mental state, x, is conscious if you have an (unconscious) 'higher-order thought' about that mental state, roughly to the effect that 'I am having state x'. A state is conscious just in the case that it is being thought about. For example, if the conscious state is seeing my computer, the thought that makes this state conscious is 'I see my computer'. For a desire to be conscious, I must have the thought 'I want . . .'. In the normal case, the mental state causes the thought, which in turn makes the mental state conscious.

Rosenthal's theory is very contentious, and philosophers have raised many objections to it. We shall concentrate on just one, which turns out to be an objection to all functionalist theories of consciousness. If we think about sensations, for example pain, being conscious, it seems very counter-intuitive to say that consciousness of the pain is the thought 'I am in pain' – that is, you feel the pain (consciously) because you have that thought. It is more plausible to say that you make the judgement 'I am in pain' *because* you feel the pain. If this is right, Rosenthal has not explained what it is to be conscious of the pain.

To develop the discussion, we need to think further about our consciousness of sensations and feelings.

'Two Concepts of Consciousness'

Explain the claim that a mental state is conscious if one has a higher-order thought about it. Why is this a functionalist theory of consciousness?

Qualia

The issue of 'qualia' is a complex and wide-ranging one in contemporary philosophy of mind. The concept itself is not very clear, and different philosophers use the term with slightly different meanings. There is no general agreement about whether qualia exist; or about what the implications are if they exist; or what it is for them to exist.

The idea of 'qualia' (single: 'quale') starts with the idea of 'phenomenal consciousness'. Consciousness, especially the sort of consciousness involved in perception, sensation and emotion, has a 'feel' to it, a distinctive 'experiential quality'. The phrase often used to try to capture this experiential quality is 'what it is like'. There is something it is like to taste beer, to see a red rose, to feel sad. 'What it is like' here isn't meant to compare the experience to others; it is meant to pick out how the experience is for the subject. When we make comparisons between experiences – for example, 'Seeing a red rose is like seeing a ripe tomato' – we do so *in virtue of* what it is like to see a red rose in the sense meant here. It is the experience of redness that allows us to compare roses and tomatoes; and there is something it is like to experience redness. We can call the properties of an experience that give it its distinctive experiential quality 'phenomenal properties'.

Some people think qualia just are phenomenal properties. But this isn't accurate. Philosophers all agree that there are phenomenal properties; what they disagree about is whether the concept of qualia is the best explanation for these properties. Philosophers who believe there are qualia argue that phenomenal properties are best understood as *intrinsic, non-Intentional* properties of experience.

1. An intrinsic property is one that its possessor (in this case, the experience) has in and of its own, not in virtue of its relations to anything else. Think of the smell of coffee. It is the smell 'of coffee' because of its relation to the substance of coffee. That it is 'of coffee' is not an intrinsic property. But how that smell smells is an intrinsic property (people who believe in qualia argue), because it would be that smell even if it wasn't caused by coffee. The smell can't be reduced to some relationship *between* the experience of the smell and something else. Intrinsic properties of experience, then, also relate to the *identity* of the experience. On this account, pain wouldn't be pain if it didn't *feel* painful.

2. Intentional properties are properties of a mental state that enable it to represent what it does. Many philosophers, for example functionalists, believe that Intentional properties are based on causation. The smell of coffee wouldn't be of *coffee* if it wasn't reliably caused by coffee and not by other things. Intentional properties, then, are relational rather than intrinsic. They depend on the way the mental state 'hooks up' to the world and other mental states. Qualia, because they are intrinsic properties, are non-Intentional properties.

We saw the difficulties facing this claim in INTENTIONALITY, p. 31.

What are qualia?

Qualia and functionalism

It seems that if qualia exist, functionalism cannot be a complete account of mental states. If phenomenal properties are qualia, then they don't fulfil any causal functional roles; so functionalism can't explain phenomenal consciousness. The objection suggests that there is something about consciousness – how pain feels, how red looks, how a rose smells – that can't be analysed in terms of functional role. Yes, of course, how pain feels is important to what it causes; for example, it causes you to cry out or withdraw your hand from the fire. But the feeling of the pain isn't *just* these causal relations. Two kinds of examples are used to show this:

1. Absent qualia: the Chinese 'mind'. Suppose the mind just is the functioning brain. Suppose the population of China was fitted with radios which were connected up in just the same way that the neurones in the brain are connected up, and messages passed between them in the same way as between neurones. According to functionalism, this should create a mind; but it is very difficult to believe that there would be a 'Chinese consciousness'. If the Chinese system replicated the state of my brain when I feel pain, would something be in pain?

We can compare this to Searle's argument against artificial intelligence, p. 33.

2. Inverted qualia: suppose that you and I are looking at ripe tomatoes and fresh grass. We both say that the tomatoes are red, the grass is green. But the particular way tomatoes seem to me is the way grass looks to you, and vice-versa. Functionally, we are identical, and yet we have different colour experiences.

One standard reply is to say that in these examples, the brain and the Chinese population, or me and you, are *not*, in fact, functionally identical. There are going to be small, but very important, differences. There is a complexity about the causal relations of phenomenal qualities that the functionalist can appeal to. For example, 'red' is a warm colour, 'green' a cool colour. If you see grass the way I see tomatoes, will you describe the colour of the grass as 'warm'? To say there is no functional difference between you and me, yet we see colours differently, we have to change a great deal (you have to think of (what I call) green as a warm colour and so on). Whether this is possible is unclear. If we specify the functional role of 'red' in enough detail, says the functionalist, maybe we'll see that whatever plays that functional role must be the phenomenal property 'red' and can't be 'green'. The same goes for other phenomenal properties, such as pain. For example, pain causes one to nurse the part of one's body that is in pain – what plays this role in the Chinese mind?

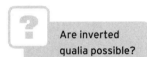

Are inverted qualia possible?

Other functionalists accept the objection and modify their theory. Not *everything* about the mind can be explained in terms of functions. Qualia depend not just on functional states, but also on the specific *physical* properties of the system that realises the functional states. How pain feels to us isn't (just) a matter of what causes it and what effects it has; it also depends on our physiology and the specific chemicals in our brains. However, mental states are still nothing more than physical states playing a functional role.

The difficulty with this response is that it starts to say that pain is identical with a physical-functional state *in us*; and this point was used against the type identity theory (p. 24). Is pain multiply realisable or not?

The point is that what makes pain pain is *how it feels*. In the world as it actually is, that might depend on particular facts of physiology. But it doesn't seem *metaphysically* impossible that some other physical state could feel just like pain. And to feel just like pain is to *be* pain. Qualia can't be reduced to physical or functional properties, or even a combination of the two. If this argument is correct, we will have to embrace some kind of property dualism. We'll see another argument for this conclusion in the next section.

Critically discuss the claim that phenomenal properties are qualia.

Key points • • •

- One functionalist theory of consciousness claims that a mental state is conscious if the person is conscious of it. To be conscious of mental state x is to have a 'higher-order' thought that 'I am having state x'.
- We can object that when we are conscious of pain, for example, this is not because we have the thought 'I am in pain'. Rather, we have thought 'I am in pain' because we feel the pain.

- Phenomenal properties are those subjective aspects of experience that we try to capture by saying 'what it is like' to have this or that experience.
- Some philosophers argue that phenomenal properties are qualia – that is, intrinsic, non-Intentional properties of experience. If they are, then functionalism cannot be a complete theory of the mind, as qualia are not functional properties.
- The thought experiments of absent qualia (the Chinese 'mind') and inverted qualia are designed to show that phenomenal properties are not functional properties, but qualia.
- Some functionalists reply that if we specify the functional role of experiences of pain or seeing red in enough detail, the thought experiments fail. Others argue that phenomenal properties are fixed by functional *and physical* properties, taken together.
- We can object to this last answer by appealing to multiple realisability. What makes pain pain is how it feels, which can be multiply realised, so can't be identical with physical properties.

The 'hard problem' of consciousness: reduction, physicalism and property dualism

Property dualism is the view that although there is just one kind of substance – that identified by physics – there are two different kinds of property, mental and physical. Mental properties depend on physical properties and substance to exist; but at least some mental properties cannot be reduced to or explained in terms of physical (or functional) properties. For this reason, property dualism challenges physicalism. The previous section raised the possibility that phenomenal properties are an example. In this section, we expand the argument to consciousness generally.

We discuss property dualism further in PROPERTY DUALISM AND EMERGENCE, p. 56.

Anyone who claims that the mind is just the brain, that mental states are just brain states, faces a very difficult challenge. How could conscious experience have arisen in the brain? Consciousness involves a 'point of view', and there is something it is like, for a conscious creature, to be that creature. Consciousness is available to us first-personally, 'from the inside'. This 'first-personal' view on to the world doesn't fit into a scientific account of how the brain works, because that account is entirely 'third-personal'. To say that experience *is* a brain process is completely puzzling: how *could* it be, given that conscious experience and brain processes can only be described from different points of view? When we describe a brain process scientifically, we remove all reference to the first-personal. But consciousness is first-personal. So, we can't be talking about consciousness when giving a scientific description.

This is known as the 'explanatory gap'. We cannot explain the phenomena of consciousness, especially phenomenal properties, using the terms available to us from science. This is an epistemological argument, about explanation and understanding.

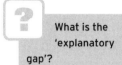

What is the 'explanatory gap'?

Going further: zombies

A famous thought experiment puts the argument metaphysically, claiming that the properties of consciousness cannot be physical properties.

A 'zombie', in the philosophical sense, is a physical replica of a person - you, for instance - but without any experiential consciousness. It therefore has identical physical properties to you, but different mental properties. Of course, zombies are not physically possible - that is, given the physical laws of the universe as it is, any being that has identical physical properties to you will also have consciousness. But it seems that zombies are at least conceivable (I've just described them), and some philosophers argue that they are therefore metaphysically possible.

Now if consciousness were *identical* with physical properties, it would be impossible for a creature to have the same physical properties as you but not have consciousness. If A is identical to B - if A is B - then you can't have A without B or vice-versa; they are the same thing. So if zombies are possible - if a creature could be physically identical to you but not have consciousness - then consciousness is *not* identical to any physical properties. This is property dualism.

The standard physicalist response is that although zombies are conceivable, they aren't in fact possible. What we are able to imagine as conceivable is not always a reliable guide to questions of identity and what is possible. For example, it is imaginable that water is not H_2O; however, given that water *is* H_2O, it's not in fact possible that water isn't H_2O. Of course, there could be something *just like* water that isn't H_2O (it falls as rain, is transparent, drinkable, etc.), but if it isn't H_2O, it just isn't water. So, it's not

This was used as an objection to Descartes' knowledge argument. See KNOWLEDGE AND REALITY, p. 9.

possible for water not to be H_2O. Likewise, we might argue that if zombies are physical replicas of people with mental properties, they cannot lack mental properties themselves. We are, in fact, imagining people.

However, this analogy doesn't work. In the case of water, what we are imagining is just like water. That's why we get confused and think that it is water, when it isn't. But when we imagine zombies, we are not imagining something just like a person. Zombies lack consciousness, and a creature without consciousness is *nothing* like a creature with consciousness. For example, to be in pain is nothing like not being in pain.

Furthermore, we can explain how it is that water is H_2O; there is nothing puzzling here. Water is precisely the kind of thing that would have a chemical formula. But, as we saw above, we cannot explain how it is that any physical property could be consciousness. Consciousness is not the kind of thing that could be identical with a physical property. Perhaps it is really the explanatory gap, rather than what we can or can't conceive of as possible, that supports the argument for property dualism.

Key points • • •

- Property dualism claims that some mental properties cannot be reduced to physical properties.
- The explanatory gap argument notes that properties of consciousness are first-personal, while physical properties, for example of the brain, are all third-personal. Therefore, we cannot explain or understand consciousness in terms of physical properties.
- A 'zombie' is a physical replica of a person, but without consciousness. If zombies are metaphysically possible, then consciousness cannot be identical to physical properties.
- Physicalists reply that zombies are not metaphysically possible, even though they are (or seem to be) conceivable. Conceivability is not always a reliable guide to possibility.

In this section, we shall continue to talk of 'physicalism' rather than 'materialism'. On the relation between the two, see p. 20.

III. NON-REDUCTIVE MATERIALISM

In II. Reductive accounts of the mind (p. 20), we defined physicalism as the view that everything that exists is physical, or depends upon something that is physical. It will be helpful to be more precise. Physicalism claims that what is physical is metaphysically fundamental. It is not enough that the only *substance* is physical; the fundamental *nature* of the universe is physical, and this covers events and properties as well. So, physicalism should say:

1. The properties identified by physics form the fundamental nature of the universe.
2. Physical laws govern all objects and events in space-time.
3. Every physical event has a physical cause that brings it about in accordance with the laws of physics. (This is known as the 'completeness of physics' or 'causal closure'.)

(Physicalism does not have to claim that everything can be *explained* by appealing to physical properties and laws. 'Explanation' brings in all sorts of different considerations, since it relates to how we make sense of things. Physicalism is a view not about explanation, but about properties, laws and causes.)

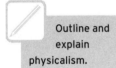 Outline and explain physicalism.

If we do not reduce mental properties to physical properties, we must therefore say something about how mental properties *depend upon* something physical; for example, what is the relationship between mental properties and physical properties?

Functionalism gives us one model: mental properties are functional properties, functional properties are properties that something physical has because of the causal relations it has, and its causal powers, on any particular occasion, are realised by its physical properties (see p. 27). This form of functionalism is a form of non-reductive physicalism.

In this section, we will discuss non-reductive models of how mental properties relate to physical ones, some physicalist, some challenging physicalism.

Anomalous monism

Monism is the view that there is just one kind of substance; it opposes dualism. Anomalous monism holds that the only substance is physical substance. It is a theory developed by Donald Davidson to solve a puzzle about mental causation, and was the origin of TOKEN IDENTITY THEORY (p. 25).

'Mental Events'

The inconsistent triad

Davidson starts with three statements, each of which he believes is true, but which taken together create an apparent contradiction.

1. Principle of Causal Interaction (PCI): Mental events interact causally with physical events. For example, my decisions cause movements of my body.
2. Principle of the Nomological Character of Causality (PNCC): Every instance of causality must be underwritten by a (strict deterministic) causal law. Where two events are related as cause and effect, there is a law that underwrites the causal relation between them.
3. Anomalism of the Mental (AM): There are no (strict deterministic) laws enabling prediction and explanation of mental events.

'Nomological' means 'relating to laws'.

An 'anomaly' is something that doesn't fit explanation.

If we take (1) and (2) together, they imply that there must be causal laws relating mental events and physical events, but (3) denies this. If we take (2) and (3) together, they imply that mental and physical events do not interact causally, while (1) says they do. If we take (1) and (3) together, they imply that not all causal relations are underwritten by causal laws, which contradicts (2).

Going further: the premises of anomalous monism

Before we look at how Davidson resolves the contradiction, why should we accept the three statements? We should accept (1) as intuitive. Surely my beliefs, desires, decisions and so on make a difference to what I do; but this involves movements of my body. Some mental events can cause physical events.

Statement (2) offers a theory of causation that is very widely, but not universally, accepted by philosophers. Causation involves the idea of regularity; the same cause will operate in the same way on different occasions.

The theory of causation derives from Hume. See THE ANALYSIS OF CAUSATION, p. 39.

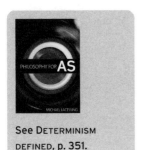

See DETERMINISM DEFINED, p. 351.

In fact, Davidson is not concerned with sensations, which might have causal laws relating to sense organs, but with beliefs, desires, emotions and so on.

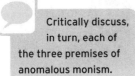

Critically discuss, in turn, each of the three premises of anomalous monism.

If a pipe bursts in the kitchen (cause), the kitchen floor gets wet (effect). If, on another occasion, a pipe bursts in the kitchen but the floor stays dry, we don't just say 'Oh well.' We insist that there must be a difference between the two occasions, because we hold the view that the same cause operates in the same way. If the effect was different, then something about the cause must have been different. (For example, the house was below freezing, so the water in the pipe was ice and stayed where it was.) Davidson says, and many philosophers agree, that the idea of regularity needs to be formalised by talking about causal laws.

Why accept (3)? First, we should note that at present, there *are* no (strict deterministic) causal laws involving mental states. The best we have are rules of thumb. For instance, if someone is thirsty and believes there is a glass of water in front of them, they will often drink it, but not always. Muslims during Ramadan abstain from food and drink during daylight hours. Someone with dropsy knows it is bad for them to drink too much. And so on.

Second, Davidson argues there *cannot* be causal laws involving mental states. We attribute mental states on the basis of rational interpretation. For example, if I know that you believe that doing philosophy is fun, and that you believe that this book is about philosophy, I can infer that you believe reading this book is fun. I don't, for example, have to check your brain to see if I'm right. Attributions of beliefs are **normative**; they are based on logical rules about what beliefs a person should rationally have. Now, if there were a law-like connection between these beliefs and brain states, then I could infer the existence of a certain brain state in the same way, and I would not have to confirm my inference by checking your brain state. But this is not how the physical sciences work. Attributions of physical states are not normative. When we make a rational inference in science, we need to check the result independently. If there were laws connecting mental events and states to physical ones, then we wouldn't need this independent check. Mental-physical laws would upset the way we do science.

The solution

Davidson solves the apparent contradiction between (1), (2) and (3) by using token identity theory and some tricky ideas in **metaphysics**:

1. Any occurrence of a mental event is also the occurrence of a physical event. There is just one event that occurs, which can be described as mental (we can refer to it using mental vocabulary, e.g. a thought, a decision) or as physical (we can refer to it using physical vocabulary, e.g. a brain event).
2. *Causation* is a relation between events. Causation involves things happening: one thing happens (the cause) and another thing follows (the effect). 'Things happening' picks out events.
3. Causal *laws* relate two events only under certain descriptions. For example, if you take out a compass and hold it still, the needle will point roughly towards the North Pole. It is a causal law that compass needles will point north. The North Pole is where polar bears live. So, the needle points towards where polar bears live. But this is not a law. (We could move all the polar bears. It would then be false to say that the needle points towards where polar bears live.)

Davidson's solution is this: mental events that cause physical events fall under a causal law, but only when the mental event is described as a physical event. Only under a physical description does the event fall under a causal law. Described as a mental event, it does not fall under any causal law. In this way, (1), (2) and (3) can all be true. So, for example, making a decision to drink causes you to reach out your arm for the glass. There is no law relating these two events as described. However, making the decision is (token) identical to some event in your brain, and there is a causal law that relates that brain event to your reaching out your arm.

> Explain anomalous monism.

The threat of epiphenomenalism

'Epiphenomenalism' is the claim that the mind is 'causally inert' – that is, mental states, events and properties have no effects. The mind is an 'epiphenomenon', a by-product of some process, presumably in the brain. According to epiphenomenalism, everything that we do and say is the effect of physical processes and events, not mental ones.

Anomalous monism is often accused of not solving the challenge of epiphenomenalism. To make the objection, philosophers rephrased Davidson's argument, in terms of properties. Davidson talks of our being able to describe events using mental or physical vocabulary. We can put this another way (goes the objection):

1. An event is the occurrence of a property (or number of properties) at an instant. Token identity theory says that the event in which a mental property occurs (e.g. making a decision) is the same event as one in which a physical property occurs (e.g. some brain event). So, every mental event is the occurrence of both a mental and a physical property.
2. Causal laws are relations between properties. The compass needle settles to point north; the law picks out a geographical property (actually, one based on magnetism). It does not pick out an ethological one (about the location of a species).
3. Events cause their effects *in virtue of* certain properties and not others. When we explain the occurrence of the effect, we appeal to the law. The needle points the direction it does because that is where (magnetic) north is (not because it is where polar bears live). Or again, if a brick breaks a window, this isn't because the brick is red; it is because the brick is solid and travelling fast.

The objection: is it because of its physical properties or because of its mental properties that a mental event causes its effects? The anomalism of the mental means that no laws connect mental properties and physical properties. If laws pick out the *causally relevant* properties, the ones we use in causal explanation, then it is the physical properties of the mental event, not its mental properties, that explain the effects it has. For example, because there is a law that relates my reaching out my arm to an event in my brain, but no law that relates it to my decision, we should say that the fact that the brain event was also a decision is irrelevant. This is epiphenomenalism.

Davidson's reply to this objection is to reject the reinterpretation of his argument in terms of properties. It is a mistake to say that causes have their effects in virtue of some properties but not others. It remains true that one event causes another no matter how the two events are described. But only when we use certain descriptions of the events do they fall under a causal law. This is all we should say.

But we can press the objection. As the examples show, we need to distinguish causally relevant properties from ones that aren't relevant, and we do this in our explanations all the time. Why would some explanations be better than others if it wasn't because events have their effects in virtue of some of their properties and not others?

The challenge of epiphenomenalism faces all non-reductive physicalist theories. We will return to the issue in ACCOUNTS OF MENTAL CAUSATION (p. 60).

?
Why does anomalous monism face the objection from epiphenomenalism? Can it answer the objection?

- Anomalous monism holds that three apparently inconsistent claims are all true. The three claims are the Principle of Causal Interaction, the Principle of the Nomological Character of Causality and the Anomalism of the Mental.
- The first is intuitive; the second is a widely accepted theory of causation, based on the idea that we capture the regularity of causal relations in laws; and the third is based on the way we understand and attribute mental states.
- Davidson argues that mental events are physical events (token identity theory), and that while causation is a relation between events (so mental events are causes), causal laws only relate events under certain descriptions, namely physical ones.
- Philosophers object that this leads to epiphenomenalism, the view that the mind is causally inert. Causal laws pick out those properties in the two events that are relevant to the causal relation. Since mental properties don't figure in laws, they are causally irrelevant (just as the colour of a brick is irrelevant to its breaking a window).
- Davidson rejects the reinterpretation of anomalous monism in terms of properties, but he then must explain why some explanations (that cite certain properties and not others) are better than others.

Biological naturalism

The theory

Biological naturalism, the theory of mind developed by John Searle, has at its heart a theory about consciousness. An investigation into consciousness should perhaps start with a distinction between 'creature consciousness' and 'state consciousness'. Some types of creatures, such as human beings, have consciousness; some, such as plants, do not. Searle argues that the mind is consciousness, and a conscious mental state is simply a matter of the subject being conscious of something. Consciousness is a 'field'; conscious states are the 'flux', modifications in the field.

As we saw in A FUNCTIONALIST THEORY OF CONSCIOUSNESS (p. 39), some philosophers have a different explanation of consciousness. We shouldn't start with 'consciousness' per se, as Searle does. Instead, we can say that a creature is conscious if it has conscious mental states. We then only need to say what

The Rediscovery of the Mind

makes a mental state conscious – for example, a mental state is conscious if the creature is conscious of it, and this means that the creature has a higher-order thought about the state. This functional analysis makes consciousness completely reducible to the ways in which mental states interact. But functionalism famously faces the objection that what pain feels like, what red looks like, can't be reduced to some *relationship between* mental states. A computer that replicated the relationships between mental states wouldn't thereby be conscious, feeling pain for instance. Consciousness is not reducible to a function.

Searle agrees with this objection. He argues that consciousness is irreducibly 'first-personal'; its reality, its phenomena exist from the first-personal perspective – that is, it is 'subjective', only visible from 'inside'. Thoughts and feelings – as thoughts and feelings – are available to the subject only. A functional analysis is 'third-personal' – it describes conscious states from the 'outside' (how they interact), not in terms of how they are like from the subject's point of view.

So if the mind is consciousness, and we can't say what this is by functional analysis, then what is consciousness? Searle argues that it is a *biological* phenomenon, a property of the brain, but not a purely functional property. Instead, it is a 'systemic' property.

Systemic properties are very common in science, and some can seem quite unexpected just looking at the parts of the 'system'. For example, water is liquid, even though none of its parts, its molecules, is liquid. Liquidity is a systemic property. But we can explain why water is liquid in terms of its parts and their causal interactions. Another example is transparency: molecules aren't transparent; what makes glass transparent is the way the molecules are organized. In each of these cases, we can explain the 'new' systemic property in terms of micro-level interactions.

Similarly, Searle argues, consciousness is a systemic property of the brain. It is the brain as a whole that is conscious, even though its individual parts – neurones – aren't. Consciousness is caused by micro-level brain processes, and if the brain and its causal powers and processes were reproduced, so would consciousness be. So, Searle says, there is nothing particularly mysterious about consciousness; it is part of the natural world – in particular, biology.

Outline and explain Searle's claim that consciousness is a systemic property.

Objection

But there seems to be a very important difference between systemic properties like liquidity and transparency, and consciousness. We can give complete scientific explanations for why liquids are liquid, why glass is transparent. In other words, we can 'reduce' these properties to what explains them: the behaviour of molecules. But Searle himself seems to provide a very good reason why we can't do this with consciousness: consciousness is irreducibly first-personal, but the activities of neurones are third-personal. Neuroscientists can see neurones and measure their activity in a way in which they cannot see or experience someone's thoughts. And so some philosophers argue that if the phenomena of consciousness are irreducibly first-personal, then properties of consciousness are *not physical*. Consciousness is not like other biological properties, because it cannot be explained in third-personal terms.

Searle rejects this argument. We could, if we wanted to, insist on redefining the facts of consciousness in physical terms, just as we have redefined liquidity in molecular terms. We could, but we don't, because then we leave out what we are really interested in, namely the first-personal conscious experiences themselves. However, this doesn't show that consciousness is something non-physical. We have explained how consciousness can be a higher-order property of a working brain. This shows that we are not talking about two different things when we talk about brain processes and consciousness. The irreducibility of consciousness is purely *pragmatic*, a matter of what our interest in consciousness is. It doesn't have any metaphysical implications.

The objection can be pressed, though. With liquidity, our explanation of why something is liquid also shows why it *must* be liquid (given the properties of the molecules and the laws of nature). But we don't have any kind of explanation of why, given the properties of the brain and the laws of nature, we *must* end up with consciousness.

Searle accepts this, but makes two points in reply. First, it is possible that as neuroscience develops, we will get such an explanation. But this seems to side-step the issue of how an explanation in third-personal terms can *ever* be an adequate explanation of something first-personal. Second, the fact that we can't say that the brain *must* give rise to consciousness isn't a problem. Science often tells us why things are the way they are without showing us that they have to be that way. An example is evolutionary explanations.

Whether biological naturalism is a form of non-reductive physicalism (as Searle claims) or property dualism (as his critics claim), we will discuss in PROPERTY DUALISM AND EMERGENCE (p. 57).

See THE 'HARD PROBLEM' OF CONSCIOUSNESS, p. 43.

Does Searle successfully defend his claim that consciousness is a systemic property?

Key points • • •

- Searle's biological naturalism holds that the phenomena of consciousness are irreducibly 'first-personal'. Therefore, consciousness is not reducible to a functional analysis.
- Consciousness is a biological property, a systemic property of the working brain. The working brain, as a whole, has consciousness, even though no part of it is conscious.
- However, with other systemic properties in science, such as liquidity and transparency, we can explain how particular micro-level properties give rise to the systemic property. We cannot explain how or why brain processes give rise to consciousness. One reason for this is the first-personal nature of consciousness. So, consciousness is not like other systemic properties in science; it may be not a physical property at all.
- Searle argues that the irreducible nature of consciousness is a reflection of our interest in first-personal phenomena. It does not show that consciousness is anything more than a biological, systemic property of the working brain.

Supervenience

We said that physicalism claims that everything that exists is physical, or depends upon something that is physical. So, mental properties depend, in some way, upon physical properties. We can develop this idea of dependence into the idea of supervenience. The essence of supervenience is this: properties of type A supervene on properties of type B if and only if any two things that are exactly alike in their B properties cannot have different A properties.

The relation of supervenience holds between properties. For example, a painting has various aesthetic properties, such as being elegant or balanced. It also has various physical properties, such as the distribution of paint on the canvas. The aesthetic properties supervene on the physical ones. We cannot change the painting's being elegant or balanced without changing the distribution of paint on the canvas. There can be no change in aesthetic properties without a change in physical properties. And two paintings exactly alike in their physical properties (i.e. duplicates) will have the same aesthetic properties. The physical properties 'fix' the aesthetic ones. We should note, though, that the notion of 'fixing' here is not causal. The physical properties of the painting don't *cause* its aesthetic properties. We might say that they realise or result in the aesthetic properties.

Many non-reductive physicalists argue that mental properties supervene on physical ones. There can be no change in an object's mental properties without a change in its physical properties, and two objects with identical physical properties would have identical mental properties. However, in contrast to the aesthetic case, it is harder to see how we can *understand* or *explain* the supervenience of mental properties on physical ones.

Functionalism provides one account. Mental properties are just functional properties, and functional properties are simply complex properties built up out of physical properties and their causal powers and relations. This explains *why* and *how* mental properties supervene on physical ones.

A stronger explanation would invoke laws that correlate mental and physical properties. Searle suggests that the relation between consciousness and the physical properties of the brain is that of systemic properties to micro-level properties. In all other cases of such a relation, there are laws that connect the two properties. Searle accepts that we don't have the laws that would allow us to explain supervenience yet. However, Davidson argues that there can be no laws connecting the mental and the physical. Davidson accepts supervenience, but he does not offer an explanation.

Many physicalists have argued that physicalism requires us to accept that there is an explanation of supervenience. If there isn't, then we don't understand how mental properties fit into a universe that is fundamentally physical. We might then start to think that mental properties are *radically* different from physical properties. And this will lead us to property dualism, which may challenge physicalism.

What is supervenience? Why is it important to non-reductive physicalism?

Key points • • •

- Mental properties supervene on physical properties if there can be no change in an object's mental properties without a change in its physical properties; and two objects with the same physical properties would have the same mental properties.
- Philosophers who believe that mental properties supervene on physical ones disagree on whether we can explain this relation. Functionalists argue that we can explain it in terms of causal roles; Searle argues that we can

explain it as the relation between systemic and micro-level properties of the brain.

- Some physicalists argue that if we cannot explain supervenience, then this could challenge physicalism.

Property dualism and emergence

Property dualism is often thought to challenge physicalism, though philosophers do not agree on whether the challenge can be met or not. So, some property dualists call themselves non-reductive physicalists, while others reject physicalism. There are also non-reductive physicalists who reject property dualism. For instance, functionalism is not usually considered a form of property dualism, because, as we have just seen, it tries to explain the supervenience relationship. Mental properties are realised, in any particular occurrence, by physical properties playing a particular causal role.

We can try to understand the relation between mental and physical properties further in terms of *emergence*. That mental properties 'emerged' from physical ones would account for both why they are not identical to them, and also why they supervene on them. The difficulty with the suggestion is that emergence is very poorly understood, and the criteria for a property being 'emergent' are very unclear. The fundamental idea is that emergent properties are 'genuinely novel'. But if they are *too* novel, we might end up accepting a form of property dualism that denies physicalism. On the other hand, if they are not sufficiently novel, it isn't clear that emergentism is the right way to describe them.

One criterion for an emergent property is whether it features, irreducibly, in causal explanations. A property is a distinct property only if it has distinct causal powers. We will look at a form of emergentism that takes this view in ACCOUNTS OF MENTAL CAUSATION (p. 62). For now, we can note that if this is the right theory of emergence, then emergence is incompatible with physicalism. Physicalism claims that all physical events have a complete physical cause (p. 46). If mental properties have *distinct* causal powers, then some physical events, for example movements of your body, have a distinct mental cause, and any physical cause is incomplete.

Many philosophers have felt that this position is at odds with science, that science is somehow committed to physicalism. Physicalists believe that there *must* be a successful explanation of mental properties, including their causal powers, usually in terms of neuroscience.

Explain the tension between property dualism and non-reductive physicalism.

Are anomalous monism and biological naturalism versions of property dualism?

BIOLOGICAL NATURALISM

Searle's biological naturalism argues for the reduction of the causal powers of mental properties to those of physical properties. However, he argues that mental properties are unique, quite distinct from physical properties, because they are related to the first-personal point of view (see p. 52). In this sense, consciousness is irreducible. Other philosophers who make the same point have argued that because mental properties are ineradicably subjective, while scientific explanations are always objective, we cannot give a complete scientific explanation of the world. We have to mention mental properties in addition, and separately.

Searle, however, denies that the subjectivity of mental properties has any *metaphysical* consequences. The irreducibility of mental properties is more an epistemological fact than a metaphysical one. Once we understand how our explanations are guided by particular interests we have in what we wish to explain, we will not conclude that the inability of science to explain consciousness implies anything strange about the world. Consciousness, he argues, is a systemic biological property, and there are, in science, many examples of this kind of property. Therefore, he denies that biological naturalism is a form of property dualism.

However, we can object that this underplays the difference between consciousness and other systemic biological properties: consciousness is unique in having subjectivity. If we can argue that this fact is not merely epistemological, but metaphysical, then Searle is wrong, and his theory is a form of property dualism.

ANOMALOUS MONISM

Davidson's anomalous monism is equally difficult to place, because Davidson rejects the metaphysics of properties that is often used to discuss non-reductive physicalism! However, he clearly states that mental predicates and physical predicates are quite different ways of identifying events, and are even governed by different standards of explanation (see THE PREMISES OF ANOMALOUS MONISM, p. 47). For Davidson, there is no possible account of mental concepts such as 'belief', 'desire' and so on in terms of physical concepts. Mental concepts have a different logic.

However (as with Searle), this is about our explanations, an epistemological point rather than a metaphysical one. To say that anomalous monism is a form

Critically discuss
property dualism
in relation to *either*
biological naturalism *or*
anomalous monism.

of property dualism, we must argue (as many philosophers have) that predicates pick out properties. The different logic of mental concepts is a result of the different nature of mental properties.

Key points • • •

- Property dualism, the claim that mental properties are a completely different kind of property from physical properties, challenges physicalism, which requires (according to some philosophers) that we can explain the relationship between mental and physical properties.
- Some philosophers argue that mental properties are 'emergent' – that is distinct, but based in the physical properties they have emerged from. But it is unclear what this means.
- Searle's critics say that because consciousness is irreducibly first-personal, it is not a systemic biological property, as Searle claims, but a new kind of property.
- Davidson does not accept the metaphysics of properties assumed in this discussion, but he does argue that mental descriptions cannot be translated into physical descriptions.

Accounts of mental causation

Substance dualism

The traditional problem of mental causation is the one posed to substance dualist theories of mind, and Descartes admitted he never solved it satisfactorily. If the mind is just thought and matter is just extension, how could one possibly causally affect the other? The mind is not to be thought of as very insubstantial matter; we can understand how something very refined, like a gas, can have causal effects. But the mind is *not in space* at all. The problem is particularly pressing for Descartes if causation is thought to involve contact of some kind between cause and effect. Clearly, nothing can come into contact with a mind that occupies no space.

However, we can reject the 'contact' view of causation in favour of a version of Hume's theory. Causation is nothing more than regular succession, and it is clear that physical events regularly succeed mental events and vice-versa.

See THE ANALYSIS OF
CAUSATION, p. 39.

However, if we interpret causal regularity in terms of laws, we face Davidson's objection (ANOMALOUS MONISM, p. 47) that it is difficult if not impossible to frame any laws that connect mental causes to physical effects. Mental events can combine in an indefinite number of ways to produce different events. For example, although I'm thirsty, I might believe there is nothing suitable to drink nearby, so don't try to get a drink. To say that 'by and large, people who are thirsty get a drink' isn't a law.

As we will see below (p. 60), this is not a problem just for substance dualism. It causes problems for non-reductive physicalism as well.

Behaviourism

Behaviourism claims that the mind is not 'something' that interacts with the body, but is a way of speaking about complex behavioural patterns. So, there is no problem of mental causation. Mental states don't cause behaviour; they are (in a sense) behaviour.

Yet it seems, from introspection, that my thoughts and sensations do cause my behaviour, such as when I make a decision and then act on it; or when I have a headache and starting looking for painkillers. Behaviourism must claim that these apparently causal claims are in fact not causal at all. And this is what Wittgenstein did. 'Because I thought it would be a good idea' and 'Because it hurts' are not causal explanations of what we are doing; they are rational explanations – that is, they cite reasons, not causes. They explain my behaviour by fitting it into a certain pattern that we can readily understand. The fact that this type of explanation doesn't attempt to give a law covering the cause and effect shows that it's not a causal explanation.

Davidson famously challenged this conclusion. Suppose I have two reasons to do something, but I act on only one of those reasons. For example, I go to the party because I want to see you and believe you'll be there, not because I believe the party is cool and I want to be seen as cool. What makes it the case that the first reason, and not the second, is the reason I act on? 'Central to the relation between a reason and an action it explains is the idea that the agent performed the action *because* he had the reason.' This 'because' must be a causal 'because'. So, behaviourism is wrong to think that there is no mental causation.

'Actions, Reasons, and Causes'

Compare and contrast substance dualism and behaviourism on the question of mental causation.

Identity theory

Type identity theory claims to solve the problem of mental causation. To understand this, we should first recast the problem in terms of properties. Causation requires things to 'happen'. 'Things happening' are events. A cause and its effect are both events, changes at a time (or over time) in the properties of objects. Events involve something changing or realising (coming to have) a property at a particular time.

According to type identity theory, mental events *just are* physical events, and mental properties just are physical properties. To say your decision is the cause of your picking up the remote control is just to say that some particular event in your brain involving purely physical properties is the cause of your picking up the remote control. Mental events and properties cause actions because they are physical events and properties.

However, the identification of mental and physical properties that solves the problem of mental causation also brings about the objection from multiple realisability (p. 24).

> Critically discuss the strengths and weaknesses of type identity theory.

Non-reductive physicalism

Non-reductive physicalism and token identity theories avoid the objections to behaviourism and type identity theory. But they have struggled with the issue of mental causation.

Following token identity theory, we might think that if a mental event, such as making a decision, is just a physical event, say a particular brain state coming into being, then surely if that physical event causes something, for example some type of behaviour, we can say that the mental state, the decision, caused it. And there is no difficult in saying how physical states can causally interact with each other.

> This point was raised as an objection to ANOMALOUS MONISM (see p. 49).

But this does not solve the problem, because we can ask, 'Was it because of its physical properties or because of its mental properties that the event caused its effects?' Do I look for aspirin because a headache *hurts* and I *decide* to look for aspirin, or because certain neurones fire in my brain? How can we defend the common-sense view that the pain of the headache and the decision are causally relevant?

Causal laws

We might try to solve the challenge raised above by rejecting the idea that causation must be covered by laws. Common-sense psychology seems to do fairly well in discovering the mental causes of our behaviour – but it doesn't do so by finding laws. It does so by *interpretation*. If we can understand the meaning of what someone is doing, the reason why she is acting as she is, we thereby discover the mental states that are causing her behaviour. This shows that not all causal investigation relies on laws. It is clear that we don't *come to know* mental causes through establishing causal laws. So why think mental causes require causal laws at all?

Philosophers have resisted this solution, since it requires us to rethink our concept of causation. Ever since Hume, philosophers and scientists have been drawn towards thinking of causation in terms of regularity, and regularity in terms of laws. How are we supposed to understand causation without analysing it in terms of these concepts?

There is an alternative that we will appeal to later (p. 62), namely using **counterfactuals**. In the circumstances, what change would mean that the effect did *not* occur? We identify causes by asking what needs to happen for the effect to occur (what is necessary), or what is enough to bring about the effect (what is sufficient).

Causal closure

Even if we can solve the problem of causal laws, we face a second problem. The 'causal closure of the physical', a commitment of physicalism (see p. 46), is the view that every physical event has a sufficient physical cause. This entails that the physical properties of the mental event must be sufficient to bring about its effects. If type identity theory is true, mental events can be causes without violating physicalism. But if token identity is true, this is less obvious.

Why believe in the causal closure of the physical? Because if we do not, we suppose that some physical events have no complete physical explanation. We could argue that events that need a non-physical explanation are miracles, from the point of view of physics. Furthermore, wherever science has so far found the cause of a physical event, it has found a sufficient physical cause. Denying the causal closure principle commits us to saying that science cannot and will not find the causes of certain physical events (in the brain, most likely).

> ? What is the philosophical significance of the view that every physical event has a sufficient physical cause?

THE OPTIONS

The problem of mental causation, as it is faced by non-reductive physicalism, brings us to four options:

1. Epiphenomenalism: mental properties have no causal effects. This is very counter-intuitive.
2. Overdetermination: *both* the physical properties *and* the mental properties of a mental event are each sufficient to bring about the effect. However, suppose I decide to walk to the fridge to find a drink. We can't say that if the neurones in my brain didn't fire, the decision to do so would have been enough to cause my walking. To walk I need muscular contractions, and these in turn require nervous stimuli from the brain. The mental properties, if relevant at all, aren't sufficient; they rely on the physical properties occurring as well. But according to physicalism, the physical properties are sufficient on their own. So, given the primacy of the physical properties, it seems that it is not in virtue of being *mental* that these states and events cause other events. This takes us back to epiphenomenalism.
3. Solving the two challenges above.
4. Abandoning causal closure, and therefore rejecting physicalism.

In the next section, we discuss these last two options.

> Critically examine the challenge mental causation poses to non-reductive physicalism.

Going further: solving the problem

In the absence of causal laws, many non-reductive physicalists have analysed mental causation in terms of counterfactuals. Suppose, on having a headache, I reach for the aspirin. Is it the pain of the headache that causes this movement, or the neurones firing? To say that it was because the headache hurt that I reached for the aspirin implies that if the headache hadn't hurt, I wouldn't have acted as I did. If we want to say that it was just the neurones firing that caused me to reach for the aspirin, we have to say that if the neurones had fired, but the headache hadn't hurt, I would still have reached for the aspirin. But this seems false. Can we suppose that the neurones would have fired anyway, without the headache hurting? If the neurones firing are one particular physical realisation of the pain of a headache, how could they have fired without the headache hurting?

There are a wide variety of theories about the supervenience relationship between the pain and the neurones, but they all attempt to secure the idea that without the pain, I wouldn't have done what I did. For example, functionalism argues that pain can be realised by many different physical states, so mental and physical properties can't be the same. However, mental states, on any particular occasion, are realised by physical states. So, the causal role of the mental state is, on any particular occasion, filled by a physical state. The physical properties fill the causal role of pain on this occasion. In this way, we can say both that it was the pain that caused me to reach for the aspirin and that it was the physical properties.

This ignores the question, discussed in QUALIA AND FUNCTIONALISM (p. 41) of whether a functionalist analysis of pain is correct.

But non-reductive physicalists face this problem: according to physicalism, the physical event of reaching for the aspirin has a sufficient physical cause, so the firing of the neurones on its own must be sufficient. If it is sufficient on its own, then the pain of the headache is not necessary. Now, of course, if the neurones firing is a realisation of the pain, then the pain will always *accompany* the firing; but it is still unclear whether the pain plays any part in bringing about my reaching for the aspirin, or whether it is epiphenomenal. If we get a complete causal explanation without mentioning the pain, then the fact that the physical properties realise pain appears to be irrelevant.

Some emergentists argue that to secure the causal relevance of mental properties, we must reject physicalism. On this view, we should say that the event of the neurones firing is sufficient for me to reach for the aspirin *only given* the presence of a headache - that is, there must be a mental cause present as well. So, the firing of the neurones is not sufficient on its own. Furthermore, it is not true that if the neurones hadn't fired, I wouldn't have reached for the aspirin, because for me to have a headache, *some other neurones* would have fired. So, it is not necessary for these particular neurones to have fired as long as some neurones fired in a suitable way. Since the physical properties of the event are neither necessary nor sufficient to explain the effect, they are not a complete physical cause.

On this account, our causal explanation *must* mention the mental property, the pain. It is true that the pain isn't sufficient, because some neurones must fire for any effect to follow. However, the pain is necessary,

Critically discuss what you consider to be the best account of mental causation.

and this secures its causal relevance. The conclusion is that physicalism is false, because the physical cause of my reaching for the aspirin is not sufficient. This account of mental causation is emergentism, and a form of property dualism, because mental properties have irreducible causal powers.

Key points • • •

- Mental causation, the view that mental events have effects, including physical effects, has formed a challenge to many theories of mind.
- Substance dualism must explain how the mind, not in space, can interact with the body, which is in space. One option is to say that causation is nothing more than law-like succession. However, it is difficult to argue that there are mental-physical laws.
- Behaviourism rejects mental causation. Mental states are analysed in terms of behaviour; they do not cause behaviour, and explanations of behaviour citing mental states are not causal, but rational.
- Davidson objects that a person can have two reasons for acting, and act on one reason and not another. We can make sense of this only by saying that one reason was the cause of the person's behaviour.
- Type identity theory argues that mental events and properties are physical events and properties. As there is no problem of how physical events and properties are causes, there is no problem of mental causation.
- However, this reduction of mental events and properties is open to the objection from multiple realisability.
- Non-reductive physicalism faces the challenge of explaining how mental properties can be causally relevant without undermining physicalism. Physicalism is committed to the causal closure of the physical, which says that every physical event has a sufficient physical cause.
- Many non-reductive physicalists analyse mental causation by using counterfactuals and then providing an account of the relation between mental and physical properties to explain how mental properties can be causally relevant.
- Some emergentists argue that this approach fails. To argue that the mental property is necessary, we must accept that the physical properties are not sufficient. This is to abandon physicalism.

POLITICAL PHILOSOPHY

2

In this chapter, we look at the nature and importance of three central concepts of political philosophy, namely liberty, rights and justice. We conclude with a discussion of these three concepts in relation to nationalism and nation-states. We begin with a discussion of the four major political theories that support different interpretations of these concepts, namely liberalism, conservatism, Marxism and anarchism. Students should be able to argue for and against different understandings of the three concepts, their relation to nationalism and nation-states, and the grounding of these understandings in theories of human nature and the state.

SYLLABUS CHECKLIST ✔

The AQA A2 syllabus for this chapter is:

Human nature and political organisation

✔ Competing views of human nature and of the purpose of the state: the state as neutral umpire, the classical liberal state; the state as an organic entity, the conservative conception of the state; the state as an oppressor, Marxist and anarchist views of the state.

Liberty

✔ What does it mean to be free? Concepts of liberty: negative freedom and positive freedom.

✔ Why is liberty valued and how can it be promoted and defended? How different political ideologies address these issues. The relationship between law and liberty.

Rights

✔ The notion of rights: the distinction between natural and positive rights. Theories of how rights are grounded and problems concerning their extent and application.

✔ How may conflicts between the rights of individuals and social utility be resolved? What is the relationship, if any, between rights, liberty, morality and law?

Justice

✔ What contributes social, economic or distributive justice? Competing principles for a just distribution of political goods: desert, need, equality.

✔ How, if at all, could redistribution be justified? The relationship between distributive justice, liberty and rights.

Nation-states

✔ The application of these concepts to nation-states and to relations between states. Nationalism, national sentiment and liberty: whether restrictions on cross-border movement and association are just; whether rights apply to groups and nations, for example a right of a nation to self-determination; whether distributive justice applies globally; the notion of a just war and how this applies in asymmetric wars.

I. HUMAN NATURE AND POLITICAL ORGANISATION

Competing views of human nature and of the purpose of the state

On ideology

Political ideologies, such as 'liberalism', 'conservatism', 'Marxism' and 'anarchism', can be studied and classified, mostly along the left–right spectrum, as providing plans of action for the creation of public political institutions, of seeking to justify various political arrangements, and as binding individuals to society. And for this reason, they are inevitably associated with power. Ideologies tend to be attached to social groups (but not necessarily classes). They provide a picture of society, one that simplifies the complexities of social reality, but this is necessary in order to provide guidance in making political decisions. Michael Freeden argues that ideologies are different organisations of political concepts that give them particular meanings.

Ideologies and Political Theory

Political concepts have, through historical usage, become complex. Each has a number of components; for example, 'liberty' includes ideas of absence of coercion, freedom from interference, opportunity, autonomy, rational choice, self-determination and so on. Different societies have understood and used the concept of liberty in these different ways. There is not one 'right' interpretation of the concept of liberty, or even of each component. Philosophers and politicians will emphasise those aspects of liberty they feel are important.

This is part of the idea of 'essential contestability'. Political concepts are essentially (not accidentally) ones that people disagree over for two reasons. First, because political concepts (e.g. equality, liberty, democracy, justice) are evaluative concepts, and people disagree over values. Second, because of the component structure. Each component has different possible descriptions, and people also disagree over which components the concept 'ought' to have.

Ideologies, then, are groups of such concepts, organised and understood in such a way as to make the interpretation of each concept support the others. Different ideologies make different political concepts central; for example, liberalism starts from liberty, socialism from community. Each ideology 'decontests' concepts, which provides them with more specific meanings, which allows them to be used in guiding political decisions. It is difficult to know what to do on the basis that liberty is absence of constraint; but if you understand the type of constraint that should be absent as physical coercion by others rather than, say, individual addictions, this provides more guidance on the type of policies to pursue.

Ideologies often use theories of human nature to decontest political concepts. The particular interpretation of liberty or rights appeals to aspects of what it is to be human – which of our faculties and what aspects of our situation are important. What these arguments are and how they work is best seen through the examples we turn to now.

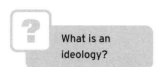

What is an ideology?

Classical liberalism: the state as neutral umpire

Liberalism holds that human beings are 'naturally' free, so any restraint on their liberty needs to be justified. The state, with its powers to pass and enforce laws that limit liberty, can be justified on two grounds. First, it is beneficial. It prevents us from harming one another and enforces punishment if we do. It encourages cooperation and trust. Second, we can retain liberty in a state that is organised in the right way. In a democracy, we help to make the laws that we live by, and we express our consent to obeying them. If the democracy recognizes the right to individual liberty, it is restricted from passing laws that undermine liberty.

This argument supports the idea of the state as a neutral umpire. We will look at these ideas further in the theories of two classic liberals: John Locke and John Stuart Mill. We won't discuss objections here, but they will arise in the discussions of conservatism and Marxism.

See THE BENEFIT
OF POLITICAL
ORGANISATION, pp. 52
and 70.

Locke

Locke argues that human beings are naturally equal and free. Equality means that no one has the right to hold power over anyone else. Our natural liberty is not freedom to do whatever we want, as it falls under what Locke calls the Law of Nature. This says that no person may subordinate another or harm his or her life, health, liberty or possessions (except in self-defence), and furthermore that we should help each other when doing so does not harm ourselves.

This Law of Nature comes from God, and it is because we are created by God that we have the duty to preserve and not to harm life. However, if we do not want to appeal to God, Locke also argues that the Law of Nature is discoverable by reason.

Second Treatise of
Government, Chs 2-5

To discover the purpose of a state, Locke imagines what life would be like without a state, or in a 'state of nature'. Without a state, if the population is not too large, people will live peacefully, each cultivating their own land. However, they may break the Law of Nature, and so it needs to be enforced. But we have no state, no police and we are all equal, with no one having more authority than anyone else. But for exactly this reason, says Locke, we *all* have the right to punish those who break the Law of Nature.

But is this enough? First, we may disagree on whether someone has broken the Law, causing tension. Second, when we punish, we are likely to be biased rather than objective, confusing punishment with revenge and being too severe. Third, we will often lack the ability to administer the punishment – so there will be no incentive for people not to break it. If we punish someone who robs us of our crops, that person may band together with other thieves and return for revenge. The only way that punishment becomes effective is if someone is so powerful that it is impossible, or at least pointless, to resist them. But this would be the end of the state of nature and the beginning of the state.

On this view, the primary benefit of living in a state is that there is a single, common interpretation of the law, that it is administered fairly and that it is enforced. The state operates as a neutral umpire when we come into conflict with one another.

See THE STATE OF NATURE, pp. 48ff. and 68ff.

Second Treatise, Ch. 9, §§ 124-7

Explain and illustrate Locke's justification for the state.

Mill

Mill develops and defends the idea of the state as a 'neutral umpire' by starting from 'one simple principle', which he then defends. This is the Harm, or Liberty, Principle, which says that 'The only purpose for which power can be rightfully exercised over any member of a civilized community, against his will, is to prevent harm to others. His own good, either physical or moral, is not a sufficient warrant.' This interprets liberty as a freedom from constraint that individuals can enjoy. Mill then connects the nature and value of liberty to the importance of personal attributes and differences, saying, 'the only freedom that deserves the name is that of pursuing our own good in our own way'.

Mill also argues that liberty is necessary for progress in discovering truth and better ways of living. In this way, liberty contributes to individual and social utility. Mill's idea of utility is utility 'in the largest sense', appealing to the interests we have as human beings who can progress and develop as individuals. So, Freeden argues, Mill places *liberty, individualism* and *progress* at the heart of his classical liberalism.

On Liberty, p. 68

On Liberty, p. 72

See THE VALUE OF LIBERTY, p. 87.

For Mill's utilitarianism, see ACT UTILITARIANISM, p. 248.

Around these three concepts, Mill places concepts that decontest them further. He emphasises both the *rational* and the *social* nature of human beings. 'Rationality' has meant many things to many thinkers: rightness (Plato, Kant), practical wisdom (Aristotle), obedience to the law of God (Aquinas), means–end decision-making (Hume) and autonomy (Kant again). Mill connects it to discerning and pursuing happiness and virtue, an essential part of self-development and human progress. Both rationality and sociability connect our personal happiness to social utility.

The tension between individualism and social utility leads to a concern with *state power*, where Mill's conception of the state as a neutral umpire emerges. Mill wants to prevent the state from interfering in people's lives. Individuals need to be free to discover how best to live; having other people's ideas imposed on one's life inhibits creativity and individuality. So, Mill presents a number of ARGUMENTS FOR TOLERANCE which suggest that imposing one's conception of the good life on other people is wrong.

Someone's 'conception of the good life' is their view of how to live. If a society adopted some particular conception, then its laws would reflect and promote the way of life of that conception. For example, in a theocracy, laws are passed on the basis of being in accordance with the will and commands of God, as a particular religion represents these (as in Islam's sharia law). Mill's arguments suggest that society must be 'neutral' between conceptions of the good life.

So while Mill advocates *democracy*, he remains concerned by the prospect of the 'tyranny of the majority', the majority of people imposing their view on the minority. In this case, the state ceases to be a neutral umpire and begins to express just one point of view: that of the majority. So, he advocates limiting the laws a democracy is allowed to pass by his 'one simple principle' that will protect individual liberty.

See arguments from fallibilism (p. 242), autonomy (p. 244), reasonableness (p. 252) and diversity (p. 253).

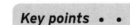

Outline Mill's ideology. Show how his Harm Principle leads to a neutral state.

Key points • • •

- Liberals argue that the state, with its ability to restrict liberty, can be justified if it is beneficial and organised in such a way as to respect individual liberty.
- Locke argues that in a 'state of nature', we are free and equal under the Law of Nature.
- Violations of the Law of Nature need to be punished, but without a state, the system of punishment will be unsatisfactory for three reasons: disagreement, bias and inability to punish.

- The state, then, is a neutral umpire between our disputes that can fairly administer punishment.
- Mill argues that the state may only justifiably exercise power over people in order to prevent harm to others. Otherwise, they should be free from constraint to live as they choose.
- He argues this freedom will lead to individual and social progress, given the rational and social nature of human beings.
- He therefore defends tolerance and a neutral state.

Conservatism: the state as an organic entity

Burke

In *Reflections on the Revolution in France*, Edmund Burke identifies a core principle of his political thought when considering whether the French Revolution should be praised for achieving 'liberty'. Liberty can't be considered 'in all the nakedness and solitude of metaphysical abstraction. Circumstances . . . give in reality to every political principle its distinguishing colour and discriminating effect.' We would not praise a prisoner for achieving liberty by escaping prison. What matters is how liberty is achieved, and what kind of liberty it is. Circumstances are everything.

Para. 10

Liberty, to be good, needs to be combined with other good things, such as government, the army, tax revenue, morality, religion, property rights, peace, order and civility. For this, changes in society that lead to gains in liberty need to be *gradual* and a *natural development* of that society. The politics of a society depend on its values, customs and therefore also on its *history*.

English liberty evolved from the Norman Conquest in 1066, with its system of law and powerful government. The aristocracy realised that they could not achieve liberty (from the monarch) unless they involved popular support. This led to the Magna Carta in 1215. The balance between strong government and the force of liberty led to gradual positive results. English liberties and rights are an inheritance, which in turn are passed on to the next generation. The French Revolution, however, did not combine liberty with other values. The new constitution did not restrain the liberty of the people. The resulting government was weak, and this made worse the attempt to achieve economic equality, which led to both instability and unhappiness. To avoid the complete disintegration of social order, the revolution moved towards a tyranny and then to Napoleon's monarchical rule.

The revolution failed, first, because it attempted change that is neither gradual nor natural to a society. Burke compares the state to a living plant and to a member of the family. Change in the state, when it is good, is like the growth of a plant or inheritance between generations of a family. It respects the past, and the authority, law, religion and customs that are traditions in society. Traditions embody accumulated wisdom, solutions to the puzzle of how to live well in society.

The second reason the revolution failed was because it tried to use a few supposedly abstract and universal principles to understand and change society. Burke argues that we cannot form clear or meaningful ideas of abstract political concepts. At best, we will have ideas based on past experiences which we have associated to them. Purely speculative thought about politics is both pointless and dangerous – pointless because it can reach no firm conclusions, and dangerous because communities are based on particular associations and interpretations of these terms, so to try to get people to respond to the words in an alien way threatens the cohesion of the community. Politics and government must proceed not by appeals to abstract values (such as 'Liberty, Equality, Fraternity', the motto of the French Revolution), but through gradual reform that makes sense to the society, with its particular values and traditions.

In summary, Burke has an organic conception of society and its evolution over time. Change should be gradual and 'natural' to that society. Second, interpretations of political concepts, and so our rights and our liberties, are specific to a society, not universal. Third, tradition should be respected, and with it authority, law and religion, as embodying the wisdom of previous generations, which we then pass on to future generations. A fourth element, that I have not explicitly commented on, is Burke's view that human beings are naturally unequal, a view embodied in many traditions.

> **Outline Burke's criticism of the French revolution.**

> **Outline and illustrate Burke's conservatism.**

The heart of conservatism

Burke does not define conservatism, which has taken many forms in different historical periods. The core issue for conservatism is making change 'safe'. 'Good' change is 'growth' and 'natural' to a society, not imposed on it. It doesn't occur faster than people's ability to adjust to it. It doesn't destroy past institutions, but respects and builds on them. It is not brought about by people *trying* to create change.

The organic metaphor presents the origins and development of the structure of society as independent of human will. It evolves naturally, and reaches its own harmonies. This idea has been developed variously – that the development of society is guided by God, or the forces of history, or facts about biology and human psychology, or economic laws and the free market. However the idea is interpreted, the claim is always that going against these rules that govern the natural development of society will lead to social instability. The role of government is to uphold rules of conduct and protect the organic process of change from interference, not large-scale reform.

Freeden notes that these core ideas are *often* complemented by the following:

1. We cannot rely on rationality. It is arrogant, overly critical of tradition and authority, and often supports abstract, not practical, knowledge. The historical development of societies is always specific and particular; so we cannot discover historical 'laws' and predict what will happen in the future. Tradition embodies more wisdom than reason.
2. The order and stability of the community, the inherited traditions, are most important; individual self-development must always take place within this framework.
3. Human beings are not perfectible. To think otherwise is false pride, and flies in the face of history. There is not enough evidence to think that we can trust individual rationality (MILL, p. 70) or that human beings act as they do only because they are 'alienated' from their nature, which would be expressed by equality in community (MARX, p. 75).
4. Power should be accountable, but the purpose of this is a harmonious political order, not the protection of individuals' freedom.
5. Liberty should be understood in terms of inherited liberties – the rights and duties developed within any particular society over time.

Compare and contrast the place of liberty in conservatism and in Mill's liberalism.

Objections

Does the state have an overarching, continuous identity, as the organic metaphor suggests? We can object that, in fact, at different times within a society there have been different traditions, cultures or interpretations of political ideas. Moreover, some understandings of society and its history have presented a false or biased image. The conservative interpretation of organic growth itself may be an illusion.

Second, other political theories are not abstract and speculative, as conservatism suggests. They are more critical of present society and set out to imagine alternative futures, but they are still focused on making a practical difference.

Third, the image of organic growth will not help us solve social conflicts. If both sides of a conflict appeal to tradition, for instance, then tradition won't solve the conflict. However, conservatives can argue that to attempt to solve the conflict by deliberately imposing a situation, rather than letting the forces that develop the social order naturally do their work, will only result in a worse situation. Understanding the state as an organic entity encourages us not to try to use government activity to force through change, but rather to allow and enable it to occur, driven by those forces that bring it about naturally.

Key points • • •

- Burke argues that in understanding political values, circumstances are everything. Any value must be combined with others.
- This requires that social change be gradual and 'natural', respecting existing traditions and values, like organic growth or family inheritance.
- Abstract and universal principles are dangerous in failing to respect particular, local traditions and interpretations.
- The core principle of conservatism is making change 'safe'. The origin and development of society occurs independent of human will.
- Conservatives often also reject over-reliance on rationality, individual self-development outside tradition, and the perfectibility of human beings.
- We can object that the image of organic change over time is false, nor will it help solve social conflicts, and that alternative theories can be practically applied.

Marx: the state as an oppressor

Theory of history

To understand Marx's view of the state, we need to start at the beginning. First, we are alive, so we need material goods, such as food and shelter. But unlike other animals, we *produce* our 'means of subsistence'. So, second, historically, the satisfaction of our original needs – how this is done and what it required, such as tools – leads to new needs, such as the means to produce those tools. Third, people create more people, they reproduce; and again, this occurs in particular ways, depending on circumstances. Finally, both production and reproduction are not only natural but also social activities – that is, they involve certain ways, arrangements, 'modes' of cooperating with others.

Marx argues that the different *modes of production* and *modes of co-operation*, which he called the economic 'substructure', determine the nature of each society. These modes develop as society evolves, in particular involving the division of labour, within the family, between mental and physical labour, between agriculture, commercial and industrial activity. These divisions of labour, and the corresponding modes of cooperation, are basic facts. Social customs, laws, education, religion, culture and the institutions of state, Marx called the 'superstructure'. It constantly evolves out of how people live their lives. To understand the state, we must understand how it is related to the modes of production in society.

The state, at any time, is based on the power relations between classes within society. The modern state is based on capitalism, with an inequality of power between the capitalists – those *who own the means of production* – and the workers. The workers get paid a salary by the capitalists, but they don't own what they produce, and the capitalists keep the profit made by selling what is produced.

The power of the dominant class is supported in two ways: through the state as a set of institutions and through an 'ideology', a set of ideas about the state and society. Both protect the interests of the dominant class and seek to justify the distribution of power. First, in capitalism, those with capital have political influence. The state is biased; it is not a neutral umpire, nor an embodiment of inherited wisdom. Second, the ideas we have are historical products, determined by the economic substructure; they are not the products of 'pure reason' or any such thing. Political theories (such as liberalism and conservatism) that defend capitalism and its liberal democratic state protect the interests of capitalists.

Oppression and emancipation

The state supports and justifies a mode of production that oppresses the workers. In capitalism, the worker suffers from 'alienation', a kind of estrange-ment resulting in a loss.

Why does Marx make modes of production and cooperation fundamental to understanding society?

The worker is alienated, first, from the products of his or her labour, which are taken away by the capitalist. Second, Marx argues that meaningful, creative work is central to a flourishing life; but the worker's activity is meaningless and repetitive – so the worker is alienated from their work. Third, this meaningless production also alienates the worker from their 'species-being', Marx's term for true human nature – our powers and needs. Fourth, capitalism alienates people from each other, because the aim is to create things to be sold, not things that will satisfy our mutual needs.

Someone who is alienated may not realise that they are, and may not consciously feel their loss. However, under different arrangements their lives would be more fulfilled. Work that is not alienated would involve the worker enjoying both their work and its product, expressing their creative powers, and would involve producing things that aimed to meet the needs of ourselves and others.

This situation cannot be remedied by liberal 'political emancipation'. Liberal ideas of rights and justice are themselves alienating, based on the thought that the individual needs protecting from harm by others, and freedom is freedom from interference. This conflicts with the fundamental nature of human beings as *communal*. We find freedom not in being separate from each other, but in positive relations with each other. Liberal rights undermine these relations, so cannot solve oppression.

A second way the state is oppressive is through the *illusion* of community, 'equal before the law'. This idea glosses over the very real power difference between classes. If a genuine community of equals came into existence, which Marx called a 'communist revolution', then the state would *cease to exist*.

Freeden identifies five core concepts in Marx's theory:

1. equality, which Marx understands in terms of people's needs being met equally, which is quite different from liberalism's moral equality or equality of opportunity;
2. welfare, fulfilling our 'species being', the importance of which is shown by the analysis of alienation;
3. the importance of meaningful creative work;
4. community, as our network of relations with others determines how our lives go;
5. history, the historical development of modes of production and cooperation and of political ideas.

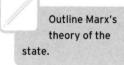

Explain and illustrate Marx's concept of alienation, and the state's role in creating it.

See NEGATIVE AND POSITIVE LIBERTY, p. 83.

Outline Marx's theory of the state.

Going further: Marx on justice . . .

Despite his analysis of the role of the state in oppressing the worker, Marx doesn't call capitalism unjust. Yet surely oppression, by definition, is unjust. This puzzle can be explained by three things.

First, Marx did not want to use liberal conceptions of justice as upholding rights in cases of conflict. The communist society would be 'beyond' justice, not having the kinds of disputes justice is needed to resolve. Each person would contribute to the community according to their ability and receive according to their need.

Second, Marx believed that the evolution of societies occurred according to historical developments in the economic substructure. For this reason, he argued that capitalism is a *necessary stage* we must pass through in order to develop the communist society.

Third, his arguments were based not on an appeal to moral ideas, but on an analysis of these historical developments in the means of production. Social change will be driven by changes in material circumstances (substructure) rather than changes in ideas (superstructure).

See JUSTICE, p. 104.

Critique of the Gotha Programme

Objections

Marx's view of the state as oppressor has been strongly challenged, both by other political thinkers and by changes in society during the past 150 years. First, the one-way relation between substructure and superstructure has been roundly rejected. Social reality certainly has an influence on ideas, at least ideas about society, but, as many Marxists quickly accepted, ideas can also influence social reality. The state, then, is not *necessarily* determined by the capitalist substructure, but can be independent of it and even affect it.

And, second, this is what has happened. Marx's prediction of a communist society has turned out false, while capitalism has changed greatly, for instance in the creation of the welfare state and in the evolution of classes. Workers own shares in companies and work has shifted from industry to information technology, services and leisure. In this evolution in society, the state has played a part.

Other theories will also challenge Marx's very strong conception of human nature and theory of alienation. Is Marx right that we can make an objective

To the second objection, Marx may respond that this has not led to emancipation, that the state continues to support a means of production that is alienating. See FALSE NEEDS AND REPRESSIVE DESUBLIMATION, p. 267.

judgement about people being alienated without taking into account their personal view on the matter? For human happiness to increase, is revolution required or only, as Mill argues, education? If we are not alienated, perhaps the state is not necessarily oppressive.

Finally, even if we agree that Marx is largely right, can we also agree that there is an alternative to the state? Is a stateless, communist society of equals humanly possible?

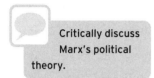
Critically discuss Marx's political theory.

Key points • • •

- Marx argues that particular modes of production and cooperation form the substructure of society, and are marked by the division of labour. The superstructure of society – laws, religion, culture and political organisation – grows from the substructure.
- The state helps secure the power of the dominant class through its institutions and ideology.
- Under capitalism, workers suffer from alienation from their labour, human nature, work and each other.
- Liberal rights and justice cannot overcome alienation, as they presuppose conflict and undermine communal relations.
- Five core concepts of communism are equality, welfare, work, community and history.
- We can object that the state is not necessarily oppressive as it is not determined by the capitalist substructure. It has, in fact, brought about changes in capitalism that Marx did not foresee.
- We can also object that Marx's theories of human nature and alienation are wrong, and that his communist society is not possible for human beings.

Anarchism: the state as oppressor

Anarchism does not name a single political theory, as different 'schools' of anarchism hold very different views about human nature and the nature of anarchist society. However, they all advocate that the state should be abolished and replaced by social organisations.

Anarchism, Ch. 1

What is distinctive about the state, such that anarchists object to it? David Miller provides an excellent summary:

1. The state is sovereign, claiming complete authority to define the rights and obligations of its citizens.
2. The state is compulsory. Members are forced to recognise their obligations.
3. The state claims a monopoly on force. No other use of force is justified.
4. The state is a distinct body. Its role and functions are separated from other social roles and functions generally, and the people composing it (politicians, bureaucrats, armed forces, police) tend to form a distinct class.

The most fundamental anarchist objection is that the state violates and undermines liberty. It exercises far more coercion than is required for human beings to live together. It enacts laws that benefit itself, not citizens. It is excessively punitive, punishing people for breaking even unjustified laws. It is also destructive, fighting wars for its own protection and aggrandisement. Some anarchists add that it is exploitative, unjustly taking wealth from those who produce it and either keeping it for its own activities or placing it in the hands of an economically privileged class.

Of course, states are useful, providing protection for individuals against others and co-ordinating productive work. But anarchists argue that for both of these essential functions, *we do not need the state*. We need some form of collective body or bodies, but these need not claim sovereignty and need no more power than is required for their specific function. They can be voluntary, with people allowed to join or leave as they choose. There need not be just one body providing these functions; there could be competition between associations. They could be run by everybody together. As noted above, there is no agreement between different anarchist theories on the nature of these collective bodies.

Despite the powerful criticisms of the state, the anarchist alternative has struck many people as too idealist. Anarchism can seem attractive only if you assume that people are peaceful, altruistic and cooperative. But this theory of human nature is clearly too optimistic! If human beings are so benevolent, then why don't we already live in an anarchist society, rather than under a state? So, even if the state is an evil, it is a necessary evil.

However, anarchists do not (all) have such a rosy picture of human nature. And they all endorse one of the following answers to why we have not yet achieved an anarchist society:

1. Enlightenment: human beings can make progress through reason, but we have not yet (or only just now) collectively achieved the point at which we

realise that our self-interest is better served by freely cooperating with one another and respecting each other's liberty.

2. Idealism: human consciousness evolves over time, and we can make progress in our moral ideas and character. We have not yet (or only just now) achieved the moral character needed to support an anarchist society.

3. Materialism: how human beings behave is affected by the material conditions in which they live, as Marx argued. Anarchism becomes a real possibility only as a response to late capitalism.

?
Why do anarchists argue that the state is oppressive?

In what follows, we briefly consider three anarchist theories to illustrate the variety of arguments made for anarchism. The similarities between certain arguments and either liberal or Marxist views should be noted.

Godwin: philosophical anarchism

Anarchism is perhaps most famously associated, in the English-speaking world, with William Godwin. He argued for 'principle of private judgement'. He argues that only one's own judgement can impose a duty on one. We must each decide what justice requires and how to bring it about. All government, with its imposition of duties through law, is incompatible with the principle of private judgement. Even a direct democracy, in which all the people vote for each individual law, doesn't respect it, because the judgement of the minority is overridden by the majority.

See p. 248.

Godwin accepted ACT UTILITARIANISM, which provides a second objection. Under a government, we are incapable of fully developing our capacity to live according to the free exercise of our private judgement. The development of people's intellectual capacity for private judgement is, in part, the greatest good. Therefore, we can never achieve the greatest good under government. As we develop our judgement, we see that we must do all we can to bring about the greatest good. Moral and political improvement will result from our understanding what the greatest good is and how to bring it about. As each person's knowledge increases, so they do not need to live under the laws of a state.

We can object that until people freely judge to seek the greatest good, then utilitarianism requires us to impose duties on them, so the state is necessary for now. Second, forcing someone to behave 'morally' is surely the way in which people learn to become moral themselves. Reason alone is not going to do this, as Godwin thought. So, the state is not incompatible with the attempt to develop their capacity for private judgement. For both reasons, laws are needed to influence the choices people make about how to behave.

For anarchy to be the best development of freedom, we must think both that people can be brought to a point of personal development such that they will voluntarily respect the freedom of others; and that such individual development can continue, down the generations, without a structure of law. Both these ideas can be questioned.

Individualist anarchism

The starting point of individualist anarchism is that each person is sovereign over their own body and property. No one can impose an obligation on another person coercively. Instead, the only legitimate relations between individuals are voluntary: by exchange, contract and gift. The liberty and sovereignty of the individual are violated by the nature of the state.

Individualist anarchists tend to assume egoism. Social harmony in society without a state will be secured by getting people to see their self-interest clearly. For example, we come to see that this is the best way to secure our autonomy. We can replace many of the functions of the state with the market, which, driven by egoism, will bring equality, ensure stability and restrain destructiveness. We pay an agency to protect us and resolve individual conflicts, and agencies compete in the market for customers. We voluntarily buy or do not buy their services.

We can object that such a society will be unjust. It is not clear that respecting other people's autonomy is in my self-interest. So, I have no reason to prefer an agency that is *fair* in its resolution of conflicts; I will prefer one that finds in my favour. And when the individuals belong to different agencies, how is the conflict to be resolved?

We can also object that the idea of individual sovereignty conflicts with natural relations of family, affection and community.

Communist anarchism

At the heart of communist anarchism is quite the opposite view of human relations, namely that our proper relationship to other people is one of solidarity. Sympathy, affection, cooperation and mutual aid should govern our behaviour.

> Critically compare Godwin's defence of anarchism with Mill's defence of liberalism.

> Discuss philosophical and individualist anarchism.

That they do not now is the *result* of living under the state and under capitalism, which emphasise competition and antagonism. The very idea that individuals are sovereign over themselves is an effect of the state. Real freedom consists in having the opportunity to satisfy what we need and desire.

Communist anarchists continue the critique of the state made by Marxists, but add that the state is not *merely* the instrument of capitalism, but uses force directly for its own purposes and benefit. What is needed, to replace the state, is no more than the extension and enlarging of existing social institutions. The basic form of association would be a local 'commune'. Communes could be arranged in a federal structure to facilitate exchange of goods, consistency of rules, etc. However, no federal decision would be implemented against the will of the local commune. The issue of punishing crimes would not really arise, as most crimes (except crimes of passion, which could be dealt with locally) would not occur, given economic equality. Furthermore, there would be no need to enforce people's contribution to the general good, as everyone naturally wants to do productive work, if they can find something they enjoy.

Many communist anarchists believe that human behaviour is motivated by a combination of egoism and sympathy. Society develops towards greater sympathy and more refined moral ideals through a confrontation between ideals and reality. Some anarchists added an evolutionary argument, namely that when groups compete, the more cooperative groups survive. There is therefore a natural pressure towards the development of greater solidarity.

As with Marxism and philosophical anarchism, we can question whether human beings can develop to a point where they can live peaceably without laws enforced by a coercive body.

> **?** Is any form of anarchism persuasive?

Key points • • •

- Anarchists object to the state as a sovereign, compulsory, distinct body that claims a monopoly on force. It undermines individual liberty and development.
- The essential function of protecting individuals and co-ordinating work can be achieved without the state.
- Anarchists argue that we have not yet achieved anarchism, despite our ability to live without a state, because we have not realised it is in our self-interest to do so, or because we are not yet sufficiently evolved morally, or the material conditions have not been right.

- Godwin defends the 'principle of private judgement', that no one can impose a duty on anyone else. The development of our judgement to see the truth of utilitarianism is part of the greatest good.
- Individualist anarchists argue that all legitimate human relations are voluntary. As we are driven by egoism, social harmony without the state will be secured by demonstrating how it is in each person's self-interest.
- Communist anarchists argue human relations are based on solidarity, and defend a communist society without a state.
- Of all three theories, we can question whether people can develop to a point where they voluntarily behave morally, without the need for coercive laws.

II. LIBERTY

The concept of liberty (or freedom – the two terms are used interchangeably) we shall discuss is that of political liberty: what is it to say an individual or society is free? This is not the concept of free will, and the metaphysical debate over whether we have free will is not normally relevant.

Different political views interpret or 'decontest' (see p. 67) liberty in different ways, appealing to different understandings of human beings, social relations, basic values and the relationship between individuals and government.

Negative and positive freedom

The distinction

Isaiah Berlin introduces a distinction between 'negative' and 'positive' liberty by saying that each interpretation answers a different question. Liberty in the negative sense is specified by answering the question 'What is the area within which the subject . . . is or should be left to do or be what he is able to do or be, without interference by other persons?' Liberty in the positive sense is specified by answering the question 'What, or who, is the source of control or interference that can determine someone to do, or be, this rather than that?' So, negative liberty is about freedom from interference, while positive liberty is about being in control or able to do something. At first, these two ideas seem very close together; if other people aren't interfering with what I do, then I am

'Two Concepts of Liberty' in D. Miller, *Liberty*, p. 34

in control of what I do, autonomous ('self-ruling'). But this isn't true. Autonomy requires that we are able to make and act on decisions that we endorse. But people can suffer from internal conflict. For example, they act to get something they want even though they know their action is morally wrong. From Plato onwards, this experience has been described in terms of a conflict between a 'higher' or rational self and a 'lower' or desiring self. To be autonomous, and so to have positive freedom, involves being able to choose and act in accordance with one's higher, rational self.

This leads to a dangerous paradox, says Berlin: if we can force people to act rationally, then we can actually force them to be free. Restricting their negative freedom can increase their positive freedom! Berlin argues that this would be a terrible political mistake, and could even justify totalitarianism (if the state claims that only it knows what is rational), so he argues that negative liberty is the form politics should be concerned with.

However, Berlin's distinction is misleading in several ways, and oversimplifies the debate. There are not two different concepts of liberty, as *all* liberty can be specified thus: 'x is (is not) free from y to do (not do, be, not be) z', where x relates to agents, y to constraints, z to actions and goals. Berlin's idea of negative liberty picks out freedom of individual people (x) from interference by other individual people (y) to act as they want (z). His idea of positive liberty picks out freedom of a person's higher self (x) from interference by their lower self (y) to act rationally (z). The difference between the two is created by differences in what they count as the relevant agent, constraint and goal. But these aren't the only options.

G. MacCallum, 'Negative and Positive Freedom', in D. Miller, *Liberty*, p. 102

Outline Berlin's distinction between negative and positive liberty.

Negative freedom

The core idea of negative liberty is freedom from interference by other people, including regulation and interference by the state. In the absence of interference, you are free – whether or not you have the *ability* or *resources* to do what you want to do. Negative freedom does not involve autonomy, only acting as one wants. According to negative liberty, freedom is just a matter of being able to do what you want to do. Everyone who is not coerced is *equally* free.

The extent of our freedom is the extent to which opportunities are available to us. However, Berlin argues that this is not a matter just of how *many* options there are, but also of *what* options there are, how *important* they are, how easy or difficult it is to take advantage of them and so on. For example, adding extra traffic lights restricts movement, but is unimportant. Denying freedom of religion removes very important options. The fullest extent of negative liberty is secured by a state that adopts Mill's Harm Principle: 'The only purpose for which power can be rightfully exercised over any member of a civilized community, against his will, is to prevent harm to others.'

Positive freedom

Adam Swift argues that there are three ideas of positive freedom, each rejecting a different aspect of negative freedom:

1. formal versus effective freedom: formal freedom is the absence of interference; effective freedom involves the power to act;
2. doing what one wants versus autonomy: someone can do what they want without being autonomous, if they are not in control of their desires;
3. freedom as freedom from political interference versus freedom as political participation.

EFFECTIVE FREEDOM

To be free to do something, you must be able to do it. The absence of interference is not enough. I'm not free to go swimming if I can't swim. You can increase someone's freedom by enabling them to do something they couldn't otherwise do, for instance through education or by giving them money.

Berlin objects that this confuses freedom with the conditions necessary for people to *exercise* their freedom. Someone is not less free if they lack money or skills; they are just less able to make the most of their freedom.

We can respond that our account of what freedom is should be based on why freedom is *valuable*. Freedom that is not valuable shouldn't count as freedom. Second, money and freedom are not that distinct. Suppose you try to travel on public transport without a ticket, because you cannot afford one. This lack of money will translate into *physical coercion*; you will be forcibly prevented from travelling. Having money gives you a right not to be interfered with that you would otherwise not have.

On Liberty, p. 68. For discussion, see FREEDOM OF THE INDIVIDUAL (I), p. 104.

Outline and illustrate negative liberty.

Political Philosophy, Part 2

We return to this in THE VALUE OF LIBERTY, p. 87.

Discuss the contrast between formal and effective freedom.

AUTONOMY

C. Taylor, 'What's
Wrong with Negative
Liberty?' in D. Miller,
Liberty, p. 146

Autonomy is not effective freedom; you can enable someone to do what they want to do, for example by providing them with money, without increasing their autonomy. Someone autonomous is able to act on their own values. They only follow others' rules (or values) if they have freely accepted them for themselves – and they are able to resist temptation. Autonomy requires 'self-awareness, self-understanding, moral discrimination, and self-control'.

Berlin tracks the historical association of positive freedom as autonomy with the division of self into higher and lower parts. The higher part is identified as the 'true' and rational self. If *someone else* is able to say what is higher or rational (as in many religious doctrines, Marx's idea of alienation (p. 75) and Rousseau's theory (p. 91)), they can define freedom for us. The state could restrict your negative liberty in any way it sees fit in order to enable you to realise what (it claims) is rational. But this implication can be avoided.

First, the most basic way to enhance autonomy is by enabling people to *think for themselves*, understand information that relates to their choices, consider consequences, and evaluate their priorities and actions. Autonomy is *not* enhanced by telling people what to do. Second, why accept that other people are *better judges* of when someone is acting autonomously than the person themselves? Third, autonomy (and so positive freedom) can be defined in terms of living according to one's values, which may not be the same as acting rationally. Fourth, even if autonomy is rational choice, we do not have to accept that just one way of living is rational for everyone.

POLITICAL PARTICIPATION

? How can the defender of positive freedom answer Berlin's claim that positive freedom leads to totalitarianism?

Distinguish and illustrate the three types of positive liberty.

Effective freedom and autonomy are models of individual positive liberty. However, 'republicanism' argues that freedom must include being involved in the political decisions that affect our lives. Freedom is not that area that politics does *not* regulate, but the freedom of citizens to *make* what rules we choose. We will return to this discussion in THE RELATIONSHIP BETWEEN LAW AND LIBERTY, p. 91.

Key points • • •

- Berlin distinguishes between negative liberty as freedom from interference and positive liberty as being in control, or able to do something.
- We can object that these are not distinct concepts of liberty, as all liberty involves someone being free from something to do something else.

- You are negatively free to do what you want as long as no one interferes with your choices, irrespective of whether you have the ability or resources to do what you want, or whether you are autonomous.
- The extent of negative freedom depends on how many options are available, but also on how important they are.
- There are three distinct interpretations of positive freedom.
- Effective freedom claims that to be free, you must have the ability and resources to do as you want.
- Autonomy claims that you must be able to act on your own values.
- Republicanism argues that freedom is found in democratic political participation, not just outside political regulation.
- Berlin objects that autonomy has been associated with acting from one's higher, rational self. If other people define what is 'higher', they can restrict your negative freedom in order to develop your positive freedom. This thought leads to totalitarianism. But we can resist this implication by arguing that prescribing one way to act for all people cannot enhance autonomy, for various reasons.

The value of liberty

Is negative liberty or some form of positive liberty the better interpretation? This section considers that question in relation to two others: What is the value of liberty? And how may it be promoted and defended politically?

Liberalism

THE VALUES OF NEGATIVE LIBERTY

Mill famously declared that 'the only freedom which deserves the name is that of pursuing our own good in our own way'. His concern here is with individuals being left alone to pursue their good, rather than the development of autonomy necessary for this. The state has a responsibility to ensure that children are educated, that there are opportunities for people to exercise their autonomy, and that there is a culture of respect for individuality. Berlin comments that without a certain area of freedom, individuals will not be able to develop or pursue an idea of the good. But securing such an area of negative liberty is as far as the state should go.

On Liberty, p. 72.
On Mill's views, see Ch. 3.

Mill argues that liberty is necessary for people to discover truth and better ways of living. Mill also seeks to protect us from the ill effects that can occur when one person imposes their vision of the good on society. As Frederick Hayek argues, 'liberty is essential in order to leave room for the unforeseeable and unpredictable . . . every individual *knows so little*, and, in particular, . . . we rarely know which of us knows best'. Liberty, then, also contributes to social utility or welfare.

The Constitution of Liberty, p. 29

See How CAN REDISTRIBUTION BE JUSTIFIED?, p. 111.

John Rawls argues that justice requires very extensive negative liberty. As long as we have enough to eat, enough clothes, a place to stay, we will value basic liberties (political liberty, the freedoms of speech, assembly, conscience, thought, personal property) above anything else, and justice recognises this.

A RESPONSE FROM POSITIVE LIBERTY

> **?** What arguments are there for interpreting liberty as negative liberty?

If the value of liberty lies in autonomy, is the state justified in seeking to enable individual autonomy by doing more than just secure freedom from interference? Is constraining negative liberty more important or worse than constraints on positive liberty that arise from a lack of the mental capacities necessary for autonomy or from a lack of resources? For example, could autonomy justify redistributing resources to those whose poverty restricts them from taking advantage of significant opportunities?

Berlin argues that this question is about the value of liberty relative to social justice. It may be that redistribution is justified even if, or though, it diminishes liberty. But positive liberty theorists are confused if they claim that redistribution is justified because it *increases liberty*.

But if freedom is more than absence of interference, Berlin is wrong. If state intervention is necessary to enable people to develop autonomy, then doing so would be justified *on the grounds of liberty*. We have argued that this appeal to autonomy does not lead to totalitarianism.

Furthermore, there should be a very close connection between what we think is valuable about liberty and what we think liberty is. Otherwise, we face the possibility that someone could be free, but that freedom would be worthless to them, and this contradicts the idea that liberty is valuable. Positive liberty as effective liberty or autonomy is a better interpretation of what liberty is because it expresses the value of liberty better. If this is right, we can defend the view that the state may do more to promote autonomy than simply secure the freedom of its citizens from interference by each other and by the state itself.

> 💬 Critically compare arguments for negative and positive liberty.

Conservatism

Burke's views on liberty were discussed on p. 71. He argues that the questions raised at the beginning of this section cannot be answered in the abstract. Liberty, in the abstract, cannot meaningfully be said to be good; to be good, liberty needs to be combined with other political goods, such as good government and the rule of law. Nor, without reference to the particular traditions and history of a society, can we say how liberty may be promoted and defended.

The best way to understand liberty, then, is in terms of inherited liberties: the rights and duties developed over time within a particular society. Certainly, we should be concerned, as Mill is, with the power that the state has over individual lives; but our concern should be that there is political and social harmony.

The liberal appeal to autonomy is dubious. Individuals are not perfectible, capable of ever more rational, more moral ways of living. Furthermore, we should not make too much of pursuing our *own* good in our *own* way; our ideas of what is good and how to live we have inherited from traditions that have been proven over time. We may develop them, but the best developments of them will be organic, integral to society, rather than some statement of radical individuality.

See also NATIONAL COMMUNITY AND POSITIVE LIBERTY, p. 128.

Marx and anarchism

Marx defends a form of positive liberty and attacks liberalism's negative liberty. Liberty lies in the realisation of our 'species-being', or true human nature. Achieving liberty means an end to alienation (see p. 76). Liberty is not a sphere of non-interference, but something we find in our connection to other people.

However, Marx's theory depends on the idea of a 'true' human nature that everyone shares. Second, in his support for a communist revolution, Marx suggests that some people can know what this is and act to help realise it for everyone. Berlin objects that these assumptions lead to totalitarianism. And the interpretation of Marx's ideas by Marxists has led to the imposition of forms of government, for example in the Soviet Union and China, that have limited negative liberty on the grounds that the state knows what is best for its citizens.

Marx can reply, however, that his theory of human nature and freedom is no more contentious than liberal theories of autonomy. Both Marx and Mill share a concern, for instance, that certain forms of work can interfere with the full development of a person's nature. Marx makes the end of alienating work central to his account of liberty, as he believes the organisation of means of production to be *the* crucial factor in the structure of society, while Mill does not. Again, Marx and Mill understand that people are naturally sociable, but Marx emphasises this much more than Mill, who equally emphasises their differences. But then Marx is not suggesting that everyone should live the same way. So-called Marxist states do not represent Marx's view of the communist society.

Anarchism criticises the state for limiting liberty unnecessarily, but different forms begin from different premises and find a different value in liberty. Communist anarchists (p. 81) endorse Marx's view of positive liberty. We find our freedom in solidarity with other people, which the state undermines. Individualist anarchists (p. 81) argue that negative liberty is required by the respect that we owe each person as sovereign over their mind and property. Godwin is closest to Mill. The ultimate value is utility, but the means to it is through autonomy, which in Godwin takes the form of the 'principle of private judgement' (see p. 80). Negative liberty is necessary for private judgement.

We can assess these accounts of liberty only in relation to assessments of the anarchist theories as a whole.

> **Discuss the relation between interpretations of liberty and theories of human nature and the purpose of the state.**

Key points • • •

- We can evaluate which interpretation of liberty is best in relation to accounts of the value of liberty and how it may be promoted politically.
- Mill defends a form of negative liberty as 'pursuing our own good in our own way'. As well as being necessary for individuality, negative liberty contributes to the discovery of truth and better ways of living.
- Rawls argues that negative liberty is necessary for justice.
- Defenders of positive liberty argue that constraints on negative liberty can be justified if necessary to promote autonomy. Negative liberty that is of no value is not liberty. The value of liberty lies in enabling autonomous action.
- Conservatism rejects an abstract debate over liberty. Interpretations of liberty and policies pursuing it are good relative to particular societies. It also casts doubt on liberal ideas of the value of individual autonomy.
- Marx interprets liberty in relation to our 'true' human nature and relations with others, a form of positive liberty. His ideas have been (mis?)interpreted in a way that led to totalitarianism.

- Philosophical and individual anarchists defend negative freedom, while communist anarchists defend positive freedom.

The relationship between law and liberty

Mill's Harm Principle states that 'The only purpose for which power can be right-fully exercised over any member of a civilized community, against his will, is to prevent harm to others.' This embodies the view that liberty and the law are in conflict. Freedom is freedom from legal constraint; the wider the extent of the law, the less freedom one has. This understanding is expressed in negative liberty.

On Liberty, p. 68

Mill's actual view, however, is subtler than this. The exercise of state power over the individual takes different forms in different societies. Where there is a complete distinction between rulers and ruled, then the liberty of the ruled is what is not constrained by law. But with democracy, the law expresses the will of the people. Liberty involves self-government as well.

Can these two ideas of liberty be brought into closer connection? Can we make sense of the idea that living under the law does not make us less free, but more free?

See DEVELOPMENT OF DEMOCRACY AND INHERENT DANGERS, p. 98.

First, individual negative liberty is dependent on the law. The law constrains other people from interfering with our negative liberty. The law is not, therefore, in conflict with negative liberty, but promotes it.

Second, the best way for citizens to ensure their negative liberty against constraint by the state is to be involved in the state. It may be that a benevolent dictator will grant an extensive area of non-interference, but this liberty will not be robust and secure. He may change his mind, or be replaced (e.g. when he dies) by a dictator who is not benevolent. However, if the citizens participate in the state, this will not happen (at least to the majority). But participating may require accepting duties, such as voting and military service, that decrease their negative liberty.

Third, liberty as political participation (p. 86) understands liberty *as* obedience to the law. Freedom is the freedom of a citizen (x) from domination by others (y) to make the rules he or she is to live under (z).

Jean-Jacques Rousseau argued that, as we live in society, society must have rules that govern behaviour. To be free, we must participate in making those rules. Individual autonomy is insufficient for real freedom, because individuals fall under the rules of society. So, we can attain it only collectively, in making

The Social Contract

the rules we live by together, and then abiding by them. Even if someone disagrees with a particular rule, the rule doesn't make them less free. They are part of a self-determining collective.

He goes on, controversially, to say that if we break the rules we have helped to make, then we aren't acting freely. The only way we can be free is through making these rules; as rules are made to be observed, to break them is to undermine the very condition of our own freedom. Paradoxically, punishing people who break rules made collectively can be understood as 'forcing them to be free'.

Rousseau has brought the individual, and a sense of what is good for the individual, completely within the social sphere. His understanding of freedom is not being subject to any *particular* other person; being subject to the collective is not a lack of freedom. But we can object that this is true only if individuals identify with the collective very strongly. If not, we need to be free *from* collective rule-making to go about our different, individual lives.

Nevertheless, Rousseau shows that liberty must mean more than having an area of one's life in which others don't interfere. By participating in the political process, we can extend our autonomy beyond making individual choices under legal constraints; we have chosen our constraints as well. In this sense, they are not constraints, but expressions of our autonomous values.

Key points • • •

- Mill's Harm Principle expresses the idea that power (law) and liberty are in conflict. Liberty increases as the extent of law decreases.
- However, in democracy, the law expresses the will of the people. Self-government is also a form of liberty.
- We can argue that the law protects negative liberty from interference by others, and that participating in making laws is the best way to protect negative liberty from interference by the state.
- Rousseau argues that liberty is living under laws we have made collectively. Individual autonomy is not enough.
- However, he also claims that punishing those who break the law is 'forcing them to be free'. We can object that we need freedom from interference by collective laws as well.

III. RIGHTS

The notion of rights

The idea of rights extends widely. I have a right to go to the cinema, a right not to be killed, a right to teach students at Heythrop College, a right to be paid, a right to have children, a right to the exclusive use of my house. Some rights are moral rights, some are legal, some are the results of contracts. We can also categorise rights by who has them (animal rights, workers' rights) or by what they are rights to (freedom of speech, the jobseeker's allowance). In general, a right can be understood as an entitlement to perform, or refrain from, certain actions and/or an entitlement that other people perform, or refrain from, certain actions. Many rights involve a complex set of such entitlements

Wesley Hohfeld provided a fourfold analysis of the 'structure' of rights that is generally accepted:

Fundamental Legal Conceptions

1. *Privilege/liberty*: I have a privilege/liberty to do x if I have no duty not to do x. I have the right to go to the cinema because I have no duty not to go to the cinema. But I have no right to steal, because I have a duty not to steal.
2. *Claim*: I have a claim right that someone else does x in certain cases in which they have a duty to me to do x. Claim rights can be 'negative' – they require that other people don't interfere with me (e.g. the right not to be killed); or 'positive' – they require that other people take specific action (e.g. the right to be paid if I'm employed).

   While every claim right entails a duty, not every duty entails a claim right. I may have a duty to give to charity, but I have not violated anyone's rights if I don't. Some duties are based on rights, but some are not. Talk of *rights* should not be confused with talk of what is morally *right*.

I shall refer to negative versus positive rights as rights of non-interference versus rights of provision respectively.

Explain and illustrate the relation between rights and duties.

Liberties and claims are the core of most rights. The rest of our discussion of rights involves rights that are, or at least involve, claims.

Going further: powers and immunities

Many rights relate to being able to alter duties:

3. *Power.* I have a power when I have the authority to alter my own or someone else's rights and duties. Judges have the right to set prison sentences; someone who is promised something has the right to enforce or waive the promise.
4. *Immunity.* I have an immunity when someone else does not have the power to change my rights and duties. So, I have the right to freedom of religion, because no one has the right (power) to impose a particular religious practice on me.

Many 'everyday' rights have a complex structure that involves all four of these aspects to a right. My property right to my books gives me the liberty to use them, a claim that no one else uses them, the power to waive that claim (lend my book to them) or transfer it (sell my book to them), and the immunity from anyone else waiving or transferring my right to my books. However, my right is not absolute; the duties and liberties are limited. For example, it does not give me the liberty to throw my books at other people, or give them permission to throw them. And if I refuse to pay taxes, my books may be seized and auctioned off to cover my debt. So, to accept a system of rights is to accept a distribution of liberties and duties.

Outline and illustrate Hohfeld's analysis of rights.

The distinction between natural and positive rights

'Natural rights' are rights people have simply in virtue of their nature, for example rationality, autonomy or certain needs. They are moral rights, and do not depend on being recognised by law. Instead, laws that violate people's natural rights can be condemned for that reason. They are universal, not relative to a particular society or set of laws. For this reason, many people think that whether there are any natural rights depends on whether there is a universal, objective morality.

By contrast, 'positive rights' are rights recognised and established in a system of rules. (This is usually the law, but also applies to religious rules and even games.) If all rights are positive rights, then rights only exist when recognised, for example in law. We can argue that a right imposes duties, which must be recognised and enforced. Rights appeal for *authoritative* recognition and *legal* enforcement. 'Natural' rights therefore do not make sense.

But surely we can say that a law fails to recognise someone's rights. In response, we can argue that, first, a law may violate someone's rights because it contradicts another law that has established those rights. For instance, UK law is required to conform to European law on what rights we have. Second, we can criticise laws for failing to recognise what *ought to be* (but is not yet) a right. Laws that do not establish the rights that people ought to have are morally wrong. But it is a confusion to say that people *have* the right before the law bestows it.

If we say there are natural rights as well as positive rights, we defend two types of right. It is simpler to reject natural rights, and talk about what rights should be established in law. Many people equate 'human rights' and natural rights, and take a rejection of natural rights to undermine human rights. But we could argue, instead, that human rights are created by national and international law. The debate continues in the next section.

> Explain and illustrate the distinction between natural and positive rights. Are there any natural rights?

Key points • • •

- A right is an entitlement to perform or refrain from certain actions, and/or an entitlement that other people perform or refrain from certain actions.
- Rights can be analysed in terms of liberties (no duty to refrain) and claims (others have a duty to refrain or perform). Many also involve powers (to alter rights and duties) and immunities (from having rights and duties altered).
- While claim rights impose duties, not all moral duties are based on claim rights. Not everything that is morally wrong violates someone's rights.
- Natural rights are universal moral rights based in human nature, and do not need to be recognised in law to exist.
- Positive rights are those established by a system of rules.
- We can argue that a right calls for legal enforcement, and so there are no natural rights. However, we can still argue that laws must establish rights that people *should* have.
- Human rights may be interpreted as natural rights or as rights created in national and international law.

Theories of how rights are grounded

On DEONTOLOGY, see p. 254.

In arguments about the basis of rights, there are two distinct issues. The first is the function of rights. Do rights exist to protect individual choice and freedom? Or to protect an individual's interests more generally? The second is what justifies rights. Is it deontological restrictions on how we treat individuals, based on individual worth or attributes? Or do rights serve some further moral or political goal, such as happiness, justice or equality?

Answers to the two questions *tend* to align, with choice defended by deontology, and interests defended by appeal to some goal. But this alignment is not necessary (e.g. we can defend the choice theory by appeal to happiness), and it is important to keep the two issues separate.

The function of rights: choice versus interests

CHOICE

Many rights relate to freedom: freedom of thought, speech, movement, freedom from murder and torture. Rights, we can argue, have the *specific* function of saying when freedom may or may not be limited. A different argument is that to have a right is to have a choice – either a liberty right to do something or not; or, for a claim right, the power to claim or waive another's duty. These claims recognise the special place that freedom and choice have in our lives. Rights protect that area of negative freedom necessary for us to live our lives according to our conception of what is good.

An inalienable right is one that you do not have the power to waive or transfer; for example, you cannot sell yourself into slavery.

However, this theory disallows many apparent rights. We cannot, on this basis, ascribe rights to beings that do not make autonomous choices, so infants, animals and comatose patients do not have rights. If to have a right is to have a choice, this limits rights even further. For example, in Australia, it is compulsory to vote. Yet don't Australians also have the right to vote? Or again, many people think that certain rights, for example to life or freedom, are inalienable. But if rights are choices, no rights are inalienable.

A second objection is that rights do more than just protect *freedom*. They tend, simultaneously, to protect other interests, such as not being physically or mentally harmed. If all, or most, rights do both, why pick out freedom as what rights protect?

One defence comes from the theory that claims rights are justified on the basis of autonomy (p. 97).

Discuss the claim that there is a special connection between rights and freedom/choice.

INTERESTS

If the function of rights is to protect individual interests, a person has a right because that will make them better off in some way. Having freedom, of course, is very much in our interests, but other interests also generate rights. Health, food, shelter and education all make us importantly better off. And beings without choice, such as infants and animals, nevertheless have interests, and these interests may generate rights. There may also be inalienable rights, as some interests may be too important for a person to exercise choice over.

But then, does *any* interest generate a right? We clearly think not. It is in my interest to be given money, but I have no *right* to this. Michael Freeden argues that

> a human right is a conceptual device . . . that assigns priority to certain human or social attributes regarded as essential to the adequate functioning of a human being; that is intended to serve as a protective capsule for those attributes; and that appeals for deliberate action to ensure such protection.

Rights, p. 7

So, not all interests generate rights. First, the interest must be closely connected to what we think it takes to live an adequate human life. Second, we must want to protect against other considerations that might conflict with it, such as preferences. I might prefer you not to have freedom of speech, if I don't like what you are saying. But if you have this right to freedom of speech, then my preferences do not provide good enough grounds for depriving you of freedom of speech. Third, we must be able to impose (and enforce) duties to protect it.

Which interests meet these criteria is a matter of debate. It could even be that our interest in an area of negative freedom is the only one!

Discuss the relation between rights and interests.

The justification of rights

APPEAL TO INDIVIDUAL ATTRIBUTES

We can argue that we are morally required to assign and respect rights because of something about individuals. One version of this claim, deriving from Locke, argues that people have natural rights bestowed by God. Another argues that to have rights is to be part of a moral community that agrees to live by certain rules.

A third version, from Kant, is that individuals are 'ends-in-themselves'. In brief, Kant argues that autonomous choice is the basis of morality itself. It is also

See RESPECTING HUMANITY, p. 262.

the source of all value; everything else has value only because it is adopted as an end by someone. So, we cannot weigh treating people as ends-in-themselves against any other end, as no other end has as much value. To ascribe rights recognises individuals as 'ends-in-themselves'; it respects their autonomy. We don't ascribe rights to someone because it is in their interests, but because it recognises what they are.

We can object, however, that our rights, even our fundamental rights, are shaped by many conditions that seem to relate not to ourselves, but to other people and social goods. My freedom of speech does not extend to saying 'Fire!' in a crowded cinema. My right to my property doesn't entitle me to do *whatever* I want with it. If my rights were grounded just in my autonomy, how can we explain this?

Explain and discuss the claim that rights are based on individual autonomy.

APPEAL TO MORAL OR POLITICAL GOALS

A second approach justifies rights by their role in securing some moral or political good. Mill argued that we could derive a theory of rights from UTILITARIANISM (p. 248). Certain of our interests, he argues, should be protected as rights. Society may use the law to regulate conduct that consists in 'injuring the interests of one another, or rather certain interests which, either by express legal provision or tacit understanding, ought to be considered as rights'.

On Liberty, p. 141

On Liberty, p. 70

Mill argues that utility is 'the ultimate appeal on all ethical questions; but it must be utility in the largest sense, grounded on the permanent interests of a man as a progressive being'. Rights relate to these 'permanent interests' we have as 'progressive beings'. Singling out these interests for protection will contribute most to utility. For example, Mill argues that freedom of thought and speech will help us to discover and understand the truth; and that 'the free development of individuality is one of the leading essentials of well-being'. On the other hand, we do not have a right to protection from economic competition, because economic competition contributes to the common good.

On Liberty, p. 120.
See THE ARGUMENTS IN SUPPORT OF FREEDOM OF THOUGHT AND EXPRESSION, p. 115, and THE ARGUMENTS IN SUPPORT OF FREEDOM OF ACTION, p. 124.

We can object, however, that if it proved that freedom of thought, etc. did *not* contribute to utility, then we would no longer have these rights. We only have rights that contribute to greatest utility. Mill's defence of rights rested on his belief that we progress through having freedom. But after two world wars and the rise of religious violence, we may doubt whether Mill is right about this. Do utility and rights conflict?

Second, a right protects the individual's interest against what may compete with it, for example the greater good. If I have a right to freedom of speech, then even if it would be better for everyone if I did not express my objectionable views, I may not be prevented from doing so. But if the ground of rights is utility, this protection seems insecure. If my rights are justified by general utility, then doesn't the general utility of overriding my rights justify violating them?

Other theories that appeal to moral or political goals to defend rights do not all face these objections. For example, John Rawls argues that we have certain rights as a matter of justice. What defines justice is not respect for the natural attributes of individuals, but fairness. Assigning and respecting rights, then, secures justice as fairness.

Mill's response is given in RESOLVING CONFLICTS BETWEEN RIGHTS AND UTILITY, p. 101.

See p. 112.

? What obstacles face justifying rights by appeal to utility?

Going further: Marx's objection

Marx argued that talk of rights - liberal rights, to liberty, property and so on - should be abandoned. When we consider the function of rights, we see that the idea of rights derives from a view of human beings as separated from each other, not communally related. It assumes that individuals have interests that can be defined as *their own*, independent of other people. Liberty rights assume that they are always potentially in conflict with each other, property rights that they may do whatever they wish so long as they don't harm others, ignoring the desperate need for resources elsewhere. These assumptions will create a society of isolated egoists. And the idea of equal rights creates an illusion that there is equality, when in reality there is not.

These are important considerations, but we can question whether the concept of rights must itself be given up. It may be that we should place more emphasis on GROUP RIGHTS (p. 122) and less on individual rights.

? How persuasive is Marx's criticism of rights?

Problems concerning their extent and application

Joseph Raz argues that a full specification of a right should tell us:

The Morality of Freedom, Ch. 7.

1. who has the right;
2. what justifies their right;
3. what it is a right to;
4. who has the corresponding duties, and what these duties are.

Our discussion so far relates to the first three points. Do rights function to protect freedom and choice only, or also other interests? Who can have rights? If rights function to protect interests, which interests? These questions all relate to the extent of rights. This issue of the extent and application of rights can also be discussed by taking up Raz's fourth requirement: what duties do rights impose?

Rights and their corresponding duties must be *practical*. This might limit the rights that we have. In THE NOTION OF RIGHTS (p. 93), we noted a distinction between rights of non-interference and rights of provision. Some philosophers have argued that the former are easier to satisfy than the latter. Rights of non-interference can be respected just by people *not* doing something, namely, interfering with each other. Rights of provision, however, require some good or service to be provided – and so it is possible that demand might outstrip supply, or that no one has the ability to make the provision. If we interpret the right to life as a right of non-interference, as long as I am not murdered, or prevented from sustaining my life, my right is not violated. But if we interpret it as a right of provision, someone has the duty to keep me alive. But suppose there is not enough food to go around? Is my right violated? By whom? It seems that duties are harder to allocate with rights of provision, leading some philosophers to reject them altogether.

However, this distinction can disappear when we consider the duty of enforcing rights. Against each individual, my right to life involves only the duty of non-interference. But the state has the additional duty of enforcing my right against other individuals who would violate it. This involves a police force and a legal system. These also involve resources (money, people willing to serve as police officers and lawyers) that may be in short supply. In fact, it may be *less costly* for the state to feed everyone than to enforce their rights of non-interference against assault. When it comes to the duties of enforcement that our rights impose on the state, all rights involve elements of provision. Rights of non-interference are not easier to enforce than rights of provision. This demonstrates the importance of specifying the duties, and who holds them, when discussing the application of a right.

In fact, to stop with the duties of the state may itself be insufficient. Democratic states, for instance, are answerable to their citizens. If the state is failing to perform its duties, we could argue that citizens, individually and collectively, have the duty to attempt to influence the state. So, for instance, while your right to life does not impose on me a duty to save you from attack, it may impose on me a duty to play my part in ensuring that the state meets its duties in preventing such attacks and punishing criminals.

Discuss the challenges to be faced in deciding on the extent and application of our rights.

Key points • • •

- In discussing the basis of rights, we must look at both the function of rights and their justification.
- The choice theory argues that rights function to protect freedom and choice. It faces the objection that this rules out many rights we think we have.
- The interest theory argues that rights function to protect individual interests. Freeden argues that rights protect just those interests necessary for adequate human functioning.
- One approach justifies rights by appealing to individual attributes, such as autonomy. But many rights take into account the interaction of individuals and social goods.
- Another approach justifies rights by their contribution to some good, such as utility (Mill) or justice (Rawls).
- But if rights are based on utility, if it turns out that certain rights, for example to freedom, do not contribute to utility, then we do not have those rights; and that if rights and utility conflict on some occasion, utility may override the right.
- Marx objects that the idea of individual rights wrongly presupposes individuals are separate from each other and in conflict.
- Rights impose duties, which it should be practical to impose and enforce. The duties imposed by rights of non-interference seem easier to fulfil than duties imposed by rights of provision.
- However, this distinction disappears when we consider the duty of the state to enforce respect for rights.

Resolving conflicts between rights and utility

If rights were based on utility, how could we defend rights claims when they conflicted with utility? A utilitarian believes that the right thing to do is what creates the greatest benefit; if violating a right did this, then what reason is there not to violate that right? But a right that can be overridden whenever it is beneficial for it to be overridden is not a right at all. The possession of a right means that the right-holder's interests cannot be sacrificed in this way.

Basing rights on an appeal to individual attributes explains why. Rights are not a means for bringing about good consequences. For instance, they are necessary to respect the absolute worth of the individual as an end-in-themselves. Social utility, if brought about through violating rights, is not good, but bad. Rights constrain the actions that the state, or people generally, are permitted to take in the pursuit of the greatest benefit.

However, we have objected (p. 98) that what rights we have, their scope and the duties they impose, take considerations of social utility into account. Likewise, many people would grant that if the consequences of not violating someone's rights are *really* bad (for example, it would lead to the deaths of many other people), then it is permissible to violate that person's rights. The force of rights is not absolute.

Mill argues that those who think rights and utility conflict are not viewing utility in the right light. Utility is a moral standard only if it is utility 'in the largest sense'. Rights protect our permanent interests, and thus serve social utility considered *over the long term*. We should establish that system of rights that would bring most utility, and then defend these rights.

But is this the correct defence of rights? If individual freedom is valuable independent of social utility, Mill's resolution doesn't work. We must instead weigh up rights against utility on occasion. We can argue that rights, though not absolute, will *generally* override social utility.

A different approach argues that the right to autonomy is not, in fact, an individual right, but a GROUP RIGHT (p. 122). If I am to be autonomous – that is, to be able to make meaningful choices about how my life goes – then certain opportunities need to be available to me. But no one is under a duty to provide these opportunities just on the basis of *my* autonomy alone. My interest, taken alone, couldn't possibly generate such large-scale duties. But everyone's interest, taken together, can. So, I have a right to autonomy only because all citizens do, collectively.

On this understanding, rights aren't independent of, or opposed to, social utility. So, there is no general rule for how we should resolve conflicts between them when they arise.

> **?** Can we formulate a general rule for resolving conflicts between rights and utility?

Key points • • •

- How we resolve conflicts between rights and utility depends on our justification of rights. Justifying rights by utility may allow rights to be overridden whenever they conflict with utility.
- Justifying rights by individual autonomy supports the idea that rights are

constraints on what we may do in pursuing utility. But rights seem to take utility into account, and are rarely (if ever) absolute.

- Mill argues that rights serve utility *in the long term*. Considered like this, there is no conflict between rights and utility.
- We may question whether I have an individual right to autonomy; the duties necessary to provide meaningful autonomy are too onerous, and can only be justified on the basis of securing everyone's autonomy. This brings utility and rights closer together.

Going further: rights, liberty, morality and law

Many core liberal rights function to protect liberty. Choice theories argue that rights in general have this function. On the interests theory, while we can connect rights to various interests, we can still analyse rights so that most protect some type of freedom. The question of whether *all* rights protect freedom is the question of whether there are any claim rights of provision concerned with interests (life, food, medical treatment?) other than liberty.

Even here, a defender of POSITIVE LIBERTY (p. 85) may argue that such interests can be understood as necessary conditions for liberty.

On the relation between rights and the law: if there are no natural rights, only positive rights, rights exist only when recognised by the law (or other systems of rules). But even natural rights relate closely to the law. Many natural rights are already recognised by law, and those that are not are rights that the law *should* recognise. This is because rights impose duties, which need to be allocated and enforced (by the state). More generally, the law distributes the liberties, duties, powers and immunities associated with rights.

Natural rights are moral rights, and appeal to morality to change the law if necessary. Many positive rights have very little to do with morality per se, and are simply ways of regulating behaviour smoothly. Natural rights theories are committed to the view that, in certain fundamental respects, the law should be based on morality, because it should incorporate our natural rights. Positive rights theories can leave open the question of how closely the law and morality should be related.

Finally, theories that justify rights in terms of individuals' attributes make rights the foundation of morality, and argue that these rights constrain the laws that a state may legitimately make. Theories that justify rights by some moral or political goal vary in their accounts of the place of rights in morality, for example depending on whether the goal is utility or justice as fairness (p. 112). They also differ in the kinds of constraints they say rights place on the law. Rawls argues that justice is the most basic political value, so rights place absolute constraints on law. Utilitarians argue that utility is the most basic political value, so rights are not so stringent.

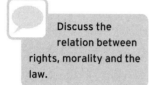

Discuss the relation between rights, morality and the law.

Key points • • •

- Whether all rights relate to liberty depends on whether there are any claim rights of provision related to interests other than liberty.
- If there are only positive rights, rights can exist only if recognised by law. Natural rights, however, are still rights that the law should recognise.
- The law distributes rights and associated duties.
- Natural rights theories argue that the law should be based on morality in some fundamental respects.
- Rights justified by individual autonomy or justice may place strong constraints on the law; rights justified by utility may be more flexible.

IV. JUSTICE

Formally, justice is the principle that each receives their 'due'. So, we are required to treat equals equally, and if what someone is due depends on some quantifiable attribute (e.g. ability in some area), we should treat differences proportionally.

The concept of justice can be divided into two important strands: justice in punishment and justice in the distribution of goods in society. We will not discuss theories of punishment. Justice in the distribution of goods divides into 'political' justice, regarding the distribution of basic liberties and rights; and what the syllabus calls 'social, economic or distributive justice', regarding goods such as money and opportunities. Our main focus will be on the latter.

Competing principles of justice

A theory of distributive justice develops and defends a principle of distribution. First, this specifies which 'goods' are being considered, such as happiness, liberty, income, wealth or opportunities. Second, the principle may indicate how to divide the good up. We shall look at three suggestions.

Equality

Different interpretations of 'equality' are relevant to justice. First, as we have already noted, justice involves *formal* equality. Second, there is the idea that, *morally* speaking, all people are equal; for example, all people deserve moral respect or have the same natural rights. This idea has not been popular historically, with many societies discriminating on grounds of sex, race or caste.

See THE DISTINCTION BETWEEN NATURAL AND POSITIVE RIGHTS, p. 94.

On the basis of moral equality, we may argue for 'assumed' equality: justice requires a distribution of strict equality unless we can give good reasons why another distribution would be better. Inequalities need to be justified. If we argue that inequalities cannot be justified, we get egalitarianism, the view that justice requires equality. Most philosophers hold this in relation to basic rights and liberties (political justice), but reject it for social justice.

Egalitarianism is certainly impractical in society as we know it, but the question is 'what does justice *require*?', not 'can we bring about justice in society?'. Our question and discussion are therefore, in the first instance, theoretical. However, the point is always to develop a theory that *can be used* in some way to inform political thinking and events.

Outline the different ways justice can be related to equality.

STRICT EQUALITY

The simplest argument for egalitarianism is that people should receive equal amounts of goods, as this is the best way to respect their moral equality. But immediately there are problems. First, what counts as the same 'amount' of goods? We could say that people should receive exactly the same goods – food, house, means of transport, etc. But this is bizarre, and it is not a good interpretation of equality, because people have *different preferences*. And suppose we do create strict equality – if we allow people any form of freedom with their money, inequalities will quickly emerge. Even if we give them the same income, since people have different preferences, for some their income may be more than enough, for others it may feel like too little.

Strict equality also overlooks inequalities in what people *need*; for example, people with disabilities may need expensive treatment. People also have different ambitions, with some working hard to achieve good things in life, others being lazy. Strict equality means that differences between people are being treated *unequally*. Finally, to live their lives equally well, people require equal *opportunities*. But what is an equal 'amount' of opportunity?

DEVELOPING EGALITARIANISM

Instead of strict equality, some philosophers argue for 'equality of welfare'. The point of equality is for people to have equally happy lives. But first, there is a real difficulty in measuring this. Second, people who have 'expensive tastes' will require more money (or resources generally) to achieve the same level of happiness as someone who has simpler tastes. Fine wine costs more than orange juice. Does justice really require that they get these extra resources?

An alternative, then, is 'equality of resources', where this includes opportunities as well as material goods. Everyone's 'bundle' of resources is equal if no one *envies* anyone else's bundle. Once we achieve this, then how people handle their resources from then on is up to them. This will lead to inequality, but the purpose of justice, as it is understood by egalitarians, is surely to eliminate any disadvantages people suffer that are *not the results of their own choices*. Differences between people that result from what they inherit genetically or through upbringing should be eradicated; but people are morally responsible for their choices and actions. If you choose to drink fine wine, you can't expect extra money to support your choice.

We can object, however, that if two people have different capacities (not resulting from their own past choices), then presenting them with equal resources will not ensure equality, because one will be able to do more with those resources than the other. To take everything into account, we should argue for 'equal access to advantage'. People should be able to make equal use of whatever makes life go better ('advantage').

OBJECTIONS

Despite the increasing sophistication of egalitarianism, there are three strong objections to it.

First, we cannot ensure equality and respect the results of people's choices, because it is impossible to distinguish between those aspects of people's lives that result from their inheritance (genetic or upbringing) and those that result from their choices. For instance, strength of will makes a great difference to a

Outline and illustrate the challenges facing strict egalitarianism.

We shall discuss a different measure of equality of welfare, NEED, as a distinct principle of justice later (p. 107).

Discuss the different forms of egalitarianism.

person's ambition and achievements. But is it itself inherited or related to choices? If both, what part each? What of people's talents – inherited or developed through choice? In what proportion?

Second, there are objections from other political principles: any egalitarian principle of justice will restrict people's freedom, especially if we try to maintain equality over time; and it will also conflict with what people deserve (p. 108).

Third, we can object that *everyone* will be better off if we do not respect equality. Economic inequality, such as a higher salary for better, or more, work, creates incentives for people to produce more wealth. This raises the *total amount* of goods in society. As a result, relatively poor people in an inegalitarian society may still be richer than people in an egalitarian society.

See Nozick's ENTITLEMENT THEORY, p. 117.

Discuss the claim that social justice requires equality.

Need

MARX (p. 76) defended a version of equality related to need. He argues in *Critique of the Gotha Programme* that theories of justice have concentrated far too much on distribution of goods and not enough on the question of *production*. The principle he proposes is 'from each according to his ability, to each according to his need'. The idea that justice lies in meeting people's needs reflects the ideals of community and solidarity. It is not, strictly speaking, a principle of equality, because what people need is not equal.

However, he argues that this is not a principle of justice, as his future communist society is one that is beyond justice (see p. 77).

DEVELOPING A THEORY OF NEEDS

What is a need? Can we distinguish between what someone needs and what they want, or is a need simply a very strong desire? We can argue that a need is not like a desire at all, because it is not a *psychological* state. Whether a child needs to take medicine doesn't depend on whether it wants to take it. And even if the child really wants more chocolate, it may need to stop eating it. A need is 'objective', while desires are 'subjective'. What someone needs depends on facts about their health, in the broadest sense, both physical and psychological. A need is what is necessary to achieve some (minimal?) level of human welfare or flourishing. So, for a need-based theory of justice to work, we need to develop a theory of human welfare.

But is there any objective theory of human welfare? Human beings are social and cultural animals, and what they need in order to flourish therefore depends on the society in which they live. The needs theorist can say either: (1) what justice in a society requires is that we meet people's needs in that society; so

This issue is discussed in RELATIVISM, p. 233.

What is a need?

justice is relative to society; or (2) needs secure some minimum level of welfare, which is universal. What else is needed to flourish relative to a particular society is not a matter of justice.

OBJECTIONS

Even if we can develop a theory of minimum welfare, it may not establish what is necessary for justice. For example, it is plausible that some human needs – even basic ones – relate to sex and others to friendship. However, we do not think that justice requires the state to meet *these* needs! But why not?

Second, there is the danger of 'needs-inflation'. For example, suppose a basic measure of flourishing is longevity. Will anything that increases longevity – diet, lifestyle, medical developments – therefore count as a need? Does justice always require making these available to everyone?

Third, should justice be concerned with needs taken 'absolutely' or should it take into account comparisons between people within a society? If we include comparative measures, then as society becomes richer, people's 'needs' increase. But if we avoid all comparison, society could contain *great* inequalities without any injustice – as long as everyone achieves a minimum standard of welfare.

Fourth, does what counts as a need within a society change over time, in response to what is available in that society? For instance, do people need TVs now, or computers, or fridges? If we say 'yes', this looks like 'needs-inflation'; but if we say 'no', given how much available entertainment, information and communication, and food depend on these three kinds of appliances, does that not make life much harder for those who can't afford them?

Finally, egalitarians will object that 'need' does not do justice to equality. Our third theory argues that people will not always need what they deserve, nor will they always deserve what they need.

Can justice be met by giving people what they need?

Desert

According to desert theories, theories of equality and need do not adequately take into account human beings as *purposive agents*, responsible for what they do and creative in response to life's challenges. People should be treated according to their specific qualities and actions. Distributed goods are rewards people receive in response to how they choose to live.

talents, intellect, etc.

What is it that makes people deserve what they do if it is not need or equality? Four possible answers:

1. *Effort*: Justice requires that people are rewarded in proportion to the effort that they make in their work. People deserve to keep what they produce as a reward for the effort they put into making it. _Nozick_

2. _Compensation_: Not only effort but *all* the costs someone incurs through their work deserve reward, and they should be compensated accordingly.

These theories ignore the question of whether the person produces anything good or useful. But promoting an evil goal surely deserves no reward! Only work (or other activities) that is _socially productive_ deserves reward.

Spencer quote! What about nurses, firemen, etc paid pittances for noble work?

3. *Contribution*: The value of the contribution that people make in terms of social productivity determines what they deserve to receive.

4. *Virtue*: Aristotle argues that justice requires that the virtuous are rewarded. So, a person's virtues in general determine what they deserve.

→ Rawls
√ debt to society incurred – paid back through taxation. Society provides resources (eg teachers, etc) that aid development of talent + thus contribute to individual's wealth

Nicomachean Ethics, Book V § 3

Compare and contrast the four bases of desert.

Going further: working out desert

We can object that the idea of rewarding desert is impractical. How can we identify what should count as effort or cost? Or how virtuous someone is? What about social productivity? Some philosophers think we can determine this through the 'free market'. The market will reward someone in proportion to how valuable their contribution is.

Unfortunately, this simply isn't true. First, the market distributes rewards not according to value, but according to how much and how many people desire what is offered. Is a footballer more socially valuable than a nurse? Second, market values are affected by other factors, such as scarcity. Gold is more valuable than iron because it is rarer, not because it is more useful. But no one deserves a greater reward for providing something just because it is scarce, unless it is also crucial to social welfare.

So, we can't use the market to work out how socially valuable a product or activity is. Then how can we? Given that any theory of social productivity will relate to human welfare, the objections faced by the needs-based theory regarding developing a theory of human welfare apply here as well.

Is there any practical way of working out what someone deserves?

OBJECTIONS

Should social justice be based on desert?

First, justice does not always require that people get what they deserve. For instance, in a competition it is the person who wins, not the person who deserved to win, who receives the prize.

Second, the initial remarks on desert suggest that we deserve only rewards that relate to our choices, etc. We don't deserve rewards based on factors outside our control. But, for instance, the value of the contribution we make to social productivity will depend on what we can do and how much others value this – neither of which we can control. And, as discussed in EQUALITY (p. 106), we cannot separate out that part of our lives or work that comes from choice from that part which comes from natural ability and upbringing.

In any case, shouldn't we disconnect desert from responsibility? Doesn't a person who is ill deserve medical care? Indeed, doesn't just being a person deserve respect? If the answer is 'yes', then the theory of desert might include the theories of equality and need: there are some things people deserve in virtue of moral equality (respect . . .), some they deserve because they need them, and some they deserve because of their particular traits and actions.

A third objection is that desert cannot define justice because it presupposes justice. You deserve something only if you deserve it in accordance with the rules – but the rules must also be just. If you contribute greatly to society, but by treating some people very badly, then perhaps you don't deserve rewards. We cannot say what anyone deserves before we know what justice requires.

Finally, if I get what I deserve, but everyone else gets more than they deserve, is this just? This idea of justice as *fairness* takes us towards a 'mixed' theory of justice, one that uses and combines a number of values, as discussed in the next section.

> **?** Does justice require that we get what we deserve?

Key points • • •

- Different interpretations of equality may be relevant to justice: formal equality, moral equality, 'assumed' equality and equality of goods.
- Strict equality of goods faces difficulty in specifying the same 'amount' of goods, and ignores differences between people's preferences, needs and ambitions.
- Equality of welfare is difficult to measure and faces the problem of 'expensive tastes'.

- Equality of resources seeks to correct inequalities that are not the results of individuals' choices, but allow those that are.
- Equal access to advantage is concerned to correct, in addition, inequalities that result from equal opportunity where people have unequal capacities.
- We can object that it is impossible to distinguish inequalities that result from people's choices from those that do not, and that everyone may be better off if we allow some inequalities in order to generate incentives.
- Needs are not psychological states, like desires, but relate to what is necessary for human flourishing.
- If there is no objective theory of flourishing, social justice may be relative to society. If there is an objective theory, it seems that only some needs relate to justice, while others (e.g. sex) do not.
- Establishing exactly what counts as a need within or across societies faces a number of difficulties.
- Desert theories argue that justice requires that people are rewarded according to their effort, or as compensation for costs, or contribution to social productivity, or for virtue.
- We can object that theories of effort and compensation fail to take account of whether someone produces something useful; and that no basis for desert can be practically measured. Even the free market does not measure contribution to social productivity.
- Furthermore, we cannot reward only what is based on our choices, as we cannot separate this from what is outside our control. And desert can only be determined once we have a set of just rules.
- We may argue that both equality and need are also bases for desert, so all three principles are needed in a theory of justice. Or that a fourth is missing, namely fairness.

How can redistribution be justified?

A just distribution of goods requires state intervention. Each principle of justice considered so far requires that goods are *redistributed* in accordance with the principle of justice – that is, that they are taken away from some people, say through taxation, and given to others. However, justice is not the only political value. So, a full justification of redistribution needs to consider justice in relation to other values, such as liberty. To address this fundamental issue, a theory needs to develop an account of, for example, the nature of society and the

See HUMAN NATURE
AND POLITICAL
ORGANISATION, p. 67.

relationship between the individual and society. We shall discuss such a theory shortly, but first, how would arguments from equality, need and desert justify redistribution?

Redistribution by equality, need, desert

According to 'equal access to advantage' (p. 106), we can argue that no one should face disadvantages that do not result from their own choices. For example, children should not gain or lose advantages as a result of their parents' choices. Respecting the moral equality of each person from birth requires that one's parents' situation does not give unequal access to advantage. Or again, someone may face disadvantage through brute luck (a genetic disease, a natural disaster); we should mitigate the effects of this disadvantage so that, as far as possible, this does not adversely affect the rest of the person's life. Providing equal access to advantage will require the state to redistribute goods (or access to goods) towards those who are disadvantaged.

The principle of need (p. 107) claims that justice requires that at least the basic needs of each person are met within society. The importance of each person being able to lead a decent life demands it. To ensure this, the state will have to provide for those who cannot meet their own needs. Since the goods necessary to meet these needs cannot come from nowhere, they will come from those who have more than they need.

One principle of desert (p. 108) claims that justice requires that people are rewarded in proportion to the value of the contribution they make to social productivity. If the free market achieved this, then there might be little need for active redistribution. However, since it does not, redistribution is needed to correct imbalances produced by the market.

Apply and defend
one principle of
justice in relation to
redistribution.

Rawls: justice and the social contract

John Rawls' theory of distributive justice is based on the idea that society is a system of cooperation for mutual advantage between individuals. As such, it is marked by both conflicts between differing individual interests and an identity of shared interests. Principles of justice should 'define the appropriate distribution of the benefits and burdens of social cooperation'. Justice is the most important political value and applies to the 'basic institutions of society' – the

A Theory of Justice,
p. 4

political constitution and the institutions that regulate the market, property, family, freedom and so on – because it is intimately connected to what society is and what it is for. If society is a matter of cooperation between equals for mutual advantage, the conditions for this cooperation need to be defended and any inequalities in social positions must be justified. And so the principles of justice, Rawls thinks, must be 'the principles that free and rational persons concerned to further their own interests would accept in an initial position of equality as defining the fundamental terms of their association'. Justice, then, is fairness.

A Theory of Justice,
p. 11

What are the terms of the 'social contract'? What principles of justice would we agree to in this situation? For our agreement to secure a fair, impartial procedure, we need to eliminate any possible bias towards, say, the rich or the poor, or the religious or the atheist. So, argues Rawls, assume that we are to agree on these principles *without knowing what our position in society will be* or what our idea of the good is. The point of this 'veil of ignorance' is to ensure that

> no one is advantaged or disadvantaged in the choice of principles by the outcome of natural chance or the contingency of social circumstances. Since all are similarly situated and no one is able to design principles to favor his particular condition, the principles of justice are the result of a fair agreement or bargain.

A Theory of Justice,
p. 12

Rawls calls this the 'original position'. Of course, Rawls is not supposing that anyone has ever made decisions on this basis. The original position is simply a hypothetical thought experiment that seeks to 'make vivid to ourselves the restrictions that it seems reasonable to impose on arguments for principles of justice, and therefore on these principles themselves'.

A Theory of Justice,
p. 18

Explain Rawls' ideas of the original position and the veil of ignorance.

Two principles of justice

The goods that are to be distributed by justice are only those that we can assume everyone will want. These include rights, liberties, powers, opportunities, income, wealth and self-respect. In the original position, Rawls argues, first, we will only agree to an equal distribution, unless a certain amount of inequality will work to everyone's advantage, for example by providing incentives that will generate more wealth for everyone. Second, once a certain level of material well-being is secured, we will value our basic liberties – political liberty, the freedoms of speech, assembly, conscience, thought, personal property – more than other goods. So, equal liberty will be preferred to unequal liberty but greater wealth.

These two ideas lead to two principles of justice, with the first (political justice) always taking priority over the second (social justice):

1. each person is to have an equal right to the most extensive total system of equal basic liberties compatible with a similar system of liberty for all; and
2. social and economic inequalities are to be arranged so that they are both

    (a) to the greatest benefit of the least advantaged . . . and
    (b) attached to offices and positions open to all under conditions of fair equality of opportunity.

A Theory of Justice, p. 302

The most controversial claim is 2(a), known as the 'Difference Principle'. Rawls argues that inequalities should be to everyone's benefit. But is he right that we would choose the Difference Principle in the original position? Which of the following two scenarios is it rational to prefer, if we have a 50 per cent chance of being either richer or poorer?

	Richer	Poorer	Average
A:	50	40	45
B:	150	30	90

Discuss Rawls' argument for his two principles of justice.

Rawls argues for A: 'maximise the minimum' level of welfare. But we can object that it makes just as much sense to maximise the average wealth (B), especially as there is equality of opportunity that will allow individuals to improve their position.

Going further: self and society

Rawls' theory is based on his view that society is a cooperative pursuit of what is in our individual interest, which can be identified prior to our existence in society. Both CONSERVATISM (p. 71) and MARXISM (p. 74) would reject this liberal individualism. It rules out any theory that sees social bonds as intrinsically good, rather than a means to our individual advantage. It assumes that we are fundamentally separate, rather than naturally social. It understands justice as arising out of conflicting claims between individuals who are uninterested in each other's welfare.

Second, in his defence of the usefulness of the original position, Rawls assumes that you and I can meaningfully exist *as ourselves* behind the 'veil of ignorance' – otherwise, the original position is useless in discerning justice for *us*. A different theory of the self, known as communitarianism, argues that our individual identities are defined by our values, what gives meaning to our lives. We cannot strip ourselves of such ideas in a thought experiment; nor would the results of the thought experiment be meaningful for us. Furthermore, our values and conception of what is good are derived from other people, and held in common with them. We gain our values in a community – another objection to Rawls' individualism.

If this is right, then even if redistribution is justified, it is not justified by Rawls' argument. In the next section, we will discuss further objections to Rawls' theory of justice.

The controversial nature of similar assumptions is discussed, in relation to morality, not justice, in MORALITY AS A SOCIAL CONTRACT, pp. 89, 102.

Discuss the role of Rawls' liberalism in his theory of justice.

Key points • • •

- A full justification of redistribution needs to relate the value of justice to other political values with which it may conflict.
- Equal access to advantage justifies redistribution by arguing that no one should face disadvantages that do not result from their own choices.
- The principle of need argues that the importance of each person requires that their basic needs are met.
- The principle of desert argues that people deserve reward according to their contribution to society.

- Rawls justifies redistribution by first considering the nature of society, which he claims is a system of cooperation for mutual advantage between individuals. Justice is therefore fairness, principles governing cooperation that free, rational, self-interested people would accept if they were equal.
- The original position, in which each person is behind a 'veil of ignorance', models these conditions.
- In the original position, people will value liberty over increases in material well-being, and will accept inequality only if it will work to everyone's advantage (the Difference Principle).
- We can object that it is not more rational to choose the Difference Principle than a utilitarian calculation of costs and benefits.
- We can also object that Rawls' assumptions about society and individuals are controversial, and fail to recognise the intrinsic value of social co-operation.
- Communitarians object that we cannot imagine ourselves behind the veil of ignorance, because it strips away our values, which define our identities.

The relationship between distributive justice, liberty and rights

The three principles of distributive justice we discussed, based on equality, need and desert, did not comment on the relationships between justice and liberty, nor did they make use of the concept of 'rights' in developing their accounts. By contrast, Rawls explicitly relates his theory to both liberty and rights.

Rawls' first principle of justice covers liberty, and he argues that once a certain level of material well-being is secured, it should always take priority over the second principle regarding distributive justice. Liberty is more important than the distribution of social and economic inequalities.

See THE DISTINCTION BETWEEN NATURAL AND POSITIVE RIGHTS, p. 94.

Rawls rejects the idea of rights prior to the principles of justice. Principles of justice *assign* rights (and duties, benefits and burdens), so people can only make a rights claim once the principles of justice are in place. We could object that justice is served when people receive what they have a right to. We could argue, for instance, that people have a right to what they need or deserve. A different theory, which bases justice on rights and liberty, is that of Robert Nozick.

Nozick's entitlement theory

*Anarchy, State and
Utopia*, Ch. 7

Nozick is primarily concerned with the distribution of property, and argues that
justice involves three ideas:

1. Justice in acquisition: how you first acquire property rights over something
    that has not previously been owned;
2. Justice in transfer: how you acquire property rights over something that has
    been transferred (e.g. by gift or exchange) to you by someone else;
3. Rectification of injustice: how to restore something to its rightful owner, in
    case of injustice in either acquisition or transfer.

Nozick's theory of justice claims that whether a distribution is just or not depends
entirely on *how it came about*. By contrast, justice according to equality, need,
desert or Rawls' Difference Principle depends entirely on the 'pattern' of distribution at that moment.

An advantage of Nozick's theory is that if a certain distribution of goods (D1)
is just (according to whichever theory you like), then if people voluntarily move
to a different distribution (D2), observing justice in transfer, D2 will also be just.
Whether D2 is patterned according to equality, need, desert or the Difference
Principle is *irrelevant*. Suppose a famous footballer whom people love to watch,
say Cristiano Ronaldo, asks to be paid 25p for each ticket sold for home games.
The club agrees and fans are happy to pay the extra 25p each. If 400,000 people
go to his games in a season, he will be £100,000 richer. According to Nozick,
this is not unjust, because everyone gave the extra money *voluntarily*. Yet the
new distribution would be deemed unjust by the other theories.

Justice, Nozick argues, is about respecting people's (natural) rights, in
particular their rights to property and their rights to self-ownership. We must
allow people the freedom to decide what they want to do with what they own.
Each person is separate, an individual, and we must respect their autonomy.
People are 'ends-in-themselves', and we cannot use them in ways they do not
agree to, even if that would lead to some supposed 'greater good' (e.g. other
people getting what they need). This has a radical conclusion: to take property
away from people in order to redistribute it according to some pattern *violates
their rights*. But this is exactly what taxation (for the purpose of redistribution)
does. To tax Ronaldo's extra earnings and return the money to the poorer fans
violates his right to the money.

See THE JUSTIFICATION
OF RIGHTS, **p. 97.**

Nozick thinks property rights are important because they derive from 'self-ownership'. A person has a right to what they produce, because they own their own labour, which they invest in creating the product. 'Justice in acquisition' places constraints on exactly when and how this occurs, but this is the basic idea. And once something is (justly) owned, then justice is all about justice in transfer.

If people have the right to do as they choose with their property, then liberty upsets patterns, as the Ronaldo example shows. So, all patterned theories of distributive justice restrict people's free actions. Either we will constantly have to intervene with the distribution of property to bring it back into line with our patterned principle of justice or we will 'have to forbid capitalist acts between consenting adults'.

Anarchy, State and Utopia, p. 162

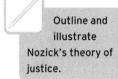

Outline and illustrate Nozick's theory of justice.

Discussion

Nozick's theory is very controversial, because it could justify *very* unequal distributions of property that may not respect what people deserve, or what they need, and may not give any kind of priority to people who are worse off. If he is right, redistribution cannot be justified except to rectify a previous injustice.

Rawls challenges Nozick's defence of property rights. Much of what people own is the result of their social position and their natural talents, both of which are morally arbitrary. Therefore, any inequalities in ownership are unjust. Furthermore, what rights people have to property can't be decided *before* deciding on the principles of justice. People don't have a right to the earnings their talents bring them, only to that share which they keep according to the principles of distributive justice.

Nozick responds that each person's talents and abilities belong to them. They therefore have a right to keep (or do whatever they want with) whatever these talents and abilities gain for them. To forcibly redistribute what they earn is to fail to respect their autonomy.

But even if people own themselves, we can argue that this doesn't entail that we have the right to do *whatever* we want with *all* of our property. A reinterpretation of 'justice in transfer' could place restrictions on property rights. Nozick supposes that any transfer, if it is freely consented to, is just. We can argue that the rules governing transfer should be sensitive to *many* political values, not just liberty. The rules we currently have (regarding tax, inheritance, transfer between married couples, gifts and so on) are a product of balancing many considerations relating to patterns of production and work, family life and political institutions.

Furthermore, we can interpret individual liberty as a goal to be pursued, not an absence of constraint. If the value of justice rests on liberty, and Nozick is right that property is so important for liberty, then surely we must ensure that everyone has sufficient property to be free. Redistribution of property from the rich to the poor will equally be a redistribution of liberty. But this is a patterned principle of justice.

A final objection to Nozick is this. History shows that a great deal of initial acquisition of property was unjust, based on theft, exploitation, slavery and colonisation. All property that derives from unjust acquisition is unjustly held. You do not have a right to transfer property you stole, nor does the new owner have a right to what they receive. But, of course, we cannot *now* rectify the injustice of the past. We have no way of establishing what belongs to whom. So, Nozick's theory has no application if we do not start from a just beginning; we must therefore work out a different theory of justice that is not so sensitive to past injustices that we cannot correct. The historical nature of Nozick's theory turns out to be a weak spot.

> Discuss the relationship between liberty, rights and justice.

Key points • • •

- Rawls argues that liberty takes priority over the distribution of social and economic goods. However, our rights are only established by principles of justice and do not precede them.
- Nozick argues that distributive justice involves property rights, established by justice in acquisition and transfer. Redistribution can only be justified if property has been acquired or transferred unjustly.
- Justice in transfer allows for any voluntary transfer of property. From any just distribution of property, any further distribution arrived at voluntarily will be just.
- This is because justice involves respecting people's rights of self-ownership and property. Each person has the liberty to do whatever they decide with their property. Taxation for the purpose of redistribution therefore violates people's rights.
- Rawls argues that self-ownership and property rights are not as absolute as Nozick argues, because what one can produce by one's natural talents is morally arbitrary, so resulting inequalities are unjust. Nozick responds that this fails to recognise people's ownership of their talents.

- We can object that justice in transfer does not rest only on liberty, but is sensitive to many political values. Therefore, property rights are not absolute.
- We can also argue that if property is necessary for liberty, redistribution can be justified on the grounds of liberty.
- Finally, we can object that Nozick's theory has no application to the real world, since almost all property was not initially justly acquired, so no one has any right to their property.

V. NATION-STATES

Nationalism and national sentiment

Nations

Nations are not states. States are political structures that are sovereign, defining the legal rights and obligations of citizens, and claiming a monopoly on the use of force. A nation is a group of people united in some way (to be explored). Some states contain more than one nation (for example, the United Kingdom, if the Scots, Welsh and English are distinct nations); some nations are spread across more than one state (for example, the Kurds, who live in southern Turkey and northern Iraq). We cannot define a nation and nationalism in terms of belonging to a particular state, because the sense of nationalism is often strongest in national groups that do not have a distinct state to call their own. So, a sense of belonging or loyalty to a state – a 'civic' allegiance – should be separately identified as 'patriotism', not 'nationalism'.

A 'nation' is not *any* group of people who aspire to a political organization in common, such as the state or something similar. A nation, distinctively, involves 'national identity', normally understood in ethnic and/or cultural terms. A nation is, normally, a non-voluntary community; members are born into and raised with a particular language, tradition and culture. This creates a 'national character' or 'form of life', a 'collective mentality' and sense of unity among the people related in this way. So, we can explain aspects of individuals' characters in terms of features of the group. In this way, 'national identity' is part of an individual's identity. National identity also connects the group to a particular geographical place and embodies a historical continuity; the group identifies with people and actions in the past, and inherits duties from them (to continue certain traditions or values) towards people in the future.

Populist nationalism often appeals to ethnic identity, but the idea of a 'common origin' of a people is almost always mythical and can support racism. Philosophers therefore stress cultural factors.

What is a 'nation'?

Nationalism and national sentiment

'Nationalism' refers to the attitude of caring about one's nation and national identity, and also the policy of a nation to pursue or sustain self-determination. It leads, further, to claiming special duties and rights based on the value of nationality. David Miller summarises nationalism in three claims: 'that a national identity is a defensible source of personal identity, that nations are ethical communities imposing reciprocal obligations on members which are not owed to outsiders, and that nations have a good claim to be politically self-determining'. These three claims, their implications and their relation to theories of rights, liberty and justice will run throughout the remainder of this chapter. The three claims, as we will see, are closely related to each other.

'In Defence of Nationality', in *Citizenship and National Identity*, p. 6

Nationalism involves individuals having a sense of national identity and, with this, feelings of belonging to a common nation. These feelings give rise to a further feeling of solidarity, which may support certain political aims, such as the defence of common liberties and distributive justice. The alternatives to nationalism – either a lack of identification with others (individualism) or an identification with all of humanity (cosmopolitanism) – can seem unfeeling or abstract by comparison.

Is national sentiment essentially irrational, and indifferent to the individual's self-interest? For instance, is it the product of a 'false consciousness', an ideology imposed on the people by those with political power for their own ends? Is it the product of a Romantic view of 'peoples' and their distinct 'essences', an idealisation of the group, and the priority of the group over the individual? Given the violence that ethnic nationalism has given rise to, we may suspect national sentiment to have irrational origins.

See MARXISM: THE STATE AS OPPRESSOR, p. 74.

However, we may also give an evolutionary defence of it. Individuals who develop a sense of belonging and identification with others do better in evolution. In species that live in groups, those groups that develop bonds of feeling and cooperation will do better than other groups. Culture has taken over the role of blood relations in forming our identifications and feelings, and so national sentiment arises.

Is nationalism 'natural' to human beings?

Key points • • •

- Nations are not states. States are sovereign political structures. Nations are groups of people united by a 'national identity'.

- A nation is usually a non-voluntary community with a collective mentality and sense of unity, into which individuals are born and within which they develop their identity.
- National identity also connects groups to places and to the past and future.
- Nationalism argues that national identity imposes special duties and rights, and that nations should be politically self-determining.
- We can question whether the origin of national sentiment is irrational, and whether human beings are naturally inclined to nationalism.

Group and nation rights

Group rights

In our previous discussion of RIGHTS (p. 93), we talked only about the rights of individuals. But many philosophers argue that groups can have rights as well. A group right is not a right held by individuals in virtue of being a member of a particular group; for example, 'gay rights' are not group rights, but the rights of *individual* homosexual people. A group right is a right held by the group *as a whole*; for example, the right of a nation to self-determination, if there is such a right, is a right held by the nation as a whole, not a right that any individual has.

What does it take for a group to have rights? First, many philosophers argue that the group needs a certain unity and identity. This could be achieved by organisation; for example, a corporation is recognised as having both legal rights and duties. Nations have an identity created by members' sense of unity and identity with one another. Second, the group must have a moral status distinct from its members. There are two criteria for this: the group can act as a group, thereby acquiring responsibilities (and duties) not held by any individual; and the group has interests as a group that can't be reduced to the interests of individual members. If rights are restricted to groups that can literally make choices (e.g. through an established decision-procedure), then many cultural groups would therefore not have rights. If rights are based on interests, we can argue that a group can have rights if it has distinct interests; for example, if as a group, it can flourish or decline.

Group rights may impose duties on people outside the group, for example duties of non-interference; on members of the group, for example to support the activities and identity of the group; and on the group itself, for example to protect its interests.

These two criteria also relate to the two main THEORIES OF HOW RIGHTS ARE GROUNDED (p. 96).

? What are group rights? How do they differ from individual rights?

Going further: group interests

There are two views of group interests. On one view, the group has distinct interests (e.g. a nation's interest in self-determination) that are not an aggregate (sum) of the interests of individuals. This view faces the objection that only individuals are, ultimately, of moral importance, so the moral status of groups must derive from that of individuals.

On another view, defended by Joseph Raz, the interests of its members, *taken collectively*, generate the group's interests. And so a group right is held by all the members in common, rather than being held by 'the group' as a distinct entity. Raz argues that a group right must meet the following criteria:

> First, it exists because an aspect of the interest of human beings justifies holding some person(s) to be subject to a duty. Second, the interests in question are the interests of individuals as members of a group in a public good and the right is a right to that public good because it serves their interest as members of that group. Thirdly, the interest of no single member of that group in that public good is sufficient by itself to justify holding another person to be subject to a duty.

The Morality of Freedom, p. 208

Raz's account explains how a group can have rights that individuals cannot, namely that the interests of individuals, taken individually, are not enough to create the relevant duty or duties, but their interests, taken collectively, are enough. He also draws attention to the fact that some goods are public: they are necessarily (at least in practice) available to all members of the group if they are available to anyone, and their enjoyment by one individual doesn't compete with their enjoyment by others. Examples include clean air, being part of a flourishing culture and national self-determination.

How can the interests of individuals ground a group right?

The rights of a nation

Do nations have rights? Two important rights a nation might have are the right to political self-determination and the right to maintain its particular culture. If a nation has these rights, then how strong are the rights? We return to these specific rights in the next section, after looking at implications of the claim that nations can have rights.

See THE NOTION OF
RIGHTS, p. 93.

? What if the
nation violates
the rights of individuals
within it? See RAWLS,
MILLER AND GLOBAL
JUSTICE, p. 132.

See NATIONALISM AND
LIBERTY, p. 127.

See NATIONAL
COMMUNITY AND
POSITIVE LIBERTY,
p. 128.

? What
implications
follow from the claim
that nations have
rights?

Rights always give rise to duties. Specifying the right involves specifying what duties it grounds, and who holds those duties. We might expect that a nation's right would impose duties of non-interference. If the nation is also a state, then other states would have the duty not to interfere with its political self-determination. If the nation is a smaller group within a state, perhaps the state has the duty not to interfere with or undermine its culture, or even the duty to grant it some self-determination.

Do the rights of a nation impose duties on individual members, for example to sacrifice their self-interest in support of the national interests? Can individuals be required to defend the nation, or to protect and preserve its traditions and culture?

If a nation's rights impose duties on its members, most nationalists think that these duties hold towards one's own nation only. We do not have the same duties towards nations *generally*. So, the duties must be grounded on what ties an individual to a specific nation, namely national identity. How can national identity impose duties? Religion, gender, sexual orientation and many other traits contribute to one's identity. So, do other groups relating to identity – 'women', 'Muslims', 'homosexuals' – also have rights that impose duties on their members? Or is the nation a group of greater importance, morally and politically, than other kinds, and so can claim rights where the others cannot?

We can argue that national identity is distinctively political, rather than personal, because a nation, unlike other groups, is identified with a geographical place and a distinct cultural and historical identity (actual or imagined). We can argue that our cultural inheritance is the basis of our values and moral identity. A nation is also a group characterised by the demand for unified political self-determination, which is not true of other groups. These special features of national identity could be argued to impose duties on members where other group identities do not.

But there are also strong objections to the idea of nations having rights. Many liberals argue that the claims of nationalism do not amount to rights. First, they cannot override individual rights claims. Second, they are subordinate to the claims that a *state* has on its citizens. Third, any false nationalist beliefs – regarding a common origin, say – should be tolerated only if they are not harmful. And fourth, the legitimacy of nationalist claims derives from the choices of individuals (e.g. expressed through association or democracy).

The right to self-determination

We can argue that a nation has the right to self-determination on the basis of utility: giving a nation its own state will promote democracy, equality and the sentiments that bond a moral community. Or we can argue that self-determination is *intrinsically* valuable to a group, just as it is to an individual. For *any* group, having the power to organise its affairs and dispose of its resources as it chooses is valuable. Where the group is formed by a shared identity, and individuals can express their views within the group, group self-determination expresses the self-determination of individuals. It also extends their self-determination, as the group will be able to achieve much more than individuals taken alone. But are these arguments enough to establish a *right*?

Does a national group within an existing state have the right to secede and set up its own state? Historically, such behaviour has led to political instability and war, for example in the Balkans. We can reply that violence is rarely, if ever, justified in the pursuit of self-determination, but this doesn't show there is no such right. However, second, there is simply too little territory for every candidate nation to have its own state (and many claim the same territory). This rules out an unconditional right to statehood. But could there be a right under certain conditions?

The argument from utility doesn't necessarily support secession, as nations can be given a degree of autonomy *within* an existing state, and this may be the best way to secure democracy, equality and moral communities. The argument from identity suggests that the most important issue is whether a nation's identity is compatible with the majority national identity in the state. If it is not radically incompatible, then it could be allowed a degree of self-determination within the state, over matters that primarily concern its interests. If its identity is radically incompatible, then secession may be justified.

(David Miller argues that even then, there are three other considerations. First, the new state and the rump state must be viable. Second, the new state should not itself contain minorities with radically incompatible identities, or the issue of secession will simply be repeated. And third, the impact of secession on other minority nations in the rump state must be taken into consideration.)

According to the argument so far, there is no clear right to self-determination for nations that are not already states; only a claim. Nation-states, however, already have a degree of self-determination. But how far does this right extend? Nationalists have traditionally claimed rights not just to the creation of a state, but also to its maintenance, strengthening and even its expansion. Does the right of self-determination involve *complete* sovereignty over both internal affairs and relations with other states? At the end of the last section, we saw a number of limitations that liberals have wanted to place on nations' self-determination and we will continue the discussion in NATIONALISM AND LIBERTY (p. 127) and GLOBAL DISTRIBUTIVE JUSTICE (p. 131).

Finally, it is worth noting that, for all this talk of rights, many nationalists have argued that a nation has not only the right, but also the *obligation* to pursue self-determination. An obligation to whom? To the nation itself and its individual members, past, present and future.

> **?** To what extent can nations be said to have a 'right' to self-determination?

Key points • • •

- A group right is a right held by a group of people as a whole. It is not a right any individual can have on their own.
- Many philosophers argue that only groups with a certain unity and identity can hold rights. And that the group must have a moral status distinct from that of its individual members, either by acting as a unity or by having distinct interests.
- A group's interests may or may not be the result of individual interests. Raz argues that group interests are the collective interests of individuals. These generate group rights when individual interests can impose duties only when taken collectively.
- A nation's rights may impose duties of non-interference on other nations and states; and may impose duties of provision, to defend the group and its culture, on its members. Members of a nation will have these duties in virtue of national identity.
- We can object that nations do not have rights, as national claims cannot override individual rights, are subordinate to the claims of the state, should only be tolerated if they are not harmful, and can only derive from individual choice.
- The right to self-determination can be defended on the grounds of utility or the intrinsic value of self-determination. However, there can be no absolute right to statehood, as there is not enough territory for every nation to have its own state.
- Whether a nation should have its own state may depend on considerations of utility and the compatibility of its national identity with the majority national identity.

- If a nation has its own state, we can question whether its right to self-determination gives it complete sovereignty over internal and foreign affairs.

Nationalism and liberty

The conflict

Must a liberal state eschew nationalist policies on the grounds that they will conflict with the liberty of individuals or disadvantaged minority groups, and undermine cultural pluralism? We can argue that nationalist policies (preserving, protecting and enhancing the national identity and culture of the majority) will come into conflict with core liberal values.

First, they will conflict with the neutrality of the state if the majority culture is promoted while the cultures of minority groups are not. A liberal state should instead provide special rights to minority groups in order to protect their cultures. Second, nationalist policies based on particular traditions and values can interfere with individual autonomy. Third, if it is a duty of individuals to promote the national heritage, this can interfere with their free creativity, for example writers or composers being told what they can and can't do. Fourth, nationalist policies will undermine diversity within the state.

Historically, nationalist states have not fostered multiculturalism, and have overlooked the interests of minority groups. But must this always be the case? David Miller argues, first, that national identities need not be exclusive, but can include the trait of welcoming foreigners and living peaceably with them. Second, national identity does not exhaust any individual's identity, so many connections can be made with others on different levels. Third, a single national identity, such as being British or American, can encompass many ethnicities and considerable cultural difference. A national identity need not require sacrificing one's distinct cultural values, as long as there is not outright conflict between the two.

However, this reply works only for *liberal* national identities that respect other cultures, individual rights and so on. Furthermore, if we distinguish between cultural and national identity, is there a real, unified national identity left of any value?

See THE ARGUMENTS IN SUPPORT OF FREEDOM OF ACTION, p. 124.

See TOLERANCE AND THE IDEAL OF A LIBERAL DEMOCRACY, p. 239, and TOLERANCE AND NEUTRALITY, p. 255.

Explain the tension between nationalism and liberalism.

Going further: national community and positive liberty

A different approach questions the conflict between nationalism and liberty, rather than trying to resolve it. First, national self-determination is a form of positive liberty, the ability to make decisions and take actions that express national values. Second, nationalism may also support the positive liberty of individuals.

We argued that THE VALUE OF LIBERTY (p. 87) lies in being able to make and act on meaningful choices. But what are the conditions under which this is possible? A number of philosophers have defended a crucial role for community (and so they are known as 'communitarians'). To make meaningful choices, an individual must acquire a set of concepts and values that create a network of meaning for them and enable them to understand the culture around them and their own life. These concepts are embedded in a language; the values are embedded in social and cultural practices. Morality is learned and acquired not in an abstract form, but in the particular form in which it is present in the community. So, it is only the community that provides a framework of meaning and value, and only within a community that an individual can make meaningful choices. Therefore, such communities are a necessary condition for individual liberty.

Second, the protection of liberty requires that individuals restrain themselves from interfering with others' liberty. Our willingness to act morally is formed within a moral community, one that recognises the obligations individuals within the group have to one another.

The nation is often characterised as the kind of community defended here. It preserves and protects its language, culture and values; it recognises special bonds of obligation between its members.

We shall not discuss whether communitarians are right about the role of community, though this has been a matter of considerable debate. Does their argument, if correct, support nationalism? First, are nations the *only* or the *best* communities for providing meaningful choices? Are there other sub- or non-national communities (based on regional, ethnic, religious or cultural identities) that could equally provide the needed framework in the absence of nationalist policies? Has the argument accepted too many of nationalism's myths? The idea that there is such a thing as a true history of

See NATIONALISM AND NATIONAL SENTIMENT, p. 120.

a national group, which suffices to distinguish it from outsiders and which unifies it as a coherent and distinctive social group over time, simply does not account for the facts of nationality and nationalism as a social phenomenon.

Second, even if nations are the right kind of community, must the values and culture of the nation be expressed via nationalist policies adopted by the state? Third, the argument only works to resolve the tension between nationalism and liberty if the values of the community support and encourage the positive liberty of individuals. Very authoritarian communities may provide meaning, but they may prevent autonomous choice. Finally, the positive liberty of its members may conflict with the positive or negative liberty of other citizens, for example if national values include forms of discrimination.

Once again, it is only a *liberal* national identity that resolves the tension between nationalism and liberty.

Discuss whether the conflict between nationalism and liberty can be resolved.

Cross-border movement

Does a nation-state have the right to control its borders, and does such control conflict with the rights of individuals to freedom of movement? On the one hand, individuals can have strong reasons for wanting to move to another state. On the other, states feel the need to control immigration to protect the way of life of their citizens.

All liberal states recognise the right of people to *leave* a state. Without a right to emigration, individuals would be effectively coerced to be part of a particular state, undermining the idea that democracy is based on consent. But if individuals have the right to leave a state, don't they also need the right to enter another state? Freedom of movement is a core liberal right. Without it, individuals will not be able to 'pursue their own good in their own way' (see p. 87). Why should it stop at borders?

However, there are many justified restrictions on movement even within the state, for example where complete freedom of movement would threaten private property, public goods, environmentally important locations or national security. Likewise, any right to immigration still recognises restrictions to protect national security, public order and the survival of liberal and democratic institutions.

Everyone agrees that states have duties to *refugees*. But what duties? We shall not discuss this issue, as our primary concern is with the conflict between nationalism and liberty.

But is there a right to immigration? First, the right to decide who may join the community is a central feature of self-determination for any group, including nation-states. Second, without this control, the solidarity of fellow nationals, their shared understandings and values, would be threatened. If anyone could join a state, over time the population would cease to have any internal cohesion and sense of national identity. Third, a strong national culture, which would be threatened by immigration without limits, supports other goods, such as redistribution and equality of opportunity.

But we can object that these arguments from national values and so on simply don't apply at the level of states. In today's world, most *states* are *multinational*. Nations do not control borders; states do. However, the arguments can be made on the basis of a *civic* or *political* culture and identity. Instead of obligations to fellow nationals, we have obligations to fellow citizens and we may appeal to the preservation of a political culture to defend immigration controls.

? Can restrictions on cross-border movements be justified?

Key points • • •

- Liberals may argue that nationalism will undermine individual rights and the rights of minority groups, interfere with individual autonomy and creativity and undermine diversity.
- Miller responds that national identities need not be exclusive, and can encompass cultural variation. However, this response works only for liberal national identities.
- Communitarians argue that our positive liberty rests on membership of a moral community. It is within a community, with a particular language and set of values, that we can give meaning to our lives and acquire the motivation to act morally.
- We can question whether nations provide the best example of such communities, and note that authoritarian communities will undermine individual liberty and may come into conflict with individuals from other communities.
- The right to freedom of movement is a core liberal right. However, it is restricted even within a state by other values, and so a right to immigration must recognise restrictions that defend the security and liberal values of a state.
- We may argue that there is no right to immigration, as nations have the right to restrict entry in order to protect national identity and culture.

- As many states are now multi-national, this appeal to national values seems inapplicable. However, a similar argument can appeal to civic culture and values.

Global distributive justice

The theories of justice we discussed were each developed to apply *within* a state. But given the moral equality of individuals, if it is unjust that the resources someone has depends on their race or gender, then isn't it wrong that it depends on their nationality or citizenship? For example, if justice requires distribution according to need, shouldn't that mean meeting need wherever it occurs in the world? In this section, we look at three positions on global justice.

See COMPETING PRINCIPLES OF JUSTICE, p. 105, and HOW CAN REDISTRIBUTION BE JUSTIFIED?, p. 111.

Cosmopolitanism

Cosmopolitanism is the view that nation-states are irrelevant to considerations of justice. We have the same duties of distributive justice towards all human beings, regardless of where they live. Some philosophers apply Rawls' theory of justice (p. 112) internationally, arguing that justice means we must place *all* individuals behind the veil of ignorance, irrespective of citizenship. We therefore end up with a global version of the Difference Principle: the only justification for inequality is that it benefits the worst-off *globally*.

Rawls himself rejects this approach (p. 132), because his theory begins from assumptions about the nature of *society*, in particular that society is a system of cooperation for mutual advantage, and that justice defines rights and duties in relation to social institutions on the basis of *social* cooperation. But these assumptions do not apply internationally. Cosmopolitans respond that international cooperation does exist, for example in economic and cultural activities. But we can object that these are too weak, and don't generate the relationship needed for Rawls' theory of justice.

We can also object that cosmopolitanism ignores the nature of the state. A just state is justified in imposing a particular distribution. For global redistribution, we would need the institutions of the state to be replaced by coercive global institutions. This would undermine the powers of the state. Cosmopolitanism conflicts with the nature of the state as a set of institutions that legitimately holds power over its citizens regarding matters of distribution.

One form of cosmopolitanism focuses on the duties of individuals generated by inequalities in development between countries. This issue of POVERTY is discussed on p. 282.

What is cosmopolitanism? Is it persuasive?

Global justice and nationalism

Nationalism involves two claims that appear to conflict with global justice as understood by cosmopolitanism. First, it says that nations have a claim to self-determination, which will include determining their principles of justice. Different nation-states may choose different principles. Second, it may claim that individuals have duties of justice owed to fellow nationals that are not owed to foreigners. States may even seek to promote their own citizens' interests through the international distribution of resources, through aid and trade. So, nationalism rejects the view that justice requires that we treat all human beings – fellow nationals and foreigners – in the same way regarding matters of distribution. The arguments for this position are the same as the arguments for nationalism generally.

See NATIONAL
COMMUNITY AND
POSITIVE LIBERTY,
p. 128.

But even if we have special duties to fellow nationals, this doesn't show that we have *no* duties to foreigners. When does justice permit us to show partiality to fellow nationals? To 'preserve' the nation, we need show partiality only *when the existence of the nation is under threat*. Global justice will not destroy nations.

Nationalists can reply that it might. First, as we saw above, global justice could considerably undermine national self-determination. Second, massive transfers of resources out of a national community would threaten the bonds between individuals in the community. The national bond is expressed in solidarity, and this in turn is expressed by special obligations that give priority to fellow nationals. If we could not show partiality, then the sense of connection to a national community would be threatened. Furthermore, solidarity provides the *motivation* for distribution in the first place.

Even if these arguments are correct, this still doesn't show that we have no duties of justice to foreigners. Can we be justified in preferring the interests of fellow nationals over those of the most needy in some other country? Unless showing such preference would break down the bonds of national community, it has not been shown that we are.

Discuss the
opposition
of nationalism to
cosmopolitan global
justice.

Rawls, Miller and global justice

The Law of Peoples

We saw in COSMOPOLITANISM (p. 131) that Rawls rejects the direct application of his theory of justice to global justice. But he develops an analogue. We need to imagine what each nation-state, or 'people', would agree to in an initial state of choice. In doing this, we cannot imagine that all nation-states are liberal, or this would make the theory quite irrelevant to our world as it is. Illiberal states must be respected, on the grounds both of autonomy and the liberal tolerance of diversity.

Rawls argues that agreement between 'peoples' would come to define global justice. First, peoples would recognise each other's freedom and independence (self-determination), including the duty of non-intervention and the right to self-defence. Second, they would agree to honour human rights – not *liberal* human rights, but with those who ruled sincerely believing that they were working for the common good, and therefore offering citizens the opportunity to express their views politically in some way (a 'decent' state). Third, peoples would recognise a limited duty of distribution to assist peoples who lived under conditions so unfavourable, such as famine, that they were prevented from having a just or decent political regime. This, of course, is a *much* less demanding principle of justice than the Difference Principle or the principles of equality, need or desert.

Rawls' conclusions depend on his assertion that we must respect the autonomy of states and peoples. But we can object that respecting the autonomy of an illiberal state could be respecting the right of those in power to deny autonomy to the citizens. Can justice require us to respect the right of those in power to deny justice to their citizens? If citizens reject and resent inequalities imposed by their government, then how can justice require us to respect these inequalities?

However, if citizens *accept and defend* inequalities between them, for example because it expresses their conception of social justice, then we can argue that justice and nationalism both require that we respect this. David Miller argues that global distributive justice cannot be the application of one principle of justice, globally, because what distributive justice requires depends upon the particular community. Each community has different understandings of what should be distributed – money, work, status, power, opportunity – and on the meaning and significance of each of these. They have different criteria for distribution, different understandings of desert, responsibility and need. Competitive societies will tend towards principles of desert, collaborative ones towards need or equality. In each case, the *right* theory of justice depends on the values of the community.

Nationalism, Ch. 10

Miller and Rawls accept that global justice still requires respect for basic human rights (which Miller expresses as conditions necessary for a minimally adequate human life) and a duty to help other nations that are struggling with conditions that prevent them from securing a just or decent political regime. However, *relative* inequality between states is not an issue of justice. Rawls

Could justice require different things in different societies? If so, what consequences does this have for 'global justice'?

argues that many differences of wealth are the results of local differences in how the states run their affairs, and there is little a foreign state can do to alter these factors. Miller argues that there is no neutral standard by which inequality can be measured, given the different understandings of goods.

Key points • • •

- Cosmopolitanism argues that boundaries between nation-states are irrelevant to justice. Principles of justice should be applied internationally.
- Rawls rejects the application of his theory of justice internationally, as it depends on assumptions about social cooperation.
- We can also object that cosmopolitanism would undermine the state.
- Nationalism defends partiality towards one's fellow nationals. Justice therefore does not require one to treat everyone alike. Global justice will undermine national self-determination and nationalist solidarity.
- We can object that this doesn't show we have no duties of justice to foreigners, or even that these duties of justice outweigh our nationalist duties in certain cases.
- Rawls argues that global justice requires 'peoples' to respect each other's self-determination, rulers to work for the common good (a 'decent' state), and there to be a limited duty of assistance for peoples living in conditions that prevent a decent state.
- Miller argues that different cultural understandings of goods and their relevant distribution entail that the right theory of justice for each state is relative to that state.
- Both argue that the relative inequality between states is not a matter of injustice. Only absolute levels of poverty (conditions that prevent a minimally adequate life or decent state) need be remedied.

Just war theory

The aggression involved in war is at odds with basic values of civilisation. It attacks people's rights to life, security, subsistence, peace and liberty. However, just war theory claims that war can, under certain conditions, be morally justified. Pacifism argues that war is never morally justified. Realism says that moral concepts cannot be applied to questions of war (or foreign policy generally).

Just war theory divides into three parts:

1. *jus ad bellum* – the justice of resorting to war;
2. *jus in bello* – just conduct in war;
3. *jus post bellum* – justice at the end of war.

Jus ad bellum

The following six criteria have been suggested for a war to be just. The first three are deontological, the last three are based on securing the best consequences.

See Deontology, p. 254.

1. War must be in a *just cause*. There is disagreement over what constitutes a just cause. Examples offered are self-defence, the defence of others from aggressive attack, the protection of innocent people from aggressive regimes, or corrective punishment for aggressive past action. All involve the 'resistance of aggression', the violation of basic rights by use of armed force.

   We can also argue that only a *legitimate* state can begin a war with just cause. To be legitimate, a state must be recognised as legitimate by its citizens and by other states; it must not violate the rights of other legitimate states; and it must respect the basic rights of its citizens.

2. The *right intention* for fighting the war is that the war is in a just cause. Any other intention, such as material gain, undermines the justice of the war.

3. The decision to go to war must be made with the *proper authority* (usually laid down in the state's constitution) and by a *public declaration*.

4. The declaration of war must be a *last resort*, following the exhaustion of all plausible alternative means to resolving the conflict.

5. A declaration of war can be just only if the state can foresee a *probability of success* in resolving the conflict through war. Violence without likely gain cannot be justified.

6. The response of declaring war must be *proportionate* – that is, the good that can be secured through war must outweigh the evil that will most likely occur. The end must justify the means. And in this calculation, the state must take into account not just the costs and benefits to itself, but those that will affect *everyone* involved in the war (e.g. including enemy casualties).

On Legitimacy, see p. 57.

Explain and illustrate the conditions under which, according to just war theory, it can be right to declare war. Explain the moral importance of each condition.

Jus in bello

Jus in bello means justice in war, and has traditionally been concerned with the treatment of the enemy. The following six rules are a general summary:

1. Weapons prohibited by international law must not be used.
2. There is a distinction between combatants and non-combatants. Only combatants may be targeted. It is wrong to intend the deaths of non-combatants. Some philosophers argue that it is wrong even to *intend* the deaths of combatants, as only the minimum use of force is legitimate.
3. Armed forces must use proportional force, i.e. proportional to achieving the end.
4. Prisoners of war must be treated well, because once captured they have ceased to be a threat to life and security.
5. No weapons or means of war that are 'evil in themselves' are permitted. Examples include ethnic cleansing and mass rape.
6. Armed forces are not justified in breaking these rules in response to the enemy breaking these rules.

> Explain the moral importance of the rules of justice during war.

Jus post bellum

There is little agreement on the rules of *jus post bellum*. However, we can apply a number of the values expressed in *jus ad bellum* and *jus in bello* to form an outline.

1. The rights whose violation justified the war should be secured.
2. Just as the declaration of war must be publicly made by the proper authority, so must the declaration of peace.
3. Proportionality governs both *jus ad bellum* and *jus in bello*, and so it should govern the peace settlement as well. It should be reasonable, not a form of revenge, which will most likely fuel resentment and further aggression.
4. The discrimination between combatants (including political leaders) and non-combatants still applies when seeking punishment. Public, international trials for war crimes should be conducted.

A fifth set of considerations relates to the rehabilitation of the aggressor state. Does justice require or permit the state to be disarmed? Does it allow for training in respect for human rights, or even political institutional reform to secure this?

Outline the main concerns of just war theory.

Can there be a just war?

'Realism' objects that justice applies *within* the boundaries of a state only. In relation to each other, states act only in terms of self-interest. This claim can take either of two forms.

According to 'descriptive realism', states are simply not motivated by justice. They are motivated by the national interest, including power and security. However, it seems unlikely that states have *no* concern with justice; they are created and sustained by individuals (and a national community) who are concerned with justice.

According to 'prescriptive realism', it is prudent for states to act without regard to morality in foreign policy. States should respect the conditions laid down by just war theory *only* if doing so would be in their best interests, for example if doing so would lead to a more peaceful world.

Pacifism argues that war is always unjust. Aggression by a state does not need to be resisted by war, as there are other means, less destructive but just as effective, such as a very widespread campaign of civil disobedience and international sanctions. However, just war theorists will reject this. There can be times when these responses work (Gandhi's campaign to free India from the British Raj; Martin Luther King's campaign for black civil rights) – but they work only when the aggressor is sensitive to claims of justice. What of an aggressor that responds to such campaigns with ethnic cleansing? War may be the only means to resist, and can therefore be justified.

A different defence of pacifism argues that war always involves violating our duties. One common response is that pacifists are too concerned with 'keeping their hands clean', with protecting their moral purity in a world that may make this impossible. But this response is unconvincing, as pacifists are no different from their opponents in arguing that we ought to do what is just. If one accepts that wars are not just but nevertheless necessary, this is to adopt realism, not just war theory.

But does war always involve violating our duties? Most theorists would agree that, in general, there is no duty not to kill another human being who is threatening one's life. Many of our deontological intuitions support this view. If Adam attacks Barry, it would be *unfair* to allow Adam to gain at Barry's cost, and Adam is *responsible* for the situation. So, it would be wrong to prohibit Barry from resisting Adam, and Barry commits no wrong in resisting. The force Barry may use should be proportionate – so if Adam is threatening Barry's life, Barry may kill Adam if no other option is available.

However, the pacifist can respond that *no actual war has met or can meet* the conditions for being just.

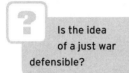

Is the idea of a just war defensible?

Asymmetric wars

An asymmetric war is one in which the two sides differ significantly in military resources or tactics. It may differ from 'normal' or symmetric war only in that one state is significantly weaker than the other; or it may involve one side not being a state or even a politically recognised body; or it may involve unconventional tactics, such as guerrilla warfare. Examples, therefore, are very wide-ranging, from the American Revolution of 1776 (a people versus an imperial force), the Second World War once the United States acquired the nuclear bomb, the conflict between Israel and Palestinians in Gaza in 2008–9 and the two Gulf Wars of 1990 and 2003.

A number of asymmetric wars are revolutionary, when a group or people seeks to overthrow or secede from a political authority. For this to be a just cause – the first condition of a just war – the political authority needs to be illegitimate, and probably also needs to treat its citizens aggressively. Holy war – a war intended to spread belief in a particular religious faith or instate a theocratic government – does not meet this criterion.

See LEGITIMACY, pp. 57 and 76, and JUST GROUNDS FOR DISSENT, p. 61.

Asymmetric wars suggest two changes to just war theory. First, if there can be just wars in which one party is not a state, then the declaration of war need not be made by a 'proper authority' or by a legitimate state. Second, we may argue that oppressed people, say, have the right to resist an oppressive state even if they are *unlikely* to succeed. With individual self-defence, my right to self-defence does not depend on whether my attempts to defend myself are likely to succeed, so why should this condition apply in cases of war? And indeed, others may legitimately come to my aid without meeting this condition as well. What matters is the justice of resisting aggression.

We can object that such a war will lead to misery without benefit. But in response, we could say that the people waging the war in resistance to aggression already face misery without benefit.

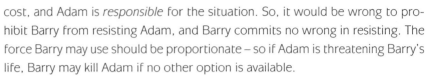

Should just war theory be revised in light of asymmetric wars?

Going further: proportionality

In many asymmetric wars, one side has far greater military might than the other. Is it required to use force that is only proportional to the force used by the other side? Just war theory says that both the declaration of war and the force used should be proportional *to the end*, not to the opposition's military ability. (Of course, the opposition's military ability will affect the degree of harm it can threaten or inflict.)

Under *jus ad bellum*, the degree of force that is justifiable is proportionate to the harm that is being threatened, and which the war seeks to avoid. However, a different reading of proportionality can be taken from *jus in bello*, namely that military action must not use more force than is necessary to achieve its end of eliminating the threat of harm. In asymmetric wars, as for example when one side uses guerrilla tactics, this can be very difficult to achieve. To end the war, the military may need to use much greater force than seems proportional to the harm threatened.

This conflict between these two interpretations of proportionality is illustrated by the debates regarding civilian deaths in the Israel-Palestine situation. In responding to civilian deaths *intentionally* caused by rockets fired into Israel, can Israel be justified in *unintentionally*, but *predictably*, causing far more civilian deaths in Palestine through the use of tanks and bombs? The aim is to secure Israel's borders against foreign attack and end the deaths of Israeli civilians. Were Israel to pursue these aims by limiting the destructiveness of its response to that caused by the rockets, it can be argued, the aims would never be achieved. But using even the minimum amount of force necessary to achieve these aims would mean deploying a force that seems disproportionate to the harm threatened by the rockets.

The Israeli government may argue that in using no more force than is necessary to secure its ends, and by not intentionally causing civilian deaths, it complies with the rules of *jus in bello*. In response, it can be objected that even if this is true, if the destruction caused by its actions is far greater than the destruction it seeks to prevent, then it fails to comply with the rules of *jus ad bellum*. On this view, war is not the morally appropriate response to the attacks in the first place.

> Discuss the nature and importance of 'proportionality' in just war theory.

Key points • • •

- Just war theory divides into *jus ad bellum*, *jus in bello* and *jus post bellum*.
- *Jus ad bellum* requires that, to be just, a war must be in a just cause and undertaken for this reason alone, declared publicly by a proper authority and as a last resort, undertaken only if likely to achieve its aims, and proportionate in response to the harm threatened.
- *Jus in bello* requires that, for a war to be just, prohibited weapons must not be used, non-combatants must not be targeted, military force must be proportional, prisoners of war must be treated well, and no 'evil' weapons must be used. Breaking these conditions is not justified by the enemy breaking them.
- There is little agreement on *jus post bellum*, but we can argue that rights should be secured, the declaration of peace must be public and made by the proper authority, the peace settlement should be proportional, and non-combatants not punished. There is debate over whether the aggressor state may be rehabilitated.
- Realism objects that justice does not govern international relations, in which states rightly pursue self-interest.
- Pacifism argues that war is always unjust, either because there are equally effective but less destructive means of resisting aggression or because it always involves a violation of duties. Both claims can be challenged.
- If pacifism cannot be defended in theory, it can still argue that no war can, in fact, meet the conditions of just war theory.
- An asymmetric war is one in which the two sides differ significantly in military resources or tactics. Asymmetric wars question whether just wars can be declared only by proper authorities or legitimate states, and whether they must have a chance of success.
- Proportionality is contentious, as the force proportional to threatened harm and the force needed to eliminate the threat of harm may be very different.

EPISTEMOLOGY AND METAPHYSICS

3

In this chapter, we look at five key debates in **epistemology** and **metaphysics**. The first, the debate over **scepticism**, raises the question of whether we have knowledge. The second asks the question 'what is knowledge?'. In the discussion, we also look at the related concepts of belief and justification. The third asks the metaphysical question about whether only particular things exist, or whether we can also say that their properties exist too. We then step back to discuss whether metaphysics is, in fact, possible. Our final topic regards the status of knowledge – can it be objective? Students should be able to argue for and against different positions within each of these debates.

SYLLABUS CHECKLIST ✔

The AQA A2 syllabus for this chapter is:

The refutation of scepticism

✔ The nature of the sceptic's challenge: how sceptical arguments connect to the problem of justifying beliefs we hold, how we can move from 'appears' so to 'is' so. Our vulnerability to error and the existence of states of mind qualitatively indistinguishable from states appropriate for acquiring justified beliefs.

✔ Responses to scepticism: mitigated scepticism, the view that scepticism is not a practical option; transcendental arguments, how experience is constituted; phenomenalism, the denial of the gap between appearance and reality; the view that the starting point for sceptical arguments is unintelligible. The strengths and weaknesses of these approaches.

Knowledge, belief and justification

✔ Belief: the dual-component view of belief (as advanced by, for example, Hume); realist and instrumentalist notions of belief, behaviour and action; whether beliefs can be voluntary.

✔ Knowledge: the tripartite definition of knowledge; 'internalist' and 'externalist' theories of justification; Gettier-type objections to the tripartite definition and responses to Gettier, for example indefeasibility, whether beliefs are appropriately caused, whether they track the truth. Whether such approaches and responses are successful.

Universals and particulars

✔ Are there only particulars such that general terms refer to the resemblances between them (nominalism)? Are general terms mind-dependent classificatory schemes? Do the referents of general terms, or universals, exist? Do we need universals in order to explain our ability to recognise, categorise and generalise about particulars? Are we bound to accept the reality of at least certain types of universal? The strengths and weaknesses of different approaches.

✔ Whether metaphysics is speculative nonsense or essential to intellectual enquiry. Can we have knowledge of a world beyond sense experience? The implications of verification and falsification for the status and meaning of metaphysical statements. The view that all epistemological positions, such as realism and idealism, are underpinned by metaphysics.

Objective knowledge

✔   Is objective and absolute knowledge possible? Can we make absolute judgements regarding alternative belief systems, for example the beliefs held in other cultures?

✔   Do different perspectives have their own internal criteria as the final court of appeal? The implications of this view: whether relativism is scepticism in disguise; whether relativism and contingency invite inertia in certain fields of human activity.

I. THE REFUTATION OF SCEPTICISM

The nature of the sceptic's challenge

To believe something is not to know it. First, we can have beliefs that are false, but we can only know what is true. For thousands of years, people believed the Earth was flat. But they didn't know this (though they believed they knew it!), because the Earth is not flat. Second, even true beliefs might not count as knowledge, because the person may have no good reason, no evidence, for their belief. If you believe someone is guilty because they dress in a funny way, you may be right – they are guilty – but your belief is not justified. How someone dresses is no evidence for guilt. So, only justified beliefs can count as knowledge.

See INTRODUCTORY, p. 159.

Scepticism is the view that our usual justifications for claiming that our beliefs amount to knowledge are inadequate, so we do not in fact have knowledge. While some philosophers have understood scepticism as a kind of theory, it is better to understand it as a kind of challenge (see p. 147). But rather than talk about scepticism in the abstract, we shall begin straight away with some sceptical arguments. Throughout our discussion of scepticism, we shall be concerned predominantly with scepticism regarding knowledge of the physical, external world – that is, the sceptical challenge to our **empirical** knowledge.

Our vulnerability to error

The argument of this section is discussed in greater detail in REALISM, pp. 201ff.

ARGUMENTS FROM ILLUSION

As soon as we reflect on our sense experience, it becomes apparent that what we perceive isn't quite the same as what we believe is 'out there'. For example, if you put your thumb up against the Moon, it looks as though your thumb is larger than the Moon, but it isn't. If you look at a red rose in sodium street lights, it looks grey, but the rose itself hasn't changed. If you half-submerge a straight stick in water and look at it from the side, it looks bent; but it isn't. So, *what* we perceive in all these cases isn't the world as it is.

We could argue that this demonstrates that perception is not a reliable guide to how things are. But this is too quick. Perceptual illusions are *special cases*. Otherwise, we wouldn't be able to talk about them as illusions; it is through perception that we know the Moon is larger than my thumb, that sticks are not in fact bent when half-submerged in water and so on. So, the argument doesn't undermine perception generally.

But some philosophers have claimed that cases of illusion show that we don't perceive the world directly; we perceive it by virtue of perceiving **sense-data**, our subjective experiences of the world. But if we only ever perceive sense-data directly, says the sceptic, we can never know what the physical world is actually like, or even that it exists. All we have 'access' to are our sense-data; who knows what lies beyond them? We can never know what, if anything, causes them.

Outline how scepticism can appeal to sense-data to challenge knowledge.

Meditations I

AN ARGUMENT FROM DREAMING

Descartes provides a different argument to undermine perception, by appealing to dreaming. Sometimes when we dream, we represent to ourselves all sorts of crazy things. But sometimes we dream the most mundane things. Yet 'there are no conclusive signs by means of which one can distinguish clearly between being awake and being asleep'. So how can we know that what we experience we perceive rather than dream?

This argument attacks all sense-perception, even the most mundane and most certain. You cannot know that you see a piece of paper because you cannot know that you are not dreaming of seeing a piece of paper.

Some philosophers argue that there are ways of distinguishing perception from dreaming, such as the far greater coherence of perception. But how do we *know* that dreams have less coherence than perception? We cannot know that what is apparently perception is not really a particularly coherent dream.

See THE METHOD OF DOUBT AND ITS PURPOSE, p. 151.

Descartes presses further the argument from dreaming. It may *seem* that 'whether I am awake or sleeping, two and three added together always make five'. But people do make mistakes about matters they believe they know certainly. And so even truths of logic and of mathematics come under attack. Are not just his perceptual experiences, but also his thoughts, open to doubt?

Discuss Descartes' sceptical argument from dreaming.

How we can move from 'appears' so to 'is' so

The two arguments above illustrate the most important move in sceptical arguments, namely that from what appears to be the case, we cannot reliably infer what is the case. There is a distinction between appearance and reality. To gain knowledge, we have to establish the truth about reality. But we only have appearance to go on. This is what makes us vulnerable to error. Two other kinds of argument support the sceptical claim.

DISAGREEMENT

In Plato's *Protagoras*, he notes that for a wide range of properties, people often disagree about how the world is. The air can seem warm to one person, cold to another; one person may judge that the sea is 'blue', another says it is 'green'. We can use this to present two different sceptical challenges. First, faced with disagreement, how can I be sure that what *I* experience is how the world is? Second, given that everyone is in the same position, does it make sense to say the air is objectively warm or cold? Aren't we forced into subjectivism?

We can respond that these disagreements apply more to some sorts of perception than to others. For example, people agree that the air is a gas, not a liquid. The disagreements presuppose a lot of agreement in our perceptions, which supports the claim that perception gives us knowledge. Second, in many cases we have objective ways of settling the disagreement. We can measure how long something is; and if one person carries on saying 'it is long' and another 'it is short', we just say they are using the terms differently. This works to some extent with 'hot' and 'cold'; for example, someone who has a fever is not a good judge of whether a room is cold or not. We say 'the air *feels* cold to them', even though 'the air is warm'. We reach objectivity by appealing to agreement again: the air is warm, the sea is blue if this is how it seems to normal people under normal conditions.

Does disagreement lead to scepticism? Why, or why not?

THE BRAIN IN A VAT

At the end of our discussions of sense-data and of dreaming, the sceptic argues that our experience could be exactly as it is, while the world is completely different from how we believe it to be; for example, only sense-data could exist, or we could be dreaming. This is the claim that there can be states of mind *qualitatively indistinguishable* from perception of an external world. When dreaming, I may have a visual experience that – if I were awake – would give me the knowledge that I was looking at a glass of water. I can't distinguish my dream from the real thing by how it seems to me.

A thought experiment makes the point. Suppose that I am not a walking, talking human being, but simply a brain in a vat. Connected to my brain is a supercomputer that feeds in just the right impulses to generate the illusion of reality as it is. I'm being deceived. I cannot know that this is not, in fact, the case; because if it were true, things would seem *exactly the same* as if I were a walking, talking person. If I were a brain in a vat, my experiences would be qualitatively indistinguishable from the experiences I have if I am not. I can't know, therefore, whether I am, in fact, a brain in a vat or not. But if I am a brain in a vat, all my beliefs about what I experience are false; I have no body, I'm not sitting at a computer, I'm not hearing the sounds of keys clicking, etc. I cannot make any inference from what appears to be the case to what is the case.

(Furthermore, I cannot trust my memories, because the computer could create 'memories' of things that never happened. So, I cannot know anything about the past, including whether it happened at all. Perhaps I have only just come into existence, and all my memories are false. In fact, if my *thoughts* are being fed to me by a supercomputer, then I can't be certain of them. Isn't it possible that every time I think '2 + 2 = ?', the computer makes me think '4' when the answer is actually 5? So, even judgements about logic and mathematics are not certain. If I have no mental *agency*, then the very idea of genuinely making a judgement, whatever that judgement is, is undermined. And if I cannot judge, then I cannot know.)

> 'If I don't know I am not a brain in a vat, I know nothing through sense experience.' Discuss.

How sceptical arguments connect to the problem of justifying beliefs we hold

Philosophical doubt can get started by reflecting on *how* we know what we think we know. We discover judgements it seems silly to doubt, but for which we seem to have no clear justification. Take the belief that I have two hands. Why do I believe this? Well, I can feel them, I can see them. But, says the sceptic, couldn't my experience – what I feel and what I see – be just the same even if I were dreaming? Or if I were a brain in a vat? If I don't know I'm not dreaming or a brain in a vat, do I really know that I have two hands? In fact, do I know that a world exists outside my mind at all? But if I don't know *that*, how can I know anything?

Philosophical doubts are peculiar. They don't make sense in everyday circumstances. Of course, if I've just been in an accident and can't feel my left arm, doubting whether I have two hands does make sense! But the sceptic is not interested in these **propositions** in cases when we have an 'everyday reason' to doubt them. The sceptic's reason for doubting them does not arise from a particular context; it is a general doubt about their justifiability. The sceptic admits that there is no everyday reason to doubt that I have two hands or that there is an external world. But that doesn't mean there isn't *any* reason to doubt these things. How do I know that appearance is a reliable guide to reality?

Is this sort of sceptical doubt *doubt*? It has no practical consequences, and a philosophical sceptic is not a very cautious person! Yet the sceptic insists that sceptical doubts are relevant; we *should* know that we are not wired up to a supercomputer if we are to know that 'this is a hand'.

Yet we might still think that it is 'unreasonable' to have such doubts. But this misunderstands the role or purpose of doubt. The sceptic doesn't suggest that there is any reason to *believe* in sceptical possibilities, but requests that we *rule them out* as possibilities. Doubt based on challenging us to rule out the *possibility* of very unlikely situations is called 'hyperbolic' doubt. And the purpose of this doubt is to help us find what we *can* know, if anything. In other words, sceptics present their challenge in order to help us discover what we know and how we know it.

The effect of sceptical doubts is not 'We can't be *certain* of our everyday judgements, although they are *probably* true.' It is to put the whole idea of our usual justifications into question. If these sceptical possibilities were true, we would have *absolutely no reason* to hold on to our usual beliefs. If I were wired up to a supercomputer, things would *seem* exactly the same, but the reality would be completely different. Sceptical arguments aim to completely undercut our usual justifications.

Scepticism is sometimes taken as the claim that nothing is known. But this is not a good definition, for it must then defend the claim that we can know nothing, which is trivially self-defeating anyway (because then we would know that we know nothing – so there is something we know). Likewise, scepticism

See also THE METHOD OF DOUBT AND ITS PURPOSE, p. 151.

does not claim that our beliefs are all false, for this would not be logically coherent. For instance, my beliefs that 'I am not at the South Pole' and that 'I am not at the North Pole' can't both be false (obviously, both can be true). Scepticism is best understood as the claim that our usual justification for claiming our beliefs amount to knowledge is inadequate.

? Why is the distinction between appearance and reality philosophically important?

Key points • • •

- Scepticism challenges whether our usual justifications for what we think we know are adequate. For example, it points out that we assume that appearance is a reliable guide to reality – but how do we know this?
- Some philosophers have argued that we do not perceive the world directly, but via sense-data. Scepticism argues that if this is true, then how do we know the world is anything like our sense-data, or even that it exists?
- Descartes questions whether we can know that we are not dreaming. If we can't, can we use our sense-experience to tell us how the world is?
- A different sceptical argument from perception appeals to disagreement. But the argument is only as strong as disagreement, and people agree a great deal about what they perceive.
- A popular sceptical scenario is that we could be brains in vats, and all our perceptual experiences are actually fed to us by a supercomputer. If we don't know this is not true, we can't know that anything our senses tell us is true.
- Sceptical doubt is odd: it is not interested in everyday reasons for doubting a proposition, it has no practical consequences and it invents very unlikely situations that we have no reason to think are actually true. But it insists that it is legitimate; we should know that sceptical possibilities, for example that I am dreaming, are not true in order to know the things we claim to know.
- Scepticism does not claim that we know nothing, nor that all our beliefs are false. It challenges our justifications and challenges us to say how we know what we claim to know.

Responses to scepticism

Attempting to refute sceptical arguments one by one does not succeed, for two reasons. First, one sceptical argument will quickly be replaced by another; and second, scepticism isn't a positive theory. It is a demand for justification, based on arguments as to why our ordinary justification fails. The syllabus lists four responses to scepticism (there are others), which we shall discuss in turn.

Mitigated scepticism

The term 'mitigated scepticism' comes from Hume's *An Enquiry Concerning Human Understanding*, § XII, Part 3. Sceptical arguments, Hume thinks, derive either from 'popular' objections or from 'philosophical' ones. The initial argument from illusion and Plato's argument from disagreement are examples of the former; the arguments from sense-data and the brain in a vat are examples of the latter. When it comes to the question of the existence of an external, physical world, says Hume, 'the profounder and more philosophical sceptics will always triumph' (*Enquiry*, p. 202).

Hume calls this kind of scepticism, the kind we have been discussing, 'excessive' scepticism or Pyrrhonism. This view holds that we should give up our beliefs, since they cannot be rationally justified. Hume asks what the meaning or point of such scepticism is, as it can have no permanent effect on how we live our lives.

Hume contrasts 'excessive' scepticism with two forms of 'mitigated' scepticism that can result from correcting excessive scepticism using common sense. The first form involves a change in how we *hold* our beliefs. It opposes dogmatic certainty, inspires modesty and caution, and attacks pride, prejudice and disdain for people who disagree with us. Philosophy shows that the basis of our beliefs in reason is insecure.

The second form of mitigated scepticism draws the conclusion that there are certain subjects that we cannot coherently enquire about. Reasoning can legitimately inform us about mathematics and *particular* matters of fact, existence and causation that can be established by experience. But metaphysical enquiries, including the attempt to show the external world exists (or does not), are impossible, while matters of religion are best founded on faith and revelation, not reason.

DISCUSSION

We can object that Hume's first form of 'mitigated scepticism' is simply a collection of intellectual virtues. We should adopt it, but we don't need sceptical arguments to support it.

In Hume's theory of knowledge, see THE DISTINCTION BETWEEN RELATIONS OF IDEAS AND MATTERS OF FACT, p. 22. And see IS HUME'S ACCOUNT SCEPTICAL?, p. 28.

Hume associates mitigated scepticism with 'academical philosophy' – that is, the philosophy of Plato. Plato's early writings attack dogmatism and certainty.

Explain Hume's 'mitigated' scepticism.

In the second form, Hume grants that we cannot have knowledge – that is, knowledge justified by reason – of the existence of the external world. But this does not entail, for Hume, that I cannot know that I have two hands. Our mental faculties are fine for establishing answers to the second, empirical question; but not for investigating the first, philosophical question. But the ('excessive') sceptic argued that if we do not know the answer to the philosophical question, about the existence of the external world, then we do not know the answer to the empirical question.

Hume can reject this on two grounds. First, we can have knowledge where we can obtain answers that can make a practical difference to our lives. Empirical knowledge is of this kind. Second, while scepticism shows that we cannot know there is an external world, the sceptical inference about empirical knowledge is something we can't know. We cannot show that if we can't know there is an external world, we can't have any empirical knowledge. Scepticism is itself part of an enquiry that we cannot engage in.

Hume's mitigated scepticism is based on his conceding that the philosophical arguments of 'excessive' scepticism cannot be answered. But is this right? If sceptical arguments can be answered, then we have no reason to accept mitigated scepticism, and its narrow view of what human beings can enquire into.

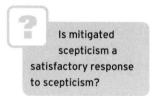

Is mitigated scepticism a satisfactory response to scepticism?

Phenomenalism

Phenomenalism responds to scepticism about the physical world by making a logical link between our experience and the world of physical objects. There are two famous defences of phenomenalism: Mill's 'metaphysical' account and Ayer's linguistic account.

MILL'S PHENOMENALISM

John Stuart Mill begins by saying we have only our experience to go on in establishing what there is. When we interact with material objects, for example when we look for something on a desk, we are presented with a series of new sensations. Certain sensations which were possible come about. I could move this piece of paper and experience the colour of the surface beneath it. There are all sorts of possible sensations that would occur under certain conditions. We have come, from experience, to expect this sequence of sensation; we are certain it will happen. And so we come to think of certain possibilities for sensation as being *permanently* available, under certain conditions. Material objects are 'permanent possibilities of sensation'.

We associate certain sensations, and the possibilities of other sensations, together, since whenever I have one sensation, the conditions of having another associated with it are to hand. These 'clusters' of possible sensations are what material objects are. A piece of paper is the permanent possibility of certain sensations that we associate together. Only some of the sensations in fact occur; but the material object is a collection of those that do and those that could occur. We derive the complexity of ideas of space, distance, perspective from the complex associations between sensations that we make (automatically – none of this need be thought through!).

We then think of material objects as the cause of the sensations that do occur. This isn't exactly wrong, though perhaps it is peculiar to think of a collection of possibilities causing an actuality. Where we do go wrong, Mill thinks, is if we think this cause is something that *could exist quite independent of sensation*. This is something we cannot know, and could only lead to scepticism. Instead, there is no logical gap between appearance and reality.

An Examination of Sir William Hamilton's Philosophy, Ch. 11

How does Mill's phenomenalism answer scepticism about the external world?

Going further: Ayer's linguistic phenomenalism

A.J. Ayer takes a different tack. He defends phenomenalism through his analysis of statements concerning material objects. He claims that the function of philosophy is to give 'definitions in use', showing how the sentences in which a symbol or type of symbol (such as 'table' or words for material objects generally) occurs can be translated into equivalent sentences that don't contain the symbol or its synonyms. (He contrasts this with dictionary definitions, in which symbols are defined in terms of synonyms.) Philosophical definitions, then, can deepen our understanding of terms in a way dictionary definitions do not – that is, they can still be informative to someone who already knows what all the terms mean in the dictionary sense.

It can happen that we discover the term is 'standing in for' something more complex. What is referred to by terms that do this are 'logical constructions'. Ayer argues that material objects are logical constructions; all propositions about material objects can be *translated without loss* into propositions about sense-data:

Language, Truth and Logic, Ch. 3

the symbol 'table' is definable in terms of certain symbols which stand for sense-contents, not explicitly, but in use. And this . . . is tantamount to saying that sentences which contain the symbol 'table' . . . can all be translated into sentences . . . which do not contain that symbol, nor any of its synonyms, but do contain certain symbols which stand for sense-contents.

Notice that Ayer doesn't claim that material objects are *constructed*, made out, of sense data; but rather that *propositions* about material objects are in fact *entirely* concerned with features and relations of sense-data. To say that a material object exists is to say that certain sorts of sense-data have been, are being, and would be experienced under certain conditions. So, there is no logical gap between appearance and reality.

Language, Truth and Logic, pp. 85–6

Outline and illustrate the differences between Mill and Ayer's versions of phenomenalism.

OBJECTIONS TO PHENOMENALISM

Very few philosophers accept phenomenalism now. What objections does it face?

First, experiences of material objects have a logical and reliable pattern. What is the *explanation* for this? Common sense claims that material objects explain our experiences; phenomenalists can only say that our experiences do have these patterns. But first, it isn't obvious that we can actually describe that pattern without referring to material objects. And second, if there is no independent cause of this pattern, what reason do we have to think that future sense-data will follow the same patterns?

Second, phenomenalism's claim that statements regarding material objects can be translated into statements about what was, is and would be experienced under certain conditions invites the challenge: 'Go on, then, prove it!' This challenge may prove insurmountable, for the specification of the conditions under which the various sense-data would be experienced must be in terms of *other sense-data*. The translation of the claim 'there is a table in the next room' must not refer to the room (as a physical space) at any point.

Phenomenalists have responded by appealing to the idea of a *sensory route*, a series of juxtaposed and often overlapping sense-data that would be experienced in 'locating' the table. But there are *many* different sensory routes to a given material object, while the statement 'there is a table in the next room' seems to claim just one thing. Furthermore, we can often understand the claim that a certain material object or set of objects exists at a certain location without having any clear idea of the relevant sensory route. An example is 'Penguins exist at the South Pole.' Finally, the conditionals in which the analysis is given may be falsified by situations that would not falsify the claim referring to the material object. For example, I won't experience certain sense-data if I suddenly go blind upon entering the room, but the table will still be there.

Key points 1 • • •

- Hume distinguishes two types of 'mitigated' scepticism from 'excessive' scepticism, which can have no practical implications. The first type is intellectual caution and humility. The second claims that reason can establish only knowledge of mathematics and matters of fact, not metaphysical claims.
- The sceptic responds that empirical claims rest on 'metaphysical' claims, such as 'there is an external world'. If I don't know the latter, I can't know the former.
- Hume can reject this by arguing that we can know what makes a practical difference; and that sceptical inference, from metaphysics to empirical claims, itself is not something reason can establish.
- Phenomenalism claims that material objects are not conceptually independent of our experiences of them. Mill claims that material objects are 'permanent possibilities of sensation'. Ayer claims that material objects are 'logical constructions' – that is, every proposition containing a word that refers to a material object can be translated into propositions that only contain words referring to sense-data.
- However, philosophers object that phenomenalism can't *explain* the regularity of our experiences, and perhaps can't even describe that regularity without referring to material objects.
- Second, the project of translating sentences referring to material objects into sentences referring to sense-data is perhaps impossible. In particular, it is difficult to translate sentences that say *where* in space a material object exists.

> **?** Can phenomenalism answer scepticism about the external world?

The view that the starting point for sceptical arguments is unintelligible

ON DREAMING

One response to Descartes' argument from dreaming (p. 144) is to say that it literally makes no sense. The concept of a dream *depends* upon a concept of reality that it contrasts with. If everything were a dream, we wouldn't be able to have the concepts of dreaming and reality.

The objection is inconclusive. First, we might argue that even in a dream, we can dream that we wake up, but we are in fact still asleep. Perhaps the development of our concepts of 'dream' and 'reality' are analogous: they refer to a difference within our experience, but this doesn't show that the *whole* of our experience can't be disconnected from reality in the way that we think dreams are. Second, and perhaps more importantly, the objection *misunderstands* scepticism. Descartes does not *need* to say, 'perhaps everything *is* a dream'; he only needs to argue that we *cannot know* when we are dreaming and when we are awake. This would allow us to develop concepts of dreaming and reality on the basis of our different experiences; but the correct application of those concepts isn't secure.

GILBERT RYLE

Gilbert Ryle argues that the very idea of 'error' presupposes that we sometimes 'get it right', for 'error' and 'correctness' are complementary concepts, like 'genuine' and 'false'. Without correctness, the idea of error makes no sense, just as counterfeit coins are impossible without real coins.

However, this fails in two ways. First, the sceptic seeks to challenge our belief that we know we've got it right when we have, not the very idea of 'getting it right'. And second, the fact that we need the *idea* of getting it right to make sense of error doesn't entail that we do ever actually get it right. Compare perfection and imperfection. We need the idea of perfection to make sense of imperfection. But that doesn't mean that anything, ever, needs to be perfect.

ORDINARY LANGUAGE

We might argue that what 'knowledge' and 'know' mean is given by how we *usually* use the terms. The sceptic's claim that, say, I don't know I'm reading this page makes no sense. It is precisely cases like this through which we learn what 'know' means at all.

Discuss Descartes' sceptical argument from dreaming.

Must we have *knowledge* in order to have false beliefs?

However, the sceptic's challenge is to point out that even in such paradigmatic cases of 'knowledge', we may be making an unjustified assumption, namely that appearance is a good guide to reality.

WITTGENSTEIN

Wittgenstein developed a more sophisticated version of the ordinary language approach. The sceptic is wrong in thinking we can doubt claims like 'there is an external world'. If there is no way of answering the question 'how do you know?', the question itself makes no sense. 'The external world exists', and other fundamental beliefs or 'background assumptions', are not things we can *either doubt or know*. We are *certain* of these 'background assumptions', but it is a mistake to say, 'I know this is a hand' in the contexts that the sceptic is talking about (it makes sense on an archaeological dig!). Knowledge claims require grounds; and to know something is to be able to establish it. But how can we establish that 'this is a hand'? What evidence is there we can appeal to? What checks are possible?

This doesn't mean scepticism is right. Background assumptions are used to teach the meaning of words. But the sceptic's situation of doubt is similar to the circumstances under which I learned 'hand'. So, 'If I wanted to doubt whether this was my hand, how could I avoid doubting whether the word "hand" has any meaning?' But if I doubt the meanings of the words I use, I can't put into words what it is I'm doubting. We can argue, then, that sceptical doubts are literally meaningless. They deprive the very words used to formulate the doubt of any meaning. Our background assumptions underpin the meanings of our words.

On Certainty, § 369

But Wittgenstein's solution is hard to accept. First, he claims that we do not know such statements as 'this is a hand'. Second, he says these statements do not even *describe* reality, because they provide examples of what words mean: 'I know this is a hand.' – And what is a hand? – 'Well, *this*, for example.' The circularity is clear. If 'this' is a hand by definition, saying that 'this is a hand' is not to describe anything. It is more similar to asserting an **analytic** truth, such as 'bachelors are unmarried'. Analytic truths help define the meanings of the terms used. Our background assumptions likewise help define the meanings of the words we use. They therefore can't be said to describe the world.

But many of the examples Wittgenstein gives of 'background assumptions', and which he says we cannot know, don't seem to be anything like analytic statements; for example, 'the world existed before my birth'. And what about 'appearance is a good guide to reality'? While Wittgenstein's remarks on knowledge, doubt and justification are insightful, his proposal about 'background assumptions' leaves us puzzled.

Is scepticism incoherent in both presupposing and undermining our knowledge of the meanings of words?

Solipsism can be seen as a consequence of scepticism. For an argument against solipsism, and therefore against scepticism, see OUR EXPERIENCE PRESUPPOSES OTHER MINDS, p. 16.

See CONCEPTUAL SCHEMES AND THEIR IMPLICATIONS II, p. 41.

Critique of Pure Reason

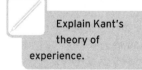

Explain Kant's theory of experience.

Transcendental arguments

Transcendental arguments are arguments about what must be true for it to be possible for us to have the kind of experience we have. For example, our experience of the physical world is structured and intelligible; our experience is of physical objects existing independently of our minds in space and time. How is this possible?

In Unit 1.1 REASON AND EXPERIENCE, we discussed an argument from Kant that answered this question. Try to imagine what it would be like to have sense experience but with no ability to *think* about it. Thinking about sense experience requires concepts – at the most basic level, being able to distinguish what comes from the different senses (vision, hearing, etc.), and then being able to distinguish types of properties, for example colour from shape. If we couldn't think about sensory experience, it would be completely unintelligible, no more than a confused 'buzz'. For instance, and very importantly, we couldn't tell that we were experiencing any*thing* – that is, *objects*. The idea of an object is the idea of something that is unified in some way – a colour, shape, position and so on, going together; or, even more fundamentally, something that exists in space and time.

A 'buzz' doesn't deserve the name 'experience'. Experience is experience *of* – experience of objects, that stand in organised relations (in space and time) to each other. So, experience has a certain 'object'-ive structure. Kant argued that such intelligible experience presupposes and requires certain very basic concepts, which he called categories. The structure of experience is made possible by certain key concepts that contribute to the ideas of an 'object' and of an objective world, including CAUSALITY, SUBSTANCE, UNITY and so on. These concepts cannot be derived from experience, because they are what make experience possible in the first place. So, they are **a priori**; Kant says they are part of the nature of the mind.

Scepticism suggests that the way we experience or conceptualise the world could be completely different from how the world is, Kant argues that the 'object'-ive nature of experience is a reflection of the nature of the mind. So, our experience of and our thoughts about everyday objects – tables, plants and so on – is not a straightforward presentation of what exists completely independently of the mind (what Kant calls 'things-in-themselves'). The idea of an object doesn't reflect the world; it reflects the mind. So, everyday objects are *defined* by our structured experience of them.

This provides an answer to scepticism. What we mean by the physical world is defined, in part, by our a priori concepts. We can know that the physical world exists and is objective – that is, that there are physical objects existing in space that correspond to our sensory experiences of them – because the world as we experience it is structured by our a priori concepts; because how things are is given by these concepts, so there is no question of a gap between our minds and how things are. This doesn't mean that the world of experience – the world of objects – isn't real. It is by definition 'objective'.

However, Kant's argument has a consequence that some might think is sceptical. We can ask: what is the relation between the physical world (structured by the categories) and how the world is, completely independent of our minds (independent of the categories)? Kant's reply is that we cannot know; in fact, we cannot even coherently think about it.

But this is not the triumph of scepticism, because there is no meaningful way in which we *could* know about reality in this sense. If Kant had argued just that our experience *is* a certain way, we could object that our concepts were a limitation to our knowledge; we weren't able to experience the world as it really is. But Kant has argued that our experience *must be* the way it is; there is no alternative to experiencing the world as a world of objects, so there is no alternative way of experiencing 'the world as it is'. Any alternative wouldn't be 'experience' at all. This makes our experience properly objective, the basis of knowledge of how things are. What we don't know – how the world is, independent of our minds – is what it is impossible to know. So there is nothing here we *could* know but don't.

> **Does Kant's transcendental argument against scepticism succeed?**

Going further: knowing what we think

A quite different transcendental argument against brain-in-a-vat scepticism (p. 146) is presented by Hilary Putnam. Scepticism requires that words mean what they do in order to formulate the scenarios which challenge our normal justifications. Many words get their meaning, in part, from causal connections to the world; 'water' successfully refers to water only because the thoughts and sentences involving the word are causally connected to water itself. The same is true of 'brain' and 'vat'. However, if I am a brain in a vat, then all my experiences are caused by the computer, and all my thoughts and 'sentences' will refer to images created by the computer. So if I am a brain in a vat, 'brain'

> **'Brains in a Vat'**

Explain Putnam's argument that brains in vats cannot have the thought 'Am I a brain in a vat?'

to me means 'brain-in-the-image'. I cannot, in fact, think about or refer to real brains; I can only think about computer-generated simulacra of brains. But according to the sceptical scenario, I am supposed to be wondering whether I am a brain in a vat. If I am a brain in a vat, I cannot have this thought. I can only wonder whether I am a 'brain-in-the-image' in a 'vat-in-the-image'! If I can wonder whether I am a brain in a vat, if this is the meaning of my thought, then I am not a brain in a vat.

Key points 2 • • •

- Ryle argues that scepticism doesn't make sense because we can't understand 'error' without 'getting it right'. But, first, the sceptic only argues that we *don't know* when we get it right; and second, although we need the *idea* of getting it right to understand error, we don't actually ever need to get it right.

- We can argue that what 'to know' means is given by how we usually use the word, so to say 'I don't know this is a book' makes no sense. But the sceptic responds that even in such cases, we may be making an unjustified assumption.

- Wittgenstein argues that sceptical doubts make no sense because they challenge the very situations in which we learned the meanings of words. Furthermore, it doesn't make sense to doubt *or to say one knows* unless we can support our claim with grounds. But 'there is an external world' has no grounds we can use as evidence.

- Kant argues that experience is of objects, and asks how it is possible for experience to be intelligible in this way, not a confused buzz. He answers that what makes experience of objects possible is certain concepts that he calls categories.

- Kant argues that the structure of the everyday world of objects is defined by our a priori concepts, and so scepticism is unjustified. However, we cannot know anything about how reality is in itself, independently of how we think of it.

- Putnam argues that words get their meaning, in part, by being causally connected to what they refer to. Brains in vats, therefore, cannot think about real objects (such as brains and vats), only about computer images of objects.

II. KNOWLEDGE, BELIEF AND JUSTIFICATION

Introductory

There are different types of knowledge: acquaintance knowledge (I know Oxford well), ability knowledge (I know how to ride a bike) and propositional knowledge (I know that eagles are birds). The first two types of knowledge are very interesting, but we are concerned only with the third, what it is to know some proposition, 'p' (see p. 160).

We intuitively make a distinction between belief and knowledge. People can believe propositions that aren't true; but if you know that p, then p must be true. You can't know something false; if it is false, then you don't know it. You have made a mistake, believing it to be true when it is not. For example, if you claim that flamingos are grey, and you think you know this, you are mistaken. If flamingos are not grey but pink, then you can't know they are grey. Of course, you believe that they are grey; but that's the difference – beliefs can be false.

There is another distinction between beliefs and knowledge. People can believe propositions for all sorts of reasons. They can have true beliefs without having any *evidence* or *justification* for their beliefs. For example, someone on a jury might think that the person on trial is guilty just from the way they dress. Their belief, that the person is guilty, might be true; but how someone dresses isn't evidence for whether they are a criminal! So, belief can be accidentally true, relative to the evidence the person has; if it is, it isn't knowledge.

Someone can hold a belief that is, in fact, true, even when they have evidence to suggest it is false. For example, there is a lot of evidence that astrology does not make accurate predictions, and my horoscope has often been wrong. Suppose, though, that on one occasion I read my horoscope and believe a prediction, although I know there is evidence against thinking it is right. And then this prediction turns out to be true! Did I *know* it was right? It looks more as though my belief is irrational. I had no reason, no evidence, no justification, for believing that prediction was true.

Knowledge, then, needs some kind of support, some reason for thinking that the proposition believed is true. Knowledge needs to be *justified*.

But what is justification? We will return to this question in 'INTERNALIST' AND 'EXTERNALIST' THEORIES OF JUSTIFICATION (p. 169).

> Outline and illustrate how knowledge differs from true belief.

> ### *Key points* • • •
>
> - There are different types of knowledge: acquaintance, ability and propositional knowledge. Theories of knowledge discussed here are about propositional knowledge.
> - Knowledge is not the same as belief. Beliefs can be mistaken, but no one can know what is false.
> - Knowledge is not the same as true belief, either. True beliefs may not be justified, but can be believed without evidence. To be knowledge, a belief must be justified.

Belief

The dual-component view of belief

The standard philosophical analysis of belief is that it has two components, 'content' and 'attitude'.

CONTENT

The content of a belief is *what* the person believes, for example that 'elephants are grey'. This content takes the form of a proposition. A proposition is what is claimed by an assertion or expressed by a complete declarative sentence. To say what someone believes, we say 'he believes that . . .', and what fills in the gap is a sentence, which states the proposition they believe, such as 'God exists', 'murder is wrong', 'seals are cute'.

As indicated, this is an analysis of belief *that* . . . However, we also talk about believing a person ('Do you believe him?') and about believing in something or someone ('I believe in love', 'I believe in God'). This suggests that the content of a belief is not always a proposition, but can be a direct object (him, love, God).

But we shouldn't draw this conclusion. Believing someone is shorthand for saying you believe *that* 'what he says is true'; so the content of your belief is a proposition. Believing *in* someone or something can be analysed in two ways: (1) in terms of believing that (e.g. 'I believe in God' = 'I believe that God exists'); or (2) in a way that makes 'believing-in' not the same as 'believing-that' anything. It is a different 'attitude'; for example, it is a form of faith or commitment. To understand this properly, we need to discuss the 'attitude' component of belief.

Attitude

Just as we say, 'she believes that she is late', so we can say, for example, 'she fears that she is late', 'she hopes that she is late', 'she is ashamed that she is late' and so on. The verb picks out the 'attitude' the person has towards to the state of affairs (being late) picked out by the proposition.

What is it to believe something? Hume described belief by contrast with imagination: 'belief is nothing but a more vivid, lively, forcible, firm, steady conception of an object, than what the imagination alone is ever able to attain'. But there are many problems with attempting to pick out belief just in terms of vividness, etc. compared with other ideas. Being afraid that the lion will pounce can be just as forceful as believing that the lion exists. So, vividness doesn't distinguish between belief and fear.

A better approach is to say that belief (belief-that, not belief-in) 'aims at' truth:

1. We can evaluate a belief as true or false – which distinguishes it from fear, hope, desire and many other attitudes.
2. To believe that p is to believe that p is true. To believe 'she is late' is to believe that it is true that 'she is late'. So if you recognise that p is false (you realise she is not late), you abandon your belief that p.
3. To say 'I believe that p' implies that p is true. For instance, it is paradoxical to say 'I believe that p, but p is false'.

All of this is also true of *judgement*. But judging that p is something you *do*, and do at a *particular moment* in time. Once you have judged that p, from then on (until you judge that not-p), you believe that p. Having a belief is not something you do and is not something that happens at a time, but over time. It is not an 'episode', but a 'disposition'. To believe that Paris is the capital of France, for instance, is not for anything to be happening in my mind. For example, I do not constantly think (consciously or unconsciously), 'Paris is the capital of France'. How we should understand belief as a disposition we discuss next.

Realist and instrumentalist notions of belief

Realism

It is perhaps natural to think of beliefs as 'things' 'in the mind'. At some point, you acquire a particular belief, after which you 'have' it. We can think of the

An Enquiry Concerning Human Understanding, p. 125

Difficulties facing Hume's analysis of belief are discussed in THE NATURE OF BELIEF AND IMAGINATION, p. 20.

See CAN BELIEFS BE VOLUNTARY?, p. 164.

What is a belief?

belief as involving a *representation* of the proposition believed. Furthermore, together with my desire to drink, my belief that 'there is a glass of water' causes me to pick up the water and drink. Anything involved in causation must be a 'thing'; so beliefs must 'really' exist.

According to this *realism* about belief, beliefs are part of the structure of the mind. Acquiring a belief changes the structure of the mind. If the mind is, or is very closely connected to, the brain, beliefs will be reflected in the structure of the brain, for example in connections between neurones.

This is a standard model for understanding dispositions in science. For example, sugar has the disposition to dissolve in water. This disposition corresponds to the molecular structure of sugar. Identifying the disposition with a structural property provides a way of explaining how dispositions are 'real'. So it is with beliefs.

What does realism about beliefs claim?

INSTRUMENTALISM

However, realism faces a serious objection. Suppose we came across an alien species who behaved in ways very similar to us. On the basis of their *behaviour*, we would say they had beliefs – without knowing anything about the internal structure of their minds or brains. Beliefs are dispositions to behave – but we don't have to find some 'real thing' that a belief corresponds to. Beliefs don't 'exist' as things at all.

See p. 20.

One version of instrumentalism is LOGICAL BEHAVIOURISM. However, this theory faces serious objections. While we can accept that beliefs are dispositions to behave, we can question the claim that this is *all* they are.

The Intentional Stance

A different form of instrumentalism is interpretationism. Daniel Dennett argues that in understanding, explaining and predicting anything in the world, we can take different approaches or 'stances'. The 'physical stance' explains and predicts how something behaves in terms of physical properties, such as the weather. The 'design stance' explains and predicts behaviour in terms of purposes, for example a plant 'seeking' sunlight, a thermostat 'keeping' the room at a certain temperature. The 'intentional stance' explains and predicts behaviour in terms of belief, desires and other mental states.

Different stances are useful for different things, and in different situations. To say that something has beliefs, says Dennett, is just to say that we can usefully use the intentional stance to explain and predict its behaviour. The intentional stance is useful when something's behaviour illustrates certain kinds of complex patterns, for example patterns that depend on the way it processes ('interprets') stimuli. On Dennett's theory, we don't have to reduce individual beliefs to individual patterns of behaviour. It is only useful to adopt the intentional stance once something's behaviour has become quite complex, and then we attribute many beliefs all at once. This avoids some of the problems of reduction faced by logical behaviourism.

We could, for example, explain the operation of a thermostat from the intentional stance ('it clicked off because it believed the room was warm enough and didn't want it any warmer'), but in this case it is obviously forced. A thermostat's pattern of behaviour isn't complex enough. But a sophisticated computer, or a robot, may well exhibit complex behaviour. If it becomes useful to talk about what the computer 'believes', then the computer has beliefs.

See IS ARTIFICIAL INTELLIGENCE INTELLIGENT?, p. 32.

Realists object: how can the intentional stance be useful unless it is picking out and describing something real? Dennett responds that instrumentalism does not imply that we can interpret something's behaviour according to any pattern. We do not *impose* the pattern by interpretation. The *pattern* is 'real', but there is no 'thing' that corresponds to the pattern. Dennett suggests an analogy between beliefs and centres of gravity or the equator. No 'thing' exists that corresponds to either of these examples; but the concepts are useful.

Instrumentalism means that beliefs do not *cause* anything – a pattern of behaviour is not a cause of a pattern of behaviour. But it is very counter-intuitive to deny that our beliefs cause our behaviour.

See ACCOUNTS OF MENTAL CAUSATION, p. 58.

Discuss instrumentalism about belief.

Key points • • •

- The content of a belief-that is what the person believes, and is expressed by a proposition.
- Belief-that is a distinct 'attitude' towards a proposition. Hume argues that a belief is a 'vivid, lively, forcible, firm, steady conception of an object'.
- A better analysis is that beliefs 'aim' at truth; unlike other attitudes, beliefs are dispositions that are true or false, and to believe that p is to believe that p is true.
- Belief-in can be analysed either as belief-that or as a different attitude from belief-that.
- Realism argues that beliefs exist as structures in the mind (or brain) and enter into causation.
- Instrumentalism argues that beliefs are dispositions to behave, and need not exist as distinct 'things'.
- Dennett argues that there are three different stances from which we explain

and predict behaviour: physical, design and intentional. To attribute beliefs is simply to use the intentional stance to understand something's behaviour.

- Realists object that for the intentional stance to be useful, beliefs must be real. Dennett replies that the explained patterns of behaviour are real, but beliefs are not.
- As patterns of behaviour do not cause behaviour, instrumentalism denies that beliefs cause behaviour.

Can beliefs can be voluntary?

Try to believe (not just imagine) that there is an elephant standing in front of you. Try really hard. Why can't you succeed? The nature of belief – that it aims at truth – suggests that forming beliefs can't be voluntary. We cannot believe at will. If we could, then we could form a belief without any regard to the truth of the proposition we believe. Furthermore, having consciously chosen to have the belief, we would know that we formed it irrespective of its truth. But to believe that p is to believe that p is true.

Of course, someone can voluntarily *say* that they believe that p. But asserting that p is not the same as believing that p – because we can be insincere. An insincere assertion that p involves asserting that p without believing that p.

All this does not mean that there is *no* connection between the will and belief. First, what people *want* to be true does tend to affect what they believe. For instance, we may pay attention only to evidence that confirms what we want to believe, and ignore evidence that undermines it. Creationists, who deny evolution, for example, might place much more weight on evidence that challenges evolution than on the massive amount of evidence that confirms it.

The fact that our desires can indirectly influence what we believe can be harmless. For instance, we might believe that our family and friends are nicer people than, in fact, they are. But again, we have formed the belief by paying attention to the evidence that they are nice, and downplaying evidence to the contrary. But someone cannot believe that p while also believing that the *only* reason they have that belief is because they want to have it. If you want to believe that p, you want to have the belief because it is *true*.

A second connection between the will and belief is that we can voluntarily undertake some action that will lead to our coming to have the belief that p. For instance, I could go to a hypnotist and ask him or her to cause me to have the belief that p. My belief, though, is not voluntary; I am caused to have it, though

? How does the connection with truth make belief involuntary?

in this case by hypnotism rather than evidence. While this is possible, it is very irrational. Presumably, I would do this only if I wanted to believe that p. But, as just noted, when I want to believe that p, usually what I want is for p to be true. But being hypnotised into believing that p will not make p true.

You might object: surely people form and hold on to all sorts of ethical and religious beliefs without any real attempt to discover the truth. Their beliefs are simply prejudices, and no form of evidence or argument changes their minds. Doesn't this show that beliefs can be voluntary?

We can make two replies. First, can someone really accept that there is *no* evidence for their belief while still holding on to their belief? This sounds peculiar. More likely, they think there is evidence, even if they don't know what it is. Alternatively, are ethical and religious points of view really *beliefs*, rather than 'beliefs-in', 'commitments' or 'faith'? These are all distinct attitudes which we sometimes confusingly call 'belief'. For example, some philosophers have argued that ethical 'beliefs' are not beliefs at all, but expressions of commitment, because there is no moral truth. If these attitudes are not belief, then they are not counter-examples to the claim that beliefs cannot be voluntary.

> It may be that, under certain circumstances, it can be rational to undertake an action or way of life that will lead to a belief. See PASCAL'S WAGER, p. 313.

> This is discussed in THE DENIAL OF MORAL TRUTH, p. 233.

> Can we literally choose what to believe?

Key points • • •

- If we could believe at will, we could believe that p without regard to whether p is true. But to believe that p is to believe that p is true.
- However, our will can influence the beliefs we form, because we can direct our attention towards confirming evidence and away from contrary evidence. But we cannot believe that p while also being aware that the *only* reason for the belief is our desire that it is true.
- We can also voluntarily undertake a course of action that will end up with our believing that p. But again, the forming of the belief is itself not voluntary.
- The fact that people's beliefs are often not responsive to evidence may suggest that belief can be directly controlled by the will. In some cases, we may question whether what they 'believe' is a genuine form of belief (for which there can be evidence), or a commitment to a value.

The tripartite definition of knowledge

The tripartite definition of knowledge applies only to propositional knowledge, knowing 'that p'. Some philosophers argue that a complete analysis of a concept, such as propositional knowledge, ought to state conditions that are together 'equivalent' to knowledge. In other words, if someone knows some proposition, they should fulfil exactly those conditions that the analysis of knowledge states. The 'justified true belief' theory of knowledge is like this. It claims that to know that p involves exactly these three things:

1.   the proposition p is true;
2.   you believe that p;
3.   your belief that p is justified.

It claims these are the 'necessary and sufficient conditions' for knowledge.

Necessary and sufficient conditions

Necessary and sufficient conditions are related to conditional statements, which take the form 'if x, then y'. Such statements relate the truth of two propositions, such as 'it is raining' and 'I am getting wet'; for example, 'If it is raining, then I am getting wet.' The conditional asserts that if the first statement (known as the antecedent) is true, then the second statement (the consequent) is also true.

Suppose the conditional is true: *if* it is raining, I am getting wet. It follows that if the antecedent is true (it is raining), then the consequent is true (I'm getting wet). It also follows that if the consequent is false (I am not getting wet), then the antecedent is false (it is not raining).

The justified true belief theory of knowledge claims that *if* all the three conditions it lists are satisfied – if p is true, and you believe that p, and your belief is justified – then you know that p. You don't need anything else for knowledge; the three conditions, together, are *sufficient*.

But the theory says more than this. It also says that *if* you know that p, then you have a justified true belief that p. There is no other way to know that p, no other analysis of knowledge. So, it claims, each of the three conditions is *necessary*. You can't have knowledge without meeting exactly these three conditions. If p is false, or you don't believe that p, or your believe that p is not justified, then you don't know that p.

So, the theory puts forward *two* conditionals: if all three conditions are satisfied, then you know that p; and if you know that p, then all three conditions are satisfied. This means whenever you have one, you have the other. And so, the theory claims, we can say that knowledge and justified true belief *are the same thing*. Justified true belief is necessary for knowledge (you can't have knowledge without it), but it is also sufficient for knowledge (you don't need anything else).

Explain and illustrate the justified true belief theory of knowledge.

Justified true belief

The claim that knowledge is justified true belief matches many of our intuitions. First, we cannot know what is false. Of course, we can *think* we know something and it turns out we don't. But that isn't knowledge; we were just wrong to think we knew it. No one disputes this.

Second, it is intuitively plausible to think that we must believe that p in order to know that p. Some philosophers have certainly challenged this, claiming that knowledge is an entirely different mental state from belief. They say that either you believe something or you know it; but you don't know something by believing it. The usual reply to this is to point to those occasions on which we make mistakes. Suppose I thought I knew something, but it turned out that I didn't. We would usually say that I had, nevertheless, *believed* it. I believed it, but I thought I knew it; this shows that we can mistake belief for knowledge. If knowledge isn't a kind of belief, this would be puzzling.

Finally, as we saw in INTRODUCTORY (p. 159), we want to make a distinction between knowledge and true belief. The distinction seems to be a matter of justification.

Justified true belief theory is a theory about knowledge. It doesn't tell us what *justification* is, or how strong it must be. We will discuss what justification is in INTERNALIST AND EXTERNALIST THEORIES OF JUSTIFICATION (p. 169) and look at how strong it should be in INFALLIBILISM (p. 172).

Why think that knowledge is justified true belief?

Gettier-type objections to the tripartite definition

Edmund Gettier famously presented cases in which we want to say that someone has justified, true belief but *not* knowledge. These cases became known as 'Gettier cases'.

'Is Justified True Belief Knowledge?'

Here's a typical example: I awake in the middle of the night and, wanting to know what time it is, I reach to where I believe my watch to be. My belief that it is there is justified, as I always put it in the same place, and I remember putting it there before sleeping. However, while I was asleep a thief stole into my room and knocked my watch from its usual position, but replaced it – as it happens, just where I had put it. Although my belief regarding where my watch is is both true and justified, it does not amount to knowledge, says Gettier.

It's obvious that my belief is true: my watch is where I believe it is. Is it justified? Well, I have all the evidence that I usually have. If you think that my memory of where I put my watch, and my habit of always putting it in the same place, are not enough justification, then you have to say that I *never* know where my watch is when I wake up at night. Gettier assumes we don't want to adopt this type of scepticism. If we can't use memory as good evidence, there is a great deal we don't know (what you had for breakfast, what your name is . . .)! So, usually, I do know where my watch is. In the case in which the thief knocks off my watch and replaces it, I'm relying on exactly the same evidence – so my belief *is* justified. But, says Gettier, *it isn't knowledge*. The connection between the reasons why I have my belief (its justification) and my belief's being true is, in this case, too *accidental*.

See INFALLIBILISM,
p. 172.

Gettier cases all have the same structure: they portray situations in which we have justified true belief, but not knowledge, by demonstrating how it is accidental, relative to our evidence, that our belief is true, even though the belief is justified by that evidence. So, justified true belief is not *sufficient* for knowledge. But that means it is not the *same* as knowledge. If knowledge isn't justified true belief in these cases, then knowledge is *never* justified true belief. Something else must be required to turn justified true belief into knowledge.

The result we want is that in normal cases, I know (where my watch is), but in Gettier cases, I don't, even though I have exactly the same evidence in each case. This shows that for knowledge, we need to connect what makes the belief true and what justifies it. We shall consider RESPONSES TO GETTIER later (p. 172).

? **What do Gettier cases show?**

Key points • • •

- The justified true belief theory of knowledge claims to give necessary and sufficient conditions for knowledge. If you have a true belief that p that is justified, you know that p (the conditions are sufficient for knowledge); if you know that p, you have a justified, true belief that p (the conditions are necessary for knowledge).

- If justified true belief is both sufficient and necessary for knowledge, it is the same thing as knowledge.
- The claim that knowledge is justified true belief initially matches many of our intuitions. However, the theory tells us nothing about justification.
- A Gettier case is a situation in which a person has justified true belief but not knowledge because their belief, even though it is justified, is only *accidentally* true relative to their evidence. So, Gettier concluded, justified true belief is not knowledge.

'Internalist' and 'externalist' theories of justification

Internalism and externalism: evidentialism versus reliabilism

Evidentialism is the theory that justification is about having evidence. To have evidence for the belief that p, some argue, is to have another mental state that represents p as true. It could be sense experience; you believe the rose is red because you see the rose, and it looks red. Or a memory; you remember where you left your keys. Or it could be that p is 'self-evident'; you just 'see' the truth of 'if the dog is behind the cat, the cat is in front of the dog'.

Evidentialism is a version of internalism about justification. Internalism claims that if your belief is justified, then you can know what justifies it directly. You have direct access to, and directly recognise, your grounds for that belief. So, whenever your belief is justified, you can know that it is justified. It could be that justification is a matter of evidence, and evidence takes the form of a mental state you can access and recognise as evidence.

> Explain and illustrate internalism about justification.

Going further: internalism and knowing that you know

Internalism is very similar to the view that if you know something, then you know that you know it. It is different in two ways. First, it doesn't apply just to knowledge, but, more broadly, to justified belief. (Not all justified belief is true. It is possible to have very good evidence for a belief, but it is nevertheless false; think of trials in court.) Second, it doesn't claim that if you know (or have a justified belief) that p, then you *do* know that you know it; it only claims that you *can* know what justifies it. The process of reflection by which you come to know the grounds for your belief may take some time, and could be difficult. But it is always possible, claims internalism.

A different (and more popular) form of reliabilism is reliabilism about *knowledge*, not justification. See KNOWLEDGE AS APPROPRIATELY CAUSED BELIEF, p. 174.

Externalism about justification simply denies internalism. It argues that, at least sometimes, you can have a justified belief without knowing what justifies it. The most common version of externalism is reliabilism.

In its simplest form, reliabilism about justification claims that someone's belief in p is justified if, and only if, it is produced by a reliable cognitive process – that is, one that has a tendency to produce a high percentage of true beliefs. Usually, what makes a process reliable is a causal connection between p and the belief that p. For example, it is the fact that the rose is red – or, more accurately, the rose's redness – that causes me to believe that the rose is red.

Reliabilism rejects evidentialism. It is not the evidence that the person is able to produce that justifies a belief; it is the source of the belief. Second, reliabilism doesn't require the person to *know* that the process is reliable. The fact that a process is reliable is not evidence the person needs to have that their belief is true. The person may have no idea how their belief was caused and whether it is reliable or not.

Compare and contrast reliabilism and evidentialism.

Discussion

Internalists object to reliabilism's separation of justification from evidence. First, in order for your belief to be justified, you must be able to justify it. But this means that you must have access to what justifies your belief. So, internalism is true.

Externalists point out that this entails that animals and babies cannot have justified beliefs. Justifying your beliefs requires considerable intellectual ability and self-awareness, which animals and babies don't have. But surely they do have justified beliefs – because the way in which they form beliefs is reliable.

A second objection is that reliability is not necessary for justification. Suppose you are a brain in a vat, and that the computer is programmed so that most of your beliefs are false (for example, you believe that grass is green, but actually it is red and so on). Your beliefs are formed in a very unreliable way; yet we should say that your beliefs are justified. You have all the evidence for your beliefs that you have in the real world. So, reliability is not necessary for justification; evidence is.

See How we can move from 'appears' so to 'is' so, p. 145.

Externalists reply that this has nothing to do with what justification is in the real world. The concept of justification internalists are defending might be philosophically interesting, but it doesn't help us understand non-sceptical cases.

A famous thought experiment presented by Laurence BonJour is intended to show that reliability is not sufficient for justification. Norman is clairvoyant. He is a very reliable clairvoyant; most of the beliefs he has through clairvoyance are, in fact, true. But he's never checked up on these beliefs, and has no idea how he comes by them. He doesn't even believe that they are usually true. Norman has *no evidence* for his beliefs. He even has evidence *against* his beliefs, given what he knows about science and how we normally come to know things. Suppose he suddenly believes that the head of McDonald's is in a secret meeting about the recipe for burger sauce. Is this belief justified? It just doesn't seem right to say that it is. Why? Because Norman has no evidence.

The Structure of Empirical Knowledge, Ch. 3

Some reliabilists insist, counter-intuitively, that Norman's belief is justified. Others reply by adding an additional condition: not only must the process be reliable for the belief to be justified, but the person must not have evidence that their belief is *unreliably* caused. That the belief is caused in a very unfamiliar way, going against a general scientific understanding of how the world works, is evidence that the belief is unreliably caused (even though, in fact, it is reliable). So, it is not justified.

This reply allows that the justification of beliefs produced by a reliable process can be *undermined* by evidence against them. But it maintains that in the absence of evidence against a belief, the fact that it is produced by a reliable process is enough to justify it. So, this is still a form of externalism.

Can belief be justified in the absence of evidence?

Key points • • •

- Internalism claims that for my belief to be justified, I must know what justifies it.
- Evidentialism claims that what justifies belief is evidence. Some evidentialists argue that having evidence is a matter of having mental states that represent p as true.

- Internalism is similar to, but not the same as, the view that to know that p requires that you know that you know that p.
- Externalism rejects internalism; beliefs can be justified without the person knowing what justifies them.
- Reliabilism claims that a belief is justified if, and only if, it is produced by a reliable process – that is, one that has a strong tendency to produce a high percentage of true beliefs.
- Internalists object that if I cannot justify my belief, my belief is not justified; that my belief could be justified without being caused by a reliable process, for example if I am a brain in a vat; and that my belief can be reliably caused without being justified, for example in the case of reliable clairvoyance.
- Externalists reply that animals and infants have justified beliefs, but can't justify their beliefs; and that sceptical cases don't inform us about justification in the real world.
- Many reliabilists accept that reliable clairvoyance does not produce justified belief, because there is strong evidence against the beliefs formed this way. However, beliefs can still be justified if reliably caused provided there is no strong counter-evidence.

Responses to Gettier

Infallibilism

Some people argue that knowledge involves certainty. One way of expressing this is to claim that a belief is not justified unless you can be certain of it. 'Certainty' here doesn't mean a psychological feeling (which could vary from one person to another), but refers to the belief being certain. We could use this view of justification to argue that Gettier cases demonstrate that we cannot be certain of our beliefs in normal cases. Because we can't tell whether we are in a normal case or a Gettier case, our beliefs in normal cases are not certain, and so are not justification. Gettier doesn't show that knowledge is not justified true belief. What he shows is that our beliefs are rarely justified.

This argument suggests infallibilism, the view that for my belief to be certain is for it to be impossible that I have made a mistake. Infallibilism seems plausible, because if I know that p, then I can't be mistaken about p, because no one can know what is false. If I know that p, I am justified in believing that p. So if I am justified in believing that p, p *must* be true; I *can't possibly* be mistaken. So if it

See Is CERTAINTY
CONFINED TO
INTROSPECTION AND
THE TAUTOLOGICAL?,
p. 37.

is possible that I am mistaken, then I can't be justified in believing that p. This rules out Gettier cases (because I do not have *justified* true belief), while defending the justified true belief theory of knowledge.

However, it is rare that our evidence rules out the *possibility* of error. So, infallibilism leads to scepticism. We can object that a belief can be justified without being true. For instance, you can have very good evidence, but still be mistaken. Or again, according to reliabilism, the reliable process may occasionally produce a false belief without ceasing to be reliable.

Explain the appeal of infallibilism.

How does infallibilism respond to Gettier? Is the response persuasive?

Going further: rejecting the argument for infallibilism

The argument for infallibilism rests on a logical error. Infallibilism is the claim that 'if I know that p, then I can't be mistaken about p'. But this claim has more than one possible meaning, depending on how one understands the 'can't':

> Reading 1: 'It can't be the case that if I know that p, I *am* mistaken that p.'

We should agree with this; in fact, it is analytically true. By definition, you cannot know what is false.

> Reading 2: 'If I know that p, (I am in a position that) I *can't possibly* be mistaken that p.'

This is what infallibilism claims. It is a much stronger claim than Reading 1, because it says that not only am I *not* mistaken, but I *can't possibly be* mistaken that p. Obviously, there are many cases in which I *could* be mistaken that p, but in fact I am not. Furthermore, if my true belief rests on evidence, there are good reasons why I am not mistaken. Nevertheless, I *could be*; this isn't impossible.

The first argument for infallibilism used Reading 1 to support Reading 2. But this is a mistake. The two claims are distinct, since one is a claim about whether I *am* mistaken, and the other is a claim about whether I *could be* mistaken. So if we are going to accept infallibilism, we need some other, independent reason for believing Reading 2.

Does infallibilism rest on a mistake?

'Indefeasibility'

My memory of where I put it and my habit of always putting it in the same place justify my belief about where my watch is. In normal cases, this justification is adequate. In the Gettier case, it is 'defeated'. The facts in this case – that the thief came in, knocked my watch and replaced it – make my usual justification insufficient. This has inspired philosophers to accept that knowledge is not justified true belief, but requires a fourth condition:

4.   My justification for believing that p is not defeated by the facts.

If my justification is not defeated by the facts, it is 'fully justified'. In a normal situation, my belief is fully justified, so I know that p. In a Gettier case, my belief is justified, but not 'fully justified', since it *is* defeated by the facts; so I don't know that p. This was the result we wanted.

There isn't any *subjective* difference between normal cases and Gettier cases. In both, I believe what I do (where my watch is) for exactly the same reasons. According to the fully justified true belief theory of knowledge, whether I know where my watch is depends not *just* on my evidence, but also on the situation I am in. So, it makes knowledge dependent on something that is not available to me (since I can't tell which situation I am in).

Knowledge as appropriately caused belief

From Alvin Goldman, 'Discrimination and Perceptual Knowledge'

If Gettier cases show that knowledge is not *justified* true belief, perhaps we can argue instead that knowledge is true belief that is 'appropriately caused'. But another Gettier case suggests this is inadequate: Henry is driving through the countryside and enters an area, Barn County, in which, unknown to him, there are many façades of barns. From the road, they look just like real barns. Henry believes they are barns. Now, in one instance he happens to be looking at the one and only *real* barn in the area, and he believes it is a barn.

It is very plausible to say that he doesn't know it is a barn, since he falsely thought all the façades were barns, and it is sheer chance that he is looking at the only real barn. But what is 'inappropriate' in how his belief was caused? For instance, it was caused by precisely *what makes it true*. It was even caused by a very reliable process, namely vision. It's just that in Barn County, this generally reliable process has produced a true belief in circumstances in which the belief still seems only accidentally true.

Let us assume that 'appropriately caused' means 'caused by a reliable process'. The theory that knowledge is true belief that is caused by a reliable process is reliabilism about *knowledge*. This is a distinct theory from the claim that knowledge is justified true belief, and to be *justified*, a belief must be caused by a reliable process. The Barn County example attacks both theories: Henry's belief about the barn is true and caused by a reliable process, but it is not knowledge.

The trouble with Henry is that, in Barn County, he can't discriminate between *relevant* possibilities – is he looking at a barn or a façade? In other situations, he can discriminate between barns and things that aren't barns just fine, so he knows a barn when he sees one. We can use this thought in any of three ways:

1. To be knowledge, a true belief must be caused by a reliable process, but also the subject must be able to use the process to discriminate between relevant possibilities in the actual situation. In Barn County, Henry can't reliably discriminate between real barns and façades. That's why he doesn't know that what he sees is a barn when it is. Justification (whatever that is), however, doesn't come into it.
2. Knowledge is justified true belief plus the fourth condition that the subject can discriminate between relevant possibilities in the actual situation. Unlike the first option, this position retains the connection between knowledge and justification.
3. Knowledge is justified true belief. To be justified, the belief must be caused by a reliable process. However, if I can't use the process to rule out real alternative possibilities, then it isn't sufficiently reliable, and so the belief *isn't justified*. In other words, we could say that whether a process counts as reliable is relative to the actual situation. Henry's vision is *not* a reliable process for producing beliefs about barns when he's in Barn County. In Gettier cases, my beliefs aren't justified, because the usual processes that cause them are unreliable, which is why I don't know. However, the justified true belief theory is right.

Knowledge as tracking the truth

Robert Nozick presents a form of reliabilism about knowledge (option 1 above). He argued that instead of a true belief that p needing to be justified to qualify as knowledge, it needed to 'track the truth'. What he meant was that

What is the relation between knowledge and beliefs that are 'appropriately caused'?

Philosophical Explanations, pp. 172ff.

a. if p were not true, then the person would not believe that p; and

b. if p were true, then the person would believe that p.

The first condition tends to be more important: Henry does not know he is looking at a barn, because he would believe it was a barn even if it were a façade.

We might argue that this undermines normal cases as well. For example, when outside Barn County, Henry *doesn't* know he's looking at a barn because he *could* be in Barn County without knowing it. But this misinterprets the first condition. It doesn't imply that I *could not* be mistaken, no matter what. Instead, it should be understood to mean that, given how the world is, in situations which are likely to come up, I am able to tell when p is true and when it is not. I know that p if there are no *relevant* situations in which either a. or b. is false.

This is INFALLIBILISM, p. 172.

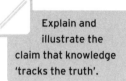

Explain and illustrate the claim that knowledge 'tracks the truth'.

Going further: denying the principle of closure

The claim that knowledge is 'closed' under logical entailment (the Principle of Closure) says that: If proposition 1 logically entails proposition 2, and I know proposition 1, then I know (or can know, by deduction) proposition 2. The thought here is that if I know a truth, I can know any truth that I can validly deduce from it. This seems very uncontroversial. Surely deduction gives us knowledge.

However, reliabilism and truth-tracking have to deny this principle. The following deduction is sound. If the Principle of Closure is right, then I can know the conclusion. But the theories claim I do not know the conclusion:

1. In a normal case, I know where my watch is.
2. I know that if I know where my watch is, I am not in a Gettier situation.
3. Therefore, in a normal case, I know that I am not in a Gettier situation.

The theories accept that if I am in a normal case, I know that p, whereas if I am in a Gettier case, I do not. This establishes the premises. However, they accept that I may *not know* whether or not I am in a Gettier case. Which means I can't always know what I can deduce from what I do know. This is a bizarre result; surely logic is reliable, tracks the truth and gives us knowledge!

However, denying the Principle of Closure can be used to defeat scepticism. The sceptic uses the Principle of Closure to argue that in order to know that I have two hands, I must know that I am not a brain in a vat:

1. I know that if I have two hands, I am not a brain in a vat.
2. Therefore, if I know I have two hands, then I know I am not a brain in a vat.
3. However, I do *not* know I am not a brain in a vat (for the usual sceptical reasons).
4. Therefore, I do not know whether I have two hands.

Many answers to scepticism reject 3. However, reliabilism and truth-tracking reject 2. I can know I have two hands without knowing that I am not a brain in a vat. I don't have reliable means for telling whether I am a brain in a vat; if I *were* a brain in a vat, then I would still believe that I was not. So I don't know that I'm not a brain in a vat. However, if I am *not* a brain in a vat, the possibility of being a brain in a vat is not a *relevant* alternative. If I am not a brain in a vat, then the process that causes my belief that I have two hands is reliable, or it tracks the truth. So, I can know I have two hands without knowing whether I am a brain in a vat.

The sceptic responds: if I were a brain in a vat, I would have no hands. And I don't know that I'm not a brain in a vat. How could I know that I have two hands and not know that I do not have no hands?!

Is it coherent to deny the Principle of Closure?

Is there a satisfactory solution to Gettier problems?

Key points • • •

- Infallibilism argues that to be knowledge, a belief must be certain. It argues that since I cannot know what is false, if I know that p, p must be true, so I *can't be* mistaken. But this argument is wrong. If I know that p, then it can't be that I *am* mistaken. But it can happen that I am not mistaken even though I *could* be.
- Infallibilism leads to scepticism, because most beliefs are not certain.
- The 'fully justified true belief' theory of knowledge adds the fourth condition that the person's justification is not 'defeated' by the facts. In a Gettier situation, this condition is not met. The theory entails that whether

my belief is knowledge depends not just on my evidence, but on my situation.

- Gettier cases suggest that a belief caused by a reliable process can still be accidentally true, so won't be knowledge.
- Reliabilism about knowledge responds that knowledge is true belief caused by a reliable process, when the subject can use the process to discriminate between relevant possibilities.
- Justified true belief theorists respond that unless the subject can use the process to discriminate between relevant possibilities, their belief is not justified.
- Nozick argues that knowledge 'tracks the truth'; in particular, if p were not true, then the subject would not believe that p.
- Reliabilism about knowledge and truth-tracking deny the Principle of Closure, the claim that I (can) know whatever I can deduce from what I know.
- While this is counter-intuitive, denying the Principle of Closure can be used to reject scepticism.

III. UNIVERSALS AND PARTICULARS

Introducing universals and particulars

One branch of **metaphysics** is **ontology**, the study of 'being', or what exists. We can classify what *sorts* of things exist. Start, for example, with whales, which are mammals, which are animals, which are living things. Each whale is an individual thing, a 'particular'. Living things are examples of physical things, which are all 'particular things'. Each class – of whales, animals and so on – contains many particular things, but we usually suppose that each of these classifications has 'internal unity' – that is, that the class is not formed by some arbitrary imposition.

What each class has in common – 'being a whale', 'being a mammal', etc. – identifies a *property* or quality of particular things: all whales have the property of being a whale in common, while whales and elephants have in common that they are mammals. Our language commonly identifies particular things as subjects and properties by predicates: x *is a whale*; whales *are mammals*.

Predicates indicate (at least) two types of property: qualities, which we've been looking at; but also relations, for example 'to the north of', 'larger than'

> Compare the class of 'pets' – what's in and what's out?

and so on, for example 'whales are larger than mice'. These relations are also something particular things have in common, but now in ordered pairs: <whales, mice> and <elephants, mice> both exemplify the relation 'are larger than'.

Can we say that properties (qualities and relations) 'exist', though obviously in a different way from particulars? 'Being a mammal' and 'is larger than' don't sound as though they refer to 'things'; they aren't *nouns*. However, we do have nouns that don't refer to particular things, but to what they can have in common: 'size', 'blue', 'honesty', 'rarity' and so on. So, it seems that there are two sorts of thing: particulars and properties. Some philosophers think of properties as '*universals*'. Words and phrases that refer to universals apply generally, to more than one thing; words that refer to particular things pick out just that one thing.

> Explain and illustrate the distinction between particulars and universals.

Nominalism: general terms as mind-dependent classificatory schemes

A 'nominalist' is someone who argues that only particulars exist in any meaningful sense. Universals do not exist separately or independently from particulars. Words for 'universals' do not refer to any distinct *thing*. There is no (one and the same) thing, such as 'blue', or 'being a whale', that is exemplified by two different particulars. Instead, the particulars simply *resemble each other*, and we pick this up in thought and language. Certainly, there are blue things – the sky, blueberries; these exist. But 'blue' itself doesn't exist. Because a number of particulars resemble each other in a certain way, we call them all 'blue'. William of Ockham, Berkeley and Hume all argued for this position.

The meaning of general terms

If we adopt nominalism, what do general terms mean? If universals don't exist, do they refer to nothing at all? But then how do they get their meaning? There are two popular options.

The first is that general terms mean the set of all those particular things to which they apply; for example, 'blue' means 'all blue things'. But there are three objections to this claim. First, many general terms, such as 'honesty', are often used in ways that don't allow us to substitute 'all honest people'; for example, 'honesty is the best policy' has not successfully been paraphrased in a way that refers only to sets of particular honest people. Surely it is simpler to say that 'honesty' refers to the universal, honesty. Second, which things are blue can change – so the set of all blue things can change. But this doesn't change the *meaning* of 'blue'. So, the meaning can't just be the set. Third, two predicates, for example 'has a shape' and 'has a size', can apply to *exactly* the same set of things but have different meanings.

The second option avoids these objections: general terms mean the concept, the abstract idea. We notice the resemblance between two or more particulars in our sense experience (for example, in the way they look to us); we then abstract from our experience to form an abstract idea (blue (of no particular shade)), and this gives the general term its meaning.

Consider: are we to suppose that *all* general terms get their meaning by referring to universals? What about terms that aren't true of anything, for example 'is a witch'? Should we think that the property of being a witch exists, even though nothing is or ever has been a witch? That the term 'witch' stands for the *idea* of a witch seems more plausible than saying either that it means 'all those things that are witches' or 'the property of being a witch'.

Generalising this account, nominalists argue that 'universals' are nothing but mind-dependent classification systems; they simply reflect how we think.

If universals do not exist, how can general terms have meaning?

Resemblance and explanation

However, this solution leaves us wondering where our classification system came from. What makes blue things blue? If it is *just* that we apply the term 'blue' to them, then what explains our concept? If there is nothing in virtue of which blue things are blue, our concept is completely arbitrary.

The obvious answer is that blue things are blue because they resemble other blue things. What we have picked out with the term 'blue' is a pattern of resemblance. This pattern explains our concept. However, we should try not to explain this pattern of resemblance by appealing to a universal that those particulars share. There is no universal 'blue' in virtue of which blue things resemble each other. Their resembling each other is metaphysically fundamental.

Problems of Philosophy, p. 96

Bertrand Russell objected that nominalism ends up contradicting itself. The resemblance between particulars (e.g. the similarity in colour) is a universal. Nominalists have focused too much on qualities, and forgotten relations! Resemblance is not a quality like 'being blue'; it is a relation between particulars (x resembles y). But relations are just as much universals as qualities; the relation of 'looks the same colour as' holds between many particular blue things.

Can nominalists argue that the relation is just an abstract idea? Not on the account given so far, because they argue that we form the abstract idea by *noticing the resemblance* – so the resemblance must be real and comes before the idea. So, we are bound to accept the reality of at least certain types of universal, namely those relations that are resemblances.

Nominalists respond that when two things resemble each other, the only things that exist are the two things that resemble each other. There is no third thing, 'resemblance', in addition. But take two pairs of blue things. We want to say the first pair resemble each other *in the same way* as the second pair. The resemblances are the same (or, at least, resemble each other). So, we have to talk about resemblances.

Can nominalists coherently explain patterns of resemblance?

Key points • • •

- Particulars are individual things. Universals, if they exist, are things that particulars can have in common, including qualities and relations.
- Nominalism denies the existence of universals, arguing that words for universals derive from particular things resembling each other.
- The theory that a general term, x, means the set of all x things faces three objections: there are uses of 'x' that cannot be replaced by 'the set of all x things'; the set can change while the meaning does not; and the set of all x things may be the same set as the set of all y things, but x and y are different terms.
- A second theory claims that a general term means the concept or idea formed by abstraction from our experience of particular things resembling each other.
- Patterns of resemblance should not be explained in terms of a universal that resembling particulars share.
- Russell objects that 'resemblance' is a relation, and hence a universal. Nominalism replies that there is no thing 'resemblance', only particular things resembling each other.

Realism: the referents of general terms exist

Plato and realism

The Republic,
Book V 476f.
See THE
THEORY OF THE FORMS:
METAPHYSICAL
IMPLICATIONS, p. 58.

Plato argued that since more than one thing can be beautiful, beauty is a property beautiful things share in common. Beauty manifests itself in all the different things, in all the different ways, we call 'beautiful'. But beauty itself is not a particular thing, and Plato argued that it must be something distinct from particular things. For instance, all particular beautiful things could also be destroyed, yet that would not destroy beauty itself. Universals, therefore, exist independently of particulars, outside space, time and the changing world of sense experience.

While many realists about universals don't accept Plato's arguments or his claim that they exist completely independently of particular things, they do accept two points:

1. 'one-over-many': universals are general, so that many particulars can exhibit the same universal;
2. 'instantiation': what the particulars have in common is the universal – what makes all the things that are whales whales is the property of 'being a whale'; what the universal explains, is, what they have in common.

The most popular argument in favour of realism goes as follows. Without universals, we cannot explain or understand our abilities to recognise, categorise and generalise about particulars. Our classifications are not arbitrary, yet particulars, of course, are particular, individual; for similarities we therefore need universals. Similarity is a matter of two (or more) particulars exemplifying *one and the same* property.

This explains the ability to recognise new examples. If someone has never encountered *this* particular (e.g. this banana), how can they identify its properties (e.g. yellow)? Because they have encountered these very properties before, in other particulars.

We should not say that *part* of a universal (e.g. yellow) exists in one object and a different part in another object. First, it is odd to think that yellow has parts. Second, we want to say that the *same* universal is exemplified by the two objects; referring to parts would undermine this. So, we should say that yellow exists wholly in each yellow thing.

> Explain the claim that universals exist.

Two problems with realism

On the realist account, it seems that a particular must either have a universal or not; something is or isn't a banana, is or isn't yellow and so on. But psychologists have recently argued that this 'either is or isn't' judgement isn't how our concepts work. Are plantains bananas or not? More or less? When does yellow become orange or green? Is a shark a fish? Many concepts seem to work by comparison with a *prototype*, a defining example (yellow, fish, banana), and other things are judged to be more or less similar to it – which is what a nominalist would say.

Realism also faces two problems with how particulars and universals relate to each other. First, Aristotle argued that Plato's realism faces an infinite regress. Plato claims that particulars instantiate universals. 'Instantiation' is therefore a relation between the particular and the universal. But relations are universals. So, the particular and the universal are both related to another universal, 'instantiation'. Whatever this relation is will also be a universal. And so on. One response is to deny that instantiation is a universal (just as nominalists answered Russell by denying that 'resemblance' is a relation).

Second, *how* do particulars 'instantiate' universals? How does a whale 'have' or 'exemplify' the property of 'being a whale'? This seems particularly challenging for Plato's theory, because universals are outside space and time. Other realist theories claim that universals are part of the spatio-temporal world (see next section), though this doesn't tell us what instantiation is.

> Compare the strengths and weaknesses of realism and nominalism.

Explanation

We use general terms in explanations all the time. Realism argues that if they were dependent on our minds, rather than referring to universals, the explanations wouldn't work. Take change: when a particular changes, the particular persists; it is the same thing, but it has changed. So what has changed? The obvious answer is a universal; for example, it had the property 'being blue' and now has the property 'being red'. The nominalist alternative, to say simply that it resembled blue things and now resembles red things, only *describes* the change; it doesn't *explain* it.

When we explain *why* something changed, here too we refer to universals. For example, the *weight* of the particular thing placed on the scales causes the needle to move, to indicate '1 kg'. 'Being a weight of 1 kg' is a universal. And to explain a false measurement, we have to say that its *real* weight is different from what we measured; we measured inaccurately. So, 'being of a certain weight, x' is independent of us and our measurement. (Yes, the *system* of measurement we invented; but we don't create the lengths of things themselves. Being a weight of 1 kg is the *same weight* as being a weight of 2.2 lb.)

Again, nominalism seems weaker. Two particulars never have the same weight, just exactly similar weights. So, an explanation that refers to the weight of one particular is a *different* explanation from an explanation that refers to the weight of the other, because it refers to a different thing. 'The needle moved to indicate "1 kg" because I put *a* 1-kg weight on the scale' would have to be changed to 'the needle moved to indicate "1 kg" because I put *this* 1-kg weight on the scale'; and *this* explanation wouldn't apply if I used a *different* 1-kg weight (I would have to give another, exactly similar, explanation).

The place of universals in explanation provides the realist with answers to two common objections:

1. Do all predicates refer to universals? No, only those universals that appear in explanations (or perhaps 'causal explanations') exist; other predicates (such as 'witch') are 'merely' ideas.
2. How do we know about universals? Empirically, through experience; via the particulars that instantiate them, they affect us.

? **Does the use of general terms in explanations demonstrate the universals exist?**

Metaphysics Z

Going further: what is a universal?

If realism is true, and universals exist, then we should be able to say something about what it is for a universal to exist. This is a very problematic question. Plato argued that universals are Forms. They exist completely independently of all particulars, and therefore outside space and time. This led to the problems of instantiation discussed earlier (p. 183).

Aristotle argued that universals exist only in and through the particulars that exemplify them. There is no redness independent of *all* red things. So, universals exist in space and time – but *at many points* in space at the same time. The argument from explanation above develops this idea, using science to establish what universals exist.

However, we can object that it is a little peculiar to say that if two red things are 10 metres apart, then redness exists 10 metres away from itself!

Second, there are some universals that are not (currently) instantiated, e.g. 'being 250,000 kilometres long'. Do they exist? We could argue that a universal exists if it is instantiated at some time. Otherwise, we have to say that universals come in and out of existence – which is peculiar, given the role they play in explanations.

Is the idea of universals coherent?

Key points • • •

- Plato argues that universals, which he calls Forms, exist independently of particulars, outside space and time. Aristotle argues that they exist only in and through particulars.
- Realists agree that universals are instantiated in many particulars; they are what particulars have in common.
- Realists argue that without universals, we cannot explain our abilities to recognise and categorise particulars; nominalists can respond that psychologists have argued that we categorise particulars by judgements of similarity to a prototype.
- Realists also face difficulties in explaining the relationship between particulars and universals. How are universals 'instantiated'?
- Realists argue that without universals, our everyday and scientific explanations cannot work. We can say that when something changes, this is because it loses one universal and gains another. We also explain causal effects in terms of universals, e.g. 'being of weight x'.
- We can argue that only those universals exist that play a role in true explanations. And we come to know about universals through experience.

Metaphysics as speculative nonsense

Metaphysics is the branch of philosophy that enquires about the fundamental nature of reality. This is not a very exact definition, but exactly what counts as metaphysics is not clear. The following traditional debates discussed in the A level syllabus are all metaphysical:

1. Universals.
2. The world independent of all experience: what is the world like considered independent of any sense experience we have? See Plato's theory of Forms in THE THEORY OF THE FORMS (Unit 4.2, p. 58) and Kant's ideas on CONCEPTUAL SCHEMES AND THEIR PHILOSOPHICAL IMPLICATIONS (II) (Unit 1.1, p. 41).
3. The soul: what is the soul? Do we have a soul? Can it survive death? See Unit 1.5 PERSONS and SUBSTANCE DUALISM (p. 7).
4. 'First cause': what caused everything that exists? How did it all begin? See the COSMOLOGICAL ARGUMENT (p. 258).
5. God: does God exist? If so, what is God's nature? See Unit 1.4 THE IDEA OF GOD, and ARGUMENTS FOR THE EXISTENCE OF GOD (p. 288).
6. Metaphysical aspects of ethics: do ethical values exist objectively? See MORAL TRUTH and THE DENIAL OF MORAL TRUTH (pp. 213 and 233).

To suggest, therefore, that metaphysics is speculative nonsense will have an impact on much of the philosophy that we do. Hume ends his *Enquiry Concerning Human Understanding* (p. 211) by saying, of any book,

> let us ask, *Does it contain any abstract reasoning concerning quantity or number?* No. *Does it contain any experimental reasoning concerning matter of fact and existence?* No. Commit it then to the flames: For it can contain nothing but sophistry and illusion.

See THE DISTINCTION BETWEEN RELATIONS OF IDEAS AND MATTERS OF FACT, p. 22.

Explain the importance of metaphysics for philosophy.

The point is important: can we have any knowledge of answers to metaphysical questions? We can argue 'yes' either because we think that answers can be established on the basis of experience; or because we reject Hume's view, and want to defend the possibility of **synthetic** a priori knowledge. The debate whether metaphysics is completely speculative is, in part, the debate between **rationalism** and **empiricism** discussed in Unit 1.1 REASON AND EXPERIENCE.

Verification

In the 1930s, a school of philosophy arose called logical positivism, concerned with the foundations and possibility of knowledge. It developed a criterion for meaningful statements, called the principle of verification, that enabled it to reject as nonsense many traditional philosophical debates.

On A.J. Ayer's version, the principle of verification states that a statement has meaning only if it is either **analytic** or empirically verifiable. An analytic statement is true (or false) just in virtue of the meanings of the words. For instance, 'a bachelor is an unmarried man' is analytically true, while 'a square has three sides' is analytically false. A statement is empirically verifiable if empirical evidence would go towards establishing that the statement is true or false. For example, if I say, 'the moon is made of green cheese', we can check this by scientific investigation. If I say, 'the universe has 600 trillion planets', we can't check this by scientific investigation in practice, but we can do so *in principle*. We know how to show whether it is true or false, so it is 'verifiable' even though we can't actually verify it.

Why think these are the only two possibilities for meaning? Given that everyone accepts that empirical hypotheses are meaningful, the debate is, then, over a priori statements. Ayer seeks to show that all a priori truths are in fact analytic. And this argument is completed by showing that the purported statements of metaphysics, if not analytic, are literally meaningless.

Philosophy, then, doesn't give us knowledge of a reality that transcends the investigations of science. It is not a source of speculative truth. The function of philosophy is, instead, to bring to light the presuppositions of science and our everyday claims – in particular, to show what criteria are used to determine the truth of these claims.

> *Language, Truth and Logic*

> Explain and illustrate the principle of verification.

Refining the proposal

Some logical positivists originally wanted to say that verification must be conclusive, that a statement must be capable of being *proved* true or false. However, this is far too strong, as Ayer argues; empirical hypotheses are only *ever* more or less probable, never completely certain. So, he weakened the claim to the claim that verification requires that empirical evidence can raise or reduce the probability that a statement is true.

Because empirical meaning depends on empirical verification, all statements about what is *unobservable*, therefore, must be translatable into statements that can be observed and verified in order to be meaningful. This applies as much in science as anywhere. Claims about electrons, for instance, are translatable into what is observable in laboratory conditions. This, Ayer goes on to argue, must in fact be an *analytic* truth – that is, statements about electrons *mean* statements about what is observable in the laboratory, if they are to mean anything at all.

Statements about the past provide an interesting case. They are, now, impossible to prove; should they be taken to mean that there is something we can *now* experience that is relevant to their truth? This would be odd, since the core of the claim is that something *was* the case, not that it is now. So, Ayer argues that claims about the past are claims that certain observations *would have* been possible or occurred under certain conditions.

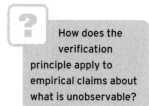

How does the verification principle apply to empirical claims about what is unobservable?

Getting rid of metaphysics

The verification principle entails that many debates in metaphysics become impossible, while others are resolved in favour of a form of empiricism.

A WORLD BEYOND SENSE EXPERIENCE

Many philosophical theories defend the idea of a reality beyond what we experience through the senses. Plato's theory of the Forms is an example, but so are religious beliefs about the soul and an afterlife. No scientific experiment can establish the existence of the Forms or of a soul that survives death. Claims that they exist can't be translated into claims about anything we can actually observe. Because these claims are also not analytic, they are, in fact, meaningless. Yet the idea of a transcendent world can be found in Augustine, Aquinas, Descartes, Spinoza, Leibniz, Kant, Hegel and Schopenhauer.

RELIGION

'God exists', and so all other talk of God also falls foul of the verification principle, claims Ayer. Despite the best attempts of the ONTOLOGICAL ARGUMENT, we cannot prove 'God exists' from a priori premises using deduction alone. So, 'God exists' is not analytically true. Therefore, to be meaningful, 'God exists' must be empirically verifiable. Ayer argues that it is not. If a statement is an empirical hypothesis, it predicts that our experience will be different depending on whether it is true or false. But 'God exists' makes no such predictions. So, it is meaningless.

See p. 129, and
THE STATUS OF THE
RELIGIOUS HYPOTHESIS,
p. 327.

ETHICS

The idea that objective ethical values 'exist' or that there can be ethical 'truths' is also ruled out as meaningless. If I say 'murder is wrong', this is not analytic, nor can any empirical investigation show this. We can show that murder causes grief and pain, or that it is often done out of anger. But we cannot demonstrate, in the same way, that it is *wrong*.

Ayer argued that ethical judgements express feelings: 'If I say to someone, "You acted wrongly in stealing that money" . . . I am simply evincing my moral disapproval of it. It is as if I had said, "You stole that money," in a peculiar tone of horror.' Moral judgements express our feelings of approval or disapproval. Feelings are not cognitions of value, and value does not exist independently of our feelings.

Language, Truth and Logic, p. 142. See EMOTIVISM, p. 236.

Discuss the implications of the verification principle.

Going further: Nietzsche on metaphysics

Nietzsche provides an argument against metaphysics very different from verificationism. He argues that metaphysical claims are, in the end, products of people's *values*. Nietzsche diagnoses the origin of the false belief in a world that transcends the world of the senses in a moral belief, namely that what is of value – truth, goodness, altruism, wisdom – cannot have its origins in its opposite: in this 'lowly, deceptive world' of the senses and desire. Values must therefore come from, and refer to, something imperishable, not this physical world. 'The metaphysicians' fundamental belief is *the belief in the opposition of values*'. Philosophers, then, have not been honest enough: they pretend that their opinions have been reached by 'cold, pure, divinely unhampered dialectic' when in fact they are seeking reasons to support their pre-existing commitment to 'a rarefied and abstract version of their heart's desire' (§ 5), namely that there is a transcendent world, and that good and bad, true and false are opposites.

Beyond Good and Evil, § 2

See MOTIVATIONAL ANALYSIS, p. 200.

Beyond the verification principle?

Responses to Ayer's claims about religion and ethics are discussed in RELIGIOUS LANGUAGE AND VERIFICATIONISM (p. 332) and EMOTIVISM (p. 200) respectively. Here we shall look at a more general objection to the verification principle, since it is the basis of his views on metaphysics as nonsense.

Some philosophers objected that the verification principle makes universal statements, such as 'All swans are white', meaningless – because although you could prove this statement false, no experience will prove it true (there might always be a swan out there somewhere that isn't white). This, though, is dealt with by Ayer's weakening of verification to only require experience to support or reduce the probability of a claim. It is rational to believe, not as a certainty but as a probability that grows with the range of experience we have, that what we haven't experienced will conform to what we have. It is irrational to expect a proof.

The main difficulty with the principle of verification is that according to it, the principle of verification itself is meaningless! The claim that 'a statement has meaning only if it is analytic or can be verified empirically' is not analytic and cannot be verified empirically. But if the principle of verification is meaningless, then it cannot be true. So, it does not give us any reason to believe that the claims of metaphysics are meaningless.

Ayer claims that the principle is intended as a *definition*, reflecting upon and clarifying our understanding of 'meaningful' uses of words. Since we do use the term 'meaningful' in a variety of ways, it is a definition just of 'literal meaning'. Ayer accepts that it isn't obviously correct, which is why he provides arguments in specific cases – ethics, religion, a priori knowledge – that support it.

But to this, any philosopher may respond by rejecting both his specific arguments and the verification principle. The verification principle is only as convincing as the arguments that are intended to demonstrate the consequences of its application. If we do not find those convincing, the principle provides no independent support. On its own, the principle does not show that metaphysics is speculative nonsense.

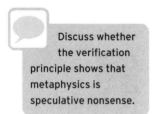

Discuss whether the verification principle shows that metaphysics is speculative nonsense.

Falsification

One response to the difficulties facing the verification principle is to replace it with a 'falsification' principle. Anthony Flew argued that for a claim to be genuinely meaningful, for it to be asserting something, it must be falsifiable. That is, there must be a test that could be used to establish that it is false. 'All swans are white' can easily be proven false; we only need find one non-white, for example black, swan. So, the claim is a genuine claim, even if it can't be shown to be true.

Flew developed his idea in relation to religious language. If 'God exists' is a real claim, then there should be some possible experience that would lead us to accept that it is false. Something should be able to 'count against it', for example the existence of evil. If you are not prepared to accept that anything *could* show that God doesn't exist, then saying 'God exists' states nothing at all. The test can be applied to metaphysical statements generally.

See THE PROBLEM OF EVIL, p. 320.

But a similar objection applies to this theory: is the view that a claim must be falsifiable to be meaningful itself empirically falsifiable? If it isn't, then it condemns itself. But we can say that it is falsifiable; if we find meaningful claims that are not falsifiable, then falsification is shown to be false. But then metaphysicians need only argue that metaphysical claims that cannot be falsified empirically are nevertheless meaningful in order to reject Flew's theory. Again, the matter can't be settled without an independent debate on the nature of metaphysical claims, which we discuss in the next section.

Is falsificationism an improvement on verificationism?

Key points • • •

- Metaphysical debates appear throughout philosophy. Therefore, the claim that metaphysics is speculative nonsense, made by Hume and logical positivism, has serious implications for philosophy as a whole.
- The principle of verification claims that only statements that are analytic or empirically verifiable are meaningful. Philosophy, therefore, cannot be an investigation of a reality beyond the reach of scientific investigation.
- Ayer argues that empirical verification does not require proof, but for evidence to be provided that makes an empirical claim more or less probable.
- Statements about what is unobservable must be translated into statements about what is observable. Statements about the past are meaningful because they are statements about what was observable.
- The verification principle undermines claims about a transcendent reality, and the existence of God and objective moral values.
- Nietzsche argues that metaphysical claims are motivated by philosophers' values, especially the view that values must originate in a transcendent reality.
- The verification principle fails its own test of meaning, being neither analytic nor empirically verifiable. Ayer argues that it is a definition, but it will be convincing only if his arguments for its consequences are convincing.
- Flew suggests that a claim must be falsifiable to be meaningful. But we can argue either that this claim is not falsifiable, or that it is shown to be false by metaphysical statements.

Metaphysics and epistemology

Can we have knowledge beyond sense experience?

One problem with thinking that religious, ethical and metaphysical language refers to things (God, values, Forms, etc.) is that we cannot see or experience these 'things' via the senses. Even if metaphysical statements are meaningful, even if they state facts, this doesn't mean that we can know whether they are true or false, unless we can test them through sense experience. In some cases, over time, metaphysical arguments may become reinterpreted empirically. Take SUBSTANCE DUALISM (p. 7): could the existence of a soul separable from the body be supported by accounts of reincarnation and out-of-body experiences? Or undermined by evidence that no neural events happen without being caused by other physical events? If so, then empiricists may allow that sense experience can establish whether there is a soul or not. But otherwise, how could metaphysical knowledge be gained? The debate about metaphysics turns towards the question of what capacities for knowledge human beings have – that is, the debate between empiricism and rationalism.

That debate was studied in depth in Unit 1.1 REASON AND EXPERIENCE, but further relates to the *entire* syllabus, and philosophy as a whole. Few, if any, of the arguments found in this book can be decided on the grounds of sense experience alone. We cannot, in one section, come to a conclusion regarding whether any of them work! So, we shall instead consider the *nature* of the arguments philosophers have made in metaphysics.

? What is the relation between the debate over metaphysical knowledge and the debate between rationalism and empiricism?

VARIETIES OF EXPERIENCE

Very few arguments have no contact at all with experience. Most attempt to *make sense* of experience. Wilfrid Sellars said that

'Philosophy and the Scientific Image of Man'

> The aim of philosophy, abstractly formulated, is to understand how things in the broadest possible sense of the term hang together in the broadest possible sense of the term. Under 'things in the broadest possible sense' I include such radically different items as not only 'cabbages and kings', but numbers and duties, possibilities and finger snaps, aesthetic experience and death.

Taking up one of these examples: is aesthetic experience a type of sense experience? Undoubtedly it involves the five senses, but these are not enough;

we need emotional responses as well. So can emotional responses – not on their own, perhaps, but when reflected upon and thought about – give us a kind of knowledge, for example that something is beautiful or elegant? Or is aesthetics *entirely* a matter of subjective taste, so there is no such thing as aesthetic *knowledge*?

Again, can emotions involved in moral experience give us knowledge of duties? Can experiences surrounding death, such as 'out-of-body' experiences, provide evidence for a soul or an afterlife? THE ARGUMENT FROM RELIGIOUS EXPERIENCE (p. 295) also claims to establish knowledge, namely of God's existence and nature.

Sense experience, then, is only one aspect of experience. To claim that there is knowledge beyond that given to us by the senses is, therefore, not necessary to argue that we have knowledge that cannot be tested against experience generally.

See How IS KNOWLEDGE OF MORAL TRUTH POSSIBLE?, p. 227.

Discuss and illustrate the varieties of human experience.

INFERENCE TO THE BEST EXPLANATION

The question of 'how things hang together' may start with the question of how our experiences of the world hang together. A strict empiricism may argue that only sense experience provides knowledge, while aesthetic, moral and religious experience are no more than subjective responses. They are fundamentally different in kind from sense experience.

Alternatively, an empiricist may allow that such forms of experience *may* represent how the world is, but, unlike sense experiences, first, we cannot show that they do (so we cannot claim to know, for example, that morality is objective); and second, we cannot tell which particular experiences are accurate and which are not (so we cannot claim to know, for example, that abortion is wrong). For both reasons, it is impossible for us to establish any knowledge in these areas.

But are either of these interpretations of human experience satisfactory? We can argue that, while we may not know *as much* or *as clearly* on the basis of aesthetic, moral or religious experience, there are *some* claims that we can know by reflecting on our experience using philosophical reasoning that appeals to coherence, plausibility, simplicity and so on. For example, moral cognitivism may argue that only the claim that there are objective moral values can make sense of THE POSSIBILITY OF MORAL PROGRESS AND MORAL MISTAKES (p. 246). THE ARGUMENT FROM DESIGN asks what best explains our experience of the world as apparently 'designed', and argues to the metaphysical claim that God exists.

What important epistemological differences are there between sense experience and other forms of experience?

See pp. 314 and 331.

See CONCEPTUAL SCHEMES AND THEIR PHILOSOPHICAL IMPLICATIONS II, p. 40.

? **Can the use of inference to the best explanation be used to defend metaphysical knowledge?**

And what is the best explanation of sense experience itself? Kant observes that sense experience presents us with a world of physical objects, existing independently of our experience in space and time. He asks how this is possible, and his answer defends a controversial metaphysical system.

These arguments assume or defend the view that *reasoning* can yield knowledge. Plato, Descartes and Kant argue that reasoning can do this on its own, and through a priori **deduction**. We have been considering the claim that the reasoning involved is inference to the best explanation. And we can argue either that reasoning by itself can establish what the best explanation is, or that the conclusions reached by reason must be tested against our experience generally before we can know whether they are sound. Occasionally, metaphysical claims may even yield empirical predictions that can, at least in theory, be tested scientifically.

At this point, empiricists may respond that unless we can use objective empirical tests, we cannot establish that any particular explanation is the *best* explanation. And so we cannot have knowledge beyond that given by sense experience.

Do all epistemological positions involve metaphysics?

A different defence of metaphysics argues that every theory of knowledge, even strict empiricism, involves metaphysical claims. So what must empiricism assume about sense experience that makes it metaphysical?

Sense experience informs us what particular physical objects exist. But it cannot establish *what* exists when a physical object exists, nor can it give a complete account of *how* we know about physical objects. The common-sense position is that physical objects exist independently of our experience in space and time. But we can argue that this is a metaphysical claim that cannot be shown to be true on the basis of sense experience alone, and three very stringent empiricists – Berkeley, Hume and Ayer – all question it.

So just on the basis of sense experience, what can we say about the existence of physical objects? Berkeley argues for idealism, Ayer for PHENOMENALISM (p. 150), while Hume adopts his MITIGATED SCEPTICISM (p. 149). However, all three responses appear to be committed to a very controversial, and metaphysical, view of sense experience itself, namely that sense experiences exist as mental 'things', as **sense-data**. Defending the possibility of sense-data against doubts about their coherence or existence involves empiricism in a metaphysical debate.

See p. 206.

Furthermore, there will be an issue of how these claims about sense experience fit in with the claims *of* sense experience. Scientific investigation indicates a close connection between the brain and sense experience. But the issue of how the brain gives rise to experience appears, at present at least, to be a metaphysical question.

We can argue, therefore, that it is inevitable that reflecting on even just our sense experience leads to metaphysical questions and the use of reasoning that cannot be tested directly by sense experience. So, metaphysics is essential to intellectual enquiry.

But empiricism may respond that all that we have demonstrated is that we are unable to form a complete or coherent account of the world. These debates about the nature of sense experience simply show that we cannot know what sense experience itself is. The claim that we can only know what sense experience reveals is not committed to any form of metaphysics; as soon as metaphysics begins, it refuses to defend any claim at all.

> Discuss the claim that metaphysics is unavoidable, and therefore needs no special defence.

Key points • • •

- Even if metaphysical statements are meaningful, can we have knowledge of their truth? If they are not discovered through sense experience, how are they known?
- Many metaphysical statements arise in trying to make sense of experience, in seeing 'how things hang together'.
- Human beings have many forms of experience, not just sense experience, but aesthetic, moral and religious, all of which involve our emotions. Can these give us metaphysical knowledge?
- Strict empiricists may argue that these other forms of experience involve our responses to the world, not representations of how the world is. Even if they do represent the world, we cannot know which experiences are **veridical**.
- We can respond that the best explanation of these experiences leads to the view that they do give us knowledge. Similarly, we can argue that the best explanation of sense experience involves metaphysical claims.
- We can also argue that every theory of what we know involves some metaphysical claims regarding the ontological status of physical objects and/or sense-data.
- Empiricists can respond that as soon as an explanation of experience reaches a metaphysical claim, we must recognise that our knowledge runs out.

IV. OBJECTIVE KNOWLEDGE

Is objective and absolute knowledge possible?

The syllabus refers to the possibility of 'objective and absolute knowledge'. 'Objective' and 'absolute' are intended as synonyms, contrasting with 'relative'. The idea of 'objective and absolute' knowledge (from now on, 'objectivism') is the idea of knowledge that is not conditional or qualified. In particular, it is knowledge that is not relative to a system of beliefs, practices or concepts.

On MORAL RELATIVISM, see p. 233.

Relativism about values and religion is commonly defended. But we should not generalise; even if there is no objective knowledge of morality, this does not mean that there is no objective knowledge *at all*. Take, for example, the claim that 'Mount Everest is the highest mountain on Earth'. Is this truth relative to cultures? If someone belonging to a culture that had never heard of Mount Everest claimed that Mont Blanc was the highest mountain on Earth, would they be mistaken? To argue that objectivism is mistaken, you have to show that even scientific knowledge can't be objective.

See IS RELATIVISM SCEPTICISM IN DISGUISE?, p. 208.

It is important to note the difference between relativism and scepticism. Scepticism denies there is knowledge; relativism claims that there is knowledge – that is, that there are beliefs that can rightly be said to be true and known to be true – but that knowledge is relative to a society, theory or conceptual scheme. The standard argument for relativism is that societies and theories can disagree over knowledge claims without there being any way in which the disagreement can be resolved in favour of one or the other.

Define objectivism, relativism and scepticism.

Plato's objectivism

Plato argues that knowledge of 'particular things' gained through the senses cannot be objective and absolute. Particular things will always be both x – have some property, such as beauty or largeness – and not-x, either at different times, or to different observers, or in different contexts. They are what they are (beautiful, large, etc.) only *relatively* and *transiently*, so there cannot be *knowledge* of them. Knowledge needs more *permanence* and *certainty*.

Part of Plato's argument is that knowledge cannot be mistaken. However, if you believe of anything that it can change, that it is one way rather than another – that it is beautiful rather than ugly, say – you could be wrong, because it is possible for it to be either. It is only contingently beautiful. Everything that we experience with our senses is **contingent**; it can exist or not, it can have this property or not, and it will change from one state to another. But knowledge, says Plato, cannot change (though beliefs can).

However, this does not mean that there is no objective and absolute knowledge. There is; we can have such knowledge of the Forms. In contrast to particular beautiful things, the Form of beauty is beautiful under all conditions, to all observers, at all times. The Form of beauty is pure beauty; it alone is not both beautiful and not beautiful.

Plato argues that if we consider the many things that are x, we shall form beliefs about them, but cannot acquire knowledge; whereas if we consider the unchanging Form of x, we acquire knowledge and understanding. As science investigates the world through sense experience, Plato would claim science cannot produce knowledge, but only belief.

Plato is making two claims: that we can have knowledge of the Forms, and that we cannot have knowledge of particular things. We shall discuss only the second claim.

Knowledge and contingency

Plato might be right that *knowledge* cannot change (*it* can't go from truth to falsehood), but that doesn't mean the *object* of knowledge can't change. For example, I can know (it seems) that a particular object of sense experience – this book – has a particular property; for example, it is a certain size, *at a particular time*, even though its size can change. Once we understand the relation between knowledge and time correctly, we can see that knowledge doesn't change even if *what it is knowledge of* changes. 'Mount Everest is the tallest mountain on Earth' – this was not always true, but it is true now – so it is *always* true that 'Mount Everest was the tallest mountain on Earth in 2009'.

What about his idea that knowledge must be certain? Hume argues that most of our beliefs about matters of fact can never be certain, but only probable. Our most certain empirical beliefs are about what we ourselves have experienced. However, past experience can give me '*direct* and *certain* information of those precise objects only, and that precise period of time, which feel under its cognizance'. Much of what we think we know, for example about Mount Everest, goes beyond personal experience. This presents two challenges to objectivism about scientific knowledge.

First, how can we infer from what we have experienced to what we haven't

Outline Plato's argument that we cannot have objective and absolute knowledge of particular things.

See THE THEORY OF THE FORMS, p. 58, and EPISTEMOLOGICAL IMPLICATIONS OF THE THEORY OF THE FORMS, p. 66.

See PROBABILITY AND BELIEF, p. 32.

An Enquiry Concerning Human Understanding, p. 114

See THE SCOPE OF
MATTERS OF FACT,
p. 27.

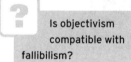

Why think that
much empirical
knowledge is not
certain?

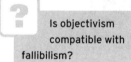

Is objectivism
compatible with
fallibilism?

experienced? We have to assume, says Hume, that the two are similar; for example, that the future will be like the past, that parts of the world we haven't experienced operate the same way as parts we have. But, of course, things may not be the same, or they may change. But this poses a particular problem for science, which claims to discover *universal laws* of nature. We can never establish these with certainty, because we can only show, at best, that they apply to what we have experienced. Any claim about what we haven't experienced can only have a better or worse degree of probability.

Second, we may have made a mistake even about what we have experienced. Scientific progress shows that even what people believe to be obviously true at one point in time may turn out to be false. For example, the Sun does not move around the Earth. So is it not possible that anything we are currently certain of could in the future be shown to be false? Furthermore, as so much of our knowledge depends on testimony – what other people tell us – we also have to assume that people are generally reliable. But people are fallible, and sometimes deliberately deceptive; important mistakes in experiments have been made. Again, at best, we can only hold our beliefs as probably true.

However, none of this shows that we don't have objective scientific knowledge *unless* we assume, with Plato, that knowledge must be certain. This assumption is INFALLIBILISM (p. 172), which we rejected in favour of the view that knowledge only requires good grounds. To argue that our beliefs are fallible is neither to show that they don't amount to knowledge nor to show that knowledge is relative. What it does show is that no claim is established finally, once and for all, and that those claims which are overturned in the future, we cannot be said to know now. Yet we still have very good reason to believe that certain claims will not be overturned, for example the claim that stars are burning balls of gas or that water is H_2O. The evidence is so decisive that what could overturn these claims is simply unimaginable to us now.

Conceptual schemes and objective knowledge

Objective knowledge, we can argue, should be knowledge of how things (really) are. All knowledge uses concepts – 'mountain', 'highest', 'electron', 'table' and so on. Concepts only identify 'how things are' if there is a correlation between reality and the set of concepts. A claim can amount to objective knowledge only if the concepts it uses are concepts that correspond to reality. Claims employing concepts that don't correspond to reality, such as 'witch', can't give us knowledge because the concept has no application. So, objective knowledge is possible only if we have the concepts that correspond to how reality is.

We can, then, argue that it is impossible to claim that there is a *single* set of concepts that describes reality 'as it is', and better than any other set of concepts, or that our concepts are part of such a perfect set. Therefore, the knowledge we have is relative to our conceptual scheme, and not objective.

These ideas can be illustrated by the idea of scientific progress, as described by relativism. The concepts science has employed have changed, with old concepts being abandoned and new ways of thinking being developed. For example, for around 100 years from 1667, there was a theory that aimed to explain how and why things burn in terms of an element called 'phlogiston'. But it was shown that there is no such thing as phlogiston, and burning actually involves (the newly discovered element) oxygen. Or again, the difference between living and non-living things was explained in terms of a 'vital force'. The rise of modern biological theory in the mid-nineteenth century showed that there is no 'vital force'. Even concepts of space and time have changed, from Newton's theory that they are 'absolute' to Einstein's theory that they are 'relative'. So, concepts that were once central become abandoned or reinterpreted. How, then, can we think that the set of concepts we now use identify how reality 'really' is?

We can develop the argument. Conceptual schemes are schemes of classification. Concepts identify similarities and differences. But while some schemes of classification can seem more natural or useful or simple, these values are ours, and are not given to us by reality itself. So how can we identify the 'true' structure of reality? Prior to classification, we cannot speak of reality as *itself* composed of different kinds of things. Unless there is a conceptual scheme that we must have, that 'carves nature at the joints', then we cannot claim that our knowledge is 'objective'. It is relative to our conceptual scheme, and this is, in an important sense, optional. First, it can change, so that we cease to believe in a classification we used previously. Second, it depends on our particular types of sense experience. Creatures with different forms of perception could form different concepts to describe reality without in any way being mistaken. No *one* set of concepts and theories can be said to classify reality absolutely.

But scientific progress can also be understood in a way that undermines this argument. As science develops, it creates concepts and theories that come closer and closer to identifying how reality is 'in itself'. It approaches an 'absolute conception of the world'. We discover that certain concepts, such as phlogiston and vital force, fail to make sense of the world, and we replace them with *better* concepts. And we also develop concepts that depend less and less on our

See also CONCEPTUAL SCHEMES AND THEIR PHILOSOPHICAL IMPLICATIONS, p. 21.

How does the argument from conceptual schemes undermine the idea of objective knowledge?

particular sensory abilities, such as the concepts of sub-atomic physics. Concepts of electrons, leptons and so on, we can argue, pick out the *fundamental* structure of reality, and so they are not optional in any true description of the world. They are not specifically related to vision, touch, hearing and so on. Our knowledge is becoming more and more objective.

? **Does scientific progress support or challenge relativism?**

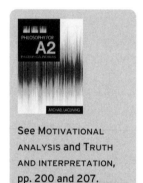

See **Motivational analysis** and **Truth and interpretation**, pp. 200 and 207.

Beyond Good and Evil, § 192

Going further: Nietzsche's perspectivism

Nietzsche argues that our beliefs are based upon our most fundamental values. He uses the term 'perspective' to capture the idea of a set of beliefs grounded on values. Different perspectives are defined by different *values*; differences in belief are not themselves enough. Two people with different religious beliefs, for instance, may occupy the same perspective if their beliefs reflect the same underlying set of values.

This applies even to sense perception, which we might expect to be *most* responsive to how the world is. First, we find it easier, argues Nietzsche, to reproduce an image we are familiar with than to remember what is new and different in our sense impression. We are averse to new things, and so already our experience of the world is dominated by an emotion. Familiar emotions – what we fear or love – will affect what we see. Second, we cannot take in everything – we do not see every leaf on a tree, but, out of our visual experience, create for ourselves an image of something approximating the tree. We do the same for everything we experience; our emotions affect this process. Third, whenever a new idea or experience arises, people become over-excited, impatient to develop or experience it. Over time, we become more cautious, see it more for what it is.

Philosophy has tended to defend objectivism and deny perspective. Many philosophers have thought that we can achieve 'unconditional' truth and represent the world as it is independent of our perspective, our values. But this is a distortion, itself based on certain values. Nietzsche's view is that perspective cannot be eliminated – that is, values cannot cease to guide our knowledge, and that the attempt to eliminate our perspective completely is misguided.

However, he argues that some perspectives are less distorting than others. First, a perspective may be aware that it is a perspective. Becoming aware of the perspectival nature of knowledge is itself an improvement in knowledge. Second, we can find a less perspectival perspective by assembling many different perspectives: 'perspectival "knowing" [is] the *only* kind of "knowing"; and the *more* feelings about a matter which we allow to come to expression, the *more* eyes, different eyes through which we are able to view this same matter, the more complete our "conception" of it, our "objectivity", will be'. We need to be flexible, not trapped by one set of values or the illusion of value-free knowing, but able to move from one valuational perspective to another, and, from these many points of view, assemble our picture of the world.

On the Genealogy of Morals, III § 12

Explain Nietzsche's argument against objectivism.

Key points • • •

- 'Objective and absolute' knowledge is knowledge that is not conditional, qualified or relative to a system of beliefs.
- Relativism argues there is knowledge (so it is not scepticism), but that it is relative to a society, theory or conceptual scheme.
- Plato argues that because particular things have their properties relatively, transiently and contingently, we cannot have knowledge of them. Knowledge requires permanence and certainty (we have knowledge of the Forms).
- We can object that even if knowledge can't change, we can have knowledge of things that do change, by relating knowledge to a particular time.
- Hume argues that (most) empirical knowledge is not certain. We must rely on testimony, which could be false, and we must assume that what we have not experienced is similar to what we have experienced.
- However, objectivism can accept that our knowledge is fallible.
- We can argue that only concepts that correspond to reality can give objective knowledge. However, there is no one set of concepts that we can have that describes reality 'as it is'.
- Scientific progress shows that central concepts have been abandoned or reinterpreted. But objectivism can reply that this is because we are developing more accurate concepts, so our knowledge is becoming more objective.
- Nietzsche argues that our beliefs and even our sense experience are influenced by our values. There is no value-free knowledge. Objectivity is approached by being able to adopt many perspectives.

Do different perspectives have their own internal criteria as the final court of appeal?

The problem of justification

Objectivism defends the view that we can judge that one conceptual scheme is – absolutely speaking – better than another. We can object that while this may be possible sometimes, it is not always so. One reason for this is that what counts as 'better' is itself relative to each conceptual scheme.

Different societies have disagreed about the nature of evidence and justification. Beliefs in one society are judged 'reasonable', while the same belief (or something very similar) in another is judged 'unreasonable' (devils, alchemy, magic, the divine right of kings). The relativist can argue that these disagreements don't show that one society is irrational, or less intelligent, or simply being dogmatic. Instead, they show that standards for judging when a belief counts as justified are relative.

This doesn't show that *truth* is relative to society. However, if knowledge is justified true belief, it shows that knowledge is relative, because a true belief in one society may count as justified while in another it does not. So even if truth is objective, there is no single objective standard for knowledge.

Objectivism can reply that standards of justification cannot vary greatly; there are universal requirements of reason, such as non-contradiction, coherence, forms of rational inference and so on. But relativism can respond that this will not secure objectivism. For instance, there is no universal standard for whether two beliefs are coherent; it depends on what else is believed – and likewise for forms of inference. For example, until 200 years ago everyone believed that geometry had to accept the laws of Euclid. Anything else was incoherent. But mathematicians have since shown this belief is false. Not only is non-Euclidean geometry coherent, it even describes what space is actually like under certain conditions!

'If there is objective knowledge, there must be objective standards for justification.' Discuss.

Going further: justification and language games

A variation on this argument, inspired by ideas from Wittgenstein, contends that standards of justification are relative to particular social *practices*. Different ways of relating to the world – in aesthetics, morality, religion, science, interpersonal relations, the self – are each coherent in their own way. We make a mistake if we think that all human intellectual activity must be assessed by the standards of physical science. Each area of endeavour is a distinct 'language game'. The rules for what counts as a recognised form of reasoning can differ, just as different games have different rules for moves within the game.

This argument is usually based on Wittgenstein's ideas about how language gets its meaning. If we use the scientific model, we may think that the basic form of language is asserting, on the basis of sense experience, that certain things exist and attributing properties to those things. Words get their meaning by referring to and describing objects. But this is much too simple. Meaning is a matter of the rules that govern how words are *used*. And these rules differ from one part of language to another.

Appreciating this requires a distinction between *surface grammar* and *depth grammar*: words or sentences that in one context describe *objects* may be similar on the surface to ones in another context that do nothing of the sort; for example, 'the glass is full of water', 'his mind is full of evil thoughts', 'the world is full of beauty'. To understand a particular 'piece' of language, one must look at how the language is used, as meaning is not given by the form of words alone.

Together with these different rules for how to use words go different standards for counts as 'rational' or 'justified' within the game. No language game can be assessed by standards of justification that belong to a different language game. So, for instance, Wittgenstein argued that religious belief cannot be criticised as 'highly improbable' on scientific grounds.

However, relativists who appeal to Wittgenstein sometimes do not notice that he defended his view by arguing that many of these different language games are **non-cognitive**. They may be justified as *ways of living*, but they do *not* ground distinct types of knowledge. The relativist must defend the view that different language games can be **cognitive**, but still have different rules for justification.

See RELIGION AS A FORM OF LIFE, p. 336.

Discuss the Wittgensteinian defence of relativism.

Can we make absolute judgements regarding alternative belief systems?

Can we go beyond relativism about justification to relativism about truth? Some ancient cultures believed that stars are pinpricks in the fabric of heaven, letting light through from beyond. Let us grant that their belief was, even according to the best standards of justification, justified. Is there any sense in which we can say that this belief was 'true for them'? To say it was 'true for them' must be more than simply to say that they believed it. We all agree they believed it, and to believe something is to believe that it is true. But to believe that some proposition is true is not the same as the proposition being true. If we say that *all* beliefs are true 'for' the person who believes them, this entails that there can be no false beliefs!

See THE DUAL-COMPONENT THEORY OF BELIEF, p. 160.

If we say that it was true, for those ancient cultures, that stars were pinpricks in the fabric of heaven, and it is true for us now that stars are burning balls of gas, the question arises how both of these claims about stars can be true. Did stars miraculously change from being holes in cloth to being giant balls of gas? It looks as though the only coherent response from relativism on this question is to argue that we cannot ask 'what are stars (really)?'; we can only ask 'what do we think stars are?'. But this is paradoxical, because each culture comes up with its account of stars by asking 'what are stars (really)?'!

When two cultures, then, give differing *empirical* accounts of some part of the world, the two accounts are in competition, and at most one can be right. Because they are empirical, the criteria for their truth are *not* internal to each belief system. It seems hard to resist the claim that the modern theory of stars is closer to the truth than the ancient theory.

We discussed CONCEPTUAL SCHEMES AND OBJECTIVE KNOWLEDGE on p. 198.

However, we can respond that this argument works only if both cultures offer empirical accounts *and* we can translate the claims of one conceptual scheme into the claims of another (for example, both are theories of *stars*).

Where one account is empirical and the other is, say, religious, or when both are religious, then the issue is far more complex. First, are both accounts claiming a form of knowledge, or is (at least) one account non-cognitive? (Does evolution contradict the account of creation in Genesis?) Second, if they are both cognitive, are their claims in contradiction or can both be true? Third, if their claims are in contradiction, does the contradiction arise from the way the claims are presented (e.g. within certain conceptual schemes)? If so, can the contradiction be removed by interpreting the claims differently? An example here might be religious pluralism; God is so beyond human concepts that each religion can be understood as a *partial* grasp of God's nature.

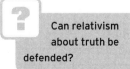

Can relativism about truth be defended?

If we have contradictory cognitive claims that cannot be resolved by rational means that both cultures agree upon, then we have relativism about knowledge.

Kuhn on scientific revolutions

In *The Structure of Scientific Revolutions*, Thomas Kuhn defends relativism about scientific knowledge. Not only standards of justification, but claims about the truth, are relative, because science does not progress by getting closer to the *right* set of concepts that matches the nature of reality.

Normal science proceeds by working within a 'paradigm', which includes a conceptual scheme, shared beliefs about theories, methodology, what counts as evidence or argument, and shared values and techniques. The development of new ideas is assessed in relation to this paradigm. However, the paradigm runs into 'anomalies' – problems that can't be solved or incorporated within the paradigm. As the number of these anomalies grows, this leads to a sense of crisis. A revolution occurs when a new paradigm is proposed and developed, breaking the old ways of thinking and, in doing so, solving a number of the anomalies. Classic examples include developments in molecular chemistry around 1800, the replacement of Newtonian physics with Einsteinian physics and the shift from Rutherford's realism about sub-atomic particles to the Copenhagen interpretation of Bohr.

Kuhn argues that, even though the new paradigm solves many anomalies of the old, we cannot compare paradigms in such a way as to judge that one is correct while another is wrong. There is no way of saying that something (e.g. genes, electrons) is 'part of reality', without implicitly relying on a particular paradigm. Three considerations support this argument.

First, we may think that a theory (paradigm) can be evaluated as true or false, or at least better or worse, by comparing its claims with evidence derived from observation. But there is no 'theory-neutral' way of describing the world that we can use to compare and judge between two paradigms. How scientists describe what they observe already depends on one paradigm or another.

Second, the main concepts of a paradigm take their meaning in relation to the paradigm as a whole. A different paradigm, even if it uses the same term, interprets the concept differently, because it plays a new and different role. They are therefore talking about different things. As a result, we cannot compare their claims to say that one is more 'correct' or 'true' than another, as they could both be correct *in their own terms*. An objective judgement needs to find neutral terms – but these don't exist.

For discussions of relativism, see CONSERVATISM, p. 171, (moral) RELATIVISM, p. 233, MIRACLES AND THE COMPETING TRUTH CLAIMS OF DIFFERENT RELIGIONS, p. 323, RELIGION AS A 'FORM OF LIFE', p. 335, and WHAT IS MEANT BY 'RELIGION'? CAN SOCIAL SCIENCE 'EXPLAIN AWAY' RELIGION?, p. 339.

Explain and
illustrate why
Kuhn's theory of
scientific progress
leads to relativism.

Third, what counts as evidence and justification also depends on the paradigm. There are no paradigm-independent rules for what is good evidence. And so again, we can't compare two paradigms to say that one fits better with the 'evidence' than the other.

Objectivism in science

Objectivists can object to Kuhn's relativism by saying that all scientists are persuaded by the new paradigm to abandon the old. There must be *reasons* for this, in particular the power of the new paradigm to resolve the anomalies of the old. Isn't this an objective measure of improvement?

The Logic of Scientific Discovery

Karl Popper argued that scientific theories make predictions which we can test through experiment against experience. If the prediction is shown to be false, then the theory is falsified, and a different theory must be developed. So, we can argue that one theory is better than another if it makes more true predictions.

But the kinds of high-level theories that form part of a paradigm are never simply 'falsified' through a single test. They are falsified slowly, over time, by failing to provide adequate explanations of observations. And Kuhn argues that the new paradigm rarely manages to carry over all the *successes* of the old. The shift to the new paradigm brings costs as well as benefits, and some phenomena that were explained become no longer explicable. This is now called 'Kuhn-loss'. Kuhn-loss shows that while a new paradigm may fill a gap, it will be subject to its own gaps.

Objectivists can nevertheless argue that Kuhn's theory is inadequate. First, even with Kuhn-loss, we can make meaningful comparisons between theories in terms of their overall capacity to solve problems. This is an absolute standard of progress. Second, if we do not assume that scientific theories are getting closer to the (objective) truth, we cannot explain the success of science. Technology has advanced considerably, and the best explanation for this is that the scientific theories that underpin technology are more accurate than before.

Kuhn agrees that there is progress, including the solving of problems, but he argues that the idea that we are getting 'closer to the truth' makes no sense. Science responds to the challenges it faces at any particular time; this does not mean that there is an 'ultimate goal' towards which it is moving.

As we saw, one reason for his view is that concepts have their meaning within a paradigm, so we cannot say that one concept (or interpretation of a concept) is more true than another. But philosophers have challenged this claim. Meaning is not given just by use, but also by *reference*. We can compare two theories of molecules or space by looking at the nature of molecules or space. Both theories are talking about the same thing, because in both theories the terms were developed in response to particular experiences. There is a causal chain from molecules to the concept 'molecule' in both theories, and this fixes *what* the concept is a concept of. Kuhn must accept this view when talking about improvements of a theory *within* a paradigm; we should also accept it when talking about how one paradigm solves the anomalies of another.

Have there, in fact, been any Kuhnian revolutions? Or have changes in scientific theory at any one time involved considerable continuity and overlap in beliefs about methodology, evidence, values and technique? If there have been no Kuhnian revolutions, then scientific theories exhibit enough similarity for us to compare them and come to an absolute judgement on which are better.

> [?]
>
> Can there be objective judgements about scientific theories, or does each paradigm have its own particular standards?

Key points • • •

- Relativism can argue that different societies have considered different beliefs reasonable or unreasonable, because they have different accounts of evidence and justification. Objectivism responds that reason is universal, so standards can't vary greatly.
- One form of relativism, inspired by Wittgenstein, argues that each 'language game' has its own rules for legitimate reasoning. It is a mistake to judge reasoning in one language game by the standards of another.
- However, Wittgenstein himself concluded that many such language games were, in fact, non-cognitive. We can therefore question whether his views support relativism about *knowledge*.
- The view that contradictory claims are each 'true for' the culture that makes them is difficult to make coherent. To believe that a proposition is true is not the same as the proposition being true.
- However, this objection to relativism works only when both cultures make empirical claims using concepts that can be translated.
- Kuhn argues that revolutions in science replace one paradigm by another. Each has its own conceptual scheme and standards for evidence, so the two paradigms cannot be compared so as to judge one 'closer to the truth'.
- We can object that only the idea that science is getting closer to the truth

can explain technological success, and that concepts can be translated between paradigms as they gain their meaning by what they refer to.

The implications of relativism

Is relativism scepticism in disguise?

On p. 196, we distinguished between relativism and scepticism. Scepticism is the claim that our usual justifications are inadequate for knowledge, so we do not have the knowledge we think we have. Relativism claims that our justifications are local to our culture, belief system or paradigm, and so there is no unconditional or universal standard of justification. A stronger form of relativism claims that truth itself is relative to a conceptual scheme, as no one set of concepts can be said to be represent reality 'as it really is'.

This understanding of conceptual schemes can suggest the idea that concepts somehow 'come between' us and the world 'as it is in itself'. No set of concepts can present reality without imposing something on it. Since we cannot get 'beyond' our concepts, scepticism argues, we cannot tell whether they represent reality more or less accurately.

The relativist can respond that in drawing the sceptical conclusion, we make an incoherent assumption. There is nothing we can *mean* by talking of 'how reality is' independent of the application of our concepts. There is no sense to the idea of 'comparing' how reality is with how our concepts represent it. Such a comparison is not simply impossible for us – as though that were some epistemological failing of ours; it is simply incoherent. (This, relativism argues, is why objectivism cannot be true.)

However, a sceptical conclusion may follow from the arguments regarding justification. If justification is relative, then how can we have any confidence that our standards of justification help us get at the truth? We see from looking at other belief systems that beliefs can be justified without being true or even close to the truth, as we understand it. What confidence can we have that our justified beliefs are any better?

But relativism can point out that the sceptic harbours an idealised model of justification in which justification in itself can secure truth. Our models of justification are not lacking, for there is no further account of how they can be improved. But this gap between justification and truth doesn't demonstrate scepticism, only fallibilism. We should lack confidence in our standards of

There is a similarity here to how REPRESENTATIVE REALISM understands sense experience, p. 205.

See INFALLIBILISM, p. 172.

justification only if we can show that they are inadequate for knowledge. But the relativist argues that knowledge is perfectly possible, understood as relative to a belief system.

Can relativism resist becoming scepticism?

Do relativism and contingency invite inertia in certain fields of human activity?

Whether relativism is true or not, we can ask whether the *belief* that it is true impacts negatively on intellectual enquiry – in particular, enquiry into how the world is. First, we should note again the distinction between relativism and contingency first discussed in KNOWLEDGE AND CONTINGENCY (p. 197). The idea of contingency is captured by Hume's observation that empirical knowledge can be held only with a degree of probability, not complete certainty; and by the complementary idea of fallibility. Contingency is compatible with objectivism, though not with arrogance.

We may argue that as long as they recognise progress in some meaningful sense, neither relativism nor contingency invites inertia. So, it is important to repeat that Kuhn argued that there is meaningful scientific progress, but that progress involves the capacity to solve problems, not getting closer to the truth. Does giving up the ideal of 'knowing the truth' undermine the motivation to enquire about the world? Not if that motivation is reaffirmed when, instead of looking forward, we look backward and see how far we have come, whether we measure this distance by what we can explain, or predict, or control through technology, or how coherent and wide-ranging our theories are, or by what we know now but didn't before.

While this answer is available for empirical theories, it is not so easily given in other areas of intellectual endeavour in which we cannot clearly identify 'progress' over time. If the truth about morality or metaphysics or religion is relative, if philosophy itself has made no 'progress' since Plato, we may wonder what the point of thinking about such questions really is.

Of course, this depends on what we think we are doing when engaging in this process of intellectual enquiry. Any student of philosophy who thinks part-time study over two years will solve the puzzles of 2,500 years will be disappointed. But relativism and contingency need not lead to inertia. First, if the truth is relative to cultural belief systems, there remains the question 'what do we believe?'. Cultures are highly complex, and not *transparent* to themselves. Philosophical enquiry is, then, a process of cultural self-understanding. Second,

Hume's MITIGATED SCEPTICISM (p. 149) defends knowledge about matters of fact, but not metaphysics.

for each individual there is still the matter of what to believe personally. Whatever the truth of the matter turns out to be, one can discover a lot about *oneself* in the attempt to discover as honestly as possible what one truly thinks about the world.

? Does either relativism or contingency invite intellectual inertia?

Key points • • •

- Scepticism can use relativism's view of conceptual schemes to argue that we cannot know whether our concepts represent the world as it really is. Relativism replies that this idea of comparing a conceptual scheme with reality is incoherent.
- Scepticism can use relativism's view of justification to undermine confidence that our practices of justification will yield the truth. Relativism can reply that scepticism is assuming infallibilism about knowledge.
- We may think that the attack, by relativism and contingency, on certainty and the ideal of knowing the objective truth would undermine the motivation to discover what the world is like. However, neither needs to deny that progress in knowledge is possible, provided this is not interpreted as 'coming closer to the truth'.
- In areas of intellectual enquiry that don't clearly show progress, we may argue that even if relativism is true, philosophy is still worthwhile as a form of self- and cultural understanding.

MORAL PHILOSOPHY

4

In this chapter, we look at two central debates in moral philosophy. The first debate concerns the question of whether there is objective moral truth. We shall look at three theories that defend the claim that there is moral truth; and then at three theories that deny this. We shall discuss challenges that each position faces. The second debate relates to deciding what the right thing to do is. We shall look at three theories, and then discuss how these theories approach a range of practical ethical issues. Students should be able to argue for and against the different positions in the two debates.

SYLLABUS CHECKLIST

The AQA A2 syllabus for this chapter is as follows:

Moral truth

✓ Moral truth as God-independent transcendent truth, the analogy with mathematical truths, the belief in Platonic forms as the archetypal example of this view, moral elitism, moral knowledge and of weakness of will; moral truth as based on natural facts, for example the view that what is morally desirable is to be understood in terms of what is in fact desired, the open question argument and the naturalistic fallacy; moral truth as based on relational properties which provide reasons for action; the analogy with secondary properties.

✓ Issues relating to the above views: the problem of how knowledge of moral truth is possible; the possibility of agreement over moral truth; the extent to which such truths can motivate or justify action.

The denial of moral truth

✓ Moral judgements as social conventions relative to a given social group, the distinction between descriptive and normative relativism; moral judgements as serving a non-descriptive function, either emotivism *or* prescriptivism.

✓ Issues relating to the above views: the possibility of judging the abhorrent practices of other cultures or individuals; the possibility of moral progress and moral mistakes; the extent to which we can value what we like.

Moral decisions

✓ The extent to which an action maximises happiness as the sole criterion by which its value can be judged, consideration of act, rule and preference utilitarianism. The strengths and weaknesses of utilitarian positions.

✓ The view that moral rights, duties and principles which are not based on consequences are required in order to make ethical decisions, and the strengths and weaknesses of these positions. Kant's attempt to provide a rational grounding for a deontological ethics, the importance of motivation in making moral decisions.

✓ Practical wisdom as the capacity to make informed, rational judgements without recourse to a formal decision procedure such as the hedonic calculus or the Categorical Imperative. The strengths and weaknesses of these positions.

✓   The above views should be discussed in relation to at least one practical ethical problem, for example the value of life: abortion, euthanasia; our treatment of the natural environment, non-human animals, and those in poverty, etc.

I. MORAL TRUTH

Moral cognitivism

Cognitivism is the view that we can have moral *knowledge*. The cognitivist believes that statements like 'Euthanasia is not wrong' are expressions of beliefs, which can be true or false. 'Non-cognitivists' argue that there is no moral knowledge, because there is no objective moral truth. One form of cognitivism, moral realism, claims that good and bad are properties of situations and people; right and wrong are properties of actions. Just as people can be 5 feet tall or run fast, they can be morally good or bad. Just as actions can be done in 10 minutes or done from greed, they can be right or wrong. These moral properties are a genuine part of the world. Whether moral judgements are true or false depends on how the world is, on what properties an action, person or situation actually has.

Cognitivists argue that our experience of morality suggests that there are moral truths. First, we think we can make mistakes. Children frequently do, and have to be taught what is right and wrong. If there were no facts about moral right and wrong, it wouldn't be possible to make mistakes. Second, morality feels like a demand from 'outside' us. We feel answerable to a standard of behaviour that is independent of what we want or feel. Morality isn't determined by what we think about it. Third, many people believe in moral progress. But how is this possible, unless some views about morality are better than others? And how is *that* possible unless there are facts about morality?

But if there are truths about morality, what kind of truths are they? Moral truths seem to be quite different from empirical truths, which we can discover using our senses. In the discussion that follows, we look at three theories. The first, that moral truth is transcendent (p. 214), emphasises the difference between moral and empirical truth; the second, that moral truths are based on

> What is moral cognitivism? In what ways does our experience of morality support it?

natural facts (p. 219), emphasises the close relationship between morality and some empirical truths about human beings; the third, that moral truths are relational (p. 223), emphasises further the distinctly human nature of morality.

Key points • • •

- Cognitivism argues that there can be objective moral knowledge. Moral realism adds that moral judgements are made true or false by how the world is.
- Cognitivism appeals to our experience of morality: we feel we can make mistakes, that moral demands are independent of us, that moral progress is possible.

Nietzsche criticises philosophers who argue for transcendent moral truth for failing to see how moral goodness, wisdom and altruism could have their origins in the empirical world of everyday human desire and sense experience. See CRITIQUE OF PAST PHILOSOPHERS and MOTIVATIONAL ANALYSIS, pp. 197 and 200.

Moral truth as God-independent transcendent truth

The idea that moral truth is 'transcendent' is the idea that it must be quite distinct and different from the empirical world, and in some way superior to it. Many philosophers have noticed that we commonly experience a conflict between what we believe is morally right and what we want to do or how we feel. In this conflict, morality is 'higher', what is 'better' in us, and it claims to have 'authority' over us, while immoral desires and emotions are a 'lower' and 'animal' part of our nature. To become morally good, we have to temper or overcome selfish desires and immediate emotional reactions and learn to consider others. Because we don't see morality in the rest of nature, among other animals, the 'higher' part of ourselves, we can argue, must have a different origin, outside the empirical world. Moral values, on this view, are not part of the natural world, but exist beyond it (e.g. science can't investigate values).

The most common way of understanding this is through the belief in God. Values are part of the 'supernatural' world, and this is also the origin of the 'higher' part of ourselves (our souls, perhaps). However, this interpretation of transcendence isn't the only one, and we won't discuss it further, as the syllabus is interested only in God-independent theories of moral transcendence.

The analogy with mathematical truths

The idea of transcendence is puzzling. We (think we) know what it is for physical things to exist, and there is nothing strange about how we discover them through our senses. But what can it be for something to exist that is not part of the empirical world? An analogy with mathematics can help.

Intuitively, mathematical truths are about numbers and other mathematical objects (such as geometrical shapes): '2 + 2 = 4' is about the numbers '2' and '4'. But what are numbers? No physical object is a number. Or again, what are triangles? No physical triangle is a 'perfect' triangle, and mathematicians don't study triangles physically; for example, the proof that the three internal angles of a triangle add up to 180° doesn't rely on measuring lots of different triangles to check. One view is that mathematical objects are 'abstract objects'. They exist, in a sense, not as physical things but as abstract things. They don't exist in space and time, but nor are they psychological things; for example, they aren't concepts, but what concepts refer to. The statement 2 + 2 = 4 was true even before we came up with the concepts of '2' and '4'. We make mathematical *discoveries*; these are discoveries about numbers. Mathematical truths don't depend on what we think; they are objective and independent of us.

How do we discover the truth about numbers and other mathematical objects? Many mathematicians believe that we have a form of mathematical 'intuition', which is a form of pure thought, a part of our capacity of reason. Although it is not based on the senses, it is a form of thought that we tend to describe by analogy with perception – as when you 'see' the proof, you 'grasp' the nature of the triangle, and so on. Like other forms of thought, it is not infallible, and it can be trained.

We can apply this model of knowledge to moral truth. Values are transcendent, outside space and time. They are objective, existing independently of us. We come to know about them using a form of rational intuition, which some philosophers identify as 'conscience', which is fallible but can be trained to become more accurate.

> Explain the analogy between mathematical and moral truths.

Platonic Forms

Plato's theory of the Forms provides one example of this understanding of values as transcendent. There are Forms that relate to moral values – Forms of justice, courage, kindness and so on. Like all Forms, they exist outside space and time,

See THE THEORY OF THE
FORMS and THE FORM OF
THE GOOD, pp. 58 and
69.

Explain the view
that moral truth
is transcendent.

independently of us, and never change. They are universal values, types of perfection – and empirical things, such as human motives and actions, exhibit moral values by partaking in the Forms. Thus, the Forms are the origin of everything moral in us.

In being perfect, Plato argues, the Forms partake of the 'supreme' Form, the Form of the Good. Why are all values values? What is valuable about them? What they all have in common, we might say, is 'Value' itself, or the 'Good'. Knowing what is good is the highest kind of knowledge.

Key points • • •

- The idea that moral truth is transcendent is the idea that it is distinct from and superior to the empirical world.
- This claim is mirrored in our experience of a 'higher', moral part of ourselves and a 'lower', 'animal' part.
- We can understand transcendence by analogy with mathematical truths, which are about abstract mathematical objects, and discovered through rational intuition.
- Plato's theory of the Forms is an example of the view that moral truths are transcendent.

Moral knowledge, elitism and weakness of will

Before we turn to our second theory of moral truth, it is worth noting some issues that arise for all forms of cognitivism. One challenge, especially for the view that moral truth is transcendent, is 'HOW IS KNOWLEDGE OF MORAL TRUTH POSSIBLE?', discussed on p. 227. Here we shall look at two other implications of the claim that there is moral knowledge.

All moral cognitivists claim that our beliefs about moral values can be true or false. For example, anyone who thinks violent rape is not wrong has a false belief, and anyone who thinks courage is good has a true belief. So, in many moral disagreements, one or both sides are simply wrong, however sincere they are. For example, our desires and emotions can bias our thinking and so lead to mistakes.

However, believing that there is moral truth doesn't mean that the truth is simple or easy. Some cognitivists argue that moral truths are very complicated, that they are sensitive to context and situation. And cognitivism doesn't claim that there is *one* clear answer to every moral problem.

'Elitism'

Plato argued that gaining knowledge of the Good is very difficult indeed. It is the culmination of knowledge of the Forms, and this requires both a very special sort of person and years of training. Knowledge of the Forms requires a complete reorientation of the mind, he argues, away from our usual desires – for the pleasure of the body, for money, for fame. The person must love learning – philosophy – above everything else.

This is clearly 'elitism': only people who have the special temperament and training really *know* the truth about morality. We can object that everyone has the capacity for moral knowledge, even if moral truth is transcendent; for example, many religious people would argue that everyone has a conscience. But to defend universal knowledge of the good, we must reject either Plato's theory of the Forms or his theory of what is required for knowledge of the Forms.

But is moral 'elitism' obviously wrong? If there can be moral knowledge, then it is plausible that some people have it while other people lack it. This distinction applies to all other areas of knowledge; are we to object that physicists are 'elitist' in claiming that they know more about physics than other people do? Instead of objecting to 'elitism', we celebrate their 'expertise'. If there is moral knowledge, then it is possible that there are moral 'experts'. We might argue that historical religious figures are examples.

However, many cognitivists have held that anyone who is capable of being a moral agent (acting virtuously or viciously), if they do not know the moral truth, can at least use their reason to *discover* what the moral truth is, if they want to. This is not to say it is easy, but at least it is possible.

Weakness of will

Moral knowledge includes knowledge of what is morally good. According to most cognitivists, what is morally good is also good 'all things considered'. In other words, it is always better to act in a way that is morally good. 'Weakness of will' occurs when someone who, knowing that 'all things considered' it is

See THE PHILOSOPHER-RULER AND HIS QUALITIES, p. 79.

See also KANT'S ATTEMPT TO PROVIDE A RATIONAL GROUNDING FOR A DEONTOLOGICAL ETHICS, p. 258.

What, if anything, is objectionable about moral elitism?

The relation between moral knowledge and motivation is discussed further in TO WHAT EXTENT CAN MORAL TRUTHS MOTIVATE OR JUSTIFY ACTION?, p. 232.

best to do x, nevertheless does y. How can, and why would, someone act in a way that *they themselves* judge is not the best way to act?

Socrates argued that weakness of will was impossible: 'No one who either knows or believes that there is another possible course of action, better than the one he is following, will ever continue on his present course.' He defended the view that moral knowledge is the same thing as virtue, so that if you know what the good thing to do is, you will do it. No one knowingly does what (they believe) is wrong. Socrates' view is still defended by both cognitivists and non-cognitivists. For example, the non-cognitivist Hare argues that moral judgements guide our decisions and actions. To say 'I ought to do x' is like giving oneself a command. Since one believes the statement, one assents to the command – but to agree to follow a command is to obey it. So, weakness of will is a puzzle for both cognitivism and non-cognitivism.

However, weakness of will does *seem* to occur. Most philosophers who deny its reality defend a version of the claim that the person doesn't *really* (deep down) believe that the right thing to do is x. For example, they actually believe that the pleasure of doing y, rather than x, outweighs what is good about x. Socrates argues that while they *say* doing x is right, they don't really *understand* that x is right; for instance, they wrongly assess the pleasure of doing y as better than x. To be virtuous, Socrates argues, is simply to (really) know the truth about what is good and what is not.

Aristotle thought weakness of will is possible. He argued that virtue is not *simply* knowledge; it is knowledge held in the right way, so that it has the right effect on one's motivation. Someone who is weak-willed is not without moral knowledge, but in the moment of being weak-willed, they do not fully grasp the significance of their knowledge.

More recently, Donald Davidson argued that the weak-willed person does not convert their judgement that x is best 'all things considered' into the judgement that x is best unconditionally or 'all-out'. We can understand how someone might say, 'I can see how all the reasons point to doing x, but I'm still not completely convinced'. Something, for example the pleasure that doing y offers, prevents them from making that final, unconditional judgement that x is best.

These solutions all argue that weakness of will involves a failure of the person to judge that x is (really) best. A different approach argues that judgement, or reason, simply does not have the final say on our decisions. Our emotions and desires, in an irrational way, can change what we do, so that we do *genuinely* and finally *judge* that x is best, but still do y. We are simply not fully rational creatures, but can be motivated to do what we do not believe in any sense is best.

Protagoras, 358b-c

See THE PHILOSOPHER RULER AND HIS QUALITIES, p. 79.

'How Is Weakness of the Will Possible?'

Is weakness of will possible? If so, how? If not, why not?

Key points • • •

- Moral cognitivism entails that in a moral disagreement, at least one side has a false belief. It does not claim that moral knowledge is easy.
- If there is moral knowledge, then there could be moral experts. Is this objectionable?
- Plato argued that knowledge of the Good requires a special sort of person and years of training. But many cognitivists have argued that anyone can discover moral truths using reason.
- Socrates argued that weakness of will – when someone judges that one action is best, but does another – is impossible. If the person does what they *say* is not best, this only shows that they do not truly believe what they say.
- Aristotle argued that weakness of will is possible, and occurs when the moral knowledge someone has is not fully active at the time of action.
- Davidson argued that a weak-willed person does not infer, from their belief that an action is best 'all things considered', the belief that the action is best unconditionally.
- An alternative view is that someone's rational judgements do not control their actions, which can be motivated by irrational desires.

Moral truth as based on natural facts

Opposing the view that moral truth is transcendent is the view that moral truths are closely tied to natural facts, especially psychological facts. Cognitivism in the past 150 years has focused on trying to clarify the nature of this relation. As we will see, there are several theories of how to understand it.

Mill: desirable and desired

One version of the claim is that moral truths *just are* natural facts. Some philosophers have interpreted John Stuart Mill's utilitarianism in this way. Mill claims that an action is right if it creates greater (or equal) happiness than any other action in that situation. So, 'right' = 'greatest happiness', and 'good' = 'happiness'. Happiness is natural property, and therefore so is goodness.

See ACT UTILITARIANISM, p. 248.

Utilitarianism, Ch. 4

To say happiness is good is to say that it should be our 'end' – what we aim at in action. Mill claims that happiness is our only end, the only good – so it could be the same thing as goodness. He admits that no *proof* is possible, but we can make an argument based on evidence. He says that 'questions about ends are . . . questions about what things are desirable'. And our evidence about what is desirable must come from what we desire. Mill argues that we all want happiness (and only happiness). From this, he concludes, happiness is good (and the only good).

However, the word 'desirable' has two meanings. Its usual meaning is 'worthy of being desired'. Anything desirable in this sense is good. But another meaning could be 'capable of being desired'. To discover what is capable of being desired, look at what people desire. But from what people actually want, how can we tell what is *worthy* of being desired (good)? People want all sorts of rubbish!

Many philosophers object that Mill has simply failed to spot the gap between the two meanings of 'desirable'. But this is unlikely. Instead, Mill is asking, 'What evidence is there for thinking that something is worthy of being desired?' He argues that people *in general* desire happiness. Unless we think that people *in general* all desire what is not worth desiring, this looks like good evidence. Is there anything that *everyone* wants that is not worth wanting? If we look at what people agree upon in what they desire, we will find what is worth desiring. Everyone wants happiness, so happiness is good.

> Discuss Mill's argument for the claim that happiness is good.

Virtues and human flourishing

Aristotle argued that moral philosophy is interested in the 'good life' for human beings as the particular sorts of being we are. 'Living well' is the ultimate aim of all human action. To 'live well' is determined by human nature. His term for 'living well' – *eudaimonia* – has been translated as 'happiness', but in fact the idea is more like 'flourishing'. We have an idea of what it is for a plant or animal to 'flourish'; we can provide an analysis of its needs and when those needs are met in abundance. Human living involves choosing and acting, but also involves the nature and quality of one's relationships with others and the state of one's mind. The facts about human nature, in particular psychological facts about our universal desires, our needs and our ability to reason, are the basis for moral truths; for example, whether a character trait, such as courage or being short-tempered, is good (a virtue) or bad (a vice).

> Explain Aristotle's view that virtues are character traits that help us live well.

However, we will question whether we can infer moral truths from psychological facts about people in How is knowledge of moral truth possible? (p. 227).

Moore: the open question argument and the naturalistic fallacy

In *Principia Ethica*, G.E. Moore objected to Mill's argument above. Moore called the attempt to equate goodness to any natural property the *naturalistic fallacy*. Goodness, he claimed, is a simple and unanalysable property. It cannot be defined in terms of anything else. Colours are similar. Blue is a simple property, and no one can explain what blue is; you have to see it for yourself to understand what blue is. But unlike colours, goodness is a *non*-natural property. It is not part of the natural world, the world of science; but it is part of reality.

Moore's main argument for believing that it is a **fallacy** – a mistake – to identify goodness with a natural property is the 'open question' argument. If goodness just is happiness, then it wouldn't make sense to ask, 'Is it good to make people happy?' This would be like asking, 'Does what makes people happy make people happy?' This second question isn't a real question (the answer has to be 'yes'), but 'Is it good to make people happy?' is a real question; the answer can logically be 'yes' or 'no'. And so goodness cannot be happiness, or any other property. 'Is x good?' is always a real question, while 'Is x x?' is not. And so goodness cannot be any other property.

> Moore did not argue that there is *no* relation between moral properties and natural properties. He thought there was a relation; he argued that in two situations, identical natural properties would secure identical moral properties. So, moral properties are, in some way, based on natural properties. But they are not identical to them.

> Explain Moore's argument against the 'naturalistic fallacy'.

Going further: is the 'naturalistic fallacy' a real fallacy?

This argument doesn't work. Here is a similar argument. 'The property of being water cannot be any property in the world, such as the property of being H_2O. If it was, then the question "Is water H_2O?" would not make sense – it would be like asking, "Is H_2O H_2O?" So water is a simple, unanalysable property.' This is not right, as water *just is* H_2O.

The reason the argument doesn't work is because it confuses *concepts* and *properties*. Two different concepts – 'water' and 'H_2O' – can pick out the same property in the world. You knew about water before you knew it was

H_2O. During this time, you had the concept 'water' but not the concept 'H_2O'. So, they are different concepts, but they both refer to the same thing. Likewise, the concept 'goodness' is a different concept from 'happiness', but perhaps they are exactly the same property in the world. We may doubt this for other reasons, but the point is that the open question argument does not show that they are different.

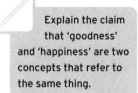

Explain the claim that 'goodness' and 'happiness' are two concepts that refer to the same thing.

The 'is-ought' gap

Even if the open question argument is too simple, we may think that Moore is right to think that, from any natural property, we cannot deduce a moral property. Whatever facts you get together to support your moral judgement (the action will cause happiness), you cannot logically infer the judgement (it is morally right). Hume noted the gap between describing the facts and saying something ought to be done: 'this *ought* . . . expresses some new relation [of which it] seems altogether inconceivable, how this new relation can be a deduction from others, which are entirely different from it'.

A Treatise of Human Nature, III.i.i

This argument has often been used to support the view that there is no moral truth. The gap occurs because morality is not a matter of fact, but a matter of attitudes that we take to the facts. However, in the next section we discuss a theory of moral truth that tries to overcome the gap.

See EMOTIVISM, p. 236, and PRESCRIPTIVISM, p. 239.

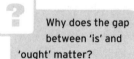

Why does the gap between 'is' and 'ought' matter?

Key points • • •

- Mill argued that goodness is happiness. To show this, he argued that what is good is desirable, and this can be inferred from what people generally desire – which is happiness.
- Philosophers object that you cannot infer what is worth desiring from what people desire. Mill responds that it is the only evidence we have.
- Aristotle argued that 'living well' or 'flourishing' is both the subject matter of morality and based on facts about human nature. Whether some character trait, such as courage, contributes to living well, and so is a virtue, is a matter of fact.
- Moore argued that the claim that moral properties are some type of natural

property (e.g. good = greatest happiness) is a 'naturalistic fallacy'. If they were, then, for example, 'Is the greatest happiness good?' would be a meaningless question. But it isn't.

- However, Moore shows only that moral concepts are distinct from natural concepts. He doesn't show that moral concepts don't refer to a natural property.
- Hume pointed out that any judgement about what is good or right is quite different from a judgement about the (empirical) facts. So, moral judgements cannot be inferred from factual ones.

Moral truth as based on relational properties

Reasons for action

The is–ought gap makes it seem that appealing to the (natural) facts when we are trying to justify a moral judgement is silly. In fact, we think of the facts as *reasons* that support our moral claims, for example that eating meat is wrong, because of the suffering it causes to animals. Now, the idea of a 'reason' makes sense only in relation to a rational creature – us. Reasons are always reasons for someone. Moral reasons are reasons for someone to do something. That some fact, for example the suffering of an animal, is a reason, for example for us not to eat meat, is a relational property; it is true (if it is true) only in relation to us.

Understanding moral properties as reasons for action can be used in arguing for objective moral truth. On this view, whether some fact is a moral reason for or against some action is objectively true or false. Compare reasons for other types of belief. If radiometric decay indicates that dinosaur bones are 65 million years old, this is a reason to believe that dinosaurs lived on Earth 65 million years ago. It is not *proof*, but it is a reason. The result of radiometric dating of dinosaur bones is a reason to think dinosaurs lived on Earth 65 million years ago, whether you think it is a reason or not. Facts about reasons are objective.

Facts about reasons are not identical with natural facts. Natural facts are not (necessarily) relational, but whether a natural fact is a reason is relational. Furthermore, there is no scientific or empirical investigation into what reasons there are. Facts about reasons are **normative** facts. They are facts about justification and reasoning.

> Reasons can come in different strengths; there can be good reasons, really good reasons and proof. Bad reasons are not actually reasons at all.

> Explain how natural facts can be reasons.

MORAL REASONS

We can now understand moral judgements like this: to say that something is wrong is to say that the moral reasons against doing it are stronger than any moral reason in favour of doing it. Because this is a statement of (normative) fact, moral judgements can be true or false. Of course, it can be difficult to establish whether a natural fact constitutes a reason for action, and how strong this reason is. But the truth is often difficult to discover.

This theory explains the connection between natural properties and moral judgements, and so bridges Hume's 'is–ought' objection. Hume is right that we cannot move directly from natural properties to moral judgements. Appealing to natural facts as reasons doesn't *prove* a moral judgement to be true or false. We cannot *deduce* moral judgements from considering the natural facts; instead, we must *weigh up* the reasons that the natural facts give us. But once we recognise that whether a natural fact counts as a reason for believing a certain value judgement is itself a matter of objective fact, we can cross the gap.

> Explain and illustrate the claim that moral truths are based on reasons for action.

Objections

But isn't the idea of 'truths about reasons' a very strange notion? No, reasons aren't strange, and we need them even to do science. Aristotle claims that certain facts about being human mean that a certain way of living is the best, most flourishing life. We therefore have reason to develop our characters in ways that allow us to live like this and meet ours and other people's needs. This isn't strange.

We can object that if reasons are related to us, dependent on us, then surely they must be subjective. Facts are part of the world. The fact the dinosaurs roamed the Earth millions of years ago would be true whether anyone had found out about it or not. But whether something is a reason or not depends on us.

This misunderstands the way in which reasons depend on us. There are lots of facts – for example, facts about being in love, or facts about music – that 'depend' on human beings and their activities (there would be no love if no one loved anything). But they are still facts, because they are independent of our judgements, and made true by the way the world, in this case the human world, is. You can make mistakes about whether someone is in love or whether a piece of music is baroque or classical.

But are reasons dependent on 'human beings' in general or on individuals? Take the case of animal suffering: surely this is only a reason for me not to eat meat *if I care* about animals. Or again, the fact that studying hard will increase my understanding of philosophy is a reason to study hard only *if I want* to understand philosophy. So, what we (individually) have reason to do depends on what we (individually) want. Thus, reasons aren't objective, they are subjective. Moral judgements are expressions of what we care about, they are not expressions of truth.

> Are what reasons for action I have dependent on what I want?

The analogy with secondary qualities

PRIMARY AND SECONDARY QUALITIES

The distinction between 'primary qualities' and 'secondary qualities' was developed during the rise of modern science. We can think of this as a distinction between properties that science says objects have – size, shape, motion – and properties that depend upon particular ways of perceiving objects – colour, sound, smell, taste. Colour, by definition, is something that is experienced in vision. According to science, what we experience as colour is wavelengths of the electromagnetic field. There are theories for sound, smell, taste and other secondary properties. But these theories – that colour is frequency of electromagnetic radiation, that smell and taste are chemical compounds – suggest that the world as we experience it through our senses and the world as science describes it – all 'particles in motion' and empty space – are quite different.

Hume thought that this showed that secondary qualities exist only in the mind. Objects aren't coloured; instead, their parts have certain properties of size and motion and so on, causing them to emit or reflect wavelengths of light (which is a type of vibration, not itself a colour). It is not until we turn to human experience – something mental – that we need the concept of colour, that we come across 'colour experience'.

> Explain the claim that secondary qualities are 'mental'.

THE ANALOGY WITH MORAL VALUES

Hume argued that moral judgement is analogous:

> when you pronounce any action or character to be vicious, you mean nothing, but that . . . you have a feeling . . . of blame from the contemplation of it. Vice and virtue, therefore, may be compar'd to sounds, colours, heat and cold, which . . . are not qualities in objects, but perceptions in the mind.

> *A Treatise of Human Nature*, III.i.i

Vice and virtue are not properties of actions and characters, and so moral judgements are not 'true' or 'false'. Instead, moral judgements are expressions of our feelings (of approval and disapproval).

But is Hume right about secondary qualities? The idea of a secondary quality, such as colour, is defined in relation to a perceptual system. But that doesn't mean the quality is subjective. John McDowell argues that secondary qualities are properties *of the object* that enable it to cause certain experiences in us. When we perceive the colour of an object, we still perceive the object, but *as it appears to us*. 'Us' means 'human beings', not 'me' or 'you'. An object's colour is not subjective, because it is independent of how any *individual* person perceives it. To be brown is to look brown to normal perceivers under normal conditions. Secondary qualities are no less real than primary qualities; it is just that they are a different *type* of property, one defined in terms of how we (human beings in general) perceive the world.

'Values and Secondary Qualities'

If secondary qualities can be understood objectively, then we can use the analogy with secondary qualities to defend the view that there is moral truth. The idea that something is a moral value (e.g. honesty) makes sense only in relation to valuers. Moral judgements are defined in the context of human responses to the world. But what values there are doesn't depend on what any individual person finds valuable or not, just as what colour something is is independent of any individual person's perception of it.

We can link moral values and reasons: a value gives us a reason to act in a particular way. So, McDowell is arguing that whether some fact (e.g. animal suffering) is a reason to act in a certain way (e.g. stop eating meat) depends *in general* on human responses; but it is independent of any individual's response, so it is not subjective.

Discuss whether the analogy with secondary qualities shows that moral values are objective or subjective.

However, we can question whether the analogy between moral values (or reasons) and secondary qualities succeeds.

Key points • • •

- Natural facts can be understood as reasons supporting moral judgements. Reasons are relational, relating features of situations to moral agents.
- If reasons are objective, then there are objective (normative) facts about whether a natural fact is a reason or not.
- On this view, a moral judgement that an action is wrong is true if the reasons against doing it are stronger than the reasons in favour of doing it. This judgement is not a matter of proof or deduction.

- We can object that whether some consideration is a reason for me depends on what I care about.
- Hume argues that moral values are like secondary qualities, existing only as 'perceptions in the mind'.
- McDowell argues that secondary qualities are objective, properties of the object relating to how it is perceived by us. Moral values are likewise objective, but relational; they make sense only in the context of human life.

How is knowledge of moral truth possible?

Models of knowledge

We have looked at different models of moral truth. Each model has a corresponding account of what moral knowledge is:

1. For Plato, moral knowledge is knowledge of the Forms.
2. For Aristotle, it is knowledge of human flourishing and how to live well.
3. On the reductionist interpretation of Mill, it is

    a. the knowledge that what is good is happiness; and then
    b. the knowledge of what actions bring about the greatest happiness.

4. For Moore, it is knowledge of the non-natural property of goodness.
5. On the reasons-based theory, it is knowing what we have most (moral) reason to do.

Because what moral knowledge is differs on each account, there are different answers to the question of how moral knowledge is possible.

The theory that goodness is a natural property can provide the most straightforward answer: we know about natural properties empirically. Once we have established *which* natural properties are relevant (e.g. happiness), there is no special problem about how moral knowledge is possible. However, establishing the connection between moral properties and the relevant natural facts is very contentious, and a matter not of empirical argument, but of philosophical reasoning.

Can Mill establish that happiness is the only good thing? Can Aristotle show what counts as a 'good life' for human beings? There have been many different ways in which people have 'flourished' in different cultures. So, from

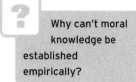

? Why can't moral knowledge be established empirically?

the biological and psychological facts alone, we cannot deduce any moral knowledge. If there is one 'best' way to live, we need some other way of discovering it.

Moral reasoning and insight

In fact, all the forms of cognitivism we have discussed argue that moral knowledge is gained through reasoning, and involves a type of rational insight. In this way, moral knowledge is different from empirical knowledge. We gain empirical knowledge through *causation*; the thing we learn about causes us to have certain sense experiences of it (e.g. a rose reflects light that enters our eyes). But moral properties do not *cause* our moral judgements. (What could the causal mechanism be?) This is one important disanalogy with secondary qualities.

Numbers and other mathematical objects similarly do not cause our mathematical judgements. We gain mathematical knowledge through (mathematical) reasoning and insight. Most cognitivists, however, think that moral reasoning and insight are not *purely* intellectual in the way maths is. Both Plato and Aristotle argue that it involves training one's desires and emotions first, because if we don't develop virtues, we won't be able to see the truth; Aristotle adds that it cannot be taught, but requires experience of life.

But what is this 'reasoning and insight'? Does it really exist? Contemporary philosophers offer two types of model, self-evidence and reflective equilibrium.

A self-evident judgement rests on the 'evidence' of its own plausibility, which is grasped directly. This doesn't necessarily mean that everyone can immediately see that it is true. 'Self-evident' is not the same as 'obvious'. Our ability to make these judgements needs to develop first, and we need to consider the issue very carefully.

The difficulty with 'self-evident' judgements is that people disagree about whether they are true or not. Moore thought it was self-evident that pleasure is good and that maximising the good is right. But other philosophers have thought it self-evident that there are times when it is wrong to maximise pleasure. The problem is, because the judgements are supposed to be self-evident, any further reasons for believing them will not be as conclusive as considering the claim itself.

Can we do without the idea of self-evidence? Suppose we *could* give reasons for thinking that pleasure is good, for example because it forms part of a

The question of the extent of reason is part of the debate between rationalism and empiricism, discussed in Unit 1.1 REASON AND EXPERIENCE.

flourishing life for human beings. Is it, then, self-evident that being part of a flourishing life makes something good? If you give a reason, we can ask whether this reason is self-evident and so on.

Another model of reasoning claims that no judgement is self-evident, because it rests on support by other beliefs. When we then question those beliefs, we can give reasons for believing them, but must in turn assume others. Our reasoning, then, involves a matter of interpreting, applying and adjusting a *framework* of reasons. We test our claims and the reasons we give by their place in the framework.

In our reflections on reasons, we will be guided by trying to make sense of our moral attitudes generally. Reflection itself will be guided by further intuitions; we will reject what seems implausible to us. We appeal to the overall coherence, the balance between our intuitions and our process of reflection, the 'reflective equilibrium' we reach. There is a lot of agreement on when something counts as a reason, even if we disagree on *how strong* a reason it is. And when there is disagreement, this could be the result of different information or experience. It is very rare for two people to *simply* disagree over whether x is a reason, and have nothing else to say about x.

The non-cognitivist's challenge

Non-cognitivists will reply that our intuitions are not insights into moral truth at all. Instead, they *reflect* our pre-existing values and commitments.

We will see two arguments for this claim in EMOTIVISM (p. 236) and PRESCRIPTIVISM (p. 239). A third argument is developed by Nietzsche. He argues that our approach to moral philosophy, and philosophy in general, is all wrong. Following Plato, we seek to give complete definitions of ideas, such as 'what is goodness?'. But Nietzsche argues that 'only that which has no history is definable' in this way. Our moral ideas have a history, so trying to give universal definitions of them is radically mistaken. In fact, the intuitions we use to defend this or that answer are themselves as historical, as contentious as the theories we give – so they offer no real support:

> most of a philosopher's conscious thinking is secretly guided and channelled into particular tracks by his instincts. Behind all logic, too, and its apparent tyranny of movement there are value judgements, or to speak more clearly, physiological demands for the preservation of a particular kind of life.

> Explain and illustrate what a self-evident judgement is.

> Explain and illustrate the method of 'reflective equilibrium'.

> See CRITIQUE OF PAST PHILOSOPHERS AND MOTIVATIONAL ANALYSIS, pp. 197 and 200.

> *Beyond Good and Evil,* § 3

Nietzsche holds that different people are 'instinctively' drawn to different kinds of life. Our values are a reflection of the type of person we are. Everybody is drawn to the way of life that suits them best. Different values, and different interpretations of these values, support different ways of life, and so people are instinctively drawn to particular values and ways of understanding them.

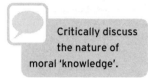

Critically discuss the nature of moral 'knowledge'.

Key points • • •

- Different models of moral truth have corresponding different models of moral knowledge.
- No cognitivist theory claims that empirical investigation *alone* can establish moral knowledge, or that moral values directly cause our moral judgements.
- Some philosophers, including Plato and Aristotle, argue that moral insight is not purely intellectual, but requires virtues of character as well.
- According to one model, moral reasoning involves self-evident judgements – judgements that rest on being grasped directly. However, philosophers have not agreed which judgements are self-evidently true.
- A second model argues that moral insight involves interpreting, applying and adjusting a framework of reasons, trying to balance intuitions and reflection to reach 'reflective equilibrium'.
- Nietzsche, arguing that there is no universal moral truth, objects that these views fail to recognise the historically situated nature of our intuitions, and the influence on our judgements of our instinctive attraction to certain values.

The possibility of agreement over moral truth

When two people disagree over a matter of fact, whether it is about the natural world (dinosaurs) or the human world (love), we normally know how we could prove the matter one way or the other. But if two people agree over all the natural facts about abortion, say, but still disagree about whether it is right, we cannot appeal to any more 'facts' in the same way. What we would call 'the facts' seem to be *all* agreed, but the dispute about values remains. Value judgements always go beyond the facts. As we saw earlier (p. 225), Hume argues the moral judgement doesn't pick out a fact, it expresses a feeling, which is why you can't reach moral agreement just by discussing the facts. We should doubt, then, that there is such a thing as moral truth.

The cognitivist can reply that this oversimplifies moral arguments. If two people agree on the natural facts but still disagree morally, then they must be disagreeing about reasons. For example, is the fact that the foetus will become a human being a (strong) reason for thinking abortion is wrong? If we resolved the disagreement about both natural facts *and* what counts as a reason for what, people would agree on the moral judgement as well. When two people disagree morally, at least one of them is making a mistake, because they are not seeing certain natural facts as the reasons they are. If, as many cognitivists claim, we need both virtues and experience of life to gain sound moral insight, then it is not surprising that so many people make mistakes.

We can object, first, that it is not plausible that all cases of moral disagreement involve at least one person who lacks virtue and life experience! Second, if we press this line too much, then we return to Plato's view that moral truth is very hard to come to know. And if only a few people can gain moral knowledge, then the possibility of agreement on moral truth is very small indeed. Third, there are many influences on people's moral beliefs, not just reasoning and insight. For instance, try to imagine that everyone (in a city or country or the world) actually reached moral agreement. Realistically, why would that have happened? Is it plausible to think that it is because reason has – finally! – won people over? It is more likely that throughout history, moral beliefs have changed as a result of other forces.

This is to consider the question of agreement practically. The cognitivist, however, needs only to defend the view that agreement is *theoretically* possible; they can concede that human fallibility makes agreement near-impossible in practice.

> Can moral disagreement be resolved rationally?

Key points • • •

- Non-cognitivists point out that moral disagreements cannot be settled by appeal to the facts, and argue that this casts doubt on whether there is moral truth.
- Cognitivists reply that when people agree on the natural facts but disagree morally, they are disagreeing over whether the natural facts are reasons. At least one person is making an objective mistake.
- We can object that it is not plausible to think that moral agreement can be secured by reason alone, as disagreement is the result of many factors.

To what extent can moral truths motivate or justify action?

Justifying action

Justifying action and motivating action are not equivalent. To justify an action is to show why it is morally right or good. But the reasons that justify an action *may not* be the same reasons that actually motivate someone to do the action. For example, according to ACT UTILITARIANISM (p. 248), an action is right if it brings about the greatest happiness. Suppose that helping a friend is right for this reason. Nevertheless, you might be motivated to help your friend not because doing so will bring about the greatest happiness (this doesn't enter your thoughts), but simply because you love your friend.

If there are moral truths, then it is uncontentious that they justify actions. So, we shall concentrate on the more difficult question of whether moral truths motivate action.

> There is a question of whether moral truths provide complete guidance on how to act – but this is not a question of justification. See CONFLICTS OF DUTIES, p. 256, and OBJECTIONS, p. 267.

Motivating action

Moral judgements guide our behaviour. If I think pleasure is good, I aim to bring about pleasure. If I think abortion is wrong, I will not commit or encourage others to commit abortion. Moral motivation can seem puzzling if the moral cognitivist is correct. A truth, in and of itself, doesn't lead to action. For example, the fact that it is raining doesn't motivate me to pick up my umbrella unless I don't want to get wet. It seems that I need to *care* about the truth, and then the motivating force comes from the caring.

Hume argued that in order to act, we need beliefs, about how the world is and how to change it, and a desire, in order to be motivated to change it. But surely statements about right and wrong, good and bad, are motivating *in their own right*. But in that case, they are not like beliefs (about truths), they are like desires.

Cognitivists have made two different responses to this objection. The first is to claim that moral judgements are *not* motivating. There certainly seem to be people – and perhaps all of us at certain times, for example when we are depressed – for whom statements about morality are not motivating. They just don't care about morality. Moral judgements, then, are motivating only to people who care about morality.

The second response is to agree that moral judgements are motivating, and this would be a puzzle if they were judgements about natural facts or Platonic

Forms. But if we argue instead that moral truths are based on *relational* properties, we can explain how they are motivating. If moral judgements are about what we have reason to do, they will be motivating, because judgements about reasons are judgements about reasons *for us*. As long as we are rational, reasons will motivate us directly. Of course, that motivation can be interfered with because we are not completely rational, so we will not always do what we have most reason to do.

See WEAKNESS OF WILL, p. 217.

How, if at all, can moral truths motivate us?

Key points • • •

- The reasons justifying an action and the reasons motivating an action can be different.
- If actions are motivated by our desires, how moral truths (or beliefs in those truths) can be motivating is puzzling.
- One answer is to say that we must care about morality – and it is this, not moral truths themselves, that motivates us.
- Another answer is to say that moral truths are about what we have reason to do – and the judgement that we have reason to act in *this* way will motivate us to act in *this* way, because we are rational.

II. THE DENIAL OF MORAL TRUTH

Non-cognitivism argues that there is no moral knowledge, because there is no objective moral truth. RELATIVISM (below), EMOTIVISM (p. 236) and PRESCRIPTIVISM (p. 239) each make this claim in some form. We will discuss objections specific to each theory, and end with three further issues that challenge non-cognitivist accounts generally.

Relativism

The distinction between descriptive and normative relativism

Relativism is a set of views about the relationship between morality and a culture or society. Descriptive relativism claims that, as a matter of fact, moral codes differ from one society to the next. According to one society, slavery is permissible under certain conditions; according to another, it is never permissible.

Again, one society will say that female circumcision is right, another that it is wrong; or that all people should be treated as equals or, alternatively, that people should be treated according to their caste. Descriptive relativism is a factual claim, and one that certainly seems correct.

From this factual claim, some people infer *normative* (or 'cultural' or 'metaethical') relativism. This is the view that there is no objective moral standard independent from what a culture endorses. There is no objective moral truth that is true for all people at all times. As a result, we cannot say that a moral value or practice of a society is objectively right or wrong. Instead, to talk of what is 'morally right' *makes sense only in relation to a specific, culturally relative morality*. 'Right' in a culture is 'right according to the culture's morality'. To use any other standard of morality to judge what is right or wrong in a culture is misguided. We cannot meaningfully use the standards of our society or appeal to 'objective' standards to judge a different culture.

The inference from descriptive to normative relativism is not straight-forward, however. Disagreement is not enough for relativism. If two people disagree, one could be wrong. It's the same with cultures. There could be objective moral truth about which one culture is mistaken.

Relativism is a form of non-cognitivism, *but at the social level*. There is no objective moral truth, and morality is an expression of a culture. However, for individuals there *is* moral truth; what is right or wrong, for any individual, is defined by what their culture says is right or wrong. Relativism does not make morality 'subjective', but relative to culture. It does not deny that people act wrongly. But it claims that to condemn an action or practice as wrongful, one must use resources from *within the culture* to which that practice or individual belongs. You can't judge a practice from outside a culture.

> **Explain and illustrate the difference between descriptive and normative relativism.**

> **Why doesn't disagreement entail relativism?**

Moral judgements as social conventions relative to a given social group

There are two ways of understanding ethical disagreements between cultures. The cognitivist must argue that different cultures, with their different ethical values and practices, are all trying to get at the *truth* about ethics. The relativist argues that this is implausible, and ethical practices are simply part of a culture's *way of living*. It claims that two cultures that disagree over a moral practice or judgement are actually making claims that are each 'true for them'.

We can support relativism by comparing the idea of moral truth to the idea of scientific truth, and looking at the nature of disagreement in science and ethics. How we can understand what would explain an *end* to disagreement in each case? With science, the best explanation is that the scientific theories we have agreed upon represent how the world is; the world has *guided* our investigations, confirming or falsifying hypotheses through experiment. Science investigates the *one* physical world.

By contrast, the idea that two cultures which disagree are both trying to find 'the truth' about ethics doesn't sit well with an understanding of the history of culture and how ethical practices develop. And since in a disagreement at least one culture is wrong, we also need to explain why that culture had 'got it wrong': why couldn't people in that culture see what was independently right and do that? This is a very awkward question.

Relativism understands ethical practices as part of a culture; ethical practices have developed to help people find their way around a social world. But there are *many* social worlds, many cultures, and they have developed different social conventions. There is not just one social world which can guide ethical practices towards agreement.

> How does the comparison with scientific disagreement support relativism?

Objection

Cognitivists argue that normative relativism does not follow from descriptive relativism. First, they draw attention to just how many general ethical principles and virtues different cultures share. For example, most cultures have prohibitions on killing, lying and theft, and encourage care of the weak. If disagreement supports the view that there is no universal moral truth, then agreement supports the view that there is. Second, they can say that different ethical practices reflect the different particular conditions in which different cultures are situated, but not different ethical principles.

Suppose, as Aristotle argues, that the aim of morality is to achieve the best life for human beings. All human beings live in some culture or other; and we need to be able to lead our lives in the culture we find ourselves in. To some degree, what traits we need to live a good life will vary from one culture to another. But because we have a common human nature, some traits will always be important, such as courage, loyalty, self-control and so on. On the basis of these ideas, we may be able to criticise different cultures for having the 'wrong' list of virtues and values on the grounds that they don't really help people lead a good life.

The relativist can respond that there is no *one* idea of the 'best life' for human beings. This idea is itself culturally relative. Furthermore, not all cultures agree that human beings are equal (Aristotle himself supported the idea of slavery!); the best life might be 'rightly' reserved for a privileged few, according to that culture.

Further objections to relativism are discussed from p. 244.

Key points • • •

- Descriptive relativism argues that cultures disagree on moral judgements. Normative relativism argues that this disagreement is not resolvable by appealing to objective moral truth. Morality is just part of a culture's way of living, its social world.
- Cognitivism needs to explain how and why cultures can make mistakes and have the wrong values. If moral values are objective, why weren't they able to discover the truth?
- Cognitivists can argue that different cultures share many general ethical principles and conceptions of virtue, and that differences simply reflect different situations.

Emotivism

Ayer and the principle of verification

See METAPHYSICS AS SPECULATIVE NONSENSE, p. 186.

In the 1930s, a school of philosophy arose called logical positivism. The cornerstone of their beliefs was the principle of verification. This claims that a statement has meaning only if it is either **analytic** or empirically verifiable. It entails that statements about right and wrong are *meaningless*. They are neither true nor false, because they do not actually state anything. If I say, 'murder is wrong', this is not analytic, nor can any **empirical** investigation show this. We can show that murder causes grief and pain, or that it is often done out of anger. But we cannot demonstrate, in the same way, that it is *wrong*.

But if ethical statements don't state truths, and are therefore literally meaningless, what do they do? A.J. Ayer argued that ethical judgements express feelings: 'If I say to someone, "You acted wrongly in stealing that money" . . . I am simply evincing my moral disapproval of it. It is as if I had said, "You stole that money," in a peculiar tone of horror'. This theory is 'emotivism'.

Moore would agree that moral judgements are neither analytic nor empirically verifiable. But he believed that they are nevertheless true or false, because they are about non-natural properties. But Ayer responds that 'self-evident intuitions' are simply our feelings of approval or disapproval. Feelings are not cognitions of value, and value does not exist independently of our feelings.

The main difficulty with logical positivism is that according to the principle of verification, the principle of verification itself is meaningless. The claim that 'a statement has meaning only if it is analytic or can be verified empirically' is not analytic and cannot be verified empirically. But if the principle of verification is meaningless, then what it claims cannot be true. So, it does not give us any reason to believe that the claims of ethics are meaningless.

Stevenson's theory

But emotivism does not depend on the principle of verification. Charles Stevenson argued that moral words have *emotive* meanings, which are neither descriptive nor analytic. The sentence 'You stole that money' has a purely descriptive meaning, namely that you took money that did not belong to you without permission from the owner. But it can be used with an emotive meaning ('You *stole* that money!'), a meaning that expresses disapproval. Many moral terms ('steal', 'honesty', 'respect') have both descriptive and emotive meanings. The central ones, though – 'right', 'wrong', 'good' and 'bad' – have only emotive meanings.

Stevenson analyses emotive meaning by connecting meaning to *use*. The purpose of moral judgements is not to state facts, but to influence how we behave through expressions of approval and disapproval. Words with emotive meaning do just that. If moral language is just descriptive, how can moral truths motivate us (see p. 232)? Emotivism, by contrast, connects caring, approving, disapproving, with the very meaning of ethical words.

But, we can object, the key moral terms 'good', 'right', 'wrong' and 'bad' *aren't* particularly or necessarily emotive. They *may* arouse emotions in others or express ours, but this depends on context, as it does with 'steal' and 'honesty'. Yet if their meaning is emotive, then the connection should be stronger than

Language, Truth and Logic, p. 146

See How IS KNOWLEDGE OF MORAL TRUTH POSSIBLE?, p. 228.

Explain and illustrate Ayer's theory of emotivism.

Facts and Values, Ch. 1

Explain and illustrate what is meant by the claim that moral language is used to express feelings rather than to describe facts.

that. So perhaps, like 'steal' and 'honesty', 'good' and 'right' have a descriptive meaning as well, related to moral facts, for example facts about what we have most reason to do. If so, emotivism has confused the emotional *use* of moral terms for their meaning.

Going further: emotivism and moral disagreement

One of the most powerful objections to emotivism is that it oversimplifies ethical discussion. If I say 'abortion is wrong' and you say 'abortion is right', I am just expressing my disapproval of it and you are expressing your approval. I'm just saying 'Boo! to abortion' and you're saying 'Hurrah! for abortion'. But about this there can be no *discussion*, no *reasoning*. Even worse, emotivism claims that we are trying to influence other people's feelings and actions. But trying to influence people without reasoning is just a form of manipulation.

Ayer responded that ethical discussion is about the facts. When arguing over animal rights, say, we are constantly drawing facts to each other's attention. I point out how much animals suffer in factory farms. You point out how much more sophisticated human beings are than animals. And so on. If we both agree on the facts but still disagree morally, there is nothing left to discuss.

Stevenson rejects this. The moral disagreement that remains is a disagreement in attitude, a practical disagreement; no one can live both by the attitude that 'eating meat is wrong' and by the attitude that 'eating meat is right'. Attitudes *can* be discussed, because people do not have feelings or make choices in isolation. Any attitude has implications for other attitudes. If I disapprove of an action, I must also have similar feelings about similar actions, or my attitudes will not provide consistent guidance about how to live. Moral disagreement, then, can be about the relations between different attitudes. For example, deciding whether abortion is right or wrong is complicated because there are many attitudes involved: sympathy towards the mother, sympathy towards the foetus, feelings about human life, death and parenthood. It is difficult to work out how these attitudes can all be acted upon, and that is why people disagree.

We may still object that *rationality* in weighing up which attitudes to give up, which to keep, is still missing. We have no sense of one set of attitudes being part of a 'better life' than any other.

Further objections to emotivism are discussed from p. 242.

Can emotivism satisfactorily account for moral discussion?

Key points • • •

- Ayer argued that a statement has meaning only if it is either analytic or empirically verifiable. Moral statements are neither, so they are meaningless, neither true nor false. Instead, they express emotions – in particular, moral approval or disapproval.
- However, the principle of verification, according to itself, is not meaningful, because it is neither analytic nor empirically verifiable.
- Stevenson argued that, nevertheless, moral statements have only emotive meaning. They express emotions, and are intended to influence the emotions and actions of other people.
- But 'good' and 'right' aren't always emotive. We may object that Stevenson has confused use for meaning.
- We may object that emotivism doesn't allow for moral reasoning. If moral judgements are attempts to influence others' feelings without appealing to reason, this is just manipulation.
- Ayer argued that all moral discussion is disagreeing over the facts, while Stevenson argued that there is also disagreement in attitude. As any attitude has complex implications for other attitudes, these disagreements can be complex.

Prescriptivism

R.M. Hare argued that moral words are not descriptive and *emotive* in meaning; they are descriptive and *prescriptive*. This difference, he claimed, allows a greater role for reason in moral discussion.

The Language of Morals

Prescriptive meaning

In claiming that moral judgements are imperatives, Hare's theory is like Kant's. See KANT'S ATTEMPT TO PROVIDE A RATIONAL GROUNDING FOR A DEONTOLOGICAL ETHICS, p. 258.

Prescriptive meaning works like commands, also known as imperatives. If I say 'Leave the room', I am telling you to do something. Hare argued that if I say 'Eating meat is wrong', I am saying 'Don't eat meat'.

We use the idea of 'right' and 'wrong' to command. We use the word 'good', says Hare, when we want to *commend* something to someone. There is a difference of emphasis between 'good action' and 'right action': 'good action' *commends* the action without necessarily *commanding* it; we are saying it should be praised, but not necessarily that you *have* to do it to be a good person. If we say an action is the 'right action', then we are commanding it; it is a guideline for behaviour that people should follow.

We can talk about good chocolate, good teachers and good people. In each case, we are saying the chocolate, teacher or person is praiseworthy in some way. In each case, there is a *set of standards* that we are implicitly relying on. Good chocolate is rich in the taste of cocoa. Good teachers can explain new ideas clearly and create enthusiasm in their students. A good person – well, a good person is someone who is the way we should try to be as people. When we use 'good' to mean 'morally good', we are appealing to a set of standards that apply to someone as a person.

So, the prescriptive meaning of good relates to the fact that it commends. What about its descriptive meaning? This comes from the set of standards that is being assumed. Its descriptive meaning picks up on the qualities that something must have to be a good . . . (chocolate, teacher, person, whatever).

Prescription and universalisation

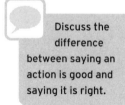

Discuss the difference between saying an action is good and saying it is right.

Because 'good' is always used relative to a set of standards, it always has a descriptive meaning. And since we usually use 'good' to commend, we generally use it with prescriptive meaning as well. But we don't always. This can happen with any word that both commends and describes; we can use it just to describe and not commend or disapprove. Take moral words like 'steal' or 'honesty'. We often use the word 'honest' to commend someone. But I can say, 'If you weren't so honest, we could have got away with that!' This is an expression of annoyance, not praise. Again, I can agree that a 'good person' is one who is honest, kind, just, etc. But I can still think that good people are not to be commended, because, as Woody Allen said, 'Good people sleep better than bad people, but bad people enjoy the waking hours more.'

So, Hare argues that descriptive meaning and prescriptive meaning are logically distinct. Nothing about being honest (i.e. telling the truth: descriptive meaning) can make me commend honesty (telling the truth is how to behave: prescriptive). More generally, nothing about the facts can entail a moral judgement. We are *free* in the prescriptions that we make.

However, whenever we apply a standard in making a prescription, we are committed to making the same judgement of two things that match the standard in the same way. If I say this chocolate is good but that chocolate is not, I must think that there is some *relevant difference* between the two. Likewise, we can choose what standards we live by, but the standards apply universally. If I think that it is wrong for you to steal from me, because it infringes my rights of ownership, then I must think that it is wrong for me to steal from you, because it infringes your rights of ownership – unless I can say that there is some relevant difference between the two cases.

Moral reasoning

While remaining non-cognitive, prescriptivism finds a place for reason in ethical debate.

First, we saw that emotivism is open to the objection that it makes ethical discussion a matter of manipulation. Prescriptivism sees the 'guiding' aspect of ethics as a matter of prescription, rather than a matter of influencing someone through emotion. This makes ethical discussion more straightforward and rational.

Second, we can argue about consistency and relevance. For example, Peter Singer claims there is *no relevant difference* between the suffering of people and the suffering of animals. If we are going to say that causing the suffering of people is wrong, we are committed to saying that causing the suffering of animals is wrong – unless we can find a relevant difference. Moral disagreements can be about the consistency in applying certain standards, and reason can help resolve this.

Third, we can infer prescriptions from other prescriptions. A famous argument against abortion says 'Taking an innocent human life is wrong. Abortion is the taking of an innocent human life. Therefore abortion is wrong.' This is a valid argument, even if we rephrase it as Hare would understand it: 'Do not take

Explain and illustrate the view that moral language is prescriptive.

See OUR TREATMENT OF NON-HUMAN ANIMALS, p. 276.

innocent human life. Abortion is the taking of an innocent human life. Therefore, do not commit abortion.' To disagree with the conclusion, we must disagree with at least one premise. And so our prescriptions are logically related to one another. Thus, we can use reason to discuss these relations.

Objections to prescriptivism are discussed in the next three sections.

Key points • • •

- Hare argues that moral words are not emotive in meaning, but prescriptive. Prescriptive language commands ('right') or commends ('good') certain objects, actions or traits, according to a set of standards.
- Moral language can be used purely descriptively, if the speaker doesn't agree with the standard. Description and prescription are logically distinct, which is why you cannot infer a moral judgement from natural facts.
- Standards apply universally, so to be consistent, speakers must be willing to universalise their moral judgements. If not, they must point to a relevant difference between cases. This allows moral disagreement to be about relevant differences as well as the facts.
- Prescriptivism also enables us to infer one moral judgement from another, as prescriptions are logically related to each other.

To what extent can we value what we like?

We have discussed the issue of moral reasoning in emotivism and prescriptivism. A further, and very important, difficulty these two theories face relates to the fact that they don't place limits on what we can approve or disapprove of. They identify moral judgements with a particular *type* of judgement – approval, disapproval, a commanded or commended principle – rather than a particular *content*. But isn't morality about sympathy, loyalty, courage, happiness and so on?

Because emotivists and prescriptivists understand moral judgements in terms of their form, not their content, they seem to allow that *anything* could be a moral judgement. Non-cognitivism claims, first, that a judgement is a value judgement if it has a particular form; and second, that value judgements 'create' values rather than 'discover' them. Values are a reflection of our value judgements. But if values depend entirely on our will, it seems we could value anything we chose to. But this is difficult to make sense of. Outside certain limits, we would consider people mad rather than thinking that they just had a different set of values to us.

Imagine someone believed in maximising the number of florists in Kensington, and all their 'moral' feelings and actions related to this: they were willing to do anything to pursue their goal (even murder), they tried to stop florists from closing down, they tried to change the law to protect florists in Kensington, they felt no disapproval towards theft, lying, disloyalty, no approval of kindness or courage – unless they related to florists in Kensington. Such a person would be classed as a psychopath!

Not just any set of expressions of approval or principles can count as 'morality'. Morality is about what is good or bad for human beings generally, given our nature and the types of problems life throws at us. It must relate in some way to what is good for people (or, more broadly, animals, the environment, God).

Emotivists and prescriptivists can respond that while 'valuing' is an activity of the will, the will is guided by *its nature*. We can't value just anything, precisely because human beings have certain needs and a particular nature. But there is no *logical* restriction on possible 'moralities'; there is just a considerable *factual* one. We are all set up, by evolution perhaps, to value actions and people in particular, familiar sorts of ways. This is why we call only particular sets of feelings or principles 'moral'. A common human nature underlies our feelings and choices. But it is still these feelings and choices that create morality.

The objection can be pressed in a different direction. If we don't distinguish morality by its content, how can the non-cognitivist draw a distinction between *moral* approval and disapproval and, say, *aesthetic* approval and disapproval? Given that 'approval' is the central concept in a non-cognitivist theory of morality, we really need an account of what makes approval moral or not moral.

> Can a non-cognitivist accept that our moral judgements are guided by facts about human nature?

> Assess the view that moral judgements are a matter of personal values and preferences.

Key points • • •

- Emotivism and prescriptivism do not identify moral judgements by what they are about, but by their form (emotive or prescriptive). This seems to allow that the content of morality could be anything.
- Emotivists and prescriptivists may respond that there is no logical restriction on what morality is about, but there is a factual one, for example psychological facts regarding human nature.
- We may object that emotivists and prescriptivists are still unable to

distinguish between types of emotional expression or commendation, for example aesthetic and moral.

The possibility of judging the abhorrent practices of other cultures or individuals

If there is no objective moral truth, then doesn't it follow that 'anything goes'? If morality is a reflection of our choices, feelings or social conventions, and my choices, feelings or social conventions are different from yours, then who are you to tell me that my morality is wrong? The denial of moral truth implies tolerance, many people claim, because no one can correct anyone else.

This can become an objection to the theory, since although tolerance can appear to be a virtue, it can also be a vice. Should we tolerate every practice, including racism, sexism, female circumcision . . .? Doesn't morality require that we 'take a stand' against what is wrong?

If morality is the product of my feelings and choices, or simply a set of conventions relative to my society, then morality has no authority over me (or anyone else). I can do whatever I like, as long as I don't get caught. 'Morality' becomes no more than a matter of taste. And if this is so, then morality cannot provide any firm grounds for morally judging the practices of other people.

Emotivists and prescriptivists can argue that this is either an unfair simplification of their theories or a straightforward misunderstanding. Living as though there are no moral values is itself a choice or expression of feeling, and one that moral people will disapprove of morally. The theory that moral values are a reflection of our feelings, or our social conventions, does not imply that we should stop having moral feelings or stop living according to convention. We should disapprove of anyone who advocates that morality doesn't matter or is just a matter of taste.

Relativists, on the other hand, will argue that there *are* moral values, independent of any individual. Morality is not subjective. Within a culture, we can use moral standards to judge other's abhorrent practices straightforwardly. The whole point of morality is to enable us to do this. The problem for the relativist arises when it comes to the practices of other cultures. On this, many relativists have advocated tolerance. To use our standards to judge other cultures is misguided – so we should be tolerant of them.

Explain non-cognitivism's reply to the claim that if non-cognitivism is true, anything goes.

Tolerance and its limits

However, the denial of moral truth does not necessarily lead to tolerance, for two reasons. First, tolerance is itself a moral value. 'You ought to tolerate other people's values, because there are no moral values' is self-contradictory. We ought to be tolerant only if tolerance is a good or right thing to be. So, turning the tables, who are you to tell someone else to be tolerant? This is no different from saying they ought not to eat meat or ought not to be racist. It is a moral claim. The denial of moral truth doesn't entail that we ought to be tolerant or that we ought not to be tolerant. This causes a problem for relativism. Different cultures have different conventions relating to tolerance: some cultures endorse tolerance, some are not tolerant at all.

Second, if my morality is different from yours, then not only will I disagree with you about whether a particular action is right or wrong, I may also disapprove of people who disagree with me and try to persuade them to change their mind. Morality does not present itself as simply a matter of conventions, relative to a particular society. We apply our morality (if not all, then parts of it) to everyone, not just our own society. Can relativism coherently *disapprove* of this practice?

Emotivism and prescriptivism avoid these problems. Our attitudes don't exist on their own, so disapproving of abortion leads to disapproving of people who approve of abortion. Tolerance is a moral attitude towards other people's attitudes, so it may conflict with other moral attitudes I have. I might feel that tolerance is a moral value, but this tolerance will have its limits. Very few people think that tolerance is a more important value than preventing a racist murder, say.

So, emotivism and prescriptivism can argue that we can (and should) judge other people's abhorrent practices. But can I really justify interfering with how other people behave just because their actions don't accord with my feelings or choices? This seems very petty. But this isn't the reason I am interfering, claims the non-cognitivist. It is not because it offends me, but because they are being racist or cruel or cowardly or whatever. Of course, that I think racist discrimination is a good reason to prevent an action is an expression of my moral feelings. For the cognitivist, by contrast, that this is a good reason to interfere is a fact about reasons. The cognitivist claims to have the backing of reality.

Outline the relationship between non-cognitivism and tolerance.

Can non-cognitivists coherently disapprove of the moral practices of other people?

Key points • • •

- Does non-cognitivism reduce morality to an optional matter of taste?
- The objection from tolerance argues that non-cognitivism implies that we should wrongly tolerate moral differences, no matter how abhorrent.
- Relativism faces the challenge that some moral codes endorse tolerance of other cultures, while some are intolerant.
- Emotivists and prescriptivists can reply that their theory does not necessarily entail tolerance (or intolerance). What we think we should tolerate depends on how important we think tolerance is as a moral value.

The possibility of moral progress and moral mistakes

A final objection to the denial of moral truth is that it does not allow for the idea of moral progress. If there is no moral reality, then our moral beliefs or feelings cannot become better or worse. Obviously, they have changed; people used to believe that slavery was morally acceptable and now they do not. But how can we say that this is *progress* if there is no objective moral truth? There are two responses non-cognitivists can give.

First, they can claim that there can be very real improvements in people's moral views (individually or as a culture) if they become more rational. This can happen in several different ways. First, people may come to know certain facts that they didn't know before. In the case of slavery, people believed many things about slaves that were not true (one popular false belief was that they were stupid). Moral progress here means basing one's morality on the facts, not mistakes. Second, people can become more consistent, more willing to universalise their principles. Some utilitarians, such as Peter Singer, argue that if we were consistent in our feelings about preventing suffering, we would not eat meat. If he is right, then vegetarianism would be moral progress. Third, people can become more coherent in their moral judgements. Many of us have moral feelings that come into conflict with each other, for example over abortion. Moral progress here would be a matter of working out the implications of our views, and changing what needed changing to make them coherent with each other.

Because people are ignorant, do not always think logically and have not resolved the conflicts between their different feelings and conventions, there is plenty of room for moral progress. But moral progress just means becoming

Cognitivists can say that we have become more humane than in the past, and there is greater agreement about moral judgements than before because we are discovering real moral truths.

Practical Ethics, Ch. 1

more rational in our moral thinking, not becoming more 'correct' in our moral judgements.

The second response non-cognitivists can give is this: if we disapprove of past moral codes and approve of our own moral code, then we will say that we have made moral progress. Society has moved from moral principles that were bad (i.e. principles we disapprove of) to moral principles that are good (i.e. principles we approve of). That is what moral progress is.

This response means that moral progress is relative to a particular moral point of view. If you disagree with me, you might claim that today's moral principles are much worse than those 200 years ago and so we have not made moral progress. But this is now just the familiar problem of how to make sense of moral disagreement, not a special problem about moral progress.

> Explain and discuss the objection to non-cognitivism from moral progress.

Key points • • •

- We may object that if there is no moral truth, as non-cognitivism argues, we cannot talk of moral progress, because changes in moral beliefs are neither right nor wrong.
- Non-cognitivists reply that moral beliefs can improve by becoming more rational – that is, changing in the light of previously unknown facts or becoming more consistent or coherent.
- From our perspective now, we can only say that the change from previous views to current views is morally good (that is, we express our approval of it).

III. MORAL DECISIONS

Morality is intended to guide our actions, and should therefore be something that assists us in making decisions. '**Normative** ethics' discusses theories of what we should do, and the application of these theories to particular issues, such as abortion, is 'practical ethics'.

Act utilitarianism: the extent to which an action maximises happiness as the sole criterion by which its value can be judged

Jeremy Bentham defended the 'principle of utility' or 'greatest happiness principle', 'that principle which approves or disapproves of every action whatsoever, according to the tendency which it appears to have to augment or diminish the happiness of the party whose interest is in question'. Or again, 'that principle which states the greatest happiness of all those whose interest is in question, as being the right and proper . . . end of human action'.

If we simplify this a little, we can say that act utilitarianism claims that an action is right if it leads to the greatest happiness of all those it affects – that is, if it *maximizes* happiness. Otherwise, the action is wrong. The greatest happiness should be the goal of our actions, what we hope to bring about. Our actions are judged not 'in themselves', for example by what *type* of action they are (a lie, helping someone, etc.), but in terms of what *consequences* they have.

'Greatest happiness' is comparative (great, greater, greatest). If an action leads to the greatest happiness of those it affects, no other action taken at that time could have led to greater happiness. So, an action is right only if, out of all the actions you could have taken, this action leads to more happiness than any other. Just causing *some* happiness, or more happiness than unhappiness, isn't enough for an act to be morally right.

Act utilitarianism seems to have the advantage of providing a clear and simple way of making decisions: consider the consequences of the different actions you could perform and choose that action which brings about the greatest happiness. It makes complicated decisions easy – the only thing that matters is happiness (and surely everyone wants happiness).

Introduction to the Principles of Morals and Legislation, Ch. 1 § 2

Explain and illustrate act utilitarianism.

Objections

But is the guidance offered helpful? How can we know or work out the consequences of an action, to discover whether it maximises happiness or not? Bentham does not say that an action is right if it *actually* maximises happiness. He says it is right according to 'the tendency which it appears to have' to maximise happiness. We don't need to be able to work out the consequences precisely. An action is right if we can reasonably expect that it will maximise happiness.

This still means we must be able to work things out roughly. John Stuart Mill, who defended a different version of utilitarianism, thought this was still too demanding. Happiness is 'much too complex and indefinite' a standard to apply directly to actions. But we don't need to try, he claimed, because over time, people have automatically, through trial and error, worked out which actions tend to produce happiness. This is what our inherited moral rules actually are: 'tell the truth', 'don't steal' and 'keep your promises' are embodiments of the wisdom of humanity that lying, theft and false promising tend to lead to unhappiness. Mill called these moral rules 'secondary principles'. It is only in cases of conflict between secondary principles (for example, if by telling the truth you break your promise) that we need to apply the greatest happiness principle directly to an action.

A second criticism of act utilitarianism is that no type of action is ruled out as immoral. If torturing a child produces the greatest happiness, then it is right to torture a child. Suppose a group of child abusers find and torture only abandoned children. Only the child suffers pain (no one else knows about the abusers' activities). But they derive a great deal of happiness. So, more happiness is produced by torturing the child than not, so it is morally right. This is clearly the wrong answer.

Act utilitarians can reply that it is *very probable* that someone *will* find out, and then many people will be unhappy. Because we should do what is *likely* to produce the greatest happiness, we shouldn't torture children. However, the theory still implies that *if* it were very unlikely anyone would find out, then it would be right to torture children. But other people finding out isn't what *makes* torturing children wrong.

Utilitarianism, Ch.2

This contrasts with DEONTOLOGY, p. 254.

?

If we always try to maximise happiness, will we act morally?

Going further: integrity and demandingness

Act utilitarianism says that my happiness doesn't count any more than anyone else's when I'm considering what to do. Obviously, I am affected more often and more deeply by my actions than other people. But that's it. My actions are just a *means* of generating the greatest overall happiness.

So what if my conscience and moral integrity tell me not to do something that act utilitarianism says it is right to do? Act utilitarianism says that I am supposed to calculate how unhappy it would be make me to perform the action, and see whether that changes what I should do! If it doesn't, I should go ahead with the action anyway. This doesn't 'respect' the importance of people's integrity.

Second, act utilitarianism is too demanding. For example, every time I buy a CD, I could have given the money to charity; and surely that would create more happiness, since other people need food more than I need music. But because people will always need food, it will *never* be right for me to buy myself music. It will never be right to do something just for myself if I have more than the bare minimum.

Critically discuss act utilitarianism.

Key points • • •

- In its simplest form, act utilitarianism claims that an act is right if, and only if, it maximises happiness – that is, if it creates more happiness than other acts in that situation.
- But how do we know which act will create the most happiness? Bentham replies that an act is right if we can reasonably expect that it will cause the greatest happiness, while Mill argued that our common-sense moral rules ('secondary principles') are a guide to what maximises happiness.
- A second objection is that some acts, such as torturing children for pleasure, are wrong even if they cause the greatest happiness.
- Third, act utilitarianism fails to respect people's moral integrity when deciding what to do.
- Finally, it makes morality too demanding.

Rule utilitarianism

By contrast, Mill's secondary principles are *rules of thumb* – that is, not strict rules that we must follow, but helpful guidance in our thoughts about what to do.

Rule utilitarianism claims that an action is right if, and only if, it complies with those rules which, if everybody followed them, would lead to the greatest happiness (compared to any other set of rules).

Rule utilitarianism has some advantages over act utilitarianism. First, a rule forbidding torture of children will clearly cause more happiness if everyone follows it than a rule allowing torture of children. So, it is wrong to torture children. Second, we don't have to work out the consequences of each act in turn to see if it is right. We need to work out which rules create the greatest happiness, but we need to do this only once, and we can do it together.

Third, the rule that we should usually allow people to act on integrity is a rule that will promote more happiness than any other. Finally, morality is not so demanding: I am only required to act in a way that, *if everyone acted like that*, would promote the greatest happiness. In the case of charity, I only need to give as much to charity as would be a 'fair share' of the amount needed to really help other people. In all these ways, it looks as though rule utilitarianism provides better guidance for making moral decisions.

However, act utilitarians object that rule utilitarianism amounts to 'rule fetishism'. The point of the rules is to bring about the greatest happiness. If we give only as much to charity as we would need to if everyone gave to charity, then many people will not be helped, because not everyone will give what they should to charity. Surely, knowing this, I ought to give much more to charity; spending the money on myself would not be right. Or again, if I know that, for example, lying in a particular situation will produce more happiness than telling the truth, it seems pointless to tell the truth, causing unhappiness. The whole point of the rule was to bring about happiness, so there should be an exception to the rule in this case. But then *whenever* a particular action causes more happiness by breaking the rule than by following it, we should take that action. And then we are back with act utilitarianism, weighing up the consequences of each action in turn.

Rule utilitarians respond, first, that only rule utilitarianism can provide real guidance for making moral decisions; and second, that deciding according to act utilitarianism will break down our trust that people behave morally. So, following a rule, even when in the particular case it will cause less happiness than breaking the rule, is still justified, because if people kept breaking the rules, that would cause less happiness in the long run.

> Explain precisely the difference between act and rule utilitarianism.

> Outline and illustrate *two* ways in which rule utilitarianism improves on act utilitarianism.

> Discuss whether rule utilitarianism can successfully guide decisions.

Key points • • •

- Rule utilitarianism claims that an act is morally right if, and only if, it complies with rules that, if everybody follows them, lead to the greatest happiness.
- This theory avoids many objections to act utilitarianism.
- However, act utilitarians object that it amounts to 'rule fetishism'. If breaking a rule would create more happiness on a particular occasion, we should break it.

• Rule utilitarians respond that people need to trust that others will abide by the rules, so we shouldn't break it.

Variations on 'happiness': hedonism versus preference utilitarianism

Hedonism

If we are to bring about happiness, we should consider what happiness is. Bentham and Mill were 'hedonists', claiming that happiness is pleasure and the absence of pain, and that this is all that matters. Bentham argued that we can measure pleasures and pains and add them up on a single scale by a process he called the 'felicific calculus'. If a pleasure is more intense, will last longer, is more certain to occur, will happen sooner rather than later, or will produce in turn many other pleasures and few pains, it counts for more. In thinking what to do, you also need to take into account how many people will be affected (the more you affect positively and the fewer you affect negatively, the better). The total amount of happiness produced is the sum total of everyone's pleasures produced minus the sum total of everyone's pains.

Mill rejected Bentham's view that pleasures and pains are all equally important. Some types of pleasure are 'higher' than others – more valuable, more important to human happiness. But which ones? Mill thought there was an objective test: if almost everyone who knows what they are talking about compares two pleasures and agrees that the first is 'more desirable and valuable' than the second, then the first is a higher pleasure.

But how can we tell if a pleasure is *more valuable* (quality) than another, rather than just more *pleasurable* (quantity)? To tell if a pleasure is more valuable, people have to prefer it *even if having that pleasure brings more pain with it*. For example, the pleasure of being in love carries the pain of longing and the possible pain of breaking up. But people still prefer being in love to, say, eating delicious food. Happiness is not contentment.

Mill argues that as long as our physical needs are met, people will prefer the pleasures of thought, feeling and imagination to pleasures of the body and the senses, even though our 'higher' capacities also mean we can experience terrible pain, boredom and dissatisfaction.

> **Compare and contrast Bentham and Mill on happiness.**

Pleasure and preferences

Preference utilitarianism claims we should maximise not pleasure, but the satisfaction of people's preferences. Two reasons favour this theory. First, it is easier to know whether someone's preference has been satisfied than how much pleasure someone experiences. So, it provides better guidance. Second, it can be right to satisfy someone's preferences even when they don't know this has happened, and so don't derive any pleasure from it. For example, I can want you to look after my ant farm when I die. You should still look after my ants, rather than kill them, even though I cannot gain any pleasure from your doing so.

> Is preference utilitarianism an improvement on hedonism?

Objections

But is happiness the right standard for morality at all? Utilitarianism weighs the unhappiness of one person against the happiness of another, whether this is in deciding which action to do or which rule to adopt. Philosophers object that it is concerned with people not as individuals, but as 'receptacles' for happiness, which fails to show them proper respect. Furthermore, the *distribution* of happiness – who gets happy by how much – is irrelevant, which fails to respect justice.

Second, Kant argued that happiness (or satisfying people's preferences) is not always morally good. For example, the happiness child abusers get from hurting children is morally bad. The fact that the abusers are made happy by what they do doesn't make their action better *at all*, but worse. So, there must be some other standard than happiness for what is morally good.

Third, is happiness the only thing that matters? Many philosophers argue that there are other values (freedom, justice, etc.). Even if pursuing these values gives us happiness, it is not the happiness the value brings which is important, but the value itself.

> Critically discuss utilitarianism.

Key points • • •

- Bentham and Mill defend hedonism, claiming that happiness is pleasure and the absence of pain, and all that matters for human well-being is the quantity of happiness.
- Mill argues that some pleasures ('higher' pleasures) are more valuable than others.

- Preference utilitarianism argues we should maximise preference satisfaction.
- We can object that utilitarianism doesn't show respect to individuals as persons.
- Kant objects that happiness is not always morally good.
- We can also argue that happiness is not the only value.

Deontology: the view that moral rights, duties and principles, which are not based on consequences, are required to make ethical decisions

Deon (Greek) means 'one must'.

Deontologists believe that morality is a matter of duty. We have moral duties to do things that it is right to do and moral duties not to do things that it is wrong to do. Whether something is right or wrong doesn't depend on its consequences. Rather, it is something about any particular action that makes it right or wrong *in itself*. In order to make moral decisions, we need to consider our duties.

The syllabus connects deontology to 'rights, duties and principles'. However, our discussion will focus only on duties. 'Principles' are not connected to deontology alone; for example, act utilitarianism has the *principle* of utility, while rule utilitarianism can claim that the rules we should follow are all principles. A deontological principle simply states that x (some act) is our duty.

For further discussion, see Rights, p. 93.

We can also discuss rights in terms of duties. If someone has a right, say the right to life, then other people have duties, the duty to respect that right. However, people also have duties that go beyond rights. For example, many deontologists argue that we have a duty of charity; but this does not mean that the poor have the *right* to receive charity. Rights entail duties, but not all duties entail rights.

Duties

Most deontological theories recognise two classes of duties. First, there are general duties we have towards anyone. These are mostly prohibitions; for example, do not lie, do not murder. But some may be positive; for example, help people in need. Second, there are duties we have because of our particular personal or social relationships. If you have made a promise, you have a duty to keep it. If you are a parent, you have a duty to provide for your children. And so on.

We each have duties regarding our *own* actions. I have a duty to keep *my* promises, but I don't have a duty to make sure promises are kept. Deontology claims that we should each be most concerned with complying with our duties, not attempting to bring about the most good. In fact, all deontologists agree that there are times when we *should not* maximise the good, because doing so would be to violate a duty. Most deontologists also argue that we do not have a duty to maximise the good, only a duty to do *something* for people in need. As this illustrates, many deontologists think our duties are quite limited. While there are a number of things we *may not* do, we are otherwise free to act as we please.

How does deontology differ from rule utilitarianism?

Discovering our duties

If we need to consider our duties when making moral decisions, how do we find out what our duties are? Deontologists tend to appeal to moral reasoning and insight. For example, W.D. Ross argued that it was self-evident that certain types of actions, which he named prima facie duties, were right. He listed seven classes of prima facie duties: duties of fidelity (such as keeping a promise), reparation (when we have done something wrong), gratitude, justice, beneficence (helping others), self-improvement and non-maleficence (not harming others).

See How IS KNOWLEDGE OF MORAL TRUTH POSSIBLE?, p. 228.

The Right and the Good

Aquinas started from insight into what is good and the nature of human flourishing. We have direct rational insight into what is good; and this informs our idea of what human nature is. It lays down that what is good is truly desirable, and what is bad is truly undesirable. Aquinas then argued that certain things, such as life, marriage, living in friendship and harmony with others, and practical reasonableness, are truly desirable, and that this is self-evident.

By contrast, contractarians believe that morality derives, in some way, from what people would agree to if making a contract with each other about how to behave. Different theorists give different accounts of what the conditions for making the contract should be, and of how morality derives from this contract. One version, defended by Thomas Scanlon, argues that moral principles are principles of behaviour which no one can reasonably reject. If an act is permitted by a principle that could be reasonably rejected, then it is wrong. How do we know what is 'reasonable'? Scanlon develops an intuitionist theory of moral reasoning, which was discussed in How IS KNOWLEDGE OF MORAL TRUTH POSSIBLE?, p. 228.

See MORALITY AS A SOCIAL CONTRACT, pp. 89 and 102.

What We Owe to Each Other

Conflicts of duties

A duty is absolute if it permits no exceptions. This causes problems in cases where it seems that two absolute duties conflict with each other: anything we can do will be wrong. Should I break a promise or tell a lie? Should I betray a friend to save a life? One response is to say that a *real* conflict of duties can never occur. If there appears to be a conflict, we have misunderstood what at least one duty requires of us. If duties are absolute, we must formulate our duties very, very carefully to avoid them conflicting.

Another response is that (most) duties are not absolute. For instance, there is a duty not to lie, but it may be permissible to lie in order to save someone's life. Duties can 'give way'; Ross argues that our usual duties are not absolute, but 'prima facie' duties – they are duties 'at first sight'. In cases of conflict, one will give way and no longer be a duty in that situation.

But how do we know how to resolve an apparent conflict of duties? Ross argued that there are no hard and fast rules about this; we have to use our judgement in the situation in which we find ourselves. But if we have no criteria for making these decisions, won't disagreements about what to do be irresolvable?

Deontologists may reply that this lack of guidance is a *strength* of the theory. Choices in life *are* difficult and unclear; a moral theory should not pretend to provide all the answers. A moral life calls for insight and judgement, not knowledge of some philosophical theory.

We may object that this is an unsatisfactory answer for a *deontologist* to give, because one of the two acts is *wrong in itself* while the other is not. If one act were good but the other act better, the issue of not being able to tell which was which might not be so pressing.

See PRACTICAL WISDOM, p. 265, for another discussion.

Explain and discuss the challenge to deontology that arises from the conflict of duties.

Going further: rationality and consequences

Utilitarians object that deontology is irrational. If it is my duty not to murder, for instance, this must be because there is something bad or wrong about murder. But then if murder is bad, surely we should try to ensure that there are as few murders as possible. If I *know* that unless I kill someone deliberately, many people will die, how can I justify *not* killing them by appealing to duty? Surely it is only my duty not to kill because death is bad. So, I should prevent more deaths. To insist that *I* don't do anything 'wrong' seems a perverse obsession with 'keeping my hands clean'.

Utilitarianism understands all practical reasoning – reasoning about what to do – as *means-end* reasoning: it is rational to do whatever brings about a good end. The utilitarian thinks it is just *obvious* that if something is good, more of it is better, and we ought to do what is better. The deontologist disagrees and offers an *alternative* theory of practical reasoning. We have looked at intuitionist versions above and will discuss another account in KANT'S ATTEMPT TO PROVIDE A RATIONAL GROUNDING FOR A DEONTOLOGICAL ETHICS (p. 258).

> Why does deontology reject the view that it is rational to do whatever maximises what is good?

Going further: actions and intentions

Deontology says that certain types of action are right or wrong. How do we distinguish types of action? For example, a person may kill someone else. A conventional description of the action is 'a killing'. But not all 'killings' are the same type of action, morally speaking. If the person *intended* to kill someone – that is, their victim's death is what they wanted to bring about – that is very different from a case in which the killing was accidental or if the person was only intending to defend themselves against an attack.

Actions are the result of choices, and so should be understood in terms of choices. Choices are made for reasons, and with a purpose in mind. These considerations determine what the action performed actually is. So, deontology argues that we do not know what type of action an action is unless we know the intention. We should judge whether an action is right or wrong by the agent's intention. This does not make moral judgement subjective. What matters is the *real* reason why the person made the choice to act as they did. It may be difficult to know what the real reason is, but that is a different point.

> See also THE IMPORTANCE OF MOTIVATION IN MAKING MORAL DECISIONS, p. 263.

> Explain and illustrate why the relation between intention and action is important in deontology.

Key points • • •

- Deontology claims that actions are right or wrong *in themselves*, not depending on their consequences. Deontology identifies different types of action, and so judges whether they are right or wrong, on the basis of the agent's intention.
- We can have general duties, for example do not lie, and duties that depend on our specific relationships to others, for example keep your promises.
- Our duties are concerned with *our* actions, not attempting to bring about the most good. It can be against our duty to do what maximises the good.
- Different theories defend different accounts of how we discover our duties. Ross argues that there are, self-evidently, seven types of duty; Aquinas argues that we know what is good, which is related to human nature, through rational insight; Scanlon defends the view that what is wrong is what can be reasonably rejected, and defends an intuitionist account of our knowledge of what is reasonable.
- Deontologists disagree whether duties are absolute or prima facie.
- We can object that deontological theories don't provide guidance when duties conflict.
- Utilitarians argue that it is irrational not to maximise what is good.

Kant's attempt to provide a rational grounding for a deontological ethics

Kant: the basics

Groundwork of the Metaphysic of Morals

Immanuel Kant argued that moral principles could be derived from practical reason alone. We only need to understand what it is to make a decision in order to discover what decisions we should make. To understand his claim, we need to put some premises in place.

First, Kant believed that whenever we make a decision, we act on a *maxim*. Maxims are Kant's version of intentions. They are our personal principles that guide our decisions, for example 'to have as much fun as possible', 'to marry only someone I truly love'. All our decisions have some maxim or other behind them.

Second, morality is a set of 'laws' – rules, principles – that are the same for everyone and that apply to everyone. If this is true, it must be *possible* that everyone could act morally (even if it is very unlikely that they will).

From this, Kant devises a test for working out whether acting on a particular maxim is right or wrong. The test, the 'Categorical Imperative', is 'Act only on that maxim through which you can at the same time will that it should become a universal law.' (An 'imperative' is just a command. The moral command is categorical because we can't take it or leave it, as we choose.) If I act on a maxim that it is impossible for everyone to act on, I must be acting immorally – because it is always possible for everyone to act morally. For example, suppose you want a gift to take to a party, but you can't afford it, so you steal it from the shop. Your maxim is something like: 'To steal something I want if I can't afford it'. This can be the right thing to do only if everyone could do it.

Categorical Imperative = universality

> Outline Kant's argument for the Categorical Imperative.

THE TWO TESTS

There are two different ways in which we could fail to be able to will our maxim to become universal. The first, which Kant calls a 'contradiction in conception', is if the situation in which everyone acted on that maxim is somehow self-contradictory. If we could all just help ourselves to whatever we wanted, the idea of 'owning' things would disappear. But, by definition, you can't steal something unless it belongs to someone else. Stealing presupposes that people own things. But people can own things only if they don't all go around helping themselves whenever they want. So, it is logically impossible for everyone to steal things. And so stealing (at least just because one wants something) is wrong.

The second way our maxim can fail is a 'contradiction in will'. Kant's example relates to helping others. It is logically possible to universalise the maxim 'not to help others in need'. The world would not be a pleasant place, but this is not what Kant focuses on. Kant does *not* claim that an action is wrong because we *wouldn't like* the consequences if everyone did it. His test is whether we *could will* for our personal maxim to be a universal law, not whether we'd like the results.

Kant argues that we *cannot will* that no one should ever help anyone else. First, a will, by definition, wills its ends (goals). Second, to truly will the ends, one must will the necessary means. And so, third, we cannot will a situation in which it would be impossible for us to achieve our ends. It is possible that the only available means to our ends, in some situations, involves the help of others. We cannot therefore will that this possibility is denied to us. So, we cannot will a situation in which no one ever helps anyone else. To do so is to cease to will

Explain and illustrate Kant's tests of 'contradiction in conception' and 'contradiction in will'.

the necessary means to one's ends, which is effectively to cease to will any ends at all. This contradicts the very act of willing.

The Categorical Imperative is based on reason

Kant argued that it is not just morally wrong to disobey the Categorical Imperative, but also irrational. It must be possible for all rational animals to choose to behave rationally. So, deciding to behave in a way that it is impossible for everyone to follow is irrational. As the tests show, disobeying the Categorical Imperative involves a self-contradiction. Through the Categorical Imperative, reason both determines what our duties are and gives us the means to discover them.

But why should morality be about behaving rationally? Morality is supposed to guide our actions, which it can do only if it motivates us. Kant argues that there are, ultimately, only two sources of motivation: happiness and reason. But happiness can't be the basis of morality, for two reasons.

First, what makes people happy differs from person to person. If morality were about happiness, then different people would be motivated to act in different ways. But morality is the same for everyone. A utilitarian would object that morality can be the same for everyone and be about happiness if morality is about creating the *greatest* happiness. Kant would respond that everyone else's happiness does not necessarily motivate me; only my own happiness does. And, in fact, utilitarians usually appeal to reason here themselves, saying that caring about other people's happiness is *rational* or *reasonable*.

Second, happiness is not always morally good. If someone is made happy by hurting others, this is no reason to say that it is morally good to hurt others. In fact, that person's happiness is morally bad. So, we evaluate happiness by morality. That means the standard of morality must be independent of happiness.

Since morality can't be based on happiness, then it must be based on reason. This is confirmed by the characteristics that morality and rationality share. Morality is universal, the same for everyone; so is reason, says Kant. Morality and rationality are categorical; the demands to be rational and moral don't stop applying to you even if you don't care about them. Neither morality nor rationality depends on what we want. Finally, we intuitively think that morality applies to *all and only* rational beings, not just human beings. In Douglas Adams' *The Hitchhiker's Guide to the Galaxy*, Arthur Dent protests to the Vogons, aliens who are going to destroy the Earth, that what they are doing is immoral. Morality doesn't apply to beings that can't make rational choices, such as dogs and cats (pets misbehave, they don't act *morally wrongly*).

Outline Kant's argument that morality is based on reason.

Objections to the Categorical Imperative

In addition to the objections posed to deontology generally, Kant's theory faces the objection that the Categorical Imperative is a flawed test. First, couldn't any action be justified, as long as we phrase the maxim cleverly? In stealing the gift, I could claim that my maxim is 'To steal gifts from large shops and when there are seven letters in my name (Michael)'. Universalising this maxim, only people with seven letters in their name would steal only gifts and only from large shops. The case would apply so rarely that there would be no general breakdown in the concept of private property. So, it would be perfectly possible for this law to apply to everyone.

Kant's response is that his theory is concerned with my *actual* maxim, not some made-up one. It is not actually part of my choice that my name has seven letters, or perhaps even that it is a *gift* I steal. If I am honest with myself, I have to admit that it is a question of my taking what I want when I can't afford it. For Kant's test to work, we must be honest with ourselves about what our maxims are.

However, Kant's test delivers some strange results. Say I am a hard-working shop assistant who hates the work. One happy Saturday I win the lottery, and I vow 'never to sell anything to anyone again, but only ever to buy'. This is perhaps eccentric, but it doesn't seem morally wrong. But it cannot be universalised. If no one ever sold things, how could anyone buy them? It is logically impossible, which makes it wrong according to Kant's test. So perhaps it is not always wrong to do things that requires other people to do something different.

Kant argues that it is not rational to act in a way that not everyone could act in. This is not means–end reasoning, but picks up on other formal features of reason (universal, categorical, independent of desires). However, some philosophers argue that Kant has wrongly taken the features of *theoretical* reason – reasoning about facts, science, logic and so on – as features of *practical* reason. Practical reason does not require us to follow a rule that everyone can follow. Instead, being irrational involves taking the wrong means to one's ends.

Assess Kant's Categorical Imperative as a test for making decisions.

Respecting humanity

Kant gave an alternative formulation of the Categorical Imperative, known as the Formula of Humanity: 'Act in such a way that you always treat humanity, whether in your own person or in the person of any other, never simply as a means, but always at the same time as an end.'

Kant does not say we cannot use people as a means, but rather that we can't use them *simply* as a means. We rely on other people in many ways as means to achieve our own ends; for example, people serving me in a shop are a means to my getting what I want to buy. What is important, says Kant, is that I also respect their humanity as an end in itself. By 'humanity', Kant means our practical rationality, our ability to rationally determine which ends to adopt and pursue. To treat someone's humanity simply as a means and not also as an end is to treat the person in a way that undermines their power of making a rational choice themselves. Coercing someone, lying to them, stealing from them, all involve not allowing them to make an *informed choice*.

Key points • • •

- Kant argues that choices are made according to maxims, and that morality is a set of principles everyone can follow.
- He therefore concludes that it is morally right to 'Act only on that maxim through which you can at the same time will that it should become a universal law' (the Categorical Imperative). Acting on a maxim that does not pass this test is morally wrong.
- A maxim can fail the test in two ways: (1) it cannot be consistently universalised; a situation in which everyone acted on it is impossible; and (2) it cannot be willed in a universal form, because a situation in which it was universally followed would undermine the operation of the will.
- Kant argued that only happiness or reason can motivate us to act. Morality cannot be based on happiness, since what makes people happy differs, and happiness is not always morally good. The Categorical Imperative is based on pure practical reason. Reason and morality are categorical, universal and independent of our desires.
- However, the Categorical Imperative delivers some counter-intuitive results, and we can object that practical reason does not have the universal form Kant assumes it does.

- Kant reformulated the Categorical Imperative as the Formula of Humanity: 'Act in such a way that you always treat humanity, whether in your own person or in the person of any other, never simply as a means, but always at the same time as an end.' This requires us to respect others' ability to make rational choices.

The importance of motivation in making moral decisions

At the heart of deontology is the idea of the 'good will', a will that intends and chooses what is right because it is right – one's duty – to do so. To do what is morally right because it is morally right is to act from the *motive* of duty. Much of the time we do things just because we want to. However, if we do not *care* whether what we do is right or wrong, we are motivated *only* by what we want. But if we wouldn't do what we want to do if it were wrong, then we are, at least in part, motivated by duty. The clearest case of being motivated by duty is when we do something we don't want to do, because we feel we ought to.

Kant compares two shopkeepers who both give the correct change to their customers. The first is honest because he is scared of being caught if he tries to cheat his customers. The second is honest because he believes it is morally right to be honest. The first shopkeeper doesn't act from duty; the second shopkeeper does. Suppose the first shopkeeper gives correct change because he wants people to like him, or even because he likes his customers. He still isn't acting from duty, because the fact that it is his duty to be honest is not his reason for being honest.

One aspect of the importance of motivation in making moral decisions, namely intention, was discussed in ACTIONS AND INTENTIONS, p. 257.

Explain and illustrate the motive of duty.

Objection

Many philosophers object to the idea that we should be so concerned with 'doing the right thing'. Surely, if I do something nice for you, such as visiting you in hospital, because I like you, that is also a morally good action. Much of the time we do good things because we feel warmly towards the people we benefit. Kant seems to say we have to want to benefit people because it is our duty to do so, not because we like them. Some philosophers have thought putting duty above feelings in our motives is somehow inhuman.

Kant can respond that he is not trying to *stop* us from being motivated by our feelings. His point is that when we are choosing what to do, how we feel should not be as important as what it is morally right to do. But when you do something for a friend, should you think, 'I'll do this because he is my friend; and it is morally right to do so'? Perhaps Kant can reply that you need to be willing to refuse to help your friend only if helping your friend involved doing something morally wrong.

The objection does not apply to other deontological theories. Aquinas, for instance, argues that practical reasoning starts with what is good, and that the right response to what is good is to choose to act in accordance with it. To *intend* to do something bad, such as lie or kill (even in order to bring about some good consequence), is not to order one's will in accordance with what is good. A good will aligns itself with what is good, and that includes friendship. If we do something out of friendship, this is morally good. We do not need an additional motive of duty to make the action morally good.

> **Discuss the role of the motive of duty in morally right action.**

Key points • • •

- As discussed in ACTIONS AND INTENTIONS (p. 257), according to deontology the intention with which an action is done makes that action right or wrong.
- Deontology also emphasises the importance of a good will, choosing what is right *because* it is right. To act on this basis is to act from the motive of duty.
- Philosophers object that acting from certain emotions and desires is also praiseworthy. Aquinas would agree, as any desire for what is good involves the will aligning itself with the good.

Practical wisdom

The syllabus defines practical wisdom as 'the capacity to make informed, rational judgements without recourse to a formal decision procedure'. As we saw in DISCOVERING OUR DUTIES (p. 255), many deontological theories argue that there is no formal decision procedure, and in fact even Kant, who has a formal decision procedure, argues that applying the Categorical Imperative correctly involves 'judgement', which cannot be formalised. However, the idea of practical wisdom is today most strongly associated with Aristotle, so we shall focus our discussion on his view of how to make moral decisions.

Practical wisdom, says Aristotle, is 'a true and reasoned state of capacity to act with regard to the things that are good or bad for man'. So, while practical

> **Greek *phronesis*; sometimes translated as 'prudence'.**

wisdom involves knowledge of what is good or bad, it is not merely theoretical knowledge, but a capacity to act on such knowledge as well. This capacity requires:

Nicomachean Ethics
VI.5

1. a general conception of what is good or bad, which Aristotle relates to the conditions for human flourishing;
2. the ability to perceive, in the light of that general conception, what is required in terms of feeling, choice and action in a particular situation;
3. the ability to deliberate well; and
4. the ability to act on that deliberation.

See *Virtue and human flourishing*, p. 220.

Aristotle's theory makes practical wisdom very demanding. The type of insight into the good that is needed and the relation between practical wisdom and virtues of character are both complex. Practical wisdom cannot be taught, but requires experience of life and virtue. Only the person who is good knows what is good, according to Aristotle.

Insight and making decisions

Aristotle argues that practical wisdom involves more than one kind of insight. First, there is insight into 'what is good or bad for man', namely insight into human flourishing. Second, practical wisdom involves understanding what is required in a particular situation in light of a general understanding of what is good. The question that faces us on any occasion is how to achieve what is good – part of a good life – in the here and now, in this situation. But there are no rules for applying knowledge of the good life to the current situation. What is right on a particular occasion is in accordance with 'right reason' (*orthos logos*), but this can vary from one occasion to another. Furthermore, this kind of insight is inseparable from making a good decision: we must understand not only the situation (which can involve considerable sensitivity), but also how to act well in it.

This makes it impossible to make true generalisations – ones that will hold in all cases – about right and wrong, good and bad. Our reasoning on 'variable' matters, our deliberation, is a form of intuitive reason. Practical wisdom 'grasps' the particular facts involved in the case. This does not make ethics subjective, as there is a truth of the matter to be discovered. However, proving the truth of one view against another is not possible by argument alone. If you are blind,

I may not be able to convince you of the colour of moonlight; if you lack insight into what is good, I may not be able to convince you of the goodness of being kind.

And so, Aristotle argues, ethical understanding is not something that can be *taught*, for what can be taught is general, not particular. Rules and principles will rarely apply in any clear way to real situations. Instead, moral knowledge is acquired only through experience.

A third kind of insight relates to what is a virtue. In one way, this is like insight into human flourishing, since it involves knowing what character traits are necessary for a good life; on the other, it is like insight into the particular situation, since it involves knowing how to respond emotionally here and now. If we feel emotions and desires, and make decisions, 'well' – that is, virtuously – we feel and choose 'at the right times, with reference to the right objects, towards the right people, with the right motive, and in the right way'.

> Explain the nature of insight in Aristotle's theory of practical wisdom.

Going further: the doctrine of the mean

In a situation in which you are being bullied, you could feel angry too much or too little, 'and in both cases not well'. There are lots of ways in which we can act and feel 'unreasonably'. Aristotle defends the 'doctrine of the mean', the idea that a virtuous response or action is 'intermediate'. Just as there is a right time, object, person, etc. at which to feel anger (or any emotion), some people can feel angry too often, about too many things, and towards too many people, or they get too angry, or get angry to scare others. Other people can feel angry not often enough, regarding too few objects and people (perhaps they don't understand how people are taking advantage of them). Someone who gets angry 'too much' is short-tempered. We don't have a name for someone who gets angry too little. Someone who has the virtue relating to anger is good-tempered. The virtue is the 'intermediate' state between the two vices of 'too much' and 'too little'. Aristotle's doctrine of the mean does *not* claim that when you get angry, you should only ever be moderately angry. You should be as angry as the situation demands, which can be very angry.

Many virtues fit this model, Aristotle argues. Some, like good temper, work with feelings. Other virtues, like honesty, work with motives for actions.

Telling the truth 'too much' is tactlessness. Telling it 'too little' is lying when you shouldn't. The virtue of honesty involves telling the truth at the right times, to the right people, etc.

This knowledge, of what is the right time, objects, people, motive and way for certain emotions or choices, is practical knowledge of how to live a good life.

Outline Aristotle's doctrine of the mean. What are its implications for making moral decisions?

Objections

Aristotle argues that practical wisdom requires virtue. Without a good character, we cannot understand what is truly good. But this means that knowledge of the good is not within everyone's reach. By contrast, many philosophers argue that everyone is sufficiently rational to understand what is right, or know what is right or wrong through their conscience.

Virtue theorists can respond that knowledge of the good can come in degrees. If someone has a completely depraved character, perhaps they really don't know what is good or bad. But most people will have enough understanding of the good to make moral decisions. Furthermore, people can improve their knowledge of what is good by becoming more virtuous people. This involves reforming their characters.

A second objection is that the doctrine of the mean isn't much help practically. First, 'too much' and 'too little' aren't quantities on a single scale. The list of 'right time, right object, right person, right motive, right way' shows that things are much more complicated than that. Second, this gives us no actual help with understanding, say, how often should we get angry, and how angry should we get. But perhaps Aristotle didn't mean the doctrine of the mean to be of real guidance. He repeatedly emphasises that the mean is where the person of practical wisdom judges it to be.

But can his theory of practical wisdom provide any guidance about what to do? If I have practical wisdom, I simply know what to do. But if I do not have practical wisdom, telling me to do what a virtuous person would do doesn't help me because I don't know what the virtuous person would do!

But just because practical wisdom is not a set of rules, that doesn't mean it provides no guidance at all. It suggests we think about situations in terms of the virtues. Rather than ask 'could everyone do this?' (as Kant suggests) or 'what will bring about the best consequences?' (as utilitarianism suggests), we can ask a series of questions: 'would this action be kind/courageous/loyal . . .?' If we think of actions as expressions of virtue, this could be very helpful.

What about cases in which virtues seem to conflict? For example, can we show justice and mercy, or do we have to choose? Here, the theory of practical wisdom is in the same position as deontology; you need practical wisdom to understand what each virtue actually requires you to do in this particular situation.

🖉 Assess the theory of practical wisdom as an account of how we should make moral decisions.

Key points • • •

- Aristotle argues that we know what is good through practical wisdom. This involves insight into what is good or bad, insight into how to achieve in that a particular situation and the ability to act on that insight in the situation.
- There is no set of rules for applying general knowledge of what is good to particular situations. Practical wisdom simply grasps the particular relevant facts directly.
- So, knowledge of what to do is so practical that it can't be taught, but requires experience.
- Aristotle's doctrine of the mean claims that virtuous traits, choices and emotions commonly lie between two vices. However, this is of little use in helping us discover what is virtuous, since the mean is not the 'middle', nor the 'average', nor the 'moderate'.
- To know what is good, Aristotle argues, you must first acquire virtues of character.
- We may object that this makes moral knowledge and the good life available only to some people, but whether this is true depends on whether most people have enough virtue for a basic understanding of what is good.
- The theory of practical wisdom can't provide a method for making morally good decisions, though thinking in terms of the virtues can be helpful. If the virtues conflict, only practical wisdom will help.

The value of life: abortion

Abortion is the termination of a pregnancy. We usually use the term to refer to the deliberate termination of a pregnancy, but in medicine a miscarriage is also called a 'spontaneous abortion'. We will be concerned with deliberate abortion.

A woman becomes pregnant when a sperm fertilises one of her eggs ('conception'). The fertilised egg is a 'zygote' until it implants in the wall of her uterus, five to seven days later. It is now called an 'embryo' until it is eight weeks old, when it is called a 'foetus'. However, I shall use the term 'foetus' for the developing organism at all stages from conception to birth.

The right to life

People who oppose abortion usually claim that the foetus has a right to life, because it is a human being and all human beings have a right to life. This is a deontological argument. But why should we think that all human beings have a right to life?

A first argument is this: if we say a foetus does not have a right to life, we are faced with the difficulty of trying to find a point at which to draw the line. The foetus develops a little each day until it is born, and after that the child develops a little each day until it is an adult with reason and rights. So how is it possible to say 'now the foetus does not have a right to life; now it does'? At any point where we draw the line, the foetus is not very different just before this point and just after this point.

But what is the *basis* for having a right to life? One answer is having a soul. The traditional point at which we are said to acquire souls is at conception. Two facts are worth noting. First, two-thirds of zygotes are spontaneously aborted – that is, rejected naturally by the uterus. If each is made special by the presence of a soul, that seems a moral tragedy. Second, some types of contraception, such as the intra-uterine device (IUD) and certain types of contraceptive pill, work by changing the lining of the uterus so that fertilised eggs cannot implant in it. These methods of contraception do not stop eggs from being fertilised. If abortion is wrong because a being with a soul is prevented from developing, then these types of contraception are equally wrong.

What else might give us a right to life? The things that come to mind – such as reason, the use of language, the depth of our emotional experience, our self-awareness, our ability to distinguish right and wrong – are not things that a foetus has (yet). And many other human beings, including those with severe mental disabilities and senile dementia, also don't have these characteristics. Yet we might think that they still have a right to life.

There is one important characteristic we do all share, and that a foetus acquires around 18–22 weeks, and that is *sentience*. Sentience is the primitive consciousness of perception, pleasure and pain. If the right to life depends on sentience, then a foetus has a right to life from around 18 weeks, but not before. However, if we choose this quality as the basis for a right to life, it means that many *animals* have a right to life as well.

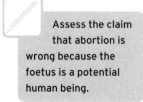

Does a foetus have a right to life? What implications follow from your answer?

THE ARGUMENT FROM POTENTIAL

If the foetus does not have the characteristics that give someone a right to life, we might argue that, unlike animals, it *will* have them if it is allowed to develop. It has a right to life now because it has the *potential* to become a person with a right to life in the future.

But we may object that, first, the sperm and the egg that combined to form the foetus also had the potential to become a person. If it is potential that matters, then contraception of any form would be as wrong as abortion. An obvious reply to this is that the sperm and egg don't form a natural 'unit' for us to ascribe potential to. But why think only the potential of natural units matters?

Second, it is not normal to treat potential as though it were already realised. Someone who has only the potential to become a teacher is not yet a teacher, and should not be put in charge of lessons. Someone who has the potential to become a millionaire cannot spend the money yet. So why think having the potential for those qualities that ground a right to life gives a foetus the right to life now?

Assess the claim that abortion is wrong because the foetus is a potential human being.

The right to choose

We generally think that people have a right to do what they want with their bodies and what to do in their lives. The foetus is part of (or at least within) the woman's body; it cannot survive without her body. If she has a right to choose what to do with her body, and the foetus has no right to life, then she is not acting wrongly if she chooses to have an abortion. Second, having a child will make a very big difference to her life. We can argue that since she has the right to choose how to live, she has the right to choose not to have a child, especially if she is not responsible for becoming pregnant (for example in cases of rape or failed contraception).

However, we may object that this argument does not apply once the foetus is able to survive outside the woman's body, a stage known as *viability*. After viability, the foetus could be delivered, kept alive outside the woman's body and put up for adoption. This could make it wrong to abort the foetus.

What if the foetus *does* have a right to life? This doesn't mean abortion is automatically and always wrong. Before viability, at least, the rights of the woman may outweigh the foetus's right to life.

Act utilitarianism

Act utilitarianism asks us to consider happiness in the two situations of abortion and giving birth. The possible consequences are so complex that it is difficult to say what might happen. However, we normally believe it is better to be alive than not alive. So, the future life of the foetus weighs heavily in its favour, and certainly outweighs the inconvenience to the woman of carrying the pregnancy to term and then putting the baby up for adoption. But there is a question as to whether the *future* experience or preferences of the foetus *count now*, because before sentience the foetus is not a being with the ability to experience pleasure and pain. Utilitarianism doesn't give us an obvious answer about future beings.

Practical wisdom

The discussion so far seems to treat women as containers for a foetus rather than creators of a life out of their own bodies. The *meaning* of pregnancy and abortion are not explored. Rosalind Hursthouse argues that to think of an abortion as though the foetus does not matter is callous and shows a lack of appreciation for the type of being a foetus is – that it is quite literally one's flesh and blood, developing from oneself. It shows the wrong attitude to human life, death and parenthood. But this doesn't automatically make all abortions wrong. If a woman has an abortion because she fears she cannot afford to feed the child or because she has a very demanding job and may neglect the child, this is not a callous thought. However, the fact that she prioritises her job above children may indicate that her priorities in life are wrong, that she hasn't understood the value of parenthood. But it depends on the particular case. It may be that the

Discuss the importance for abortion of a woman's right to choose.

Assess whether utilitarianism can help us decide whether abortion is ever morally right.

'Virtue Theory and Abortion'

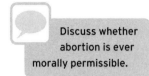

Discuss whether abortion is ever morally permissible.

woman leads a very worthwhile, fulfilling life, and cannot fit motherhood into the other activities that make her life as good as it is. From this perspective, then, each abortion is an individual case, involving an individual woman in a unique set of circumstances. Each case must be judged on its own merits.

Key points • • •

- Unless we give all human beings, including foetuses, a right to life, we have to say that we acquire it at some point. But when, and on the basis of what property?
- Some philosophers argue that foetuses have a right to life because they have the potential to become human adults. But we do not extend rights to something that is only potentially a future rights-holder.
- A woman's right to choose what to do with her body and her life supports the claim that she is not wrong to have an abortion, at least before viability. These same rights may even outweigh any right to life the foetus has.
- Act utilitarianism considers whether abortion would create more happiness than giving birth. However, it is unclear whether we should count the potential happiness of the foetus if it isn't sentient at the time of the abortion.
- Virtue theory emphasises the meaning of birth and abortion in human life. It suggests that there may be virtuous motives for having an abortion, and whether a particular abortion is right or wrong will depend on these.

The value of life: euthanasia

The *New Oxford Dictionary of English* defines 'euthanasia' as 'the painless killing of a patient suffering from an incurable and painful disease or in an irreversible coma'. 'Euthanasia' comes from two Greek words: '*eu-*', a prefix meaning 'good' or 'well', and '*thanatos*', meaning 'death'. Literally speaking, when someone undergoes euthanasia, their death is good. Normally, for death to be good, living would need to be worse than death. Incurable, painful disease and irreversible coma are two ways in which living can be worse than dying. In these cases, we might say life is not worth living.

We can distinguish six types of euthanasia.

Involuntary euthanasia is euthanasia when the patient does not want to die. *Non-voluntary* euthanasia is euthanasia when the patient has not expressed their choice, for example if they are too young to express choices, or they can't express choices now – for example, because they are mentally impaired through senile dementia – and did not express their choices earlier. *Voluntary* euthanasia is euthanasia when the patient wants to die and has expressed this choice.

Each of these three types can be either *active* or *passive*. Active euthanasia is when the patient is killed, for instance by a lethal injection. Passive euthanasia is when the patient is allowed to die, for instance by the withholding of treatment for a disease, which then kills them.

Passive euthanasia does not fit the dictionary definition above, because it involves letting the patient die rather than killing them. It also doesn't fit because it can sometimes be very painful and prolonged. Active euthanasia, by contrast, is almost always painless, since very high (fatal) doses of painkillers can be given with the injection.

> Explain the difference between active and passive euthanasia.

Morality, legality and utilitarianism

One of the most common arguments against euthanasia is the possibility of abuse. Patients might feel pressured into agreeing to euthanasia by families that didn't want to look after them or by doctors who wanted to use the hospital resources for other patients. Alternatively, patients who feel depressed might choose euthanasia, when with help they could become less depressed.

These are important points. But we should distinguish the question of whether voluntary euthanasia can be *morally permissible* from the question of whether it should be *legalised*. The question of whether euthanasia should be legal is not our question here. However, we might think the argument is relevant if we adopt a rule utilitarian approach, as rule utilitarians seek those rules that will create the greatest happiness. If making a rule that allows voluntary euthanasia could make people unhappy, this is relevant.

However, the case from abuses describes what may happen when people *don't* follow the rule on voluntary euthanasia – that is, when they act immorally. So, it turns out not to be an argument against the *morality* of voluntary euthanasia after all.

Act utilitarians consider euthanasia on a case-by-case basis. They argue that the differences between types of euthanasia are not morally important unless they involve different consequences. The only important question is whether euthanasia creates more happiness (or less suffering) than preventing it. Involuntary euthanasia is clearly different from voluntary euthanasia, since the person does not want to die – so is 'made unhappy' by their death (or at least by the prospect of their death). It might still be right, if the person's life really will contain more unhappiness than happiness. But if a person wants to stay alive, it is very difficult to make this claim. People commonly agree that, because it is important for us to be able to make choices about things that are important to us, involuntary euthanasia will almost always turn out to be wrong. Voluntary euthanasia, however, will be right in those cases in which it maximises happiness. The only question is whose happiness should be considered.

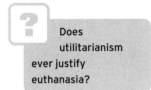

Does utilitarianism ever justify euthanasia?

Deontology

Kant argued that people who commit suicide destroy their rationality in service to something else: pain. So, suicide and asking for euthanasia do not show respect for our own rationality; they do not treat it as an end in itself. But this doesn't deal with cases in which the reason why someone requests euthanasia is because they are about to lose their rational faculties (as in advanced Alzheimer's disease) or cases in which someone doesn't have any rational faculties (as when children are born without a complete brain).

We may agree that rationality is what bestows *dignity* on human beings, and we must respect people's dignity. Therefore, a human being who may lose their dignity and their rationality through illness and pain may legitimately request euthanasia. We respect and protect their dignity by helping them die in circumstances of their own choosing. This is one of the most powerful arguments for voluntary euthanasia.

But deontologists don't argue that we should always respect someone's choice when what they want is morally wrong; sometimes it is morally right to prevent them from doing what they want. So, voluntary euthanasia could still be wrong if wanting to die is morally wrong.

Can euthanasia be justified as a 'dignified' death?

Active versus passive euthanasia using deontology and practical wisdom

If voluntary euthanasia is ever morally permissible, is there a moral difference between active and passive euthanasia? An act utilitarian may argue not. In both cases, the person dies. All that matters is that they don't suffer. However, other theories argue there is.

Not killing someone is related to the virtue and duties of *justice*. Justice requires that we *respect* people, their choices and rights. Not letting someone die is related to the virtue and duties of *charity*. Charity requires that we help other people's lives go well. For example, people all over the world are dying from hunger and disease. It is difficult to argue that because you did not give more to charity, you have done something as bad as if you had actually *killed* them yourself.

However, there are some cases in which letting someone die is equivalent to killing them, for example when you have a duty to provide food or medicine to someone and you do not. A parent who didn't give their child food would be guilty of murder. In such a case, both justice and charity require the same thing, and so there is no practical difference between killing and letting someone die.

Is there a practical difference in the case of euthanasia? Normally, killing is forbidden by justice as it violates the person's choice; but in voluntary euthanasia, respecting the person's choice means killing them. But some deontologists argue that we have a duty not to kill human beings even if the person who dies requests death. This is one interpretation of the idea of the *sanctity of life*, that we must respect someone's right to life even when they want to die. These deontologists may allow passive euthanasia, but not active euthanasia.

Many doctors think that the idea of administering lethal injections goes against the idea and duties of practising medicine. However, in addition to the duty to protect the lives of their patients, doctors also have the duty to do what is best for their patients, including relieving pain. One way of trying to respect both duties at once is to allow the patient to die while doing everything possible to ensure that their death is painless. In cases in which passive euthanasia is painful, giving large doses of painkillers is permissible, even if this actually causes the patient to die sooner. (So, to *intend* to kill someone is always wrong; but the intention here is to relieve pain.)

This argument appeals to a famous deontological principle, 'the doctrine of double effect'. There is an important moral distinction between a harmful effect occurring as a *side effect* of pursuing a good end and causing the harm as a *means* to the good end. Sometimes this is expressed as the view that it is permissible to cause a harmful effect we do not *intend*, but is an inevitable result of doing something good (if the good thing sufficiently outweighs the bad), but it is wrong to intend the harmful effect, even if we intend it only in order to achieve the good result. So, it is all right for a doctor to inject a large dose of morphine into a patient to relieve their pain, knowing that it will make them die sooner, but it is wrong to give that injection with the intention of killing them.

But does the duty to protect life involve the duty to prolong life for as long as possible, even if the quality of life is very poor? If so, then active euthanasia is permitted if doctors must always do what is best for their patient, and death can be what is best. At this point, virtue theory may appeal to virtues such as mercy and compassion to permit euthanasia.

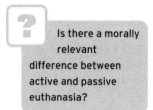

Is there a morally relevant difference between active and passive euthanasia?

Key points • • •

- Act utilitarianism argues that there is no relevant difference between types of euthanasia unless they lead to different amounts of happiness. Involuntary euthanasia is likely to cause much more unhappiness than voluntary euthanasia. However, there is little difference between active and passive voluntary euthanasia; in fact, passive euthanasia tends to cause more pain, so active euthanasia should be preferred.
- Rule utilitarianism takes into account whether a rule permitting voluntary euthanasia would lead to more happiness than one prohibiting it. Opponents argue that the permitting of euthanasia could be open to abuse. However, this is only an objection to legalising euthanasia, not to its being morally permissible.
- Deontological views present arguments both for and against voluntary euthanasia. One argument against is that seeking euthanasia values pain more highly than rationality. But a response is that when one is about to lose one's reason, euthanasia enables a dignified death.
- Is there a difference between active and passive voluntary euthanasia? Killing someone usually violates the duty and virtue of justice, while not letting someone die does not. We may therefore violate no duty in letting someone die.
- However, it may not be unjust to kill someone who requests it, so active voluntary euthanasia may also be permissible, and may also be more compassionate.

Our treatment of non-human animals

Utilitarianism

Animal Liberation

Peter Singer argues that the way we commonly treat animals – for food, clothing and medical experimentation – is not morally justifiable. We do not think that it is right to treat women worse than men just because they are women (this is sexism), or to treat one race worse than another (this is racism). Likewise, it is wrong to treat animals differently just because they are not human. This is 'speciesism'.

We can object that with women and men, and different races, there is no difference in those important capacities – reason, the use of language, the depth of our emotional experience, our self-awareness, our ability to distinguish right and wrong – that make a being a person. But there is a difference between human beings and animals with all of these.

Singer responds that these differences are not relevant when it comes to the important capacity that human beings and animals share, namely sentience. For a utilitarian, an act (or rule) is wrong if it produces more *suffering* than an alternative. Who is suffering is irrelevant. When it comes to suffering, animals should be treated as equal to people.

Does this mean that we should prohibit the eating of meat, the wearing of leather and animal experiments? Not necessarily. First, there is the question of whether stopping these practices would reduce the amount of (animal) suffering in the world more than it would increase (human) suffering. Second, the utilitarian position objects only to suffering, not to *killing*. If you painlessly kill an animal and bring another animal into being (as is done when rearing animals), you haven't reduced the total amount of happiness in the world. We need only ensure that animals are happy when they are alive, and slaughter them painlessly. This would make eating meat much more expensive, because animals would have to be kept in much better conditions. Eating meat is wrong only when animals are not treated as well as they could be.

Discuss the implications of utilitarianism for our treatment of animals.

Deontology

Some deontologists argue that killing human beings is wrong because they have a right to life. Having rights is related to our rationality and choices; they protect the 'space' that we need in order to make free, rational choices. Animals don't make choices the way we do, so they don't have rights.

But babies also aren't rational and don't make free choices (yet), and some people with severe mental disabilities never do. If they have a right to life, and do not have different psychological capacities from certain animals, then to deny those animals a right to life would be speciesist. For any property unique to human beings that justifies a right to life, some human beings won't have it. With any property that all human beings have, some animals have it as well.

The Case for Animal Rights

Tom Regan argues that to have a right to life, a creature only needs to be a 'subject of a life'. By this he means having beliefs, desires, emotions, perception, memory, the ability to act (though not necessarily free choice) and a psychological identity over time. If a creature has these abilities, there is a way its life goes *for* it, and this matters *to* it. A right to life protects this. Although we can't know exactly which animals meet this criterion, we can be sure that almost all mammals (including humans) over the age of 1 do so.

Because these animals have a right to life, Regan argues, we cannot kill them for any reason less important than saving life. Because we do not need to eat meat or wear leather to live, we should not use animals for these purposes. Regan also argues that an animal's right to life is equal to a human being's. We do not normally discriminate between 'more valuable' and 'less valuable' human lives, even though some people are capable of much greater things than others. So, we should not discriminate between 'more valuable' human lives and 'less valuable' animal lives. This means we cannot justify medical experiments that involve killing animals by the human lives the experiment may help save.

Regan's view is very counter-intuitive. Our intuitive judgements that the lives of human beings are more valuable than those of animals, and that it is permissible to kill an animal when we *need* to, are very strong. But what are the arguments supporting these intuitions?

? Could some animals have a right to life?

Practical wisdom

Is the speciesism argument valid? Perhaps it is not *just* the capacities of the being that determine how we should treat it, but also our *relationship* to it. There is a moral importance to bonding, the creation of special ties with particular others. We 'naturally' privilege those closest to us. Our bond to other human beings is special because we share humanity.

Of course, not to recognise that an animal can suffer is to show a lack of compassion. To treat it as a meat-growing machine or experimental object is to display a relationship with it that resembles selfishness, because we reduce it from what it is in itself to something that exists only for our sake. Does this mean that eating meat and animal experiments are wrong? We are left without a clear answer, but a sense of the difficulty of the question.

? What relationship between human beings and animals is morally appropriate?

Key points • • •

- Singer argues that what matters is suffering; who is suffering is irrelevant, and to think otherwise is speciesism.
- Utilitarianism claims that whether eating meat or animal experimentation is wrong depends on whether it produces more suffering than alternatives. Killing an animal painlessly, if you bring another animal into existence, won't reduce happiness, so is permissible.
- Many deontologists argue that rights protect our rational choices; as animals don't make rational choices, they don't have rights. But this is also true of babies, so do they not have rights?
- Regan argues that any creature that is a 'subject of a life' has a right to life. The right to life is equal in all cases.
- Further reflection brings out the dependence of morality on relationship (not just capacities). It also emphasises the importance of compassion in our treatment of animals.

Our treatment of the natural environment

One central question in environmental ethics is whether to think about the issues, such as overpopulation, depletion of resources and pollution, in terms of the effects on human beings or in terms of changes to the environment itself or both. For example, pollution can undermine the quality of life and even kill human beings, but also has many effects on other species. Carbon emissions from human activity appear to be an important cause of global warming, which is affecting almost everything on the planet one way or another. But which effects matter morally, and why?

Utilitarianism

Hedonist utilitarianism (p. 252) claims that the only things of moral value are pleasure and pain. So, only human beings and animals count. Plants, ecosystems, natural objects and resources like mountains and icebergs, and species – none of these experiences pleasure and pain. If Mill is right that higher pleasures are worth much more than lower pleasures, then we should focus mainly on human beings, as only they experience higher pleasures. So, hedonist utilitarianism approaches a question like global warming in terms of its effects on people now and in the future.

Preference utilitarianism (p. 253) is broader, because people want more than their own pleasure. Someone might want the rainforests not to be demolished – not because they will have any experience of the rainforests, nor because they think this will affect the experience of people in the future, for example by new drugs being discovered, but because they simply want them to continue existing. Our desires relating to the natural environment are not just concerns for ourselves.

On this view, plants, ecosystems, species have value because we value them; but they have only as much value as we give them. Some philosophers have argued that this is enough to support a very 'cautious' policy towards the environment, so that we should minimise pollution and the use of non-renewable resources. The adverse effects on people alone dictate this, they claim; if you start counting all the animals that are affected as well, and the preferences people have for the natural environment to continuing existing 'unspoilt', then surely we must move towards a more 'sustainable' way of relating to the environment.

But others argue that utilitarianism does not support this. Instead, the effects of how we now treat the environment may not be as bad as some predict, and technology will provide solutions to the problems that arise. Furthermore, preferences for an 'unspoilt' environment are outweighed by urgent needs for food and other resources. So what action utilitarianism supports depends on what you think the consequences will be.

If you think that the natural environment matters in itself, independent of how we care for it, then you must defend a different view from utilitarianism.

Discuss utilitarianism's approach to environmental issues.

Deontology and practical wisdom

A good person respects the values that things have. If something is good, then they will seek not to destroy it. When something has a value in itself, then we have a duty to respect that value. But does anything apart from human rationality and well-being have value in itself? Some philosophers have claimed that all life has value in itself and even that ecosystems do, as complex life-supporting systems.

A second approach makes an analogy between exploiting and polluting the natural environment and vandalism. Even if something doesn't matter in itself, destroying it can be bad if done from a bad motive. We could argue that much environmental destruction involves greed, or lack of concern for others, or wantonness, or an inability to appreciate beauty. If this is right, then even if the natural environment isn't of value 'in itself', certain ways of treating it could still be wrong.

A third approach considers the relationship between human beings and the natural environment. We are who we are because of relationships to other people and society – and so there are virtues like justice and concern of others. Likewise, we are who we are because of our relationship to the natural environment. This is partly a physical relationship – the physical needs of breathing, eating, recycling waste – but it is also obvious in our aesthetic and personal relationships to animals, plants and landscapes, and in science. Something about the human spirit is caught up with and responds to the environment. A sustainable, respectful relationship with the environment is part of a good life for us.

These arguments are all contentious. Historically, the relationship between human beings and the natural environment has been one of mastery as well as respect. Great benefits to us have resulted from the development of technologies that use and control the natural environment. Any duties to the environment must be weighed against duties to human beings.

> How can we best support the claim that it matters morally how we treat the natural environment?

Key points • • •

- A central question in debates about how to treat the natural environment is whether only the effects on human beings matter morally.
- Hedonist utilitarianism says the only effects that matter are experiences of pleasure and pain.
- Preference utilitarianism notes that people have, for example, desires for 'unspoilt' environments that they will never experience. However, the value of the natural environment depends entirely on how much we value it, compared to other things.
- Some philosophers argue that all life has value in itself, which must therefore be respected.
- Even if the natural environment is not valuable in itself, destroying it may display vices of greed, selfishness and a lack of aesthetic appreciation.
- We can argue that a sustainable, respectful relationship with the natural environment is part of a good life for human beings. However, historically our relationship has been exploitative.

Poverty

The debate about poverty raises the question: what are we morally required to do to *help* other people? Everyone accepts that it is good to help those who need help. But is it obligatory? If so, are we required to help those near to us, or also people far away?

We must distinguish this question from the different and very difficult question of what the *best way* to help the poor is. This second question is the one most often discussed in debates about whether we should give to people begging on the street; or whether we should give aid to people in other countries who are dying from lack of food or natural disasters. Of course, if we have a duty to help the poor, it makes sense to help in the most effective way, over the long term. But what the most effective way of helping is, is not our question, and we will not discuss it.

Utilitarianism

Act utilitarianism claims that if we do not do what maximises happiness, then we act wrongly. So, if we can prevent something bad, such as the suffering caused by poverty, then we should prevent it (unless preventing it will cause more unhappiness). So, for example, if a child is drowning in a pond, and I can save her, then I should – even though I will get my clothes muddy. But what is the moral difference between saving a drowning child and saving a starving child in another country? If I can save that child, for instance by giving all the money to charity that I would otherwise spend on things I don't need – like nice clothes and DVDs – then this is what I should do.

We can object that if I am morally required to try to help all poor children, then it will always be wrong for me to spend anything on myself. True – but aren't other people's lives more important than our clothes and DVDs? The balance between looking after ourselves and helping other people is itself determined by what will bring about the best consequences overall. The act utilitarian argues that *whenever* we can help someone, without a greater cost to ourselves, we should.

Rule utilitarianism agrees that we have a duty to help the poor. However, our duty is to help only as much as would be needed if *everyone* helped, because what is morally required is following rules that would maximise happiness if everyone followed them. Act utilitarians object that this rule will lead to much less happiness – because we know that not everyone will help as they should. So, we must help more.

Deontology and practical wisdom

Compare and contrast act and rule utilitarian on the question of helping the poor.

People have a *right* not to be harmed, so it is always wrong to harm them. But, many deontologists argue, people do not have a similar right to be helped, so it is not always wrong not to help them. While we may have some duty to help others, we are not required to help on every possible occasion. For instance, we may say that if you have gained what you own, for example your money, without harming others, then you have a right to keep it or do with it as you choose. If you have a right to your money, that means that you don't have a *duty* to give it away to help the poor. Aquinas, however, argues that the point of material goods is to satisfy our needs. If they are not being used to satisfy needs, then they are not being used rightly. Whatever we don't need, therefore, in a sense belongs to the poor more rightly than it belongs to us.

See, on rights, PROBLEMS CONCERNING THEIR EXTENT AND APPLICATION, p. 99.

The act utilitarian approach overlooks or perhaps rejects the strong sense we have that each person has a special relationship to their own projects and lives. To say that helping the poor is required conflicts with the idea that our own flourishing, our own lives and what we want to do with them matter to each of us in a unique way. The happiness of others does not (need to) play the same role in making our decisions as our own happiness. Poverty places a duty on us to help – so that it is wrong *never* to be charitable, but we are not required to make great sacrifices in our own lives.

What duties do we have to the poor?

Key points • • •

- The question of whether we have a duty to help poor people, and the question of how best to help them, are distinct.
- Act utilitarianism argues that we are required to help the poor as much as possible, until the cost to ourselves is equal to the amount of happiness we cause.
- We can object that act utilitarianism overlooks the special relationship we each have to our own lives. We cannot live as happiness-generating machines.
- Rule utilitarianism claims that we are required to help only as much as would be necessary if everybody helped.

- Many deontologists argue that people do not have the right to be helped, so while we have some general duty to help others, we are not required to help all the time.

Answering exam questions on practical ethics

Unlike other areas of philosophy, practical ethics touches on everyday life immediately. So, it is easy to slip out of doing good philosophy into thinking in more 'everyday' ways. Doing well in exam questions on practical ethics involves thinking hard about the question in a philosophical way. Here are some tips to help:

1. While the facts are important, just talking about the facts is not philosophy. Nor is repeating what people generally say or feel about these cases. You are not doing social science, but discussing *justifications* for certain ways of making decisions.
2. Whether an action is right or wrong can depend on the facts, and as philosophers, we may not know all the facts. So, philosophical arguments are often 'conditional'. It is not just acceptable, but good, to say 'if it turns out like this, then this follows (the action is right/wrong)'. For example, you might say 'if a woman's life is harmed by having a child now, abortion is right'; don't discuss whether her life would actually be harmed, how it 'might happen' that she comes to love the child and so on.
3. Avoid oversimplification wherever possible. Practical moral issues are very complex. In particular, if you are evaluating a theory, say deontology, by its success in practical cases, the complexity is crucial to being fair. Consider whether practical ethics 'ought' to be easy or not. Can we expect clear rules and algorithmic decision procedures in life? Is the presence of grey areas really a failure? Deontology and practical wisdom suggest not.
4. Likewise, try to avoid objections that just point out our ignorance. For example, 'who knows what consequences follow from an abortion?' is not helpful. This move is simply a refusal to do philosophy. A utilitarian will quickly reply that we must simply do our best to work out the consequences. The same with 'who is to say what is right?'. *You* as a philosopher are to say what is right, as you see it and to the best of your ability (this is not arrogance, but the contribution of a rational human being to a rational debate).

5.   Make a distinction between morality and legality. Whether a practice should be legalised is a separate debate from whether it is morally acceptable.
6.   Separate metaethical issues from practical issues. So, relativism and non-cognitivism should be kept out of discussions of practical ethics as far as possible. The premise of practical ethics is that we are searching for the (or a) right thing to do. Challenging this premise is unhelpful in this context.

5

PHILOSOPHY OF RELIGION

In this chapter, we shall look at four debates in the philosophy of religion. The first covers two arguments for the existence of God: from the existence of the universe and from religious experience. The second considers the nature of religious faith and its relation to reason. The third discusses the nature of miracles and whether we have good reason to believe miracles occur. The last looks at a number of interpretations of religion and religious language that may suggest they are non-cognitive. Alongside these debates are reflections on the assumptions made in them about the nature of religion and the appropriateness of using reason to support or criticise religious belief. Students should be able to argue for and against different positions within each of the four debates, and reflect on the assumptions involved in each.

SYLLABUS CHECKLIST ✔

The AQA A2 syllabus for this chapter is as follows:

Arguments for the existence of God

✔   The cosmological argument for the existence of God.
✔   The argument from religious experience to the existence of God.

✔ Students should consider the background assumptions (ontological, epistemological and semantic) that motivate the arguments, their interpretation and the criticisms aimed at them.

Reason and faith

✔ How should we understand 'faith'? Is 'faith' a special kind of cognitive state, engendered by divine grace, illuminating truths that would otherwise be inaccessible? Alternatively, is 'faith' more like an attitude or commitment characterising the way we approach and interpret experience?

✔ Is it more rational to choose to believe in God than choosing atheism or agnosticism? To what extent can we 'choose' what to believe?

✔ Students should consider issues raised in this section not only in their own right, but also in their application to other aspects in this unit.

Miracles

✔ The role and significance of miracle stories in religions. What do we mean by 'miracle'?

✔ Sceptical arguments regarding the occurrence of miracles.

✔ Miracles and the competing truth claims of different religions.

✔ Students should consider miracles in relation to the normative dimensions of belief, potential incommensurability and the possibility of religious pluralism.

Making sense of religion

✔ The extent to which religion might be 'explained away' by social science.

✔ The various problems and solutions regarding the status and interpretation of religious language that have been motivated by verificationism.

✔ Whether religion should be understood as a language game or an autonomous 'form of life'.

✔ Students should consider what is meant by 'religion', whether it is a well-defined or integrated phenomenon and the relation between 'religion' and other kinds of discourse and activity.

I. ARGUMENTS FOR THE EXISTENCE OF GOD

The cosmological argument

The question at the heart of the cosmological argument is 'Why does anything exist? Why something rather than nothing?' The argument is that unless God exists, this question is unanswerable. There are different forms of the argument. Two central ones are the *Kalam* argument and the argument from contingent existence. They are usually presented as **deductive** arguments; an **inductive** variation is given by Richard Swinburne (p. 292).

The Kalam *argument*

The *Kalam* argument observes that:

1. of anything that begins to exist, you can ask what caused it. For example, what caused me (my birth)? In a sense, my parents. But then, we can repeat the question: 'What caused my parents?' And so on. We can go back to the beginning of the universe, and then ask 'What caused the universe?'. If
2. the universe began to exist, then
3. it must have a cause of its existence. Something can't come out of nothing.
4. What we need is something that causes things to exist, but the existence of which isn't caused itself.
5. Only God could be such a thing.

There are three key issues that need to be addressed to defend the argument. First, is the causal principle, that everything that begins to exist has a cause, correct? Second, does the universe have a beginning? Third, must the explanation be God? We will leave this third question to the very end of this section.

THE CAUSAL PRINCIPLE

Must every event have a cause? David Hume famously argued that we cannot know this. It is not an **analytic** truth (by contrast, 'every effect has a cause' *is* an analytic truth; but is every event an effect?). 'Something cannot come out of nothing' is also not analytic. And Hume argued that **synthetic** truths are known **a posteriori**, through experience. And although our experience is that everything so far has a cause, can this principle can be applied to the beginning of the universe?

First, the beginnings of universes are not something we have any experience of. Second, the beginning of the universe is not an event like events that happen within the universe. It doesn't take place in space or time, since both come into existence with the universe. Even if everything within the universe has a cause, that doesn't mean that the universe as a whole does. We cannot apply principles we have developed for events *within* the universe to the universe as a whole. As Bertrand Russell famously put it, 'the universe is just there, and that's all'.

DOES THE UNIVERSE HAVE A BEGINNING?

Rather than challenge the causal principle, we can reject the idea that the universe has a beginning at all. Because time came into existence with the universe, the universe didn't 'happen' *at a time*, so in a sense it *has no beginning*. We can reply that even if this is true, science suggests the universe has a finite past (it is about 15 billion years old). Whatever has a finite past must have a cause of its existence. In the case of the universe, that cause can't exist *in* time if time didn't exist before the universe. But that doesn't mean there was no cause, only that the cause must exist outside time. Which God does, according to many theists.

Alternatively, even if *this* universe has a beginning, perhaps it was caused by a previous (or another) universe, and so on, infinitely. In other words, rather than infer that God exists, we may think there is just an infinite regress of causes. Something has always existed.

It is, however, difficult to imagine what infinity is; it is not, for instance, simply 'a very long time'. It is very different from 'a very long time'; it means, quite literally, that there was no beginning, ever. Because the universe exists, this response claims that an *actual* infinity – something that is in fact infinite – exists. This is quite different from talking about the *idea* of infinity. The idea of infinity makes sense; but does it make sense to think that something infinite exists?

Explain the *Kalam* argument.

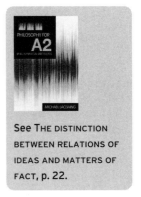

See THE DISTINCTION BETWEEN RELATIONS OF IDEAS AND MATTERS OF FACT, p. 22.

Must every event have a cause?

Going further: infinity

For example, the universe gets older as time passes. But this couldn't happen if the universe were infinitely old, because you cannot add any number to infinity and get a bigger number: $\infty + 1 = \infty$. So if the universe is infinitely old, it is not getting any older as time passes! Or again, to have reached the present, an infinite amount of time would need to have passed. But it is not possible for an *infinite* amount of time to have passed, since infinity is not an *amount*. So if the universe were infinitely old, it could never have reached the present.

Given that science tells us that the (this) universe has a beginning, this discussion of something *always* existing means that we must think of preceding universes. But given that the beginning of this universe was also the beginning of time as we know it, we may wonder what sense to make of talking about anything existing *before* this universe. We should not talk about an infinity of time, therefore, but an infinite series of causes (some operating outside the time of this universe).

But the puzzles arise for an infinite series of causes, too. Each new cause doesn't add one more cause to the series, since $\infty + 1 = \infty$. And we would never have reached the point in the series at which we are now if it were an infinite series.

What problems face the view that we can reject the idea of a beginning to the universe?

We noted that the question at the heart of the cosmological argument is 'Why something rather than nothing?' If we have an infinite series of causes, although each cause can be explained in terms of the previous cause, we may wonder what explains the *whole series*. If we say something exists because something has always existed, we still haven't answered the question why anything exists at all. This takes us to the next form of cosmological argument.

Discuss the *Kalam* argument.

The argument from contingent existence

This version of the cosmological argument, defended by Frederick Copleston in a radio debate with Bertrand Russell, emphasises the need to *explain* what exists:

1. Things in the universe exist **contingently**; they might not have existed or they might stop existing.
2. Something that exists contingently has (and needs) an explanation of why it exists; after all, it is not inevitable.
3. This explanation may be provided by the existence of some other contingent being (as in the example of me and my parents). But then we must explain these other contingent beings.
4. To repeat this *ad infinitum* is no explanation of why anything exists at all.
5. So what explains why contingent beings exist at all can only be a non-contingent being. A non-contingent being is one that cannot not exist – that is, it exists **necessarily**, and doesn't need some *further* explanation for why it exists.
6. This necessary being is God.

> Explain and
> illustrate the
> argument from
> contingent existence.

OBJECTIONS

Russell accepts that of any particular thing in the universe, we need an explanation of why it exists, which science can give us. But it is a mistake to think that we can apply this idea to the universe itself. A form of explanation developed for the *parts* of the universe needn't apply to the universe as a *whole*.

However, we can reply that the universe is itself a contingent being. If every part of the universe ceased to exist, so would the universe. So as a contingent being, the universe is like its parts. What is wrong with the principle that all contingent beings require an explanation for their existence?

A second objection is that although, as philosophers and scientists, we should *look for* explanations of contingent beings, we cannot know that in fact every contingent being *has* such an explanation. Without this, the argument fails as a deduction. However, this objection can be avoided if we give up the idea that the cosmological argument is deductive, and claim that it is an inference to the best explanation instead (see below).

A third objection attacks the conclusion. It is not God but matter/energy (in some form) that is a necessary being. A fundamental law of physics is the conservation of energy: the total amount of matter/energy in the universe remains constant; it cannot be increased or decreased. If a version of this law applied even at the beginning and end of universes, then matter/energy is a necessary being. However, we have no reason to believe that this law *does* apply at the beginning (and possibly the end) of the universe. The Big Bang theory

? **Is the cosmological argument from contingent existence more or less successful than the *Kalam* argument?**

The Coherence of Theism

See pp. 314 and 333.

suggests that matter/energy was created, along with time and space. That is, the universe came into existence – so it is contingent.

Swinburne: an inductive argument

Richard Swinburne claims that the cosmological argument is better understood as an inference to the *best explanation*. God's existence isn't logically proven, but it is probable, given the premises. Considered on its own, the claim 'God exists' is very improbable, says Swinburne. But in the light of the cosmological argument, it becomes more probable, because God's existence is the best explanation for why the universe exists.

An inductive argument for God's existence needs to take into account *all* the evidence, both for and against. Swinburne does not defend God's existence on the basis of the cosmological argument alone. He combines it with other arguments. There is also a similar version of THE ARGUMENT FROM DESIGN, namely that God is the best explanation of the order and purpose that we find. We can add THE ARGUMENT FROM RELIGIOUS EXPERIENCE (p. 295) and an argument from MIRACLES (p. 321). Each works the same way: the existence of God is the best explanation for these phenomena. When we put all these arguments together, he claims, it becomes more probable that God exists than that God doesn't.

SWINBURNE'S COSMOLOGICAL ARGUMENT

If we look over the two cosmological arguments above, it is apparent that we can't deduce God's existence. But the premises are plausible, and the inferences are intuitive. So although it is not an analytic truth that everything that begins to exist has a cause, it is extremely probable; our experience supports it. And the theory of the Big Bang and the problems with the infinite existence make it more plausible that the universe (or matter/energy) has not existed without beginning, but came into existence. If we reject God as an explanation for the existence of the universe, we run into problems: if not God, then what?

The second part of Swinburne's argument is that we have reason to believe that no other explanation of the universe will be satisfactory. For instance, any scientific explanation must already assume that something exists, and that whatever exists is governed by scientific laws. If we explain this universe in terms of another universe, we then have to explain the existence of that universe. And science can't explain scientific laws – where they come from or why they are the way they are – because all scientific explanations presuppose laws. Scientific laws are 'brute'; they have no explanation unless we can find some other kind of explanation for them.

Explaining the existence of the universe in terms of God doesn't suffer this problem, because it is not a scientific explanation, but a 'personal' one. We explain the products of human activity – this book, these sentences – in terms of a person. I'm writing things I *intend* to write. This sort of explanation explains an object or an event in terms of a person and their purposes. The hypothesis that God exists and intended to create the universe (including its laws) provides a personal explanation for the existence of the universe. So, Swinburne argues, it is probable that God exists and caused the beginning of the universe.

> How does Swinburne's cosmological argument differ from other versions?

Going further: best explanation

But is this the *best* explanation, or does it face as many difficulties as scientific explanation? Does invoking God's existence just make us more puzzled?

First, does the argument support the existence of God, as we normally think of God? It doesn't show that there is only one cause of the universe; nor does it show that that cause is perfect, omniscient, omnipotent or cares about people. The cosmological argument only needs 'God' to be able to create the universe. It doesn't say anything else about God.

However, a good explanation will be simpler than its rivals. 'Simplicity' means not invoking more different kinds of thing than you need to; and attributing only those properties that they need for the explanation to work. So, simplicity requires that we shouldn't suppose that two possible causes exist when only one will do. Supposing that there is more than one cause of the universe is a worse explanation, because it is not as simple. It is also simpler to suppose that the cause of the universe is itself uncaused, or we have a problem of regress. It is also simpler to suppose that God has infinite power and intelligence, or we would have to explain why God had just the amount of power and intelligence he has (enough to create the universe, but no more) - that is, what limits God's power and intelligence.

(Swinburne adds infinite goodness to the properties of God, but we can question this; why does God need to be *good* in order to create the universe? This objection becomes more pressing in light of THE PROBLEM OF EVIL.)

> Is God the best explanation of the universe?

See p. 320.

The limits of explanation

We can object that Swinburne has not demonstrated that God is the best explanation for the existence of the universe, because we are left with the question 'What explains God?', and this seems to be an even more puzzling question than 'What explains scientific laws?'

Swinburne responds that science will introduce an entity – such as a type of sub-atomic particle – in order to explain something, even though that entity needs explaining itself, and scientists don't yet know how to explain it. So, we can still say that God is a good explanation for scientific laws even if we can't explain God.

But if we will always have *something* we can't explain, why invoke God? Why not just say we can't explain scientific laws? Russell, for instance, rejects the idea of trying to give an explanation for the universe *at all*. But Swinburne responds that explanation is a principle of science and philosophy. If you give up on this, you give up on pursuing these forms of thought. If we invoke God, we can explain scientific laws and the existence of the universe, and we should explain as much as we can.

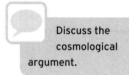
Discuss the cosmological argument.

Key points • • •

- The cosmological argument tries to answer the question 'Why does something exist rather than nothing?' The arguments from cause and contingent existence try to *deduce* that God exists; Swinburne argues that God's existence is the *best explanation*.
- The *Kalam* argument claims that everything that begins to exist has a cause, and that the universe began to exist. The only way to avoid an infinite regression of causes is to say something exists that did not begin to exist, namely God.
- Hume objects that we can't know that everything that begins to exist has a cause. Russell objects that we can't apply this principle to the universe itself. Other philosophers argue that an infinite regression of causes is possible, so we can't infer that God exists.
- The argument from contingent existence claims that the existence of anything that exists contingently has an explanation, and that an infinite regress of explanations is not an explanation for why anything exists at all. So, we can deduce that some non-contingent being exists, namely God.

- We can object, with Russell, that there is no explanation of the universe as a whole; or that matter/energy exists non-contingently, so we can't infer that God exists.
- Swinburne claims that although the cosmological argument fails as a deductive proof of God's existence, the best explanation for the existence of the universe is the existence of God. However, showing that it is the best explanation is difficult.

The argument from religious experience

The argument

Many people have experiences they identify as 'religious'. Experiences that are part of a religious life include the ups and downs of faith, doubt, sacrifice and achievement. We are interested in only those experiences in which it seems to the person as though they are directly aware of God, or God's action.

Some philosophers have argued that these experiences are importantly similar to perception, an immediate awareness of something other than oneself. We usually treat perceptual experiences as **veridical**, unless we have good reason to doubt them. Furthermore, the fact that other people have similar perceptual experiences supports the claim that perceptual experiences show the world accurately. Some philosophers have argued that religious experiences are also similar to each other, despite occurring to very different people in very different circumstances. The best explanation of these experiences, and their common nature, is that they are veridical – that is, they are experiences of something divine. Therefore, God exists.

Outline the argument from religious experience.

There are three important questions to discuss. First, what is the similarity between religious experiences, and how do their characteristics support the existence of God? Second, what philosophical problems are there for thinking that these experiences can give us knowledge of God? Third, is there an alternative explanation for the experiences?

James: what is religious experience?

William James argued that, for all the apparent differences between religions and religious experience, it was possible to detect a 'common core' to all (genuine) religious experiences:

The Varieties of Religious Experience

1. Religious experiences are *experiential*, like perception. They are quite different from *thinking* about God or trying to *imagine* God's nature.
2. However, they aren't connected to any particular mode of sense perception (sight, hearing, etc.). Sometimes they can be – for example, the person may feel God is speaking to them – but the 'inner words' are not normally everything about the experience. They are part of an awareness that transcends sense perceptions, that doesn't have sensory content.
3. The person feels they are *immediately* aware of and connected to God.
4. This awareness tends to block out everything else temporarily, perhaps even to the degree that the distinction between the person and what they are aware of disappears ('mystical union').

The heart of religious experience, James argues, is an immediate sense of the reality of the 'unseen'. By this, he means to contrast what we are aware of in a religious experience with the usual 'visible world'. Our awareness of the 'unseen' may be inarticulate, beyond even an ability to think in any usual terms about it. Conceptualisation, an attempt to describe it, say *what* was experienced, comes later.

> **?** What are the main features of religious experience, according to James?

EXPERIENCE AND CONSEQUENCE

If we are to take such experiences seriously, as something other than momentary insanity, we must connect them up to the rest of our lives, thinks James. Religious experiences are connected to having a religious attitude to life; those experiences that have no impact on how someone understands life are dubitable, and may not be genuine. James argues that a religious attitude is 'solemn, serious and tender', and has five main characteristics. We should understand religious experiences in relation to them:

1. The visible world is part of a spiritual universe that gives it meaning.
2. Having a harmonious relation with the spiritual universe is our true purpose in life.
3. This harmony enables spiritual energy to flow into and affect us and the visible world.
4. A new zest adds itself like a gift to life.
5. We gain an assurance of safety, a feeling of peace and, in relation to others, a preponderance of loving emotions.

All religion, he argues, points to the feeling that there is something wrong with us as we stand, and that this is corrected by becoming in touch with a higher power. Realising this is connected to an awareness of being in touch with something 'more' in religious experience.

All of this, notes James, is very interesting psychologically, but does it show that religious experience is experience of God? In being aware of something 'more', is this 'more' just our own 'higher self', or something objectively real? We should think it is something real for two reasons. First, there is 'more' to us than we consciously realise – so in religious experience we are in touch with something external to ourselves as we usually experience ourselves. James is happy to call this reality, considered abstractly, 'God'. Second, religious experience has real effects upon us. 'God is real since he produces real effects.'

James claims that if we try to say more about God than this, then we speculate. But we might argue that we can know something about God by the *type* of effects produced: a zest for life, the predominance of love, the sense that there is something wrong with us without God. We may also argue that God is not only the spiritual side of people. For example, how could human beings have a spiritual side if there is no divine being? Philosophers may argue that although it remains a hypothesis, the existence of God is the *best explanation* for the experiences James describes.

Philosophical issues

We noted that religious experiences are similar to perception and that we usually assume perceptual experiences are veridical unless we have reasons to think otherwise. However, philosophers have argued that religious experiences are not really like perception, so we shouldn't assume they are veridical; and that there are, in any case, other reasons to doubt them.

RELIGIOUS EXPERIENCE IS NOT LIKE PERCEPTION

First, sense experience is universal among people, and is continuously present to us when we are awake. It provides a very rich amount of detail and information ('a picture is worth a thousand words'). By contrast, only some people have religious experiences, and only rarely. They find it very difficult to say anything that is very informative.

However, only a small number of people can correctly identify an eighteenth-century piece of furniture, but that doesn't mean they aren't right or reliable. We can't tell the truth of something from its frequency. Furthermore, while the experience doesn't give *much* information, that doesn't mean it doesn't give *any*.

> **What reasons are there to think that religious experiences are genuine?**

However, the objection is that because religious experiences are rare, we shouldn't *assume* they are veridical until we have reason to doubt them. Surely, part of the reason we trust perception *is* because it is so widespread, common and informative.

Another reason we trust perception is that we have intersubjective agreement; if you and I start seeing things very differently, we wouldn't be so sure. And if I'm not sure about what I see, I can check with you. This isn't true of religious experience, which is more private.

In response, we may appeal to James' five characteristics of a religious attitude. If a religious experience has no transformative consequences, we may doubt it was veridical; if it does transform the person, then we have reason to think it was. Second, we can argue that religious experiences are more like experiences of what we *feel* than of what we perceive. And I don't check how I'm feeling by seeing how you feel, nor do you have direct access to what I feel. But we can respond that our feelings, unlike perception, are not assumed to be veridical, as they can often be misguided.

REASONS TO DOUBT THAT RELIGIOUS EXPERIENCES ARE OF GOD

By and large, people from different cultures have used similar ways of understanding the world, in terms of objects with colour, size, solidity and so on. By contrast, religious experience has produced very different ideas of what the 'divine reality' might be, from the Christian idea of God to Buddhist ideas of 'nothingness'.

James would respond that we shouldn't think that religious experience can give us a whole theological system. At most, we can argue for the reality of something spiritual, and perhaps reach tentative conclusions about what that reality is like. We may also argue that people can experience the same thing while disagreeing about what it is they have experienced (think of witnesses in court). So, disagreements between religions don't show that religious experiences aren't veridical, only that they can tell us very little about the nature of the divine.

However, we may still wonder whether the existence of God is the *best* explanation of religious experiences, or whether some other explanation is as good. For example, we might argue that people who have a religious experience are simply imposing certain religious ideas or expectations onto an emotional experience that is not awareness of the divine at all. One response to this points out that there are many cases of conversion as a result of religious experience in which the person wasn't expecting anything religious to occur.

Discuss the strengths and weaknesses of the analogy between religious experience and perception.

See THE DIVINE ATTRIBUTES, p. 125.

How plausible is it to say that we are aware of something 'more' in religious experience?

Freud: a psychological explanation

Sigmund Freud presents a different explanation of what might be happening in religious experiences. He argues that they could be hallucinations, like dreams, caused by a very deep unconscious wish that human beings have. This wish goes back in history to the emergence of the human race, and in each individual to their earliest infancy. The wish is for consolation and reassurance.

The Future of an Illusion

In the face of the uncontrollable forces of nature, we feel vulnerable, afraid and frustrated that there is so little we can do. We want to rob life of its terrors. Likewise, when we are infants we are completely helpless and dependent, and need protection. Both motives come together in the thought that there is a God, a protector, a means by which we can control nature (for early religions) or feel safe in the face of danger and uncertainty. Our relationship to God takes on the intimacy and intensity of our relationship to our parents.

Religious beliefs are 'fulfilments of the oldest, strongest and most urgent wishes of mankind. The secret of their strength lies in the strength of those wishes.' Isn't it remarkable, Freud says, that religion describes the universe 'exactly as we are bound to wish it to be'? A belief that is based on a wish, rather than on evidence, Freud calls an 'illusion'. It isn't necessarily false; it's just that it isn't based on seeking the truth.

Just as religious beliefs are based on wishes, so religious experiences are as well. Freud argues that dreams are caused by deep desires we are unaware of, and he argues that religious experiences are similarly caused. They are hallucinations that happen when we are awake, caused by the wish for security and meaning, for things to 'be OK'.

Freud's theory seems to account for many of the characteristics James noted about religious experiences. If they are hallucinations, then we can expect them to be experiences, rather than thoughts, in which the person seems to be aware of something directly. Given the nature of the wish, we can expect them to involve intense feelings; and because the wish is abstract, they won't be particularly related to any mode of perception. They will feel as though there is something beyond or outside the person that can offer security, upon which one can depend.

Explain and illustrate Freud's explanation of religious experience.

OBJECTIONS

James argues that Freud's theory doesn't undermine the possibility that religious experiences are experiences of God:

1. We can't evaluate the truth of an experience just by its origin. We should look at its effects, its place in our lives. We must evaluate it by other things we feel are important and what we know to be true. Religious experiences produce real effects, which are positive.
2. We can agree that religious experiences come to us in the first instance from the unconscious. But it is entirely possible that the unconscious is a *conduit* of spiritual reality. Almost everyone who believes in a spiritual dimension to human beings thinks this goes beyond what we are aware of.
3. *Even if* religious experiences are caused by a wish for security and meaning, if God does exist and we do need him, then our wish for contact with God would be realistic. If we are made by God, then a relationship with God would be one of our deepest desires. The wish Freud identifies may not be the result *only* of the experiences he describes.

Freud would agree with much of this. Knowing why an artist paints may be no help at all in saying whether the painting is beautiful; knowing why a scientist dedicates their life to research won't tell us whether what they discover is true. Freud only argues that religious experience, in itself, gives us *no reason* to think it is an experience of God. It is perfectly possible for religious experience to have an entirely psychological cause, and seem exactly as it does now. Until we have some *independent* reason to think God exists, then we cannot use religious experience to support the claim that God exists.

Another objection is that Freud's account of religion is inadequate. For instance, religion is not as comforting as he supposes.

> **?** **What support does religious experience lend to the claim that God exists?**

> See **WHAT IS MEANT BY 'RELIGION'? CAN SOCIAL SCIENCE 'EXPLAIN AWAY' RELIGION?**, p. 339.

Key points • • •

*   The argument from religious experience claims that in (genuine) religious experiences, people are directly aware of God. This claim is supported by two considerations: religious experiences exhibit great similarity in certain core aspects; and they are similar to perceptual experiences, which we usually trust unless we have reason to doubt them.
*   James argues that religious experiences are an immediate sense of the reality of the unseen, often blocking out everything else from the person's mind.
*   He argues that we should evaluate religious experiences in relation to the life and attitudes of the person more generally. The religious attitude

understands human beings as needing connection to a spiritual world, which can provide feelings of love, peace and safety.

- Religious experiences are of something 'more' – in the first instance, a transformative spiritual dimension to human beings.
- Philosophers have objected that religious experience is not like perception: it is much rarer, it has little detail and we can't check our experiences for intersubjective agreement. However, this doesn't show that religious experience is not veridical, though we may argue that we shouldn't automatically trust it.
- Religions make different claims about God, but this doesn't show that religious experience isn't experience of God. People can experience the same thing, but interpret it differently.
- Freud argues that religious experiences are hallucinations caused by a very deep wish for security and meaning in an uncertain world. Because of this, we cannot tell whether they also contain some truth. We therefore cannot use them to argue for the existence of God.

Going further: background assumptions (ontological, epistemological and semantic)

In these arguments for the existence of God, what assumptions are being made? In particular, how do they understand the claim 'God exists'? The syllabus identifies three types of assumptions to consider: ontological, epistemological and semantic.

Ontological assumptions relate to the question of what exists. What is being assumed here about the *nature* of God's existence? It is assumed that God is a being, or at least a force, that exists independently of (and prior to) human beings and religious beliefs. For example, to be the cause of the existence of the universe *in a literal sense*, God must exist independently of the universe. Or again, religious experience is taken to put us in touch with something *outside* our minds.

Semantic assumptions relate to the meaning of words and language – what does it mean to say 'God exists'? For example, is this meant to be a statement of fact? In line with the ontological assumption, the semantic

Ontology is the study (-ology) of what exists or 'being' (ont-).

Other understandings were discussed in THE RELIGIOUS POINT OF VIEW, pp. 324 and 344.

assumption of the arguments is that the word 'God' refers to a being that exists. To believe in God's existence is to have a belief that can be objectively true or false.

Epistemological assumptions relate to evidence and knowledge. The epistemological assumption is that we can (and need to) support belief in God using rational arguments. The existence of God can be deduced or inferred as the best explanation from premises that are more certain or plausible than God's existence.

The ontological and semantic assumptions are a traditional part of religious belief. However, not all philosophers or believers have accepted them. In RELIGIOUS LANGUAGE AND VERIFICATIONISM (p. 332) and RELIGION AS A 'FORM OF LIFE' (p. 335), we will discuss alternative understandings of the claim 'God exists'. Suppose that 'God exists' does not state an objective fact, but expresses an attitude that someone takes towards life. Or again, suppose that to believe in God is not to make a claim about some being independent of religious practice; to talk of God is to talk of how to understand and live life. The question of belief in God is then a question of whether the religious approach towards life makes sense.

On this view, the cosmological argument is either nonsense, or, more profoundly, explores the *meaning* of the universe. 'God' explains the universe not as cause, but as its point. And whether religious experience supports belief in God becomes a question about whether religious experience is 'truthful', revealing some important aspect of human life.

What of the epistemological assumption? Our next topic, REASON AND FAITH, looks at a variety of positions that challenge this assumption. We might argue that reason is incapable of supporting belief in God in the absence of faith (p. 304) - so arguments for the existence of God can only meaningfully occur between those who already believe in God and are simply trying to understand their belief better. Or we might argue that religious belief is not inferred from other beliefs, but formed directly in response to experience (analogous to beliefs about what we perceive; p. 306). Or we can argue that reasoning, while not inappropriate, cannot settle the matter, so belief in God must rest on a commitment, a 'leap' or 'gamble' (pp. 309 and 313).

? Why is it important to identify and discuss the assumptions made by arguments for the existence of God?

Key points ● ● ●

- The cosmological argument and argument from religious experience usually assume that the word 'God' refers to a being that exists independently of human beings, and that belief in the existence of God can be supported by rational arguments.
- A number of interpretations of religious belief, and of the relation between reason and faith, reject these assumptions. Some argue that talk of God is talk of important aspects of human life; some argue that religious faith cannot be established by argument.

II. REASON AND FAITH

In Christianity, the importance of faith and its role in religious life stem from its significance in the New Testament. In that context, the term is most closely related to 'trust' – trusting God and God's promises. In this sense, faith is more of an attitude than a state of belief or knowledge. It is described as a 'virtue', along with hope and charity (or love). However, when you trust a person, you also believe what they say. And this connects faith to belief, which is a cognitive state. Those who emphasise faith as belief argue that God reveals truths that faith accepts. Those who emphasise faith as an attitude argue that God reveals God's self, and that the question of truths arises at the level of human interpretation of that revelation.

See BELIEF, p. 160

> Explain and illustrate the difference between faith as trust and faith as belief.

One position on faith, which we shall not discuss further, is that it is simply religious belief, and, like all belief, religious belief is (or should be) based on evidence and argument. This view understands faith as cognitive, but not a special kind of cognitive state.

'Faith' as a special kind of cognitive state

Faith and revelation

If faith is not *simply* religious belief formed on the basis of evidence, through the usual rational processes, what kind of cognitive state is it, and how does it relate to questions of evidence?

St Thomas Aquinas argued that faith and reason must cohere together. As rational beings, our greatest happiness will be found in worthwhile rational activity. Therefore, our greatest happiness lies in rational contact with God. However, some truths about God are beyond our ability to grasp rationally. Our intellect is dependent on our senses, and from what we experience, we are not able, for instance, to infer God's nature. We are, however, able to demonstrate that God exists and to know some of God's attributes (e.g. through THE COSMOLOGICAL ARGUMENT, p. 288). Reason can support faith.

Aquinas understands faith as believing what someone says because you trust them. Now, if you *need* someone's testimony to believe something, that must be because you cannot work it out for yourself. Because our intellect is limited, we need faith to be in contact with God. Rationally understanding a truth is better, in a sense, than believing it on someone's testimony. So, it is good to seek understanding of God. But one cannot hope to achieve this understanding without the presence of faith first.

Because what we believe by faith is beyond rational understanding, then our belief isn't rationally compelled by evidence or argument. So, faith is voluntary; it involves, to some degree, *choosing* to believe. Anyone who doesn't believe what God has revealed (which Aquinas took to be Christian doctrine) lacks faith.

We can object that there is a tension between saying faith involves believing a set of truths and saying that it is voluntary. Can we choose what to believe? Aquinas replies that the disposition to believe is given to us by God (see FAITH AND DIVINE GRACE, p. 307). We can still question whether this solves the question, discussed further in TO WHAT EXTENT CAN WE 'CHOOSE' WHAT TO BELIEVE?, p. 317.

> **?** Why does faith depend on revelation, according to Aquinas?

Religious belief as 'basic'

> 'Reason and Belief in God'

Alvin Plantinga agrees with Aquinas that faith is a type of belief, but he defends a different relation between faith and reason.

EVIDENCE AND BASIC BELIEFS

The view that all beliefs should be proportionate to the evidence is 'evidentialism'; we should believe only things we have evidence for, and we should believe them only with the degree of certainty that the evidence supports. It is irrational to believe anything on insufficient evidence. So, we should not believe that God exists unless we have good evidence that God exists.

Plantinga argues that not *all* beliefs can be based on evidence, because then every belief would rest on other beliefs. So, some beliefs, says Plantinga, must be acceptable without evidence. A belief is 'basic' if it is not accepted on the basis of other beliefs.

Many philosophers have argued that two sorts of beliefs are rightly or 'properly' basic: 'self-evident' beliefs, and beliefs that are based on 'what is evident to the senses'. If I see a brown tree, I believe 'the tree is brown'. I don't, even subconsciously, *infer* this belief: I don't think, 'I seem to see a brown tree', 'What I seem to see is often accurate', 'Therefore, I believe the tree is brown'. I form the belief immediately in the presence of sense perception.

Going further: on evidence

Plantinga says that a belief is 'basic' if it doesn't rest on other beliefs, which he equates with not resting on evidence. A belief is supported by evidence, according to him, only if it is supported by other beliefs. But this is a narrow interpretation of 'evidence'. After all, the two types of properly basic beliefs foundationalists talk about are what is self-*evident* and what is *evident* to the senses. The evidence in each of these cases is something about the belief itself or about the circumstances in which it is formed (for example, believing 'the tree is brown' when looking at a brown tree). The evidence is not other beliefs, but that doesn't mean there is *no evidence* for these beliefs. The evidence for believing the tree is brown is your experience, that you see a brown tree.

The distinction between basic and non-basic beliefs, then, is not between beliefs that rest on evidence and ones that don't. Instead, basic beliefs rest on a form of evidence that isn't itself a belief (e.g. a sense experience).

We can, then, argue that a belief is justified if, and only if, either it is properly basic or it is accepted on the basis of other beliefs, which eventually come to rest on properly basic beliefs. Any belief that is neither properly basic nor based on other beliefs is not rationally justified.

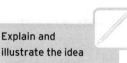

Explain and illustrate the idea of a basic belief.

RELIGIOUS BELIEF

Plantinga argues that religious belief is basic. But how so? The existence of God is neither self-evident nor evident to the senses; belief in God isn't properly basic. Surely, then, we should believe that God exists only if we support this belief with other beliefs. Plantinga argues that this argument is self-defeating. How do we know that 'only what is self-evident and what is evident to the senses is properly basic'? This claim is not itself self-evident nor evident to the senses, so it is not properly basic. It also is difficult to see how we can deduce it either from self-evident beliefs or from what is evident to the senses. So, it may be that other forms of belief are also properly basic.

Many theologians, particularly in the tradition of Reformed theology (theology that came out of the Reformation), argue that religious belief is not usually accepted or held on the basis of arguments. Some argue that arguments for the existence of God don't work; but even if they did, religious faith in God is not dependent on them.

So, faith is not inferred from other beliefs, but this does not mean that it is without justification. Instead, religious beliefs are comparable to beliefs based on sense perception. We don't believe in the existence of physical objects because we have good arguments for them; we don't infer them from experience; they are simply given to us in experience. Likewise, the existence of God is simply *apparent* to the believer.

How? John Calvin argues that God implanted a direct awareness of himself in every mind. We only lose touch with this awareness through sin. Other theologians argue that we see God in creation. We don't *infer* God's existence from nature; we *see* God in nature. Others argue that we have a direct awareness of God in religious experience. Again, this is distinct from saying that we infer God's existence from religious experience.

On any of these views, religious belief is basic. Faith is a *distinct* cognitive state, just as each of the senses provides a distinct way of knowing about the world.

See THE ARGUMENT FROM RELIGIOUS EXPERIENCE, p. 295.

Explain and illustrate the view that religious belief is basic.

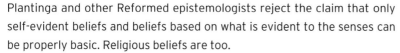

Going further: what is properly basic?

Plantinga and other Reformed epistemologists reject the claim that only self-evident beliefs and beliefs based on what is evident to the senses can be properly basic. Religious beliefs are too.

One way to support this belief is to develop the analogy with perception. Perceptual beliefs are properly basic, Plantinga suggests, because they are caused by the circumstances in which they are formed (e.g. the experience) and are a product of 'proper functioning'. My belief that 'the tree is brown' when I'm looking at a tree is caused by my looking at the tree, and is a product of my senses and cognition working properly.

So we can ask: is the belief that God exists *caused by* the circumstances Reformed theologians appeal to or are people's beliefs in the existence of God caused by something else entirely, such as upbringing? Second, is forming this belief an example of *proper* functioning? Is it part of the proper functioning of the human mind to see God in nature? Is religious experience an example of proper functioning? Arguments from psychology and the social sciences that try to explain religious belief and experience could suggest that they are not.

See Freud, p. 299, and Can social science 'explain away' religion?, p. 339.

Is religious belief analogous to perceptual beliefs?

Faith and divine grace

Properly basic beliefs can be defeated. For example, if I know that I'm in a museum of optical illusions, I won't believe what I see. Perceptual experience gives us prima facie justification; we treat perceptual experiences as veridical *unless we have reason to doubt them*.

Plantinga argues that the same is true for religious belief. Even if it is properly basic, that does not mean that it is immune to arguments against the existence of God. These may defeat our belief in the existence of God if they are not answered.

However, if perception were always faulty, generally unreliable, then it would be unreasonable to form beliefs about the world on the basis of perception alone. Such beliefs, then, would not be properly basic. An objection of this kind can be made to religious faith. People do not *generally* agree in the beliefs they form about God (either God's existence or God's nature). So whose faith (or lack of it) is an example of *proper* functioning and whose is faulty? And why do so many people 'malfunction'?

Plantinga appeals to the idea that our cognitive abilities are damaged by 'original sin'. For example, what we think to be reasonable or rational to believe might be a reflection of our pride or self-centredness. This is why so many people 'malfunction' in forming their basic beliefs about religious matters.

Aquinas rejects the strong version of this, since he claims that our limited intellect can at least know that God exists using reason (p. 303). Plantinga emphasises more strongly the idea that faith is a gift from God, a matter of divine grace. By God's grace, Plantinga argues, we come to be able to function properly, and so form the right basic beliefs.

The thought that faith is given by divine grace comes from the New Testament book of Romans, Ch. 4, in which St Paul asks how we can be 'justified before God'. He answers that we could never be 'justified' through good deeds; we can only be justified by faith. This entails that faith itself cannot be 'worked at' or 'earned' – so it must be a gift from God.

That faith requires divine grace for proper functioning does not make it irrational. Just as perception is rational, in the sense of being part of normal cognition, Plantinga argues that the sorts of experiences that support belief in God are likewise part of reason (functioning properly). If he is right, then faith is a form of reason, and trying to draw a contrast between the two is mistaken.

> **Warranted Christian Belief**

> This idea raises many difficulties; for example, how could anyone be blamed for lacking faith? Isn't it arbitrary that God gives faith to one person and not another? And so on. But these are not our concern here.

> Assess the claim that religious belief is properly basic.

For a third cognitive account of faith, see DIFFERENT PERSPECTIVES, pp. 324 and 344.

Key points • • •

- Aquinas argues that reason can infer God's existence and some of God's attributes, but much about God's nature can be known only through revelation.
- Faith is a matter of believing what someone you trust tells you. Faith in God's revelation is voluntary.
- Plantinga argues that religious beliefs are 'basic', not inferred from other beliefs we have. Traditional examples of basic beliefs include self-evident beliefs and those based on what is evident to the senses. Plantinga argues that the claim that these are the only basic beliefs is self-defeating.
- Reformed theologians argue that the existence of God is apparent to the believer in nature or in religious experience, and cannot be inferred by rational argument.
- We can question whether religious belief is *properly* basic, or simply

unjustified. Plantinga argues that perceptual beliefs are properly basic because they are caused by the circumstances in which they formed and are a product of proper functioning. Religious beliefs may be properly basic for the same reasons.

- To explain why so many people 'malfunction', Plantinga appeals to original sin. Faith (proper functioning) is a gift, a matter of divine grace, that corrects the malfunction. As such, faith remains a form of reason (cognition), just as perception does.

Faith as an attitude or commitment

The view that faith is an attitude or commitment rejects the claim that faith is essentially about beliefs. The attitude most associated with faith is trust in God. But just to say this is not enough. For instance, surely we can only trust someone who we *believe* exists. So, faith would rest on the belief that God exists. But what if this belief involves a commitment that does not rest on the evidence? How does someone acquire this commitment? Is it rational to do so?

> In this section, we consider two accounts of faith as commitment. The view that faith is a **non-cognitive** attitude is discussed in THE MEANING OF RELIGIOUS LANGUAGE, p. 334, and RELIGION AS A 'FORM OF LIFE', p. 335.

James

W.K. Clifford argues that it is 'wrong always, everywhere, and for every one, to believe anything on insufficient evidence'. Belief, he argued, must be earned through patient investigation, not by stifling doubts. No real belief is insignificant, and this will be especially true for religious beliefs. A belief inclines us to believe other similar things, while it weakens beliefs that are contrary to it. Forming beliefs on insufficient evidence makes us credulous, it weakens our cognitive powers and it makes other people less concerned about telling us lies. Religious faith, if it amounts to belief without sufficient evidence, is therefore always wrong.

> 'The Ethics of Belief'

William James argues that Clifford is wrong; it *can* sometimes be right, and in fact *reasonable*, to believe something without sufficient evidence for its truth, namely when we face a 'genuine option' that cannot be decided on the basis of evidence. A 'genuine option' involves three conditions:

> 'The Will to Believe'

1. The alternatives for what to believe, for example 'God exists' and 'God does not exist', are 'live'; the person feels they really could believe either. Some people may not feel this way, in which case one or other alternative is 'dead'.

Explain and illustrate James' idea of a 'genuine option'.

2. The alternatives exclude each other (not more than one of them can be true) and there are no other alternatives; the choice between them is 'forced'.
3. The alternatives are 'momentous' rather than trivial; for example, this is your only opportunity to get it right, or the stakes are high.

If these three conditions apply, and we cannot decide on the basis on evidence, then it is not unreasonable for us to incline towards one belief or another on other grounds.

In belief, we have *two* goals: to avoid error, as Clifford argues; but also to *secure the truth*. Although avoiding error is important in science, in other areas of life we often need to form beliefs with some risk of error. For example, in forming a friendship with someone, you need to trust them, which will involve the belief that they are trustworthy *before* you really have good evidence of this. And it is reasonable to do this, given that we want to form the friendship. It is not always wrong, then, for our wills to influence our beliefs.

In the case of genuine options, if our intellect can't decide, then our emotions and will can and *must*. To not form a belief, for example for fear of getting it wrong, is itself a decision made on the basis of an emotion. But given what is at stake in a genuine option, getting it wrong might be less bad than losing out on truth: 'worse things than being duped may happen to a man in this world'. Clifford opposes reason and emotion in forming beliefs, arguing that we must form beliefs only on the basis of reason. But his argument is itself supported by emotion and moral values. Emotions come into what we believe, or don't, whichever way we argue.

Religious faith, for many, involves a genuine option. The 'religious hypothesis' is that the best things are eternal, and we are better off now if we believe. James says it clearly presents an option that is forced and momentous; if it is live for the individual as well, then it is reasonable for them to believe.

However, while religious faith clearly deals with things that are important, it is not obvious that the choice between having religious faith and not is either forced or momentous. There are many religions, so the question arises as to *which* religious faith to adopt. And some of these faiths, such as Buddhism, do not say that God exists. So, the options are not forced. Second, if believing in God is not necessary for God to reward one with eternal life, then the choice is not momentous.

See Is IT RATIONAL TO CHOOSE TO BELIEVE IN GOD?, p. 316.

James is *not* arguing that faith is *more* rational than agnosticism or atheism. He is only arguing that it is *not less* rational. He is arguing that there is a place for faith that reason can respect. Reason can recognise its limitations, and can recognise that faith may rightly act when reason is limited. Having faith on the basis of the will does not fly in the face of reason; it simply goes where reason cannot.

Kierkegaard

Søren Kierkegaard argues that we are wrong to think of religious beliefs in the same way as other beliefs. Religion is not a type of philosophical system, and we shouldn't weigh up religious beliefs in a philosophical way. Instead, faith is characterised by passionate commitment. Beliefs formed 'objectively' are not; they may have no impact on one's life. To believe that God exists, but to treat this as just another fact, about which we feel nothing, is not to have faith. Faith isn't (just) a matter of what, but of *how*, we believe.

The commitment that characterises faith requires a decision, a 'leap'; it is not something that can be established intellectually. This leap actually *requires* objective uncertainty: 'If I am able to apprehend God objectively, I do not have faith; but because I cannot do this, I must have faith. If I want to keep myself in faith, I must continually see to it that I hold fast to objective uncertainty.'

Some philosophers argue that reason can't determine whether God exists *because* God wants us to have this type of committed, passionate relationship with him. If we felt we knew the answers, something would be lost. Kierkegaard emphasises the importance of this: objective certainty will not have the same impact on one's life as faith in the face of uncertainty. But without reason to guide us, why should we 'leap' in the direction of religious *belief* rather than unbelief? And *can* we just believe whatever we choose to? Is the leap of faith possible?

Philosophers disagree about what Kierkegaard thought about the relation of reason to religious belief. He remarks that we 'cannot believe nonsense against the understanding, which one might fear, because the understanding will penetratingly perceive that it is nonsense and hinder [us] in believing it'. Neither James nor Kierkegaard thinks that belief is completely under the control of the will, but we can form beliefs without relying on reason in certain circumstances. For Kierkegaard, religious faith in its trust and commitment is 'incomprehensible' in that it lies outside the limits that reason can reach for itself. But, like James, he thinks reason can recognise that it has limits, and that faith might *legitimately* lie outside these limits. To achieve it, we must leap. By contrast, if faith were just nonsense, reason would inhibit our ability to leap.

> **?** Does James show that religious belief can be reasonable even if not based on sufficient evidence?

> *Concluding Unscientific Postscript to Philosophical Fragments*, p. 204

> See To what extent can we 'choose' what to believe?, p. 317.

> *Concluding Unscientific Postscript to Philosophical Fragments*, p. 568

> **?** Is Kierkegaard's 'leap of faith' possible? Why does he argue that it is necessary?

An objection

If faith goes beyond reason, then it must accept that we do not have *any reason* to believe in God. The arguments of James and Kierkegaard only show that faith is not unreasonable. They don't show that we *should* leap in a particular way. But many religious believers think that they do have *some* reason to believe in God, appealing to some argument that says God is the best explanation, for example THE COSMOLOGICAL ARGUMENT (p. 288), THE ARGUMENT FROM RELIGIOUS EXPERIENCE (p. 295) or an argument from MIRACLES (p. 321). But they are willing to accept that the evidence for God's existence is not very strong, so they say it is a matter of faith.

This seems inconsistent: it accepts that belief in God *is* a matter of evidence and argument, but says that we don't need to justify our conclusion by the balance of evidence, because belief rests on faith. If we are getting into the question of evidence, shouldn't we be consistent and believe in God only if the evidence suggests it is *more* likely that God exists than not – that is, if belief in God is supported by reason?

But there are other possibilities:

1. Belief in God is precisely as reasonable as not believing in God (the evidence is exactly balanced).
2. We cannot tell what the balance of evidence is.
3. For some reason, our belief needs to be more certain than the evidence (either way) allows, so we should consider not just the evidence, but other issues as well.

Philosophers have not tended to argue for (1), but some of their arguments support (2) and (3). So, we could argue that while reason cannot settle the question of belief in God, and so it must rest on faith, this does not mean we have no reason at all for such belief.

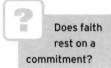
Does faith rest on a commitment?

Key points • • •

*   James argues that it is reasonable to decide what to believe when faced with a genuine option – that is, a forced and momentous choice between claims that are live, a choice that is not settled by intellectual enquiry.

- We can object that religious faith is not a genuine option, because it is not forced or momentous.
- Kierkegaard argues that faith is distinct from 'objective' belief in involving a passionate commitment. Faith requires a 'leap' in the face of uncertainty.
- Faith is incomprehensible to reason, but it is not rejected by reason. If it were, we would not be able to believe by making a decision.
- Both James and Kierkegaard argue that faith is not unreasonable. But we need independent considerations to suggest that we *should* believe in God.
- We can object that few religious believers think there is *no* reason to believe in God, but appeal to arguments. But then consistency requires us to believe in God only if the evidence is sufficient.

Is it rational to choose to believe in God?

Pascal's Wager

Pascal's Wager doesn't claim that we have good evidence for God's existence, so it isn't *theoretically* or *cognitively* rational to believe in God. Rather, it argues, we have good *practical* reason to believe in God, because we stand to benefit greatly from such a belief. It is an attempt to justify belief in God quite independently of any attempt to prove God's existence. Here is Pascal's argument, though the format and numbering are mine:

Pensées, § 233

1. 'God is, or He is not.' But to which side shall we incline? Reason can decide nothing here. . . . Since you must choose, let us see which interests you least.
2. You have two things to lose, the true and the good; and two things to stake, your reason and your will, your knowledge and your happiness; and your nature has two things to shun, error and misery.
3. Your reason is no more shocked in choosing one rather than the other, since you must of necessity choose . . .
4. But your happiness? Let us weigh the gain and the loss in wagering that God is . . .
5. If you gain, you gain all; if you lose, you lose nothing . . .

That is very fine. Yes, I must wager; but I may perhaps wager too much.

6. Since there is an equal risk of gain and of loss, if you had only to gain two lives, instead of one, you might still wager. But if there were three lives to gain . . . you would be imprudent, when you are forced to play, not to chance your life to gain three at a game where there is an equal risk of loss and gain.
7. But there is an eternity of life and happiness . . . there is here an infinity of an infinitely happy life to gain, a chance of gain against a finite number of chances of loss, and what you stake is finite . . .
8. wherever the infinite is and there is not an infinity of chances of loss against that of gain . . . you must give all . . .

Pascal says (1) we cannot use reason to prove that God exists nor that God does not exist. But we must believe one or the other. In this sort of case, it is perfectly acceptable to decide your belief on practical grounds. The pros and cons can be summarised in a decision matrix (a table of the benefits and losses of each possible decision):

	God exists	**God does not exist**
Wager for God	Infinite gain	Finite loss
Wager against God	Finite or infinite loss	Finite gain

The potential gain of wagering for God and being right is infinite. As long as there is *some* chance that God exists – that is, the probability that God exists is not zero – this outweighs any finite gain that may come from wagering against God and any finite loss that may come from being wrong. It is irrational, therefore, not to wager for God. For now, we will treat 'wager for God' as including 'believe in God'; but we'll return to this point in the last objection to Pascal's argument.

> **Explain the structure of Pascal's Wager.**

Going further: two inconsistencies

Pascal first says (2) that what is at stake is 'the true and the good'. We want to avoid error and believe what is true; but we also want to secure our happiness. He then claims (5) that if we believe in God, but God does not exist, we lose nothing.

This seems wrong on two counts: first, we have believed a falsehood, so we have 'lost' truth. However, by (3) – that reason is indifferent to which way we wager – this might be counted as no personal loss; we have not violated or undermined our rational capacities. But the second loss could be to our happiness: belief in God is usually thought to carry certain burdens of piety and morality. Pascal doesn't provide any argument to suggest that we will be as happy believing in God as not believing in God. But it turns out that it doesn't matter if belief in God carries a loss, because it will be finite. Against the infinite possible gain, this carries no force.

The second inconsistency relates to the probability of God's existence. For the argument to work, Pascal must suppose the probability is not zero. Absolutely no chance of an infinite gain is no incentive! But he says (6) there is an equal chance of loss and gain. This is unwarranted: by his earlier assertion that (1) 'reason can decide nothing here', we cannot know that the probability of God's existence is 0.5. Worse, (1) also questions whether we can *know* that the probability of God's existence is not zero.

But Pascal's assertion in (1) could be taken as an assertion that we cannot know that God does *not* exist. We cannot establish what the objective probability of God's existence is; *subjectively*, then, the probability of God's existence cannot be zero. We must assign some positive probability to God's existence; this much reason can decide, even if it cannot establish what that probability should be.

But why shouldn't we refuse to assign any figure of probability to God's existence? If we do this, then the wager does not work. As Pascal notes in (7), there must be *a chance* of gain; if we cannot say whether there is such a chance or not, there is no decision we are rationally obliged to make.

Does Pascal illegitimately assume that we can know God *might* exist?

Analysis of the argument

The main argument comes in (6)–(8). In (6), Pascal explains the rationality of gambling. (He measures utility in terms of 'lives', perhaps intending to capture the contrast between this one life and eternal (infinite) life.) If there is an equal chance of winning or losing, it is rational to bet 1 to gain 3. If we are betting money, then

	Win £3	Lose	Expected utility
Bet £1	3	-1	$(0.5 \times 3) + (0.5 \times -1) = 0.5$
Don't bet	0	0	0

Since $0.5 > 0$, it is rational to bet if the chances are 50:50 and the gain is three times the stake.

In wagering for God, Pascal cannot claim that the chances are 50:50. We don't know what the chance is of God's existing. However, (7) the gain is infinite, while the stake remains finite. So, no matter how small the chance of God's existence, $\infty \times$ any finite chance $= \infty$. Therefore, (8) infinite gain is the choice to wager for.

> Explain Pascal's argument for the claim that it is rational to gamble that God exists.

Objections

Philosophers have raised four types of objection to the argument. First, the decision matrix is wrong; if there are more options than Pascal allows for, or the weightings are different, the argument doesn't work:

1. The utility of eternal life can't be infinite, either because infinite utility makes no sense or because infinite utility couldn't be appreciated by finite beings like us. Whether we should wager for God depends on (how large the potential gain is) $\times$ (the probability of God's existence). Since we don't know either, we aren't rationally compelled to wager for God.
2. Why think that God bestows infinite utility on all and only those who wager for him? Perhaps all are saved. Or perhaps only the Predestined are. Or perhaps God bestows different utilities on different people, depending on other factors.

3. Which God should we believe in? If Pascal's wager works, doesn't it work for any god? So shouldn't we believe in Roman, Greek and Hindu gods as well? But we can't be rationally required to hold inconsistent beliefs.

A second objection is that rationality does not require us to maximise expected utility. Beliefs are a matter of *theoretical* rationality, while maximising utility is a criterion of *practical* rationality if it is a criterion of rationality at all. Theoretical rationality doesn't apply here (by (1)), but that is no reason to assume that the criterion of practical rationality takes over. We could instead argue that there is no belief it is rational to adopt.

Third, we might argue that it is immoral to wager for God. To form beliefs by wagering, rather than by evidence, is to corrupt oneself (Pascal is wrong to think we do not corrupt reason). Or again, if God condemned all those who do not wager for Him, including honest non-believers, God is immoral. Or the entire matter of 'wagering' is simply unworthy of such a grave issue as belief in God.

Finally, we can object that Pascal's Wager wrongly assumes belief in God can be a matter of will. We discuss this in the next section.

> Does Pascal's Wager show that it is rational to choose to believe in God?

To what extent can we 'choose' what to believe?

Try to believe that there is an elephant standing in front of you. Try really hard. Why can't you succeed?

Belief by its nature aims at truth:

1. We can evaluate a belief as true or false. This is not the case with other kinds of mental states, such as fear, hope or desire.
2. To believe that p (some proposition) is to believe that p is true. To believe that 'God exists' is to believe that it is true that 'God exists'. So if you recognise that 'God exists' is false, you abandon your belief that God exists.
3. To say, 'I believe that God exists' implies that 'God exists' is true. For instance, it is paradoxical to say, 'I believe that God exists, but "God exists" is false'.

The nature of belief suggests that forming beliefs can't be voluntary. If we could choose what to believe, then we could form a belief without any regard to the truth of the proposition we believe. Furthermore, having consciously chosen to have the belief, we would know that we formed it irrespective of its truth. Yet

Of course, you can choose whether to *say* that you believe that God exists. But this is not the same as believing that God exists – because we can be insincere.

to believe that God exists is to believe that 'God exists' is a true statement. But I cannot choose what is true.

However, this is no objection to Pascal, as he does not claim that we can choose to believe in God in this way. Instead, he says that to 'wager for God' is to take steps to cultivate a belief in God, for example by adopting a religious lifestyle, attending worship, observing rituals. These are things we can choose to do, and over time they will bring about belief. But *how* can what we choose to do affect our beliefs, and does this show that beliefs can be voluntary?

First, what people *want* to be true does tend to affect what they believe, in various ways. For instance, we pay attention only to evidence that confirms what we want to believe, and ignore evidence that undermines it. For instance, we might believe that our family and friends are nicer people than in fact they are by noticing when they are kind and ignoring when they are not. But this only shows that belief is not voluntary, but formed in relation to evidence. Someone cannot believe that their friends are kind while also believing that the *only* reason they have that belief is because they want to have it. The same applies to believing that God exists.

We might object: surely people form and hold on to all sorts of ethical and religious beliefs without any real attempt to discover the truth. They believe what they do for all sorts of individual and social factors, but their beliefs are simply prejudices, and no form of evidence or argument changes their minds. Doesn't this show that beliefs can be voluntary?

Even in these cases, the idea that someone can believe that there is no evidence for their belief while still holding on to their belief is peculiar. (Most people assert that there is evidence, even if they can't say what it is!) And certainly their beliefs are not *rational* – but Pascal wants to establish that belief is God is not a mere prejudice.

However, even if we want God to exist, this is not the way in which Pascal suggests we acquire belief in God. So, a second connection between the will and belief is that we can voluntarily undertake some action that will lead to our coming to have the belief that p. For instance, I could go to a hypnotist and ask him to cause me to have the belief that p. My belief, though, is not voluntary; I am caused to have it, though in this case by hypnotism rather than evidence. The case of coming to believe in God through adopting a religious lifestyle is analogous, not with hypnotism(!), but in that we can choose to act as if we believe in God. Over time, says Pascal, a genuine belief in God will form.

For this to happen, we cannot think that the *only* reason we believe in God is because we adopted a religious lifestyle. In retrospect, we may see this as a *cause* of our belief; but through our new lifestyle, Pascal thinks, we will become sensitive to experiences that *justify* our new belief. These experiences are not available to anyone, but only to someone who has set themselves on the path to belief. That does not make them less genuine, only restricted to those who sincerely seek God.

Discuss whether Pascal's Wager wrongly assumes that we can choose what to believe.

Key points • • •

- Pascal argues that because reason cannot prove the existence or non-existence of God, we should decide what to believe by the possible benefits of our beliefs.
- If we believe in God and are right, the possible benefits are infinite. If we are wrong, we have lost little (only a finite amount). If we don't believe in God and are right, we have gained little (a finite amount). If we are wrong, we could lose a great deal. Whatever the chances of God's existence, we should believe in God, because a very small chance of an infinite gain still outweighs a very large chance of a finite gain.
- We can object that the decision matrix is set up wrongly. For example, we don't know that believing in God, if God exists, will produce an infinite gain. We don't know which God to believe in.
- We aren't rationally required to hold beliefs that maximise potential benefit.
- It is immoral to form beliefs about God in this way.
- We cannot directly influence what we believe by what we want. Beliefs aim at the truth, and are responsive to evidence.
- But Pascal argues that we should act in a way that will lead to belief in God. This can be voluntary and, he argues, it provides experiences that justify that belief.

Going further: reason and faith in philosophy of religion

Our discussions of the relationship between reason and religious belief have implications for how we should understand and conduct philosophy of religion. Philosophy is normally thought of as a discipline that is based on reason, drawing on empirical information where relevant. But if religious belief is necessarily or correctly based on faith, and faith is based on neither reason nor on empirical facts, this raises the question of how we should do philosophy of religion.

In BACKGROUND ASSUMPTIONS (p. 301), we briefly discussed the epistemological assumptions of the arguments for the existence of God, and noted that they attempted to provide rational grounds for belief in God through deduction or inference to the best explanation. The same assumptions apply to THE ROLES OF MIRACLE STORIES (p. 321) – that is, that miracles improve the evidence for belief in God – and HUME'S ARGUMENT AGAINST MIRACLES (p. 329). Furthermore, people who think social science can 'explain away' religion (p. 339) tend to think that if we can demonstrate that religious belief is not based on reason, we have to some extent undermined it.

The views we have discussed – of Plantinga, James, Kierkegaard and Pascal – all reject this epistemological assumption. And we will see further arguments against it in discussions of religious language (RELIGION AS A FORM OF LIFE, p. 335) and social science (BEYOND SOCIAL FUNCTION: THE QUESTION OF MEANING, p. 343). In the discussion of miracles, we will also see theories that argue that miracles are 'signs', understood only by those who already have faith, and are not intended to provide objective evidence.

One of the issues, then, in philosophy of religion is whether certain debates within philosophy of religion are possible or meaningful, or whether they misconceive the nature of religious belief and its relation to reason.

> Outline and discuss the implications for philosophy of religion that faith is not based on reason, but is nevertheless justifiable.

III. MIRACLES

The role and significance of miracle stories in religions

There is no one role that stories of miracles have in the major world religions, and there is strong disagreement over their significance, even within any one religion. At the outset, it is worth noting that none of the scriptures of Judaism, Christianity and Islam uses the word 'miracle' (or equivalent). Instead, all three use words that mean 'wonder', 'power' or, very often, 'sign' to describe those events that we might now judge to be miraculous. So, there is even a question over whether a particular story is, in fact, a 'miracle' story.

The roles of miracle stories

Nevertheless, it is fair to say that the understanding of miracles, in most religions, has been dominated by the following three roles, relating to God's activity in history, the lives of particular holy men and divine revelation:

1. Miracles are signs that demonstrate God's underlying activity in the world and his purposes. They reveal God's character and plan. Miracles performed by individuals illustrate the meaning and impact of their mission. While some miracle stories tell of apparently random demonstrations of power, most tell of events such as healing, rescuing, resurrection, conversion and so on, and relate to the values of the religion and its understanding of God.
2. Miracles are intended to support the development of religious faith. The performance of the miracle is supposed to demonstrate the truth of what the miracle worker says; the power to work the miracle shows the message comes from God. Miracles can be intended to generate conviction in particular individuals, or they can occur at a historical period in order to establish a religion generally. (Many Protestant Christians argued that God allowed and enabled miracles in the early Church, but not since.)
3. Miracle stories are intended to highlight revelation through scripture. The miracles confirm what else is said in scripture, and gives scripture God's seal of approval.

However, (stories of) miracles also function in other ways:

4. They demonstrate the connection of the physical world to a spiritual world.
5. They support the belief that supplicatory prayer can be meaningful.
6. They support the belief in the ability of a personal God to respond to the world.
7. They enhance the reputation of a saint or holy person, proving their connection to God and, in some cases, their status as a protector of a particular geographical area, such as a town.
8. Miracle stories also function to move the audience emotionally, as the characters and events described are 'larger than life'.

Rather than events that contravene the laws of nature – see WHAT DO WE MEAN BY A MIRACLE?, p. 325.

What roles do miracle stories play?

The significance of miracle stories

A debate over the significance of miracle stories marks a number of religions. For example, when early Christian thinkers appealed to the miracles of Jesus and the Apostles to try to convince others of the truth of their teachings, they were faced with two powerful objections: first, that the miracles they reported were no more amazing than those reported by believers of pagan religions; and second, that the miracles they reported were the result of sorcery, not the intervention of God. In response, rather than appeal to miracles to support Christian teachings, some early Christian thinkers tried to defend their accounts of miracles by appealing to the truth of the teachings! Others disregarded appeals to miracles entirely.

A similar debate broke out between Protestants and Catholics 1,600 years later. Protestants argued that God had restricted miracles to the time of the New Testament, and the Catholic belief in continuing miracles went hand in hand with Catholics' false belief in saints. Catholics replied that the fact there weren't any Protestant miracles demonstrated that Protestantism was not the true religion.

Similar concerns and disagreements appear in many religions. On a popular level, miracle stories can form an important part of people's religious faith and their attachment to particular beliefs or holy people. On a reflective level, religious thinkers have recognised that appealing to miracles may be no use at all as a form of evidence in support of religious conviction or revelation. Or again, while many of the founders of religion are reported to have performed miracles, they are also reported to have warned *against* the temptation of seeking miracles. There is no need of such sensationalism in true faith. And so miracles can seem to be both crucial to a religion and beside the point!

What remains untouched by this debate is the idea of miracles as 'signs' of God's activity, purpose and character. In this sense, miracle stories are integral to the nature and message of the religion, for example the idea of God as healer or giver of life. These signs are not meant to convert the unbeliever; they are perceived as signs only by those who already believe. They confirm and strengthen faith, but they don't create it. However, some religious thinkers have reservations about thinking of miracles as specific acts of God, because doing so can undermine the idea that God is active throughout creation. We need to realise that God and the miraculous are present in everything.

Discuss the significance of miracles for religious belief.

Key points • • •

- Many religious scriptures talk not of 'miracles', but of 'wonders' and 'signs'.
- The three main roles of miracle stories are to function as signs of God's activity, plan and nature; to support the development of religious faith; and to support belief in revelation through scripture. However, they play a number of other roles as well.
- There is little agreement on the significance of miracle stories, even within one religion. While the stories form part of popular faith, many religious thinkers realised that they could not provide evidence for religious claims, and a number of religious founders warned against seeking miracles.
- Miracle stories nevertheless indicate the religion's understanding of God's activity, purpose and character.

Miracles and the competing truth claims of different religions

There is a common assumption among many religious believers that only the 'true' religion could have 'true' miracles. Some have maintained that other religions have no miracles, others that the miracles of other religions are 'false' (the product of magic, sorcery or devils). From a neutral standpoint, it is difficult to agree with any conclusion of this sort. Hume pointed out that every religion proclaims its miracles as indications of the truth of its message. But not every religion can be true. So if miracles support the truth claims of the religion, then the miracle stories of one religion are evidence *against* the miracle stories of another. On these grounds, we should not accept *any* miracle story as true. An alternative response, of course, is not to appeal to miracles in support of the truth claims of one's religion.

> *An Enquiry Concerning Human Understanding*, p. 178

The understanding of miracles as signs provides a different connection between miracles and truth claims. It has been a standard criticism of certain alleged miracle stories (of other religions, or within one's own) that the story is merely sensationalist, revealing nothing about God, and should therefore be dismissed as ungenuine. What kind of God, we may ask, would bring about this *kind* of event? Debates about the nature of God occur between religions; and one religion may evaluate and criticise the miracle stories of another for failing to accord with God's true nature.

> Discuss Hume's argument that miracle stories of competing religions cancel each other out.

Religious pluralism

But another possible response to the issue of miracle stories across religions is that of *religious pluralism*. There is no one definition of religious pluralism – it may mean (from weak to strong):

1. merely the fact that different religions coexist in society;
2. religious tolerance;
3. inter-religious dialogue;
4. inter-religious cooperation;
5. the belief that religions other than one's own make *some* valid or true claims;
6. the belief that religions make *equally* valid or true claims.

The first four forms of religious pluralism are compatible with believing that one's own religion is the only true religion. If one believes that miracles support the truth of a religion, it is possible that the miracle stories of other religions lead one to remain open-minded about the possibility that other religions also make true claims, and this open-mindedness may display itself in tolerance, dialogue and a willingness to cooperate on projects of importance to both religions.

The fifth form of religious pluralism may take the evidence of miracles occurring in other religions to support the claim that they are true in some respects. Further, the miracle stories may promote an understanding of God's character and nature that accord with (some aspect of) one's own religion.

The last form takes the evidence of miracles across religions to indicate that each is true. But it rejects Hume's assumption that they cannot all be true. There is no reason why God should not work miracles within any religion, as each contains a valid (if partial, perhaps) response to the reality of God.

> **?** What role do miracle stories play in debates about which religion is true?

Key points • • •

- Hume argues that each religion claims that its miracles indicate that it is the true religion. Since not all religions can be true, we should not believe any miracle stories. But an alternative response is to think that miracle stories do not support truth claims.
- Religious pluralism, in a weak sense, is compatible with believing that all other religions are false. However, their miracle stories may incline some people to be open-minded on whether they are true.

- Stronger forms of religious pluralism allow that truth can be found in more than one religion. If miracle stories support truth claims, they could support religious pluralism.

What do we mean by 'miracle'?

There are different ways to define what a miracle is. Three important definitions are:

1. an event that has religious significance;
2. an event caused by God;
3. an event that violates (or is otherwise not in accordance with) the laws of nature, caused by God.

The appeal of the first definition is that people talk of events as miracles even when the event isn't outside the laws of nature. This is the sense of miracle as a 'sign' discussed above, without any further commitment to the sign being extraordinary. It allows an element of subjectivity or interpretation as to whether an event has 'religious significance' or not. However, some religions specify the idea of religious significance further. For instance, in Christianity, miracles are connected to the events reported in the Scriptures, such as healing. Therefore, not every event can be said to have religious significance. Nevertheless, the event may have religious significance only for religious believers, and then only those of a particular religion.

The second definition rules out subjective interpretation, as miracles are only those events that are *in fact* caused by God. The theologian Paul Tillich points out that this view fits smoothly into a pre-rationalist understanding of the world. Until people formulated scientific laws of nature, and believed that everything happens in accordance with them, there could be no way of thinking of miracles as violations of such laws. Instead, miracles are events directly connected with the divine.

> *Systematic Theology,*
> Vol. I.

However, as it stands, the definition says that *every* act of God is a miracle, for example God's continuous creation in sustaining the existence of the universe or all genuine religious experience. Tillich is more specific: a miracle must also be an astonishing, shaking event, and one that points to 'the mystery of being'. Miracles are given only to those for whom they are signs, and are received in faith.

The third definition has been most common with philosophers. Aquinas says a miracle is 'beyond the order commonly observed in nature', while Hume talks of it as a 'transgression' or 'violation' of a law of nature. It is also clear from many miracle stories that even if they are described only as signs, if events unfolded just as described, then something that violated the laws of nature must have taken place.

The third definition allows for greater objectivity. Whether an event violates the laws of nature may secure more agreement than whether it is of religious significance; and it is very hard to show that some event is genuinely an act of God. But for this reason, we should also add that a miracle should be a *public* event.

Miracles and the laws of nature

It can seem merely technical, but if we adopt the third definition it is important to be very precise about the relation between miracles and the laws of nature. If we say a miracle is a *violation* of the laws of nature, we risk defining miracles out of existence. Here's how: a statement is a law of nature only if it is true, general (or universal) and **contingent**. (It must be general to be a law, and it must be contingent to be a law of *nature* rather than a law of logic – 'all bachelors are unmarried' is true and general, but not a law of nature!) However, the occurrence of a natural event that violates the law makes the statement either not true or not general. But if it is not true or not general, it is not a law. Any statement that is a law of nature cannot be violated while remaining a law. Therefore, by definition, there can be no violations of a law of nature; if a miracle is a violation of a law of nature, then a miracle is a contradiction in terms. But this is wrong. Miracles are not *logically* impossible.

So how are miracles related to laws of nature?

1. A miracle is a violation of *known* laws of nature. *Objection*: If the miracle occurs, then it would be wrong to call what we *believe to be* laws of nature laws. Instead, we should say that

2. A miracle is a violation of *what we believe* the laws of nature to be. *Objection*: This means that whether an event is a miracle depends on what we believe. Suppose God causes an event that is in accordance with the *real* laws of nature: if we know these laws, it isn't a miracle, but if we don't know these laws, it is. This isn't right. It also implies that miracles are not exceptions to the real laws of nature.

> **Compare and contrast the strengths and weaknesses of the three definitions of miracles.**

> **Explain why defining miracles as violations of laws of nature threatens to make them logically impossible.**

3. A miracle is an event that is *outside, or not in accordance with*, the laws of nature. This definition preserves both the idea that miracles are somehow 'at odds' with the laws of nature, and the idea that they are still laws.

One argument for (3) is this: the laws of nature apply only to *natural* events. If an event is caused by God, it is not a natural event. So, the event doesn't *violate* the laws of nature; it just falls outside them. (You aren't *breaking* the US speed limit of 55 mph if you drive at 60 mph on a motorway in Britain.) Because it is outside the laws of nature, a miracle is *physically* impossible. But that doesn't mean it is logically impossible.

> Discuss the relation between miracles and laws of nature.

Going further: non-repeatable exceptions

Richard Swinburne defends a fourth definition. He argues that the 'generality' of a 'law of nature' is not absolute; the law describes what happens in terms of regularity and predictability. A miracle, therefore, is *not* logically incompatible with a law of nature as a counter-instance to it. So if an event 'violates' a law of nature, we should not conclude that the law is not genuine unless we think that the counter-instance could or would *recur* under similar conditions. To formulate or revise laws of nature, science needs to be able to test and repeat events. If we think the miracle is a one-off event, then we shouldn't revise the law; it remains a good and accurate predictive tool.

So Swinburne argues that we shouldn't say (3) miracles aren't natural events, because then they aren't genuine exceptions to the laws of nature. They are natural events because they happen within the natural universe to natural objects. So, we should say miracles are genuine, non-repeatable exceptions to the laws of nature.

However, some philosophers reject Swinburne's notion of 'laws'. They argue that the laws of nature are not *just* descriptions of what normally happens, but define the limits of what is physically *possible*. On Swinburne's account, miracles aren't physically impossible, strictly speaking; they just fall outside the usual and regular pattern of events.

A second objection to Swinburne's analysis is that while *we* may not be able to repeat the miracle, we might think that if God acted in the same way

?   Are miracles
non-repeatable
exceptions to laws of
nature?

again, then the miracle would happen again. For example, could the many cures of diseases count as 'repeatable' events from the perspective of God's activity? If so, then miracles aren't non-repeatable events. It's just that we can't repeat them.

Key points • • •

- To say that a miracle is an event of religious significance does not capture the exceptional nature of miracles, and makes whether an event counts as a miracle subjective.
- To say that a miracle is an event caused by God, without indicating that the event breaks the laws of nature, fits with a pre-rationalist understanding of the world. However, we should add that the event is astonishing and points to 'the mystery of being'.
- The most common philosophical definition of miracles is events caused by God and not in accordance with the laws of nature.
- Some philosophers claim that a miracle is a *violation* of the laws of nature. But a law is true and general, so if an event is a violation of it, the law is not a genuine law. Therefore, no event can be a genuine violation of a law of nature.
- Another definition claims that the laws of nature apply only to natural events, while events that are caused by God are not natural events. Miracles, then, are not in accordance with the laws of nature (they are not physically possible), but they are not violations of the laws of nature.
- Swinburne argues that miracles are genuine violations, non-repeatable exceptions, to laws of nature. He argues that laws are only regularities, and if the event is non-repeatable, the law remains a true description of natural regularities.

Sceptical arguments regarding the occurrence of miracles

In MIRACLES AND THE COMPETING TRUTH CLAIMS OF DIFFERENT RELIGIONS (p. 323), we gave this argument from Hume: given that every religion claims miracles, but not every religion can be true, we should not accept any miracle story as true.

The evidence cancels out. However, we also saw two alternatives to Hume's conclusion: miracle stories do not confirm the truth claims of a religion; and religious pluralism.

Before turning to Hume's other arguments against belief in miracles, we'll discuss reasons from within religious thought itself to doubt their occurrence.

Three theological objections to miracles

At the end of THE SIGNIFICANCE OF MIRACLE STORIES (p. 322), we noted the argument that thinking of miracles as specific works of God undermines the idea of God's activity *throughout* creation. Second, this understanding of miracles suggests that God acts selectively, and this considerably sharpens THE PROBLEM OF EVIL. If God cured your son from cancer, why did He not cure mine? If God gave you a premonition not to board the doomed plane, why did He not share that information with the rest of the passengers, who then died? Many theologians argue that God's activity in the world is not selective in this way, so miracles in this sense don't occur.

See p. 320.

We can reply, however, that if the *purpose* of the miracle is not so much to benefit some particular person, but rather to support their and other people's religious faith, the theory is not so objectionable. Selective benefit may make evil harder to understand; selective revelation does not.

Other religious thinkers object to the idea that God would use miracles to support religious faith. It suggests that people are incapable of recognising moral and religious truth when presented with it. We can reply that this may be true, but it is no objection. People are not always capable of recognising the truth, and may need some 'wonder' to move them towards religious faith.

> What theological reasons are there to doubt that miracles occur?

Hume's argument against miracles

Hume defines a miracle as 'a transgression of a law of nature by a particular volition of the Deity'. However, we have seen that if this definition is true, a miracle is a contradiction in terms. But Hume doesn't argue this. He argues instead that we never have a good reason to believe that miracles occur.

An Enquiry Concerning Human Understanding, p. 173

He claims that 'as a firm and unalterable experience has established these laws [of nature], the proof against a miracle, from the very nature of the fact,

See PROBABILITY AND BELIEF, p. 32.

is as entire as any argument from experience can possibly be imagined'. By definition, a miracle goes against our very regular and extensive experience of how the world works. Therefore, on the basis of experience, the probability that a miracle has occurred must always be less than the probability that it hasn't. Because it is rational to believe what is most probable, we never have good reason to believe that a miracle has occurred.

In fact, Hume only considers the evidence for miracles from *testimony*, rather than from experiencing an alleged miracle oneself. (This is because the debate at the time was whether we should believe the miracles reported in the New Testament.) Now, we can often rely on testimony, and we have established by our experience that what people tell us is true, we can later confirm directly is true. For us to rationally believe testimony, though, it needs to be more probable that the testimony is true than not.

Hume argues that this is never the case with miracles. It is always more probable that the testimony is false than that the events reported actually occurred:

1. There is no miracle attested to by people of good sense, education, integrity and reputation where the miracle is witnessed by many such people (the attributes listed describe people we can trust not to be easily fooled and to tell the truth without exaggerating).
2. Human nature enjoys surprise and wonder, which gives us a tendency to believe unusual things when the belief isn't justified.
3. Tales of miracles abound among ignorant peoples, and diminish in civilisation; and the tales of miracles are often given in explanation of everyday events, such as battles and famine, that don't need a miraculous explanation.

However, Hume's argument really rests on the conflict between miracles and laws of nature, since he argues that even if there were good testimony for a miracle, we should not believe it. It is our experience that establishes the reliability of testimony. But it is also our experience that establishes the laws of nature. The evidence on the two sides cancels out.

We can understand the importance of these arguments if we compare miracles to unexpected events. After all, these *also* go against our experience, so do we ever have good reason to believe some unexpected event has occurred? Yes, says Hume, on two conditions: first, that there is widespread, consistent agreement that the event occurred; and second, that there are 'analogies' of the event in our experience. Our experience leads us to expect the unexpected, *within limits*. These may vary from person to person; Hume presents the case of an Indian who, never having lived anywhere cold enough, refused to believe that water turned into ice. Hume thought he was right to do so until more evidence appeared. If we heard of someone coming back from the dead, we would be in a similar situation, and should not believe it.

If the evidence mounts up, we should, then, not believe that a *miracle* has occurred; we should try to find what the natural cause of the event is. The only rational response is scientific discovery, not religious belief.

Objections

Suppose we investigate an event and are unable to find any natural causes that would explain it. Can't we reasonably conclude that a miracle has occurred? According to Hume, we have only two choices: reject the claim that the event happened or look for a natural cause of it. But does experience support his claim? Is there *no* experience that could support a belief in a non-natural cause?

Hume would claim that no *experience* is evidence for a non-natural ('miraculous') explanation, because we never experience a non-natural *cause*. To suppose that God caused some event will always be speculative, for we have no experience of God. So even if we don't find a natural cause, we can only conclude that *we don't know* what the cause is, not that the cause is non-natural.

On Hume's account, if I personally witness someone undoubtedly killed before my eyes get up, wounds healing and walk off, I *still* shouldn't think there is a non-natural cause of this. All the rest of my experience casts doubt on the belief that what I am seeing is actually taking place. Is it not more likely that I cannot trust my eyes? To have a good enough reason to believe the event actually happened, I must think it is sufficiently analogous to my experience. But then if it is sufficiently analogous, it will probably have a natural cause. If it is not analogous, then can my current experience be trusted? At best, the evidence cancels out.

We may argue that if I am not the only witness (so I'm not hallucinating or going mad), and the other witnesses are reliable, and there is no scientific explanation that could account for it, then it is reasonable to believe a miracle has occurred.

This conclusion doesn't justify many people believing in miracles. It also doesn't mean that miracles have ever occurred.

> Explain and illustrate Hume's attack on belief in miracles.

> Is there good reason to believe miracles occur?

Key points • • •

- Theologians have objected to miracles on the grounds that the idea of God intervening specifically undermines the idea of God's activity throughout nature, sharpens the problem of evil and suggests that people cannot recognise moral and religious truth.
- Hume argues that we never have good reason to believe, on the basis of testimony, that a miracle occurred. Experience always provides overwhelming evidence that the miracle didn't occur, so it is more probable that the testimony is false.
- If the testimony is very well supported and the event has 'analogies' with our experience, then we should believe an unexpected event has occurred and look for its natural cause. To believe there is a non-natural cause of the event is never supported by experience, since we never have experience of non-natural causes.
- We can object that under certain conditions, it is possible to have good enough evidence to believe an event not in accordance with the laws of nature has occurred.

IV. MAKING SENSE OF RELIGION

Religious language and verificationism

Ayer's argument

See Verification, p. 186.

Language, Truth and Logic

See p. 129.

In the 1930s, a school of philosophy arose called logical positivism, concerned with the foundations and possibility of knowledge. It developed a criterion for meaningful statements, called the principle of verification. On A.J. Ayer's version, the principle of verification states that a statement has meaning only if it is either analytic or empirically verifiable (can be shown by experience to be probably true/false).

'God exists', and so all other talk of God is meaningless, claims Ayer. Despite the best attempts of the ONTOLOGICAL ARGUMENT, we cannot prove 'God exists' from a priori premises using deduction alone. So, 'God exists' is not analytically true. Therefore, to be meaningful, 'God exists' must be empirically verifiable. Ayer argues that it is not. If a statement is an empirical hypothesis, it predicts that our experience will be different depending on whether it is true or false. But 'God exists' makes no such predictions. So, it is meaningless.

Some philosophers argue that religious language attempts to capture something of religious experience, although it is 'inexpressible' in literal terms. Ayer responds that whatever religious experiences reveal, they cannot be said to reveal any facts. Facts are the content of statements that purport to be intelligible and can be expressed literally. If talk of God is non-empirical, it is *literally* unintelligible, hence meaningless.

Responses

We can object that many people do think that 'God exists' has empirical content. For example, THE ARGUMENT FROM DESIGN argues that the design of the universe is evidence for the existence of God. And on the other hand, THE PROBLEM OF EVIL takes the existence and extent of suffering to be evidence against the existence of God.

John Hick argues that even if we can't verify the existence of God in this life, that doesn't mean religious language is meaningless. He develops the idea of 'eschatological verification', whereby experiences of God in the afterlife would establish the truth of the existence of God. In arguing that talk of God is meaningless, Ayer overlooked possible experiences of life after death.

These responses accept the verification principle. But the most common response has been to reject it, as it famously faces serious objections. What is the status of the principle itself? It does not appear to be analytically true; and it is difficult to know how it could be verified empirically (since it is a criterion of meaning, we cannot go around looking for sentences we already believe meaningful or meaningless and then seeing whether they accord with the principle). So if it were true, it would be meaningless; it cannot be both true and meaningless, so it's not true. If it's false, then it's false!

One response to this is to broaden the verification principle, and claim that a sentence is meaningful if it is analytic, or empirically verifiable, or empirically *falsifiable*. To be able to say 'this is a fork' *meaningfully*, we have to know what kinds of situation would lead us to say 'this is not a fork'. Anthony Flew argued that religious language is meaningless because, for a religious believer, nothing could prove that God *doesn't* exist. If 'God exists' is a statement of fact, then it must be possible to imagine the conditions under which we would say that it was not a fact. For example, the theory of evolution by natural selection is a

See THE STATUS OF THE RELIGIOUS HYPOTHESIS, p. 327.

Outline Ayer's argument that religious language is meaningless.

See pp. 314 and 320.

'Theology and Verification'

If no experience could falsify the claim 'God exists', does this claim state anything meaningful?

hypothesis; if aliens came to Earth and demonstrated that they had planted 'fossils' (which actually they had made) for us to find, we would give up the theory. What would make us give up the claim that 'God exists'? We can argue that there are no tests of this kind, so 'God exists' is not a factual claim.

The meaning of religious language

See CAN WE HAVE KNOWLEDGE BEYOND SENSE EXPERIENCE?, p. 192.

However, we can object that this argument has a very limited view of meaning. It assumes that for 'God exists' to state a fact, we have to know how to test whether that fact is true or false against sense experience. But we could argue, first, that there are more types of experience than sense experience; and second, that the meaning of 'God exists' is related to and secured by *making sense* of facts. For example, we could use the argument from design to infer that God's existence is the best explanation for the nature of the universe (or use the problem of evil to infer that God does not exist). In this case, 'God exists' is a hypothesis, but not a *scientific* hypothesis, since we use philosophy, not science, to test it. What we mean by 'God exists' will be shown by these arguments.

An alternative response is to agree that 'God exists' is not a statement of fact, but to insist that it still has meaning as an expression of a non-cognitive attitude or commitment. In support of this, we should note that people don't normally acquire religious beliefs by argument or testing evidence. Instead, they come to an understanding of the world that is expressed in values and a way of living. When someone converts to a religion, what changes isn't so much intellectual beliefs, but their *will*, what they value and how they choose to live.

On this view, religious 'beliefs' are expressions of attitude and commitment, attitudes towards other people, nature, oneself, human history and so on, that put the world in a certain light and that support commitments to act in certain ways and to mature as a spiritual being. The core of accepting a religious faith, on this view, is the intention to follow the way of life prescribed by that religion.

Explain the claim that religious language expresses an attitude.

We can object that there is much more to religious 'beliefs' than a commitment to a way of life. What can we say about different religions that recommend similar ways of life? If commitment to a way of life is all that matters, then does it matter at all what one believes? Many religions have thought that it does; some have even argued that how one lives is not the main point at all. So, religious 'belief' is not the same as an attitude towards how to live. Furthermore, many religious believers would say that they live a certain way *because* God exists and has shown us how to live. But if this statement only *expresses* the commitment to live in a certain way, then it doesn't answer the question of *why* one should live that way. If religious 'belief' is just a commitment, what supports that commitment, or is it arbitrary?

Can the view that religious language is expressive, and not descriptive, make sense of religious belief?

Key points • • •

- The principle of verification claims that only statements that are analytic or empirically verifiable are meaningful. Ayer argues that 'God exists' is neither, and therefore meaningless.
- Hick argues that experiences after death could prove the existence of God.
- The verification principle is self-defeating: it is neither analytically true nor empirically verifiable. By its own standard, it is meaningless. It therefore cannot show that religious language is meaningless.
- Flew argues that 'God exists' is meaningless because it is unfalsifiable.
- We can object that religious language takes its meaning from attempting to make sense of experience in general, even though it cannot be verified or falsified by sense experience.
- Some philosophers argue that religious language is not factual at all, but expresses the believer's attitudes and commitments towards life.
- We can object that this is too reductionist. There is more to religious belief than adopting a particular way of life, and beliefs are often cited to justify the choice of a way of life.

Religion as a 'form of life'

Ludwig Wittgenstein argued that we cannot understand language without understanding the ways in which language is used and how it interacts with how we live and what we do. Wittgenstein was greatly influenced by KIERKEGAARD (p. 311) in his understanding of religious belief. He sought to understand religious language and belief by relating them to religious activity. He agreed with Ayer that religious language is not empirical, but rejected Ayer's conclusion that it was therefore not meaningful.

Philosophical Investigations

Language games

Wittgenstein attempted to illuminate the nature of language by comparing language to games. In particular, like games, language is an activity guided by rules – in games, rules governing what one can do; in language, rules governing meaning. Second, meaning is learned from the rules governing the use of the word or sentence, just as 'pieces' in a game such as chess are understood in terms of how they can be used.

Meaning, then, is often a matter of how words are *used*. Appreciating this requires a distinction between *surface grammar* and *depth grammar*: words or sentences in one context describing *objects* or an *event* may be similar on the surface to ones that in another context do nothing of the sort, as in 'the bus passes the bus stop' and 'the peace of the Lord passes understanding'. To understand a particular 'piece' of language, one must look at how the language is used, as meaning is not given by the form of words alone.

When looking at how words are used, we need to look at the 'language game' – that bit of language and the rules it follows – which gives the words their meaning. (Wittgenstein lists as examples of language games asking, thanking, cursing, praying, greeting and so on.)

> Explain and illustrate Wittgenstein's claim that the meaning of a word is given by its use.

Religion as a 'form of life'

The idea of 'language games' emphasises the foundation of language in activity. Wittgenstein says that a language game is the speaking part of a 'form of life'. A form of life is far broader than any specific language game; it is the foundation out of which language games grow, the collection of cultural practices that embed language games. As part of forms of life, language games do not need any justification. They are rooted in natural human reactions and activities. If, then, religious faith and language are a particular language game, part of a human form of life, their claims need no justification. We only need to understand what is distinctive about them.

> The very foundation is biology, and Wittgenstein often emphasises how our natural reactions form the basis for language games. (Think of talking about pain or colour, or even responses to music.)

So, religious language must be understood as part of a religious life. Religious life and language contain the many different language games of praise and worship, prayer, miracles and so on; but religious language can also be understood as forming a game in its own right, governed by particular rules. Wittgenstein argued that religious language has a depth grammar quite distinct from its surface grammar. Its surface grammar can look empirical, as though, like science, religious language is talking about things and events. This is misleading.

A central part of Wittgenstein's analysis is that 'God exists' is not a statement of fact. It is not about a *thing*, an *object* that exists as part of the world like natural objects do. It is not a claim about an entity at all. If it is not an empirical statement, then believing it is not an empirical belief: 'a religious belief could only be something like a passionate commitment to a system of reference. Hence, although it's a *belief*, it's really a way of living, or a way of assessing life. It's passionately seizing hold of *this* interpretation.' He argued that if we look at how the statement is *used*, what it *expresses* for people who believe it, we see that it is not used as a description; it is used to express a form of commitment.

This can be illustrated by talk of the Last Judgement. This is not a hypothesis about a possible future event; if it were, it would be utterly bizarre (what's the evidence? how is such a belief formed?). The Last Judgement is a 'picture', an understanding of life by which the believer is guided through life. Another example is provided by D.Z. Phillips, who defended and developed Wittgenstein's theory. He argues that if someone thinks that prayer is a means to obtaining something, they have misunderstood the nature of religion, and their belief has become superstition.

On this view, religious language expresses an emotional attitude and understanding of life, and a commitment to living life according to that understanding. It is not a description of the way the world is. Phillips argued that this means that God is not 'logically prior' to religion, some thing to which religion is a human response. Talk of God makes sense only within religious practices. To understand religious language is to understand the place of certain statements in the life of the believer and religious community. And the nature of religious faith shows that these statements are not factual.

Culture and Value, 64

Is talk of God talk of an entity? What are the similarities and differences?

'Religious Beliefs and Language Games'

Compare and contrast Wittgenstein's account of religious language with verificationism.

Discussion

An important implication of Wittgenstein's theory is that we can't criticise or support religious beliefs by using *evidence*. *No* language game can be criticised by standards of rationality that are external to that game. Religion cannot be criticised on the grounds that it is *not true* or highly *improbable*; for this presupposes that it makes factual claims, and it does not. So, for example, both the argument from design and the problem of evil are irrelevant as attempts to prove or disprove the existence of God. Faith, then, is not founded on reason. It is a distinctive and natural part of being human.

This, we might object, cuts religious belief off from reason too severely. However, Phillips points out that the theory doesn't mean there are no grounds for accepting or rejecting religious belief. Religion is part of a form of human life: 'Religion has something to say about . . . birth, death, joy, misery, despair, hope, fortune, and misfortune.' If religious faith makes no sense in the light of such experiences, we will rightly reject it. The problem of evil could be relevant here. Not any set of attitudes and commitments makes sense.

What this means is that religion can't be isolated from other cultural and linguistic practices that criticise it. Religion is *not* a completely autonomous form of life, for it is always situated in and among many other human practices. But this does not mean that such connections to life *justify* or *refute* religious beliefs.

However, we can object that this interpretation of religious belief as not factual conflicts with how many believers think of God and their faith. Wittgenstein's account looks like a *reinterpretation* of religious belief, not an analysis of it. In defending religious faith against criticism from 'external' standards, his theory makes a claim about what religious language means that seems equally external to (and critical of) religious faith.

It also makes *what you believe* much less important, as religious faith is about how we live. Yet many religious believers who act in similar ways and hold similar values argue that there is something distinctive and important about the different beliefs they hold. Furthermore, within the history of any religion there have been heated arguments about how to interpret a particular doctrine (e.g. in Christianity, the Incarnation), when it is very difficult to see how the different interpretations could make any impact on different ways of living. All this suggests that religious language is intended to be true – that is, fact-stating – and not just expressive.

We can argue that Wittgenstein was right to point to the expressive use of religious language. But he was wrong to think that because religious beliefs express attitudes, they cannot *also* be empirical. There is no reason to think that they cannot be *both*. After all, religious believers *do* think they are saying something factual when they say 'God exists'. It has this use.

> Discuss the claim that religion is a 'form of life'.

Key points • • •

- Wittgenstein argues that the meaning of language relates to how it is used. Different uses of language – 'language games' – are governed by different rules, given by their depth grammar.
- Language games are grounded on forms of life, cultural practices that express and develop natural human reactions and activities.
- Wittgenstein argues that religious faith is part of a distinctive language game (or form of life). Language games have their own standards of meaning and justification. Religious faith is not empirical or fact-stating, so it is wrong to assess it by empirical or philosophical reasoning.
- Philosophers have objected that this cuts religious faith off from the rest of life too severely. Phillips replies that faith still needs to 'make sense' of our experiences. But this doesn't mean that our experiences *justify* or *refute* religious beliefs.
- However, many religious believers think their faith is partly empirical, and that right belief, not just a particular way of living, matters.

What is meant by 'religion'? Can social science 'explain away' religion?

The view of religion taken by social scientists has changed considerably over the past 150 years. Yet many of the earlier theories, while now rejected by social scientists, are still popular in contemporary culture. We will discuss definitions and explanations of religion together, as it is difficult to decide between definitions without looking at their supporting explanations.

Some philosophers have argued that there is no one, correct definition of 'religion', as there is no feature that all religions have in common. Instead, religions are sets of beliefs and practices, each of which have certain features in common with some, but not all, others. Of course, it is true that we cannot make belief in a supreme deity, or in judgement after death, or the practices of adoring idols or sacrifice, part of the definition of religion, or we exclude many religions. However, such philosophical arguments often do not consider the definitions actually offered by sociologists, which have become increasingly complex.

A helpful review of the first 100 years is given in Talcott Parsons' 'The Theoretical Development of the Sociology of Religion', first published in 1944.

Intellectual approaches

Primitive Culture, Ch. 11

In the 1870s, Edward Tylor argued that, minimally, religion involves the belief in spirit beings – 'animism'. This belief has two aspects: belief in the individual (human) soul, and beliefs in other spirits, who are aware of human beings and can be either pleased or displeased with them. This relationship creates the need for worship. These beliefs originate, argues Tylor, in an attempt to explain certain psychological phenomena, especially dreams.

Lectures on the Origin and Growth of Religion

Also in the 1870s, Max Müller argued that natural events (lightning, earthquakes, mountains) make a striking impact on people, creating an impulse towards religion. Events caused by the forces of nature are compared to human actions, and 'spirits' are invented as the agents who perform these events. A 'biography' is then invented for each spirit. This account of the origin of religion is 'naturism'.

Both these views understand religion as a form of irrational superstition, based on two foundations: an attempt to understand and/or control the world, and irrational aspects of human psychology. Many early theories also argued that religion naturally evolved from primitive to sophisticated forms – animism, then polytheism, then monotheism, each being more cognitively sophisticated than its predecessor. However, because religion is an attempt to explain the world, we can judge religious claims by using empirical criteria. So eventually, as we become able to explain things scientifically, belief in religion will naturally disappear.

Theories of this form are discussed in EXPLAINING THE IDEA OF 'GOD' AS A HUMAN CONSTRUCTION AND PROJECTION II, p. 151.

But the next generation of social scientists pointed out serious flaws in the assumption that early human beings were essentially objective investigators trying to explain their experiences. Vilfredo Pareto said that systems of belief that involve claims, such as descriptions of the nature of God, which cannot be tested empirically, should not be understood as 'pseudo-scientific' theories. The early theories have overlooked the non-cognitive *emotional* and *social* functions of religion. The cognitive elements – religious beliefs and explanations – must be understood through their interconnection with the non-cognitive. Religious beliefs have not been formed by drawing logical conclusions from empirical experience.

The Elementary Forms of Religious Life

Emile Durkheim also objected to both animism and naturism. If animism were true, then religion would be no more than an illusion. The idea of a spirit would have no foundation in experience, but be merely imaginary. This, he felt, was unacceptable, as religion has produced so much of our culture: morality, law, even science. There must be some aspect of religion that is 'realistic', based in our experience of the world. But naturism cannot account for this; admiration and surprise at natural events will not produce the sense of the 'sacred' that marks religious belief. Nature is uniform, so how could people come to think that *some* aspects of it are sacred while others are not? There is no natural property that everything sacred has in common.

Can religion be understood just as an attempt to explain experience?

Social function and the importance of emotion

MALINOWSKI

In the 1920s, Bronislaw Malinowski supported the arguments of Pareto, demonstrating that religion is not pseudo-science. 'Primitive' people do not confuse religious belief with empirical knowledge of how the world is and how to meet their needs. Religion relates to magic, which serves a different purpose, originating in situations in which people aren't certain of success in getting what they need. Despite their best efforts, for example at farming or catching fish, the outcome is uncertain. This combination of strong emotional investment and uncertainty, argued Malinowski, leads to psychological tension and anxiety. (This is his development of Pareto's idea of the non-cognitive elements of religion.) Magical rites emerge, aimed at ensuring success. They have two functions: they help resolve anxiety and they protect the motivation to keep trying (this motivation could otherwise be defeated by the thought 'what's the point?', which would undermine the survival of society).

'Magic, Science and Religion'

But magic is not religion. Religious rites and belief relate to anxiety in the face of situations where *nothing can be done*, such as death. The magical rite relates to a definite aim of the performer; the religious rite does not. However, like magic, religion has a useful social function: it contains and formalises the expression of emotions and attitudes that could otherwise be destructive of the group.

Malinowski's account of the distinction between magic and religion has been questioned, as many religious rites appear to have a definite purpose, and many religious beliefs relate to practical activities (e.g. a famine as punishment for sins). But his overall account shows the importance of the social function of religion.

If Malinowski's account were right, religion would relieve anxiety. But this doesn't seem to be so. First, the believer feels anxiety about whether the ritual has been performed *properly*. Anxiety has not been alleviated; at best, it has been displaced. However, we should note that religions contain further rituals relating to this, namely to do with the purification and expiation of sins. Nevertheless, we can still object that even in this complicated form, the analysis of religion remains too optimistic. Over time, religion has produced as much anxiety, for example about how to live and the effects of our actions on an afterlife, as it has alleviated. This is not to deny that religion has something to do with the experiences Malinowski discusses, but it rejects the claim that its (sole) function is to alleviate anxiety.

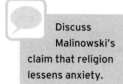

Discuss Malinowski's claim that religion lessens anxiety.

DURKHEIM

Durkheim identifies two defining aspects of religion. First, all religions are marked by the division of the world into what is sacred and what is not (not sacred = profane). Sacred things are set apart and forbidden from common use, while rites are rules on how to behave towards what is sacred. Second, all religions involve a *group*, a 'church' – individuals understand themselves as united by their faith, becoming a 'moral community'. This contrasts with magic, which doesn't generate a sense of unity.

At the heart of religion, then, is a set of attitudes: the sacred deserves respect, and it is associated with authority and morality. This again demonstrates that we cannot understand religion as logical inferences from empirical experiences. As we saw above, Durkheim argued that this attitude cannot derive from animism or naturism. Instead, the original and simplest form of religion, he argued, is totemism.

Human society was originally organised, he claimed, by clan. Members of the clan felt their bond to each other as very special, and not merely biological. Each clan had a totem, which was shared with no other clan. The totem was the paradigmatically sacred thing; everything sacred was sacred through some connection with the totem. The totem represented something impersonal, of which it was merely a symbol – the first 'religious' symbol, a symbol of authority, morality and divinity.

And yet the totem also represents the clan, society. So, society itself is the origin of religion and the idea of god. In the totem, argues Durkheim, society has deified itself. Society holds the authority and moral code that is expressed through religion. It is vastly superior in power to the individual, and the individual is utterly dependent on it. Furthermore, society imposes behaviour that will serve its ends and requires sacrifices of the individual; it imposes its values, without which social life would be impossible. Religious rites express forces that impose morality, bond society together and support and celebrate life.

Durkheim's views on the social functions of religion, and the close tie between religion, morality and authority, have been widely accepted. However, that the totem expresses both god and society is, on its own, insufficient for Durkheim's conclusion that society has effectively become its own god.

Beyond social function: the problem of meaning

There are different religions, with different religious beliefs and practices. Nothing in the theories discussed addresses this issue. If the only function of all religion is to alleviate anxiety or create social bonds, then any differences between religions must either be considered unimportant or be explained in similar terms, for example as responses to what was required for a particular society at a particular time to function well.

In the 1920s, Max Weber argued that we can explain religious beliefs only if we refer to people's attempts to *think about* and solve the issues that religion tackles. The emotion-based accounts that Malinowski and Durkheim present are not wrong, but religion also has a *cognitive* dimension, which we can call 'the problem of meaning'.

Talcott Parsons defines religion as a response to those aspects of life that we cannot rationally understand or control, but which nevertheless are felt to relate to fundamental questions about our place in the universe, values and the meaning of life. Frustration and anxiety isn't just an emotional state; it can also be cognitive. Confronted with cognitive frustration, human thought develops in different directions, and it is this that explains the differences in religious beliefs. These beliefs are integrated with many practical attitudes that people adopt towards everyday life. Religious conviction, for each individual, is created not rationally, but as supplying a way of understanding how to behave in certain areas of life where otherwise we have no guidance.

Bringing together all the theories above, Parsons argues that a religion will minimally contain:

1. beliefs about the supernatural or the sacred, including the connection of these to morality;
2. a system of symbols, objects, acts and people that are sacred;
3. a set of activities that are seen as important in the light of religious beliefs, but which don't try to accomplish anything practical;
4. a group that shares these beliefs, and is united as a group in this way.

Clifford Geertz argues that we are confronted with this problem of meaning in three forms: there are limits to our cognitive abilities (explaining the existence

What social functions did religion originally perform?

The Protestant Ethic and the Spirit of Capitalism

'Sociology and Social Psychology'

'Religion as a Cultural System'

See p. 320.

What is 'the problem of meaning'? Why is it important in understanding religion?

and nature of the world); limits to our endurance, especially in illness and death; and limits to our moral insight, especially THE PROBLEM OF EVIL. In each case, religion provides an answer, removing the threat of meaninglessness.

However, Geertz rejects the claim that (solving) the problem of meaning is the *basis* of religious belief. These solutions to meaninglessness are not arrived at from experience. Instead, we must already accept some form of religious authority, which *transforms* our experience through its system of symbols. In engaging in a life informed by religion, the believer develops a distinctive set of dispositions that change his or her activities and experiences. Conversely, the individual's emotions and motivations are made meaningful by being related to the religion, for example *Christian* charity or *Christian* hope. Religious concepts not only provide a framework for *interpreting* experience, but shape experiences. Many religions claim that we must believe before we can know.

Does social science 'explain away' religion?

How should we understand the social science account of religion? It *seems* to show that religious belief is irrational, or a solution to an emotional problem. However, Weber, Parsons and Geertz all reject the idea that social science can show whether religious belief is *true* or not.

First, the meanings expressed in the symbolic systems of religions cannot be explained just in terms of social processes and functions. Second, the sociological account of certain aspects of religious belief, such as answering the problem of meaning, is not reductive. Both Parsons and Geertz explicitly state that the account offered may be true whether or not religious faith is divinely inspired. If religious beliefs are true, then it would be surprising if they were *not* bound up with human psychology and social activity. Third, Parsons points out that there are other aspects of religion, such as its creativity and innovation, that cannot be explained so well in sociological terms.

However, we should note that social science supports the view, shared in different ways by Plantinga, James, Kierkegaard, Pascal and Wittgenstein, that faith is not based on the arguments of reason. Its conviction is either fundamentally an emotional conviction, or only available to those who are open to experience in the 'right' way.

Nevertheless, social science makes it much harder to claim that one religion is 'correct', and that all others are wrong. Even if God exists, religion is clearly a set of *human* beliefs, practices and institutions, and as such is marked by human errors and human vices.

Do social scientific explanations of religion give us reason to believe that religious claims are not true?

Key points • • •

- We cannot define religion as belief in a supreme deity or life after death as this would exclude some religions. However, social science has provided more sophisticated definitions that may cover all religions.
- Tylor argued that religious belief (belief in spirit beings) arose from attempting to explain psychological phenomena. Müller argued that religion arises from attempting to explain natural events.
- We can object that both views are too 'intellectual', understanding religion as irrational superstition. Pareto and Durkheim argued that we must take account of the non-cognitive emotional and social functions of religion.
- Malinowski argued that religion, like magic, attempts to resolve anxiety in important situations in which the outcome is uncertain or out of our control. It contains emotions that could undermine the group.
- We can object that religion does not reduce anxiety as much as Malinowski argued.
- Durkheim argued that religion is marked by a division of what is sacred from what is not, and that all religions involve a 'moral community' united by their 'faith'. The origin of religion is totemism.
- As the totem represents both society (the clan) and god, society has deified itself. We can object that this is too simple, and does not take account of the cognitive elements of religion.
- Weber argued that to explain religious beliefs, we must refer to people's attempts to think about the problems religion addresses – 'the problem of meaning'. Geertz notes that the problem of meaning arises in three forms, based on limits to our abilities to understand, to suffer and to gain moral insight.
- Parsons argued for four elements of religion: beliefs, including moral beliefs, about the supernatural or sacred; a system of sacred symbols, objects, acts and people; a set of religious activities that don't have a practical goal; and a group united by these shared beliefs.
- Geertz argued that the problem of meaning, interpreting experience, is not the basis of religion. We must first accept some religious authority, which transforms our dispositions and experience.
- Weber, Parsons and Geertz all maintain that social science cannot show that religion is false (or true). Religious meanings can't be explained in terms of social functions; and the sociological account is not reductive. But it does support the view that religious belief is not based on rational arguments.

6   PREPARING FOR THE EXAM

To get good exam results, you need to have a good sense of what the exam will be like and what the examiners are looking for, and to revise in a way that will help you prepare to answer the questions well. This probably sounds obvious, but in fact many students do not think about the exam itself, only about what questions might come up. There is a big difference. This chapter will provide you with some guidance on how to approach your exams in a way that will help get you the best results you can. It is divided into three sections: revision, understanding the question and exam technique. Before continuing to read this chapter, it is worth looking back at the Introduction to see how exam questions are structured and what the Assessment Objectives are (p. 3).

Throughout the chapter, I will highlight revision points and exam tips. You can find these collected together at the end of the chapter.

Revision: knowing what the examiners are looking for

There are lots of memory tricks for learning information for exams. This chapter isn't about those. Revision isn't just about learning information; it's also about learning how to use that information well in the exam. Being able to do this is a question not of memory, but of directed revision and concentration in the exam. If you've been doing the exercises throughout this book, then you have been putting into practice the advice I give below.

It may sound obvious, but in order to know how best to answer the exam questions, you need to think about how they are marked. The examiners mark your answers according to three principles known as 'Assessment Objectives' (AOs). These are listed in the Introduction, on p. 3.

You can use these AOs to help guide your revision. AO1 (Knowledge and understanding) leads straight to the first revision point:

> R1: Learn the arguments. Who said what? What terms and concepts did they use? How did they defend their positions?

This, you may think, is challenging enough! But this isn't enough. In displaying your knowledge, you need to show what is *relevant* to the question being asked. Knowing what is relevant is a special kind of knowledge, which involves thinking carefully about what you know about the theories in relation to the question asked. The best way to learn what is relevant is to practise answering questions, either exam questions or questions you make up for yourself or a friend. Try to make up questions that are similar to the exam questions, for example that use quotations or that use words like 'assess' and 'critically discuss'. Practising answering different questions on the same topic helps keep your knowledge flexible, because you have to think of just the right bit of information that will answer the question.

> R2: Practise applying your knowledge by answering questions about it. The best questions to practise with are past exam questions, but you can also make up questions for yourself.

AO2 (Interpretation and analysis) means that your knowledge needs to be developed in a particular way. In philosophy, there is no easy, straightforward answer to 'What did he mean when he said . . .'. So in knowing and under-standing arguments and issues, you need to be able to *interpret* them and defend your interpretation.

> R3: Revise those aspects of the issue that are hard to understand. Practise arguing that they *can* be understood in more than one way, and why they *should* be understood to have the meaning you give them.

One aspect of interpretation is knowing what is relevant and what is not to the view you are discussing. From this point, what point follows next? Or again, what would be a relevant example? You can either remember good examples you have read, or create your own. In either case, you should know precisely what point the example is making. An irrelevant example demonstrates that you don't really know what you are talking about.

R4: Prepare examples beforehand, rather than try to invent them in the exam. If you can use your own, that's great (you'll get extra marks if they are good). But they must be short and they must make the right point – so try them out on your friends and teachers first.

But this is only half of AO2. When interpreting someone, you also need to show what his arguments are and how they are supposed to work. This means being able to *analyse* an issue, finding its main claims and main arguments and then breaking down the arguments into premises and conclusions, and showing how the conclusion is supposed to follow from the premises.

R5: Spend time identifying the main claims and arguments involved in each issue you have studied, putting arguments in your own words, stating clearly what the conclusion is and what the premises are. Point out or show how the reasoning is supposed to work.

What of AO3? How do you revise for 'assessment and evaluation'? This AO tests you on how well you can relate and compare arguments, how well you build an argument, deal with objections and come to a supported conclusion. The best way to prepare for it is to spend time *thinking* about the arguments and issues. Thinking is quite different from knowing about. You might know Descartes' arguments for substance dualism, but you may never have stopped really to work out whether you think they are any good.

AO3 encourages you to do two things. One is to question what the argument actually shows: do the premises support the conclusion, or some other point of view? The second is to relate a particular argument to other arguments and viewpoints on the issue, and in particular to reflect on whether the objections

to an argument undermine it. Work through the arguments so that you understand for yourself the pros and cons of each viewpoint. As a minimum, be able
to argue both for and against a particular view.

> R6: Think reflectively about the arguments and issues. Practise arguing for
> and against a particular view. Think about the place and importance of the
> arguments for the issue as a whole.

You need to be able to construct arguments, not just report them. This means
that what you write should also take the form of premises and conclusion.
The premises will be your judgements as you go along, in response to this
view or that objection. These judgements need to add up to a conclusion. You
shouldn't end your essay with a totally different point of view from the one your
evaluations in the essay support. In other words, do the judgements you reach
reflect the arguments you have presented?

This doesn't mean that you have to find one point of view on the issue and
defend it. But if you can't come to a firm conclusion about which viewpoint is
right, try to come to a firm conclusion about why the different points each seem
right in their own way, and why it is difficult to choose. Philosophy is not about
knowing the 'right answers'; it is about understanding why an answer *might* be
right and why it is difficult to know.

> R7: Think about how your judgements on the various arguments you have
> studied add up. Do they lead to one conclusion, one point of view being
> right? Or do you think arguments for and against one position are closely
> balanced?

These first seven revision points relate to taking in and understanding information. There are two more points that will help you organise the information,
learn it better and prepare you for answering exam questions.

A good way of organising your information is to create answer outlines or
web-diagrams for particular issues. For example, from Unit 3.1 Philosophy of
Mind, you could create an outline or web-diagram for reductionism. Think about
the essential points and organise them, perhaps like this:

1. What is reductionism?
2. Which theories are examples of reductionism, and why?
3. Within each theory, what are the main arguments for that theory?
4. What are the main arguments against each reductive theory?
5. What are the main strengths and weaknesses of reductionism against non-reductive theories?
6. What is your conclusion on the issue, and why?

With an outline like this, you should be able to answer any question that comes up on reductionism.

> R8: Create structured outlines or web-diagrams for particular issues. Try to cover all the main points.

Finally, once you've organised your notes into an outline or web-diagram, time yourself writing exam answers. Start by using your outline, relying on your memory to fill in the details. Then practise by memorising the outline as well, and doing it as though it were an actual exam. You might be surprised at how quickly the time goes by. You'll find that you need to be very focused – but this is what the examiners are looking for: answers that are thoughtful but to the point.

> R9: Practise writing timed answers. Use your notes at first, but then practise without them.

There is one more thing important to revision that I haven't yet talked about, which is how the structure of the questions and how the marks are awarded can help you to decide what to focus on. This is what we'll look at next.

Understanding the question: giving the examiners what they want

The key to doing well in an exam is understanding the question. I don't just mean understanding the *topic* of the question, like 'rights' or 'scepticism'. Of course, this is very important. But you also need to understand what the question is asking you to *do*. And this is related to the three Assessment Objectives discussed above.

All three Assessment Objectives are applied to your essay answer. You therefore need to demonstrate knowledge, and analysis, and evaluation. Usually, evaluation is the most demanding – and it is worth noting that it is also the one that receives most marks.

Don't think that you need to divide your essay into parts, first demonstrating knowledge, then analysis, then evaluation. If you concentrate on making your answer evaluative, you will usually demonstrate knowledge and analysis as you go along. The reason for this is that a good evaluative answer to a question provides an *argument* for a conclusion. But for an argument to be good, it needs to clearly display an understanding of the topic, as well as analysis of each issue or point as it is discussed. It needs to start by explaining what is under discussion (what issue or theory), and then explain and illustrate points as they are made, to support the conclusion that this answer to the question is the best one.

Exam technique: getting the best result you can

Exams are very exciting, whether in a good way or a bad way! It can be helpful, therefore, to take your time at the beginning; not to rush into your answers, but to plan your way. The tips I give below are roughly in the order that you might apply them when taking the exam. You might be surprised at the number of things it can be worth doing before you write anything at all.

I'll assume that you have studied just two themes in Unit 3. So, you have a choice of four questions, two from each theme. First, for your first theme you need to decide carefully which question to answer, and this means reading the whole of both questions very carefully before making your decision. You need to be sure you can answer the question as it is set, not just talk generally about the issue it raises.

E1. Read through both questions before starting your answer. This will help you to decide which question you can answer best overall.

Before you start to write your answer, read the question again very closely. Notice the precise phrasing of the question. Because an exam is exciting (in a good or bad way), many people have a tendency to notice only what the question is about, such as rights or universals. They don't notice the rest of the words in the question. But the question is never 'so tell me everything you know about rights'! *Every word counts*. Your answer should relate not just to the issue in general, but to the *specific words* of the question.

E2. Before starting your answer, read the question again very closely. Take note of every word.

You are now ready to start answering the question. But many people find it is worth organising their thoughts first. What are you going to say, in what order? Arguments require that you present ideas in a logical order. If you've memorised an outline or a web-diagram, quickly write it out at the beginning so that you note down all the points. It is very easy to forget something or go off on a tangent once you are stuck into the arguments. Having an outline or web-diagram to work from will help you keep your answer relevant and structured. It will also remind you how much you still want to cover, so it can help you pace yourself better. However, you might discover, as you develop your answer, that parts of the outline or diagram are irrelevant or just don't fit. Don't worry – the outline is there only as a guide.

E3. Before you start your answer, it can be worth writing out your outline or web-diagram first. This can help remind you of the key points you want to make, and the order in which you want to make them.

Finding and using a good example is very important. Good examples are concise and relevant, and support your argument. But you need to explain why they support your argument. An example is an illustration, not an argument.

E4. Keep your examples short and make sure they support the point you want to make. Always explain how they support your point.

Because philosophy is about the logical relationship of ideas, there are a number of rules of thumb about presentation. Here are four important ones.

E5. Four rules of thumb:

1. Don't use a 'technical term', like 'the greatest happiness principle' or 'the cosmological argument', without saying what it means.
2. Describe a theory before evaluating it. (If you have described it in answer to a previous part, you don't need to describe it again.)
3. Keep related ideas together. If you have a thought later on, add a footnote indicating where in the answer you want it to be read.
4. Don't state the conclusion to an argument before you've discussed the argument, especially if you are going to present objections to that conclusion. You can state what the argument hopes to show, but don't state it *as* a conclusion.

It is worth noting that evaluation is more than just presenting objections and responses side by side. Get the objections and the theory to 'talk' to each other, and try to come to some conclusion about which side is stronger. Furthermore, one good discussion is worth more than many weak or superficial points, so choose two or three of the *most powerful* relevant objections, and discuss those in depth.

E6. Make sure your discussion does not just report a sequence of points of view, but presents objections and replies, and tries to reach a particular conclusion.

Finally, it is very easy to forget something, or say it in an unclear way. Leave time to check your answer at the end. You might find you can add a sentence here or there to connect two ideas together more clearly, or that some word is left undefined. These little things can make a big difference to the mark.

> E7. Leave time to check your answer at the end. You may want to add a helpful sentence here and there.

Revision tips

R1: Learn the arguments. Who said what? What terms and concepts did they use? How did they defend their positions?

R2: Practise applying your knowledge by answering questions about it. The best questions to practise with are past exam questions, but you can also make up questions for yourself.

R3: Revise those aspects of the issue that are hard to understand. Practise arguing that they *can* be understood in more than one way, and why they *should* be understood to have the meaning you give them.

R4: Prepare examples beforehand, rather than trying to invent them in the exam. If you can use your own, that's great (you'll get extra marks if they are good). But they must be short and they must make the right point – so try them out on your friends and teachers first.

R5: Spend time identifying the main claims and arguments involved in each issue you have studied, putting arguments in your own words and stating clearly what the conclusion is and what the premises are. Point out or show how the reasoning is supposed to work.

R6: Think reflectively about the arguments and issues. Practise arguing for and against a particular view. Think about the place and importance of the arguments for the issue as a whole.

R7: Think about how your judgements on the various arguments you have studied add up. Do they lead to one conclusion, one point of view being right? Or do you think arguments for and against one position are closely balanced?

R8: Create structured outlines or web-diagrams for particular issues. Try to cover all the main points.

R9: Practise writing timed answers. Use your notes at first, but then practise without them.

Exam tips

E1. Read through both questions before starting your answer. This will help you to decide which question you can answer best overall.

E2. Before starting your answer, read the question again very closely. Take note of every word.

E3. Before you start your answer, it can be worth writing out your outline or web-diagram first. This can help remind you of the key points you want to make, and the order in which you want to make them.

E4. Keep your examples short and make sure they support the point you want to make. Always explain how they support your point.

E5. Four rules of thumb:

1.   Don't use a 'technical term', like 'the greatest happiness principle' or 'the cosmological argument', without saying what it means.
2.   Describe a theory before evaluating it. (If you have described it in answer to a previous part, you don't need to describe it again.)
3.   Keep related ideas together. If you have a thought later on, add a footnote indicating where in the answer you want it to be read.
4.   Don't state the conclusion to an argument before you've discussed the argument, especially if you are going to present objections to that con-clusion. You can state what the argument hopes to show, but don't state it *as* a conclusion.

E6. Make sure your discussion is not just reporting a sequence of points of view, but presents objections and replies, and tries to reach a particular conclusion.

E7. Leave time to check your answer at the end. You may want to add a helpful sentence here and there.

GLOSSARY

a posteriori – Knowledge of propositions that can only be known to be true or false through sense experience.

a priori – Knowledge of propositions that do not require (sense) experience to be known to be true or false.

analytic – An analytic proposition is true (or false) in virtue of the meanings of the words. For instance, 'a bachelor is an unmarried man' is analytically true, while 'a square has three sides' is analytically false.

argument – A reasoned inference from one set of claims – the premises – to another claim – the conclusion.

cognitivism – The theory that knowledge of some specific type of claim is possible; for example, moral cognitivism claims that there is moral knowledge.

contingent – A proposition that could be either true or false, a state of affairs that may or may not hold, depending on how the world actually is.

counterfactual – A conditional statement in which the first clause picks out a state of affairs that is contrary to fact, for example 'if the water hadn't spilled, the table would be dry', which implies that the water *did* spill.

deduction – An argument whose conclusion is *logically entailed* by its premises – that is, if the premises are true, the conclusion *cannot* be false.

dualism – The metaphysical theory that there are two distinct types of substance (mind and body); or, as property dualism, that there are two distinct types of property (usually physical properties and properties of consciousness).

empirical – Relating to or deriving from experience, especially sense experience, but also including experimental scientific investigation.

empiricism – The theory that there can be no a priori knowledge of synthetic propositions about the world (outside my mind) – that is, all a priori knowledge is of analytic propositions, while all knowledge of synthetic propositions must be checked against sense experience.

epistemology – The study ('-ology') of knowledge ('episteme') and related concepts, including belief, justification and certainty. It looks at the possibility and sources of knowledge.

fallacy – A pattern of poor reasoning. A fallacious argument or theory is one that is mistaken in some way.

induction – An argument whose conclusion is *supported* by its premises, but is not logically entailed by them. That is, if the premises are true, the conclusion may be false, but this is unlikely (relative to the premises). One form of inductive argument is inference to the best explanation – that is, the conclusion presents the 'best explanation' for why the premises are true.

metaphysics – The branch of philosophy that enquires about the fundamental nature of reality.

necessary – A proposition that *must* be true (or if false, it must be false); a state of affairs that *must* hold.

non-cognitivism – The theory that some specific type of claim does not assert a proposition that can be true or false, and therefore there can be no knowledge of that kind. For example, moral non-cognitivism claims that moral judgements are neither true nor false, so there is no moral knowledge.

normative – Relating to 'norms': rules or reasons for conduct or belief.

ontology – The study (-ology) of what exists or 'being' (ont-).

proposition – A declarative statement (or, more accurately, what is claimed by a declarative statement), such as 'mice are mammals'. Propositions can go after 'that' in 'I believe that . . .' and 'I know that . . .'.

rationalism – The theory that there can be a priori knowledge of synthetic propositions about the world (outside my mind); this knowledge is gained by reason without reliance on sense experience.

scepticism – The view that our usual justifications for claiming our beliefs amount to knowledge are inadequate, so we do not in fact have knowledge.

sense-data (singular **sense-datum**) – In perception, mental images or representations of what is perceived, 'bits' of experience; if they exist, they are the immediate objects of perception.

synthetic – A proposition that is not analytic, but true or false depending on how the world is.

veridical – A proposition that is true or an experience that represents the world as it actually is.

INDEX

eBooks – at www.eBookstore.tandf.co.uk

A library at your fingertips!

eBooks are electronic versions of printed books. You can store them on your PC/laptop or browse them online.

They have advantages for anyone needing rapid access to a wide variety of published, copyright information.

eBooks can help your research by enabling you to bookmark chapters, annotate text and use instant searches to find specific words or phrases. Several eBook files would fit on even a small laptop or PDA.

NEW: Save money by eSubscribing: cheap, online access to any eBook for as long as you need it.

Annual subscription packages

We now offer special low-cost bulk subscriptions to packages of eBooks in certain subject areas. These are available to libraries or to individuals.

For more information please contact webmaster.ebooks@tandf.co.uk

We're continually developing the eBook concept, so keep up to date by visiting the website.

www.eBookstore.tandf.co.uk